ISBN 978-1-333-64339-3
PIBN 10530217

1 MONTH OF
FREE
READING

at
www.ForgottenBooks.com

By purchasing this book you are
eligible for one month membership to
ForgottenBooks.com, giving you
unlimited access to our entire
collection of over 1,000,000 titles via
our web site and mobile apps.

To claim your free month visit:
www.forgottenbooks.com/free530217

English
Français
Deutsche
Italiano
Español
Português

www.forgottenbooks.com

Mythology Photography **Fiction**
Fishing Christianity **Art** Cooking
Essays Buddhism Freemasonry
Medicine **Biology** Music **Ancient
Egypt** Evolution Carpentry Physics
Dance Geology **Mathematics** Fitness
Shakespeare **Folklore** Yoga Marketing
Confidence Immortality Biographies
Poetry **Psychology** Witchcraft
Electronics Chemistry History **Law**
Accounting **Philosophy** Anthropology
Alchemy Drama Quantum Mechanics
Atheism Sexual Health **Ancient History**
Entrepreneurship Languages Sport
Paleontology Needlework Islam
Metaphysics Investment Archaeology
Parenting Statistics Criminology
Motivational

Preface.

THE mode in which the papers which constitute this volume were given, having varied somewhat from that mentioned in the preface to the First Volume, it is incumbent on us to describe the change.

During the preparation of the whole of that volume the Doctor was used as a writing medium only. After its publication he was developed as a speaking medium, being thrown, for the occasion, into a trance so deep as to be unconscious alike of what he was saying and of what was occurring around him. What he said at such times was carefully recorded by the Judge, and as carefully revised by us afterward in connection with our unseen friends. Most of the communications in this volume given through him were received in this way.

Late in the year 1853 the Judge's daughter, Laura, and his niece, Jane Keyes, were developed as mediums, and were received as members of the circle—the circle from that time consisting of us two, Mr. Warren, Mr. and Mrs. Sweet, and those two young ladies.

We had occasional assistance also, of great value, from another source. In December, 1853, we became acquainted with Mrs. A. T. Hall and Mrs. Helen Leeds, of Boston, the former a medium for writing by impression, and the

2

latter a seeing and speaking medium, and occasionally writing mechanically.

Laura Edmonds' medial powers were very similar to those of Mrs. Leeds, the only difference being, that when speaking, seeing, or writing, she was never unconscious, while Mrs. Leeds most generally was so. The same difference was noticeable in the manifestations through the Judge and the Doctor, the former never being unconscious, while the latter most frequently was.

In the mean time Mr. Warren began to be developed as a seeing medium.

And in all the circle a marked improvement in the ease and accuracy of communicating has been very apparent, thus holding out to all the prospect of still greater usefulness in the future.

J. W. EDMONDS,
GEO. T. DEXTER.

NEW YORK, *December* 18, 1854.

Introduction

OF JUDGE EDMONDS.

In presenting to the world a continuation of our work on the great truth which is marking the nineteenth century, it will not be amiss for me to utter a few words in elucidation and explanation.

In a very early stage of my investigations, long before I was willing to receive it as true that the spirits of the departed could commune with us who yet remained behind, and when it seemed to me but barely probable that they might, the question occurred, To what end is it? what purpose is there in view? and what beneficial object can be attained by it?

The answer readily suggested itself, that if it be true that they can thus commune with us, they must be able to disclose to us something at least of the state of existence into which they had been and we were to be ushered.

Such disclosure had never yet been made to man. Through Moses and the prophets there had been revealed to him the existence of one God, instead of the hosts of deities which the pagan world had worshiped. Through Christ and his apostles, man's existence for eternity, and the rule by which that existence could be made a happy one, had been revealed. But what that existence was, how it was that that rule was to insure man's happiness, and what was to be his ultimate destiny through the countless ages of eternity, had been concealed from him. His future was a sealed book, and the natural longings of the heart to know could obtain a response only from his own imaginings. Vague, fanciful, contradictory, and material as these were, they left the understanding still to grope on in darkness, they left the desire for that knowledge still unsatisfied, and they left man to sink, by gradual but sure progress, from ignorance into infidelity.

I asked myself why may not that now be revealed? Surely nothing could be more important, and man was never before so well prepared for its reception. We believed, and it had been believed in all ages and among all people, that God had in his providence made to man, and through the instrumentality of man, revelations of His mighty truths. And among Christians, at least, this was believed as part of the very foundation of their religion. Wherein had man's nature so changed in the process of time that he could not again receive of those truths and again be the instrument of conveying them to the knowledge of his fellows? I could conceive of no reason why the humble and the lowly of this day could not as well become such instruments as the fishermen of Galilee, nor why the instructed of modern times could not receive and impart of them as well as him of Tarsus, of whom it was said, even from high places, that much learning had made him mad. As I have often had occasion to remark, I could see nothing in nature or revelation to forbid it, and I concluded that it was possible that a further revelation could be made to us, that perchance it might be that it was now coming, and that the prayer which had ascended for centuries from the whole Christian world, " Thy kingdom come," might now be answered.

I say that it seemed to me that it might be, and if it might, what was our duty in the premises? Did it become us to say that it could not or that it should not? that we would not receive it? or if it came in spite of ourselves, that we would not promulgate it? that we should not admit that it could be for good, but that it must of necessity be for evil only? that we should condemn without investigation, and repudiate and denounce without knowledge of what it was or what it might teach? that we should be content with our condition of ignorance, and resolve that a knowledge of the future should find no entrance to the chambers of the under standing?

I did not so conceive my duty, nor did I imagine that there were any who would oppose all investigation, and war upon the reception of any further knowledge. And I may pause a moment in passing to say, that I have marveled not a little that in a country where freedom of thought is so loudly professed there should have been displayed such determined and virulent hostility even to an investigation of what may be truth. But let that pass. My duty seemed to be plain, and that was to ascertain—not take it for granted—but inquire and ascertain if possible whether such further knowledge might not come.

The result of that inquiry we are now in part giving to the world. How far it is entitled to credit—to what extent it may be true we do not mean to say. We give it as it has come to us, as faithfully and as accurately as in our power, and we leave every one to form his own opinion upon its merits. We do not claim to be authority for any thing. We do not ask for any other credit than that of intending fairly and faithfully to give what we have received, as we have received it.

I am aware that there are some things contained in the following papers which will startle even confirmed believers in Spiritualism. I believe so, because they startled us, and there are several things which our first impulse was to withhold from insertion in the book. They were so much in conflict with all our preconceived notions, and with what we knew to be the general opinion of the world around us, that we were conscious they would not be credited at first, but would be likely to draw down upon us and on our publication a still more severe storm of denunciation—if that were possible—than we had yet experienced. But we were professing to give to the world the revelations as they came, precisely and accurately as we received them, and what right had we to withhold any of them because they did not square with our notions, or because, forsooth, we might be subjected to some personal inconvenience? No. We could not so deport ourselves—we could not allow any mere personal consideration to warp or color communications, our relation to which was but that of the conduit through which they might pass to minds to which they might be more acceptable even in the first instance. We therefore give them as we receive them, and withhold nothing. Let each one judge of them for himself.

There are, however, some considerations which tend to corroborate the revelations made to us, and which ought not to be overlooked.

There are at times contradictions and inconsistencies in spiritual intercourse, as all must be aware, but there is one remarkable fact, viz., that amid all these incongruities—through all mediums, whether partially or highly developed—from all the spirits who commune, whether progressed or unprogressed, there is a universal accordance on one point, and that is, that we pass into the next state of existence just what we are in this, and that we are not suddenly changed into a state of perfection or imperfection, but find ourselves in a state of progression, and that this life on earth is but a preparation for the next, and the next but a continuation of this.

Through all the thousands and tens of thousands of mediums in this country and elsewhere, so far as I can know, the teachings all agree in this one respect, and through this overwhelming evidence comes this mighty truth, hitherto unknown to man in general and only guessed at by a few.

If this is a truth, it surely will not require a lengthened argument to demonstrate its vast importance. If, indeed, it only may be true, no profound disquisition will be necessary to show that it is worthy of an enlightened investigation. And if its reality can once be established to the satisfaction of our dispassionate reason, it needs no one to rise from the dead to tell us that it is as novel as it is interesting, and that however much it may be corroborated by all of nature around us, it can be established only by a revelation from on high.

This fact, at once new and momentous, does not, it will be seen, depend on our testimony alone, but finds support in all the revelations of spiritual intercourse, wherever located and springing from whatever source they may.

There is another important instance in which all the manifestations through others corroborate those which we promulgate, and that is, in demonstrating that man does exist after the life on earth. And this is proved, not by abstract reasoning, not by reasoning from analogy, or by appealing to received and acknowledged revelation, but palpably, by addressing the senses. To all the senses this proof comes, with such copiousness and such overwhelming power as to be utterly irresistible to the rational mind. To those who have never doubted man's immortality, and who have regarded it as irrational to question it, this consideration may not be of much moment. But to those who have questioned it—and alas! their number has been far greater than the unthinking world imagine—it is of vital consequence, and is hailed by them with a joy inexpressible. I can not do better than give in this connection some extracts from a few of the many letters I have received on that subject.

————, MICH., *March* 26, 1854.

DEAR SIR—Pardon me for this intrusion. It is the interest which I have lately felt on the subject of Spiritualism that has induced me to address you at this time. A desire to do so has been increasing for some weeks past, until it has now become so strong that I can no longer forego the privilege, although it may be considered a breach of the rules of etiquet. Although a personal stranger to you, I am not unacquainted with your name and reputation, and therefore feel less reluctance in writing to you than I otherwise should.

Before the death of my wife, in August last, I was a most decided unbeliever; so much so, that I often said I would not go twenty rods out of my way to see the most astounding manifestations yet related. I believed it all a humbug. Therefore I am now entirely ignorant of any physical manifestations (unless the following may be considered as such): While I was standing by the corpse of my wife, the day after her death, I felt a very strange and pleasing sensation, such as I never felt before (which I am unable to describe and therefore will not attempt), and I have often felt the same sensation since then. It steals over me in my solitude both night and day, and cheers my lone hours. It has awakened in my mind an interest of inquiry into the truth of the doctrine of Spiritualism; and, although I can not yet fully believe in spiritual manifestations (I wish I could), my mind has undergone an entire change in regard to the future. The love of life and great dread of death have forsaken me, and I look forward with cheerfulness and hope to the time when I anticipate meeting that pure spirit who has gone before me, etc.

————, ILL., *April* 15.

DEAR SIR—I make no other apology for addressing you at this time than that I have perused a work from the spirit-land, which has been prepared under the supervision of you and Dr. Dexter, which has given me more satisfaction with regard to the future state, or life after death, than I had ever received from all other sources. And I take this opportunity of returning to you and the Doctor my sincere and heartfelt thanks for the light, and the many and everlasting truths I have received at your hands. And believe, that although this work has been aided in its onward progress by you, through much self-sacrifice on your part, yet you have been more than paid for all your efforts to aid the cause of truth in the satisfaction of having done right. I have been for years lecturing upon the laws of life and health, and striving for reform in medicine, but my mind has been in darkness with regard to the future until I perused your work, etc.

————, WISCONSIN, *April* 10, 1854.

DEAR JUDGE—With much consolation and delight I have just read your work on "Spiritualism," and now am almost persuaded to be a Spiritualist, but pause before I hazard my temporal as well as my spiritual welfare in adopting such a belief.   *   *   *   *   *   *   *   *

If only convinced that it was right to countenance and assist such proceedings, I would gladly bid farewell to all bright visions of earthly pleasure, wealth, and fame, and devote this life to the spiritual interests of immortal man. Until six years of age I was instructed by my parents in the Presbyterian faith, from whom I was at that time separated, and have since (which is about sixteen years) been left to take my own course through life, influenced at one time by circumstances to attend Roman Catholic worship, at another Episcopalian, at another Methodist, etc., each professing differently, yet each right and all others wrong. To consent to unite with any one of the sects I could not. I observed good and bad professors in them all, and just as honest and honorable men among those who made no religious profession. I soon became bewildered, careless, skeptical, and finally almost a confirmed infidel. I had not long witnessed these modern spiritual manifestations before I became convinced that they were produced through some invisible agency; and, although I had once laughed and ridiculed the idea of there being any ghosts, witches, or haunted houses, I was at length compelled to think otherwise, and obliged to admit the probability of those strange manifestations, and persuaded myself that all those apparently supernatural phenomena that have been exhibited in all ages of the world to the present time, viz., ghost-appearances, witchcraft, sorcery, house haunting, necromancy, mesmerism, psychology, biology, animal magnetism, clairvoyance, table tippings, and all these late spirit-manifestations were produced through the same agency, that they were different branches of the same mysterious tree. I believed that there could no good come from it. * * * But since reading your work on "Spiritualism," I do not know what to think about it. I know, however, the immortality of the soul was never more clearly demonstrated to my mind, or my belief in that fact or in the Divine authenticity of the Bible was never more strongly confirmed, though the belief is not of so superstitious a nature as it once was. Honored Judge, sympathize with the feeble, and do not disdain to answer, and oblige

Your sincere disciple.

———, Miss., 29th May, 1854.

Dear Sir—I have just finished the perusal of a work bearing your name, on the subject of spiritual intercourse with man in the flesh, and am induced to address you for the purpose of trying to fix my mind upon its important truths; for, believe me, I am anxious to know the truth that I may be able to believe. I have tried through twenty years to believe in the Christian system, and with all the aids of education, parental training, and example, and the strongest wish, I have been unable to believe, and am, of course, afloat upon an ocean without an anchor. You will appreciate, then, my solicitude for certainty on a matter of such importance as the immortality of the soul. If that can be obtained, I can begin to be happy, otherwise I shall not, of course, emerge from the gloom that has always surrounded me, etc.

———, Maine, June 8th, 1854.

My dear Sir—Having recently read a book on Spiritualism, put out to an anxious and inquiring world by yourself and Dr. Dexter, I have thought it not a sin to address you for a few moments upon the same, a subject so deeply interesting to the living, and of so much vital importance to the spiritual welfare of the world.

I have thought much and zealously upon the great subject, *Death*. My mind has seized hold with eager grasp on many and varying ideas, and it sometimes has appeared that I was fixed in some permanent belief, one which would hold me up here and buoy my sinking spirit over the waves of Jordan in safety; but no sooner found than gone. If the least appearance of trouble threatened, or the dark billows of life seemed to overwhelm me, then it was, and so it has ever been, my faith has forsaken me, and I have fell back in despair. The dark clouds of futurity came rolling in upon my mental vision, and death seemed to blast even my fondest hopes! This was when life was most pleasing. I had around me a little family—two boys and two girls—an affectionate wife, and a devoted mother. 'Tis true I had consigned to the grave a good father, a tender, doting mother, and a kind and affectionate sister. I had often thought of them, and had frequently bedewed their graves with memory's tears. But oh! the anguish of heart at the loss of a dear and affectionate child, none, none can tell but a loving parent whose heart has been lacerated and torn in sunder by the event.

I have lost my eldest son, one of the best boys I ever knew, trustworthy, well educated, temperate, and generous to a fault. Yes, he has gone! his familiar seat is made vacant by death! And oh, my family circle is broken, and I know not what to do to find peace. I go to church, all is empty! I read the Bible. In it I find much to admire, and many consoling promises to those who love God and do his commandments; but still I can't see my child! I pray with all the sincerity I am master of—but still no light appears. I am wrapped in impenetrable darkness. It seems that the shroud of death and unbelief has already enveloped me, and from whence there is no escape. The question is uppermost, Does my child live? is he happy? does he see his father, mother, brother, and sisters? does he wish to be with us again? could he have been saved here still longer? was his treatment right? All these and a thousand other ideas are constantly floating over my mind. Judge Edmonds, I am wretched. It is with difficulty that I can lay my mind down to my work. What shall I do? I have my answer, Believe in the Lord Jesus Christ. He is the resurrection and the life; He who believeth on me shall never die, etc., etc. Still I am benighted. My head is enveloped in thick fogs of unbelief.

Can you, my dear sir, give me light—even the least glimmer of hope that my son lives and is happy. I have consulted spirit-mediums, but can get nothing as yet satisfactory to my mind. Perhaps the fault is all my own. I am so blinded by sin and unbelief that it is impossible for me to get light Your writing encouraged me. It seemed that while I read I had hope, etc.

———

———, CHOCTAW Co., ALABAMA, *June 11th*, 1854.

DEAR SIR—I hope you will pardon me for the liberty I have taken, being an entire stranger, in addressing you this letter. I have hesitated a long time, fearing that probably you receive so many communications of this kind that you have not time to give attention to all. I have this day, after conversations with one or two of my friends, who are induced, as well as myself, to believe that there are actual communications from the spirit-land with this. I have never had or have never seen any thing of the kind, but have read your work entitled "Spiritualism," and with more pleasure than any book I have ever read. I would give any thing in my power to be convinced of the truth. I am satisfied I would be a happy man, and hope to be able in some way, from your advice, if you will give it, to arrive at some conclusion, etc.

————

————, LAPEER Co., MICH., *July* 25, '54·

DEAR SIR—In the flesh I am a stranger to you, and in all probability ever shall be, but in spirit I have held sweet communion with *you*. Yes, blessed be *God*, through your teachings on Spiritualism I have been delivered from the blackness of infidelity. For twenty-five long years I sought for the jewel of great price, and found it not, until my *soul* was entirely enveloped in the black pool of infidelity. But my deliverer has come. My heart swells with holy gratitude as I pen these lines. Yes, blessed be *God*, for me there is hope and gratitude which words can not express, *eternal life.* I know you will excuse me for troubling you with these few lines. *God bless you.*

————

————, LYNN Co., OREGON TERRITORY, *Aug* 9, 1854.

DEAR SIR—I take the liberty to write to you though a stranger ; but after reading your book entitled "Spiritualism," which I think a great deal of, I see that you appear to take a pleasure in comforting the afflicted when you can. If it is not asking too much, I would be a thousand times thankful for a communication through you from our dear children we have lost. I have your "Spiritualism" and the book of "Human Nature" by Leroy Sunderland, and Andrew Jackson·Davis' writings, which has been more satisfaction and comfort to me than all the riches of this earth could be if I had them. They have helped me, with what little manifestations I have witnessed of the spiritual manifestations, to settle my belief. I have studied the laws of nature all my life since I can recollect, daily and almost hourly, and I could not decide whether there was a future state of existence after this life or not. I could not believe the Bible, for it did not correspond with the laws of nature, nor common sense, nor justice; but after reading all those works, and seeing and hearing what little I have, I am a firm believer in the cause, which surely is a good one, etc.

————

————, VIRGINIA, 1*st Oct.*, 1854.

SIR—Although I am an entire stranger to you, nevertheless I have concluded to write to you relative to a subject about which I feel very much interested— it is "Spiritualism," any knowledge of which I was entirely ignorant, except some general newspaper information, until very lately I was loaned by a friend from New York your first volume on that subject. I must say my mind since its perusal has been very much relieved. I feel as though I had almost arrived at one of the "spheres" so beautifully described in said volume, the reason of which I believe is on account of the condition my mind has been in the last twenty years, an outline of which I'll give you, as my condition has been an unusual one.

When I was about seventeen years of age I became very much concerned about the eternal world, and made every effort to prepare myself for it, and was for about three weeks the most miserable being you could conceive of. Occasionally during this time, by continually humbling myself before God, I would feel for a short time a spiritual influence within me, but this would last only a very short time, when again all my condemnation and wretchedness would revive. In this way I continued night and day pretty much, until my system couldn't hold out any longer, and concluded I was lost and gave up, when, on the same day, while walking alone and bemoaning my condition, there was a sudden change come over my understanding or feelings, for it appeared *that* spirit, for which I had so long been striving to get to stay with me, was within me, not only within me, but round about me and in every living thing, in short God was everywhere, and 'twas in Him I lived and moved, and in *Him* all things consisted. I was relieved; but it didn't last over a few weeks, for I became a constant student of the Bible, and in it I found so much contradiction and cruelty—the last in the Old Testament—that I was a miserable being for three years, and never obtained any relief until I ceased to read or reflect on the subject. I now refused to be recognized as a religious man, although I continued one outwardly and longed to be one, and frequently since have commenced studying my Bible, but I would soon have to give it up again. This, with what real religion, according to the New Testament, I could see in the world, so staggered me, that I could not have credulity enough to believe in sufficient to embrace; for, according to the requirements there laid down, religion, pure religion, had nearly ceased to be.

In just such a condition have I been for many years, completely between two difficulties, that of heartily desiring to be religious, and the other, not knowing how I could possibly reconcile the inconsistencies already mentioned. At one time I read every work nearly in the language on infidelity, but here I could not find any relief, for none of said writers ever made me disbelieve in revelation. Yet, you'll say, "I contradict myself;" but what I mean is, I could not be made to believe or disbelieve; was in a complete strait; and, moreover, I never wished or desired for a moment to disbelieve in a revelation from God. In truth, I have for years longed and heartily wished for fellowship with God, and since reading your production it seems as if it is just what my condition requires; there is a load removed from me, and I feel better satisfied with myself and all creation. You can't imagine what consolation it has brought me, for I am constitutionally a religious man. I am not for a nominal religion, but one that reaches and influences continually the soul and life, and thereby making the being not only an outwardly good man, but one truly and practically, etc.

————

————, MICHIGAN, *Nov. 5th*, 1854.

MY DEAR FRIENDS—If you will permit an utter stranger thus to address you, can you with patience give a few moments of time to the inquiries of one whom you may never see on earth, one in whom you have no interest more than that you have for the whole family of man. But, gentlemen, you will excuse me for that very reason, when I say, I claim a fraternity from the glowing affections of a heart relieved, hope re-established, a mind at rest. * * * I have been for some weeks anxious to communicate with you touching one of the most momentous subjects that can interest an intellectual being.

During childhood and youth I was taught by pious and careful parents in the strictest possible manner. They (my parents) were both strict Lutherans and perfectly consistent in every point. Of course this had great influence with their children. My preliminary education was the best the State afforded, and at the age of seventeen I commenced the study of medicine. The habit of close and scrutinizing investigation, induced by this study, was soon formed in me, and thus I was soon led to re-examine the religious principles taught me in early life. The result, unfortunately, was to unsettle the whole range of my religious opinions. Since that day to the present, at the age of fifty-two, I have been in doubt and often in anxious perplexity. When I heard of the " Rochester knockings" it engaged my attention for a few weeks, but from the paucity of information that I could obtain, I threw it aside as nonsense. Lately, however, a friend put into my hand a work published by Judge Edmonds and Dr. Dexter, with an appendix by Gov. Tallmadge.

This work I read and re-read with the most anxious attention. Indeed, shall I acknowledge it, my mind was so absorbed that I could neither eat nor sleep. The third reading was a critical and close examination of principle, doctrine, object, laws of nature promulgated, its consistency with the laws of nature heretofore known, etc., etc. In candor I must say I was a ready convert. The more so, perhaps, because the whole doctrine in a singular manner agrees with many misty, indistinct, half-formed opinions I had gained by the study of astronomy, etc.

——————

———, Ky., *Nov.* 15, 1854.

DEAR SIR—I have read your work on Spiritualism with great pleasure, and also your occasional publications in the *Sacred Circle.* I have always arisen from the perusal of them with purer sentiments and stronger hopes of man's immortality than I have derived from any other production, etc.

——————

NEW YORK, *Nov.* 22d, 1854.

DEAR SIR—Impelled by emotions of the deepest gratitude, I address you these lines (although personally a stranger to you), for the purpose of rendering my sincere and heartfelt acknowledgments for the inestimable blessing which God in his infinite mercy has been pleased to bestow upon me, through your divine instrumentality.

The son of orthodox parents, and the grandson of an orthodox clergyman, I at an early age imbibed those gloomy doctrines. As I grew older, and reason assumed her prerogative, I began to entertain serious doubts of their truth. The more I studied to understand them, the more I became perplexed, until finally the conviction forced itself upon my mind, that there was something entirely wrong in the doctrines I had been taught to believe. Still there was an aching void within me; an unutterable longing for something higher and holier than this earth could give, and for a stronger evidence and more living faith in immortality. I deeply felt the necessity of a more pure and undefiled religion, which, freed from all earthly error, and clad in the simple garb of truth, our reason and our hearts could at once embrace. Long I struggled in a sea of doubts and fears, while from my inmost went up an earnest prayer for truth.

About sixteen months ago I read your letter in the *Herald*, which called my attention to the phenomena of the spiritual manifestations. I had heard of the subject before, but believing it to be one of the common humbugs of the day, I had not considered it worth investigating. But when I read the testimony of one whose distinguished name and high position placed him far above suspicion, I could no longer remain insensible to its importance. I commenced investigating, and received evidence after evidence of the truth of spirit-intercourse, until the last shadow of doubt was removed from my mind, and the sublime reality of eternal life, with all its immortal splendor, burst upon my astonished vision, and I rejoiced with joy unspeakable and full of glory.

I am now in almost daily communication with the happy spirits of those who were near and dear to me on the earth, who have proved their identity by unmistakable tests; whose heavenly influence and glad messages of undying love have quickened into life interior powers that I knew not of, and thrilled my soul with raptures inexpressible and joys unfelt before; and whose high and holy teachings have led me to a more intimate communion with my Maker; and have unfolded to my senses a new world of ever-increasing loveliness and beauty.

I feel that I have indeed passed from death unto life.

Oh! how sweetly the pure and holy teachings of Jesus, who died on Calvary for these same truths, harmonize with our interior perceptions when stripped of the false covering which bigotry and superstition have thrown around them.

I have also the gratifying evidence of its happy effects upon many of my friends, whose attention I have directed to this fountain of living waters, and whose thirsty souls are now drinking in rich draughts of immortal joy.

A respected and aged friend in the West writes me thus:

"*Dear Sir*—The evidences and very strong proofs with which you have been favored, of having communication with your departed brother and sister, have filled me with astonishment, and, as it were, made me at once a staunch believer, with a full determination to obtain all the knowledge upon the subject that my short span of remaining time will permit.

"Sir, I thank you for the papers you sent me. I have read them carefully, and with pleasure. I will now confess to you, that through a long life I have always been a kind of infidel; from my inability clearly to ascertain the mind's immortality. In this it is proved beyond a doubt. I can now see my way clear. God is good. God is love. We can now love him. A vail is as it were drawn from my vision. My life has acquired a value of which I was not before aware. I thought that life was short, and almost worthless. But thanks to God it is otherwise. Let us rejoice."

Thus having had both internal and external evidence of its heavenly influence and redeeming power; I can no longer doubt that it is indeed of God; and that all things else but truth will fall before its surpassing glory; and that its quickening power will spread through the hearts of men, until every human soul "with heaven-born love grows warm;" and the will of God is done upon the earth even as it is done in heaven; until the whole earth blooms in perennial beauty from the Arctic to the Antarctic circle; from the Orient to the Occident; and never-ending songs of love and praise to God most high ascend with the morning sun, as she rolls her flood of golden light around a world of love.

Even now, while I write, I feel the influence of holy spirits diffusing through my soul a harmony so divine, a joy so serene, that my whole interior being seems vibrating to the music of the spheres; and my glad soul seems eager to take its immortal flight to the realms of endless day.

Oh! for language to express the joys I know, the gratitude I feel. But there are emotions of the soul which mortal language can not express, which mortal lips can not utter, and which must be deferred until, freed from earthly impediments, I can address you in the language of the soul, when I meet you in the realms of glory.

—————, N. Y., *Dec. 5th*, 1854.

My DEAR SIR—I hope you will pardon the liberty I have taken in addressing this communication to you, but when you find that it is for the purpose of obtaining more light upon a subject that lies very near my heart and conscience, I think you will perceive that I have no ulterior object in view. I came to the city of Hudson to live about the year 1829, to learn the tailor's trade. * * * If you recollect —————— was what in them days was called a Freethinker, and left his impressions in regard to divine things on my mind, so that I have gone through all the scale of skepticism, until September last I obtained a copy of your and Dr. Dexter's work on Spiritualism; but I am as one laboring in the dark. I can not go back to cold skepticism; and I have not enough of light upon this great and momentous subject to send me forward rejoicing. Although born in poverty and reared in want, my mind has always been led to inquire what is truth? how shall I obtain it? I have went through all the doctrinal points of the so-called Christian creeds, and find but little of it there, and the balance error; but if this last manifestation should prove true, what a day of rejoicing to the down-trodden millions of earth, when they shall find that they all are His Children, and He is their Father, and there is no such thing as children of the Devil, no further than wrong teaching and the sway of their own passions have made them so! etc.

—————, OHIO, *May* 30, 1854.

DEAR SIR—Though entirely a stranger, I venture to address you on the occasion of reading the relation of your vision (to-day for the first), as I find it copied into the Ohio *Statesman* of this city.

You may judge of the interest I take in the matter, when it is noted that I have communicated with spirits in the invisible world daily, and frequently hourly, for the last eighteen months; but not in the satisfactory visible manner in which communications are made to you. * * * *

I was previously, and during most of the period of manhood, a confirmed but honest skeptic as to immortality and the Scriptures. I am so no longer, etc.

————

————, JEFFERSON Co., NEW YORK, *Jan.* 6, 1854.

DEAR SIR—I am almost in my seventieth year. Thirty-four years ago I joined the Presbyterian Church. I was an elder in the same for some years; but when I came to investigate the creeds on which the polity of the church was founded, I discovered that the God they presented me for my adoration was not the God before whom in the stillness of my own communing I had given a willing obeisant surrender of my heart. That God the Father, the Creator, and the Sustainer of the human family should, for his pleasure or otherwise—prior to the creation of our earth—make to himself a place of such dark damnation as they depict, and that God, even prior to this, in his own wisdom did predestinate a large mass of the human family to be occupants of this fearful place, I must confess I found myself an unbeliever, and if there had been no refuge but the church to which I might flee, I should have doubted the truths of God's Holy Word. But it pleased God to place in my way men who taught a more rational doctrine. Now that light has dawned on the world, I begin to realize some of great truths so indistinctly seen in the past. First to me came "Davis," dispelling the mists of darkness, and bidding the weary pilgrim raise his longing eyes to see the joys approach. After that came your Book of Books. And let me here take this opportunity to thank you most heartily for foregoing the pleasures of sin for a season, that you might put in the hands of your fellow-man these words of life. God bless you for the noble act. Oh, how my heart has expanded to those streams of gushing eloquence, as they fell from the spirit-lips of Bacon and Sweedenborg. Day and night, night and day, have I feasted on them, and still I turn to the banquet with renewed desire to taste again, etc.

————

————, NEW JERSEY, *Jan.* 8th, 1854.

SIR—I some time since attended your lecture at this place, and from your twice or thrice stating the satisfaction it would be to you, if but one of that numerous audience would look into and search of this great and wonderful revelation of the truth of which you had become fully convinced, but, sir, to my great disappointment, you never in any way pointed out to us how a man should search for the proof of a future existence by present spiritual manifestations. I hope, sir, you will excuse the liberty I take, being an utter stranger, in wishing to occupy a little of your valuable time; but I have all my life been strangely skeptical of a future existence, my mind being of that order requiring present and positive proof. I have read and heard of a great many accounts of the wonders of spiritual manifestations, but I have, during my life, passed through several professed new dispensations, and seeing them

all die a natural death, I paid but little attention to this until I heard that a
man of your known reputation and character had become a firm believer in
the truth of Spiritualism, etc.

————————

—————, MICHIGAN, *Jan.* 21*st*, 1854.

DEAR SIR—I am directed by a spirit of a high degree of intelligence to address you, otherwise I (a stranger to you) would not obtrude upon your valuable time.

I am directed to say that our mission of love to our fellow-men may be
much facilitated by the mediums which are scattered at remote distances
through the vineyard making themselves known to each other; this, to me,
would prove a high pleasure, if not an incalculable benefit.

I am further directed to give you a brief history of the spiritual manifestations in my family, which I proceed to do without ceremony.

I was reared in the old *severe* Presbyterian school, the result of which was,
that at the early age of ten years I turned in disgust and inexpressible hatred
from the Christian mythology and openly avowed my unbelief in the God of
Israel. Of course this open rebellion subjected me to much persecution from
that time onward; but thus early I had ample evidence of the presence of invisible intelligences, which directed my steps in the paths of virtue. Fully
appreciating my high responsibilities as a member of the great social family,
I arrived at hopeful manhood, deeply impressed with the great truth that my
theory of spiritual presences was correct and that the world was wrong, and
as deeply impressed with the enhancement of my moral obligations and duties
under this beautiful economy, which, however, was as yet indefinite in my
own mind. At twenty-two I entered upon the practice of law in Ohio; the
future promised a bright and flattering propect, but my mind was so deeply
impressed with higher truths than my profession promised, that in 1843, after
ten years devoted to my profession, I removed to this county with a young and
loving wife, to enjoy a seclusion which my professional pursuits forbid. . One
great object of this step was to adopt and cultivate those simple habits of conduct and that independency of thought and mental discipline so much at war
with the social habits of the times. My intention was to devote my life to
literature and the investigation of the laws of eternal progression, of which I
supposed myself the discoverer, and as such would have claimed no small degree of credit had I not since have discovered that my mind was but the
humble medium of the great thoughts of highly progressed spirits, etc.

————————

—————, N. H., *Feb.* 20, 1854.

DEAR SIR—I commenced the reading of your work entitled "Spiritualism"
with much solicitude for the doctrines it might teach, and have read it with
deep interest and great satisfaction. It has strengthened my belief in the all-
wise purposes of God, and more than all, in the future existence of the human
race. To the minds of many, indeed, a large majority of men, future existence
may be proven by the works of nature, or to those who possess the faith by
the Scriptures. But I saw not the evidence, nor had I the faith. Even at the
age of sixteen I well remember having serious reflections upon the subject of

religion. But thus early I found in the popular systems of worship inconsistencies with what I believed *must* be the great leading characteristics of God,
that God in whose works such wisdom, beauty, and justice are evinced. As I
grew older these convictions were strengthened, until at last I became almost a
confirmed skeptic. Still there remained in my mind an inherent desire to embrace some great general principles of religion that were not inconsistent with
what I conceived to be the character of that Being who created man with his
beautiful organism, and the vast universe obeying unerring laws and moving
in such harmony. When Davis' Revelations appeared, I read it with eager-
ness and also his subsequent publications, and found a plan, in many things
consonant with the great desire of my heart and the convictions of my reason.
These and many other kindred works paved the way for your "Spiritualism,"
and now I write to *thank you sincerely* for the sacrifices you have made for
your fellow-man, and for your honesty and independence in declaring to the
world your convictions upon this most momentous subject. I can not conceive
of any conclusion so rational as the one you have embraced, that these manifestations are from spirits. If this intelligence comes from man, through some
undiscovered channel, has the world ever before witnessed such a universal
concert *in falsehood* as these communications exhibit? Would every mind
which acts upon the medium add its testimony to the one great falsehood? It
is not possible. I dare say in your experience as a judge you have seen nothing equal to it. Man is not so base. I believe Spiritualism not inconsistent
with the doctrines of the Bible. It does not comport with the present condition of the Church. I believe many errors have grown into the popular systems of worship, that there is coldness, aristocracy, and selfishness mixed with
many things of good, and of course must, for a while, receive their opposition.
Your publication clears up many points of doubt which gave me some disqui-
etude previously. There are many believers in this new doctrine, and many
of the first minds in our State, and many others, are reading these works, etc.

————, Ky., *March* 14, 1854.

DEAR SIR—I have just read with a great deal of interest your and Dr.
Dexter's work on "Spiritualism." I am called by the Christian world a skeptic. I have at times doubted almost every thing but my own existence. It is
said that skepticism implies a want of knowledge. I admit it most emphatically in reference to what is taught by the Christian world of a future state.
The Bible, as expounded, has never satisfied my mind. I have had a thousand
doubts in reference to its teachings, and as I felt satisfied that some of them
must be erroneous, or they were erroneously interpreted, I had come to the
conclusion to reject the whole as being a revelation from God, and regard it
simply as a history of the Jewish nation, with all their superstitious vagaries
and idle fancies. But I must confess, that since reading your work, the only
one of the kind I have read, many of my doubts have been removed in reference to many of the facts of the Bible, believing yet there are many errors of
fact, and consequently wrong deductions therefrom. I make this latter admission on the presumption that Spiritualism be true, etc.

There is another respect in which the communications given to us receive corroboration from their accordance with others, and that is in demonstrating that the memory, the affections, and the characteristics which distinguish us in our earthly life follow us into the next existence, and abide with us there, at least for a season. In this, too, I believe that all the communications through all sorts of mediumship agree, and it is thus that we are enabled so often to identify the dear ones who have gone before, even though we can not see or hear them.

In all these respects the agreement in the manifestations is universal and uniform.

But there is another regard in which, though the agreement is not so general, yet it is, as a corroboration, of equal interest, to me at least. It has been repeatedly said to me, that what I was beholding in the visions described in this and the former volume was what was absolutely going on in the spirit-life, and the particular circumstances which occupied spirits at the time that I saw them.

How it was that I saw this, I do not know. With all my efforts, I have not been able to understand it. I live in hopes, that in time—as one by one the explanations come to me—I may be able to comprehend and explain it, but at present I can not. I only know that they come without any volition on my part, but of their own accord, and often when I am not expecting them; that they can not be the product of my own mind, for they often differ, *in toto cœlo*, from all my preconceived opinions; that they are not mere vague imaginings, for they impress themselves on the mind. with all the distinctness and precision which belong to the impression of material objects through the instrumentality of the senses; and that they are not manifested to me alone, but often to others who are present with me, and who do not at the moment know what I am beholding, and often to others far distant from me, and of whose existence even, I am at the time ignorant.

ᵀ can now readily lay my hand on two or three instances of this.

n the course of our travels last winter, we spent a few days at a small village in the West. There I heard, from professed believers in our faith, of a physician living among them, who was extensively engaged in the practice of his profession, and who was a Spiritualist, but was generally regarded by them as partially deranged on the subject. I thought, from the accounts I had of him, that it was one of those cases of fanaticism of which we have been pained to witness so much, and I dismissed the matter from my mind. Just before I left the place, he called on me, and during a brief conversation with him, I discovered a calm, clear, logical mind, with great good sense, and an utter disregard of the opinions of others in his reception of truth. He was aware of the opinion which was entertained of him, and said it was because he had told of the things which he had seen, and others had not; and that they had attempted to convince him that he had not seen. " But," said he, " I know whether I see or not, though it is not an easy matter to make others know it." And upon inquiring of him what it was he had seen, I was surprised to find he had witnessed many of the very scenes which I had, when I knew that he was ignorant that I had ever witnessed them.

I was struck with the corroboration, for here was a man of whose existence even I had been unconscious, who lived many hundred miles distant from me, who was ignorant of what had been shown to me, yet to whom, at about the same time, precisely the same revelations had been made.

This was in the State of Michigan. Another instance came from the other extremity of the country, from Alabama, and through an individual equally unknown to me. I will let him tell his own tale, by inserting here, with his permission, one of his letters to me, merely remarking that in a subsequent interview with him, I found the corroboration was even stronger than his letters would seem to indicate.

Livingston, Sumter County, Ala.,
May 29th, 1854.

My dear Sir—Manners and customs in all ages have to some extent been conventional, and have seemed to require an apology when one stranger addressed another by letter. I have just finished your work on Spiritualism, and though your senior in years, I recognize you as an elder brother.

I will commence by first stating why I am desirous of interchanging views and opinions with you. I had no certain knowledge, until I read your book, that what is considered a vision had ever appeared to me. I procured your work in Mobile, about the twentieth of last month, having never before seen any thing in print but what had appeared in the *National Intelligencer;* judge, then, my surprise when I read the vision which passed before you, in which was the old man attended with rays of light, and your departed friend in a porch of a cottage embowered in trees. This same vision in all the minute particulars has passed before me in the last few months, with this difference, that the porch and window disclosed the fact that several of my departed friends were the occupants. I would add, that the old man supported himself with a staff that reached higher than his head, by holding it in his right hand, the hand pointing up, his whole frame so weak that he bent to the right about the hips, and supported himself by occasionally bringing his left hand to his staff to aid in his efforts to brace himself up.

I would likewise add, that all things around, both animate and inanimate, particularly the wind, seemed endued with intelligence. You will readily conclude that I would be more than human if I did not feel greatly interested— particularly when I have given an account of the vision in your work, beginning on page 248, and again resumed on 289. (I believe those are the pages; I have loaned the book to a friend.)

This vision likewise passed before me with a slight addition, which may be called up to your recollection when I mention it. The star appeared to me nearly as large as a dinner plate, and unusually white; my attention was called to it with the intimation, The Star of Christ, with so much quickness as only to leave it on the mind, and immediately the picture of a head passed over the disk; the form of which is still so impressed on my mind, that, if I was a painter, I could make an exact copy. It was a calm, quiet, rather pensive, intellectual face; a well-formed nose; a broad forehead, not remarkably high, but smoother and whiter than the balance of the face; a fullness about the cheek bones; the chin somewhat projecting; the mouth rather wider than common, and the lips thinner than common.

The commodore, as presented to me, was a middle-aged man, and heavily built, with a fine formed nose, and white skin, and full glow of health. All *things* rejoiced at his arrival. The human figure not quite as tall as you describe it.

You conclude that this version is a picture of progress. I think with you, and likewise that progress will be greatly accelerated by events now transpir- in the world, particularly in Europe. * * * *

I conclude I have said enough on those subjects, and that I may have unnecessarily taxed you in the midst of more important demands on your attention.

I salute you in spiritual affection,   CHS. R. GIBBS.

P. S.— * * * * *

You may ask is my spirit-brother a member of any church? I answer yes The Senior Warden of St. James' Episcopal at this place.   C. R. GIBBS.

Another instance is mentioned in a letter, from which I extract:

SACKETT'S HARBOR, *Oct.* 31, 1854.

DEAR JUDGE :

*   *   *   *   *   *   *   *

My medial powers do not seem to increase much, from some cause or other. In fact I do not write as well; but I am informed they are trying to develop

me for speaking, and I often feel an influence, but it is not sufficiently con-
tinuous yet to be beneficial, as I would like. I frequently have visions, nights
or toward morning, in a moderately sleeping state.

It is not a little remarkable to me that yourself, Mrs. M——, of Watertown,
and myself, all unbeknown to each other, should have three different present-
ations of the lowest circles agreeing so well in the main. Mine was the 22d
May, previous to the publication of your first volume, and followed after some
little anxiety for a friend who had lived an unprogressive life, and died in
California. Mrs. M.'s was last spring. The only difference is, she had doubts
whether they ever would progress. I saw the possibility of their progressing,
and had the impression that they would eventually, though slowly, and not
until a long time, etc.

There is yet another consideration with the same tendency, and
that is the effect which a careful and close investigation of the
subject uniformly produces on the calm, logical, reasoning, cultivated mind.

Believers in spiritual intercourse are now numbered by millions
on earth. Not only in this country, but throughout this continent
and the eastern, the manifestations have made their appearance.
In the salons of the imperial cities of Europe, amid our own
mighty forests, in the solitary islands of the oceans, and on the clas-
sic shores of Greece they have been witnessed, and everywhere
they have produced in the candid, inquiring mind the same effect,
namely, the conviction of the reality of spiritual intercourse. Why,
even the pulpit, amid the iron bonds of its sectarianism, begins to
acknowledge it; and the press, mighty as it is as an engine of
human enlightenment, yet ever lagging behind the car of advancing
knowledge, astounded by the phenomenon which meets it at every
step, begins to ask, Can these things be? The jury-box, the bal-
lot-box, and the legislative halls begin to hear its lowly whisperings, and there stands now prominent before the eyes of the world,
the fact of the spread of a new faith, whose rapidity of progress
has no parallel in the annals of mankind.

May we not then, with propriety, point to these things as evidence
of the truth of that which we believe? May we not ask, what but a
stern reality could work such marvels before men? Could aught
but truth bend in dumb obedience to its behests the brightest and
strongest minds of an age distinguished for its enlightenment?
Could delusion or deception thus sweep across a prostrate world
and make conviction ride triumphant over the power of early edu-

cation, the prejudices of preconceived opinions, and the denunci-
ations of the accumulated knowledge of ages, and in defiance of
the universal cry which fear and selfishness have unitedly sent
forth in such warning tones ?   May we not ask what this is, which
not only thus carries conviction in its train in spite of all obstacles,
but which, coming from whatever source it may, thus accords in
its general and leading features ? that which, whether heard in the
gentle whisperings of the fireside or in the roar of the agitated
multitude—whether in the solitude of nature in her wildness, or
amid the din and bustle of city life—whether emanating from
high or low, from rich or poor, from the ignorant or instructed—
whether amid the moan of sorrow or the joyous laugh of gladness
—whether from the confiding repose of childhood or the stern
activity of manhood, still exhibits an accordance and a power which
acknowledge no equal in the history of the world ?

However these considerations may strike others, we confess that
with us they have great force, and they encourage us to go on
with our work, because they tend to convince us that we do not
err.

We have not been without anxiety on that subject, for it would be
in the highest degree painful to us to learn that we had even uncon-
sciously taught error and misled only one mind.   We have therefore
been impelled to great caution as to what we should send forth.
We have not deemed it worth while to enter into any detail of the
numerous precautions which we have used, or to explain the various
processes to which we have resorted in order to test the accuracy
of what has been communicated to us, for the simple reason that
we did not desire ever to be received by any one as authority.
We preferred that each one should examine for himself, and for
himself determine whether what we uttered was the truth.   If the
omission of these details on our part could but result in producing
a spirit of free inquiry in others we were well content, even though
it might subject us to the imputation in some minds of acting
hastily or unadvisedly ; for of what moment was it what others
thought of us in comparison with a freedom of thought which
should open the human mind to the reception of the great truths
now dawning on the world ?   Our paramount desire has been to
attain the truth, to receive it freely and impart it faithfully, leaving
its adoption by others to be governed by their own investigations,

by the inner promptings of their own hearts and by all of nature which they behold around them.*

But while on the one hand we have attached much importance to these items of corroboration to which we have alluded, we have not, on the other, been unmindful of the numerous difficulties attending the intercourse, nor of their just influence in determining the amount of credit to be given to them.

I pause here a while to dwell on that topic.

In the first place, then, I remark, that I know of no mode of spiritual intercourse that is exempt from a mortal taint—no kind of mediumship where the communication may not be affected by the mind of the instrument.

Take my own mediumship as an illustration. The visions which I have are, as I have remarked, impressed on my mind as vividly and distinctly as any material object possibly can be, yet in giving them to others, I must rely upon and use my own powers of observation, my own memory, my own command of language, and I not unfrequently labor under the difficulty of feeling that there is no word known to me that is adequate to conveying the novel idea communicated. I am often conscious that I fail, from poverty of language, in conveying the sentiment I receive with the same vigor and clearness with which it comes to me. So it is also with what I may call the didactic teachings through me. Sometimes the influence is so strong, that I am given, not merely the ideas, but the very words in which they are clothed, and I am unconcious of what I am going to say until I actually say it. At other times the thought is given me sentence by sentence, and I know not what idea or sentence is to follow, but the language used is my own and is selected by myself from my own memory's storehouse. And at other times the whole current of thought or process of reasoning is given me in advance, and I choose for myself the language and the illustrations used to convey it, and sometimes the order of giving it. But in all these modes there is more or less of myself in them, more or less of my individuality underlying it all. It must indeed be so, or why should I speak or write

---

* Perhaps as good evidence as we can give of this caution will be found in the fact of withholding this volume so long, when the whole of it could easily be written in a month, and most of it was written more than twelve months since.

in my own tongue rather than in a dead or a foreign language
ʿunknown to me?

I have noticed the same thing in the Doctor, and more than all
that, I have observed in both of us that our communications not
only at times contain what may be called Americanisms, but expressions peculiar to our respective professions.

It is, therefore, rarely that either of us can say that the communications through us are precisely what the spirits designed they
should be, and as they designed them; and consequently it will
never do to receive them as absolute authority, however agreeable
they may be or however consonant to other teachings.

It is not an easy matter to account for this, but it is easy to
know that the fact is so, and as easy to observe that it is at times
true of all mediums. Sometimes it is more apparent than at
others, owing to many causes ever at work around us; sometimes
it is owing to the physical condition of the medium, and sometimes to his mental state; sometimes to the atmosphere; sometimes to locality—some localities, such as high and hilly places
being more favorable than such as are low and swampy; sometimes to the condition of those who are present, whether in a state
of harmony or discord, and very frequently to the state and condition of the spirits who are professing to commune, and their apt-
itude to the task.

Thus I have known a spirit, who on earth had never learned to
read and write, to be unable to communicate through a writing medium. So one whose education here had been imperfect would
spell badly and use bad grammar, and one knowing but little of our
language would speak in broken English; and one, Lord Bacon,
for instance, who in life had been used to a different idiom from
from that now prevailing, would yet speak in modern English
Americanized, with here and there a relic of the expressions he
had used in the olden time.

There is another cause, and that is, the passiveness or otherwise of the mediums to the influence at work with them. Sometimes they resist with a very determined will, and it is impossible
for others, and often even for ourselves, to know when the operation of that will is entirely overcome, or how much of its influence
may hang around and stain the communication with its taint of
mortal life. Sometimes timidity and diffidence will color and

sometimes vanity and fanaticism distort the teaching of the spirits. Often the want of confidence will warp them ; for, strange as it may appear! there are mediums who are not Spiritualists, and who, unaccustomed to the examination of their own minds, can not discriminate between their operation and the spirit-influence ; and as often an overweening credulity will put awry that which was designed to be plain and straightforward.

There is, it is true, a simple remedy for much of this, and that is, entire passiveness in receiving the influence and the full and active exercise of the reason in weighing afterward what it has effected. But unhappily there are many who do not know the remedy, and more still who do not apply it. The intercourse is beyond conception fascinating, and there are not a few who indulge a selfish gratification in yielding to it. It is never safe to do so, for thus many are misled and many are disturbed and driven off by incongruities which could easily be avoided.

There is another consideration still, which even more fatally affects the reliability of the intercourse, and is very often overlooked.

We are taught that the intercourse is not supernatural—not the result of the suspension of nature's laws, but the product of those laws and of their legitimate action. As yet, we are in a great measure ignorant of those laws and of their mode of action ; but the results we see and can know—the effects are facts which, perceptible to our senses, appeal to our reason and demand the action of our judgments. From all that we have yet witnessed, we are warranted in the belief that the intercourse is in obedience to, and not in contravention of, natural laws—that so far as we are concerned on earth, mediumship is owing to physical organization, more than it is to moral causes, and that all in the spirit-world, the unprogressed as well as the progressed, have the power of communing with and influencing us in a greater or less degree.

So, too, we are taught that there are spirits in the next state of existence whose propensities are evil. Not that they are a distinct race of beings, known in the old theology as Devils, and represented as a creation distinct from, and independent of, the human family, but men and women who have lived on earth, perverted and distorted morally, and have passed away from this primary existence with those perversions and distortions unchanged and

aggravated by the desolation and misery, apparently to them without end and without hope, in which they find themselves existing.
Selfish, intolerant, cruel, malicious, and delighting in human suffering upon earth, they continue the same, for awhile at least, in their
spirit-home. And having in common with others the power of
reaching mankind through this newly-developed instrumentality,
they use it for the gratification of their predominant propensities,
with even less regard than they had on earth, for the suffering
which they may inflict on others.

Some instances of this are disclosed in the following papers, but
many, very many more are occurring to the knowledge of inquirers
everywhere, and there are perhaps few circles where first or last
this has not been in some form or other apparent.

It can not be difficult to discover in such a state of things the material, not only for much positive mischief, but the cause of many of
the crudities and contradictions which so often disturb the superficial observer, and sometimes mislead the credulous and confiding.

This influence displays itself in various forms, but scarcely ever
without tending to impair confidence in the manifestations. Sometimes it is with a clearly marked purpose of evil, avowed with a
hardihood which smacks of the vilest condition of mortal society.
Sometimes its fell purposes are most adroitly vailed under the cover
of good intentions. Sometimes it is restless and uneasy—"to one
thing constant never." At other times it is calm, considerate, and
persevering. Now it contents itself with finding amusement in
the harmless perplexities to which it subjects us, and anon it is
satisfied only when it can goad on its victim to crime, and rejoice
in the agony it produces.

But, whatever its form, its existence is too strongly demonstrated to doubt it, and while it shows to us the realization of the
" roaring lion seeking whom it may devour" of Holy Writ, or " the
instigation of the devil" preserved still in our old law forms, we
have the consolation of knowing that now we can be conscious of
its presence, and guard against its approaches. We can detect
when it is near us, and, no longer obliged to battle with it in the
darkness of our own fears and ignorance, we can meet it boldly,
and contend against it successfully. And, above all, we can expose its unhallowed intrusion upon the communion which is otherwise calculated to lift our hearts upward to our God.

It is not however alone from those evilly disposed that this element of distrust flows. There must of necessity be in the spirit-world those who are in every imaginable condition of development, and who occupy every imaginable position on the ascending plane of progression. Some are more, and some less, ignorant than others; some more prudent and careful; some more zealous and inconsiderate; some impulsive and rapid, and some calm and deliberate; in fine, with every conceivable variety of attribute and faculty. Of necessity, the communications from each of these must be affected, as all human intercourse is, by the peculiar characteristics of each individual. And while from this source must necessarily flow an element of uncertainty, we are taught to avoid its inconveniences and its hazards, by applying to it, as we do when weighing human testimony, the sagacity and searching power of our reason.

There is yet another consideration not to be disregarded. I allude to false communications and fabricated mediumship. Such instances have been known among us; some where the mediumship was entirely an assumption of the pretender, and unworthy of any confidence. In all religions ever known to man, hypocrites have been found; and while we have no reason to expect ours to be exempt from this common lot of humanity, we have abundant reason to know that it is comparatively harmless with us, and must be still more so as we advance in the power which is dealing with us and which is enabling us to read our own hearts and the hearts of our fellow-men. But there are false communications which are not intentionally so. Some arising from a mistake of the spirit who is communing, and some from the error of the medium who has not yet so studied himself as to be able to distinguish the innate action of his own mind from the impress of spirit-influence.

Another consideration is, that the character of the mediumship is frequently changing in the same individual, and that no two mediums are precisely alike. From this latter cause there must of necessity arise an effect producing some uncertainty. It is as if one on earth were sending the same message through different persons. No two would deliver it in precisely the same words, unless they had learned it by rote. The main idea might be transmitted correctly enough, but it would be liable to various shadings,

from the different capacity of the messengers to comprehend it
and from the variety of their power of language to utter it.

The changes in the medium are often imperceptible at first, and
are made manifest only in the effect produced, and at other times
they are very great, without any one's knowing when they occurred. I can best illustrate this by a brief account of one medium
whose whole progress I have witnessed with intense interest.

She was a young girl of tolerable education and warmly attached to the Roman Catholic faith. Her church told her to disbelieve
in Spiritualism, and she refused to witness any of the manifestations, though they were frequent all around her. At length the
house in which she resided became what in former days would
have been called haunted. It continued so for nearly six months,
during which she heard strange sounds and witnessed various acts,
which, she became satisfied, were not the product of any mortal
agency, but were evidently intelligent. Her curiosity was excited,
and she sought a medium. She soon saw enough to convince her
of a spiritual agency, and very soon became herself a medium.
It is now about a year since she was developed as such, and her
mediumship in that period has assumed many forms.

At first she was violently agitated in her person. She soon wrote
mechanically; that is, without any volition on her part, and without any consciousness of what she was penning. Having a strong
will, she was able at any moment, by exercising it, to arrest the
manifestation. She next became a speaking medium. She was
not entranced as some are, into a state of unconsciousness, but
was fully aware of all she was saying and of all that occurred
around her. She, however, had not advanced far enough to know
the source whence came the thoughts which she was uttering, and
she imagined they might be the product of her own mind. To
convince her upon that subject, she was shown, through the instrumentality of her own mind, all the particulars of the wreck of the
steamer San Francisco—that her upper deck had been swept off
and a certain number had thus perished; that the residue of those
on board had been taken off in three vessels, and were then on
their way in different directions for different ports, and that the
steamer had been abandoned on the sea. All this was several
days before any news had reached the land of the accident to that
vessel, and she was told to wait and see if the information which

had been given her, and which was much more detailed than I have written, was not strictly accurate, and then determine for herself whether it was her own mind. A few days brought minute confirmation of every incident which had been disclosed to her.

Since then this faculty of knowing things at a distance has greatly improved. She saw the wreck of the Arctic when it was occurring. She saw and detailed with great accuracy, as subsequent accounts showed, the recent collision on the Canada Railroad, and that a few moments after it happened, and while the dead and wounded were being lifted out of the ruins. She has seen and described the state of things at Sebastopol and its vicinity, and she has frequently described scenes and conversations going on at the moment, at the distance of several hundred miles from her; and all this, not when she was in a trance, but in a state of mental consciousness to all around her.

She next became developed to speak different languages. She knows no language but her own, and a little smattering of boarding-school French. Yet she has spoken in nine or ten different tongues, sometimes for an hour at a time, with the ease and fluency of a native. It is not unfrequent that foreigners converse with their spirit-friends through her in their own language. A recent instance occurred where a Greek gentleman had several interviews, and for several hours at a time carried on the conversation on his part in Greek, and received his answers sometimes in that language and sometimes in English; yet until then she had never heard a word of modern Greek spoken.

About the same time her musical powers became developed. She has repeatedly sang in foreign languages, such as Italian, Indian, German, and Polish, and it is now not unfrequent that she sings in her own language, *improvising* both words and tune as she proceeds—the melody being very unique and perfect, and the sentiments in the highest degree elevating and ennobling.

Her next advance was to see spirits and spiritual scenes, and now scarcely a day passes that she does not describe the spirits who are present, entire strangers to her, yet very readily recognized and identified by their inquiring friends. This has of late been witnessed by very many persons, and many an unbeliever in spiritual intercourse has been overwhelmed with the evidence of identity which thus by sight and by communion has been presented.

At one time she was used as the instrument for delivering long and didactic discourses on the principles of our faith. Now she is mostly used to give moral and mental tests, which to many are very satisfactory. At one time she saw chiefly allegorical pictures ; now she sees the reality of spiritual life. Once she wrote mechanically, but now by impression, knowing the thoughts she pens. Formerly it was difficult for spirits to converse through her ; but now conversation, with any one, however much a stranger to her, goes on with a freedom and ease most gratifying to the investigator.

These various changes have been wrought generally without any apparent external cause, and have been unknown until they appeared. But what internal process may have been going on to produce them we do not know, nor how far its workings may at the time affect the mediumship. We simply know that they are, and as they may affect the intercourse, we feel an admonition to greater care and caution.

I do not mention this case as a solitary or extraordinary instance of spirit-power, for I am aware of many others of a similar character. But I refer to it because it is an apt illustration of the view I am endeavoring to present, and because the whole development having occurred under my own observation, I incur the less hazard of being mistaken.

From this whole class of cases I draw two inferences, one which I have already mentioned—namely, that the communications may be affected by these changes ; and the other, that the faculty of mediumship is like all our other faculties, capable of advancement and increase by education and training. The original power of becoming a medium may be owing to some peculiar organization of the individual, like the organs of language, of music, of imitation, and the like ; but, like them, the faculty is capable of great improvement by a due course of treatment. If this be so, then, until the medial power be developed to its state of perfection— and what that may be we do not yet know—there must of necessity be great changes in its exercise, which can not with safety be disregarded.

The changes from this cause are not confined to individual cases, but they are visible in the whole scope of the intercourse. At first the manifestations were generally made in the rudest and simplest physical form, addressing themselves mainly to the senses. But as minds became convinced of the reality of spirit-communion, and stept over the threshold of the new school, seeking the higher truths which it was apparent must flow from that reality, there was a demand for a more elevated and more facile mode of conveying them to us. The supply at once met the demand. And there is, in my view, no stronger evidence of the divine origin of this mighty movement than is to be found in the fact, that as the mind grasps the knowledge proffered it, and craves for more, the means are at once provided for satisfying that craving, and those means very often unlike any device of man's ingenuity, and unlike aught previously known to him.

How often has the most determined unbeliever been struck down from his self-complacent but giddy height by a power which he could not control! How often has the skeptical medium been overpowered, even in his physical action, by an influence unseen, and to him before unknown! How often has the astuteness of the keenest doubter been set at naught by an intelligence whose capacity he could not measure, and whose source he could not fathom, but whose presence he could not question! How have the timid, the weak, and the halting been strengthened and sustained until they could easily brave all that the opposition of an angry world could inflict! How have the strong, towering in the might of their own knowledge, been laid prostrate at the feet of those whom they regarded as most ignorant! And how invariably and inflexibly has conviction ever followed investigation!

I for one see and acknowledge in this a power mightier than belongs to mere earthly humanity, and I bend in humble adoration in its presence, but too conscious that without its aid I can not grasp the mighty truths it can teach. But those truths come, and by instrumentalities so admirably fashioned to the work in hand, so perfectly adapted to the occasion, that to deny their spiritual origin involves the assumption of a power in the human frame which would tax the credulity far beyond aught demanded by a belief in Spiritualism.

But this is, in a measure, a digression from the topic on which I intended to dwell. My purpose was, as I invoked on the one hand certain fragments of corroborative evidence, so it was due to candor and to the spirit of fair inquiry, by which I hope I am governed, to state on the other those things which are calculated to detract from the force of that evidence.

I do not mean here to say that I have enumerated all the impeaching evidence that may be found in this matter. I am, on the contrary, aware that I have not, nor can I well do so in the limits allotted to this paper. For, as no two mediums are exactly alike in their manifestations, and there are now thousands of them; as no two communications through the same mediums are ever exactly alike, because ever liable to be affected by the existing condition of both mind and body; as the spirits who commune are no two of them alike, and are now numbered by tens of thousands; and as the variety in the source as well as in the instrumentality of the communication is as vast as that which is to be found in the human character everywhere, so there must of necessity be many other causes to warn the well-regulated mind to beware of credulity and fanaticism, and to weigh all things carefully and well before yielding belief.

To do this there is but one safe course, and that is, to apply to the evidences which Spiritualism proffers the same acuteness of reasoning, the same deliberation of judgment which it is necessary for us to apply to all other evidences presented to the human mind; to test them as we would test any human evidence on any topic, and apply to them the same touchstone which for ages we have been called upon to apply to the evidences of Christianity.* Doing this wisely and discreetly, the rational mind will find no difficulty in arriving at a satisfactory conclusion, even amid the incongruities which Spiritualism in its crude and infant existence may present.

But I dismiss this topic, lest I may dwell upon it too long for the patience of the reader. My intention was originally to devote a large portion of this paper to an enumeration of the benefits that must flow from the adoption of our faith. But my fellow-laborer has performed that task so well in his introduction, that I am saved

---

* Since I have been a Spiritualist I have occupied some of my time in reperusing "Paley's Evidences of Christianity," and I was struck with the applicability of the whole reasoning to the evidences of Spiritualism. I recommend a reference to that work, especially to those who are disposed to quarrel with our faith because it refuses to save them from the responsibility of thinking for themselves.

from doing more than dwelling a moment on one or two of its leading considerations.

One is, that Spiritualism proves the immortality of the soul. It does not ask us to believe it upon the authority of its mere assertion; it does not merely present to us the abstract reasoning which to many minds in all ages has been so unsatisfactory; it does not merely appeal to nature and her laws and their operation, which in this age have been so powerless to work out the end in view; it does not merely point to the golden vaults of the heart, and seek a response from its awakened instincts, but it proves it in a manner most satisfactory to the intellect, even when enveloped in its material surroundings—proves it by a direct and unanswerable appeal to the senses—proves it as the Creator proves that the sun shines at noonday and the stars sparkle at night—proves it as nature demonstrates the existence of the storm and the thunder—proves it as matter makes manifest to us its own reality—proves it through the instrumentality of our material organs—and proves it as many other things are made apparent to us, so that we may say, not merely that "we believe," but that "we know." And what is most interesting is, that the evidence is within every man's reach. He has but to knock, and it will be opened to him—he has but to ask, and he may receive. No man lives but he may have, if he pleases, evidence most satisfactory, that the friends whom he has laid in the grave do yet live and can commune with him.

This is a bold assertion to make, but I make it after years of careful investigation, conducted under most favorable circumstances, after having witnessed innumerable manifestations, and after having beheld the intercourse in all its known phases. I make it deliberately, and as the result to which my examination and that of many, very many others has conducted me, and I know I can not be mistaken. Whether I am or not, the means are fortunately at hand to determine. I repeat, they are within every man's reach. He has but to stretch forth his arm and be satisfied. The tree of knowledge is planted in our midst and each can pluck for himself of its fruit and eat. True, now, as of old, the serpent of evil does coil its loathsome form around its outer branches, but the fruit is at length beyond the reach of its poison—the flower blossoms in despite of its pestiferous breath, and man, when he approaches its grateful shade, may yet crush the tempter's head beneath his heel

4

If this be so, can we be sufficiently grateful to the Bounteous Giver that he has at length in His mercy removed the murky cloud of infidelity which was casting its dark pall over the human heart, crushing it out of the very form of humanity amid the crumbling ruins of its own happiness? And can we reject the precious boon which comes on angels' wings to waft us nearer to our God?

There may, indeed, be difficulties in the way, obstacles to encounter, inconveniences to suffer, but to the anxious inquirer they will not be insurmountable. It is possible to overcome them, and then will follow conviction, bearing in its train peace and love to man.

But this is not the chief benefit of Spiritualism. It not only teaches us that we do indeed live after death, but it teaches us what that life is, affording us the inestimable advantage of knowing how properly to prepare for it. A part of that knowledge has already been given, not merely in these pages, but in the numerous publications and discourses which have been used as the means of conveying it to us. More will yet in due time be given; for it is the design of this great work to open to us a view of the intimate relation ever existing between us in the mortal form and the spirit-world, and its ever-present influence over us for good or for evil, and a revelation of what the world is into which we shall be ushered when we shuffle off this mortal coil.

Can we estimate too highly the value of this knowledge? Can we set too high a price upon that which teaches us the true purposes of our existence upon earth, and how to shape it so as most effectually to secure our everlasting happiness? Can we too highly value that which rolls away from our minds the ignorance and mystery which have hitherto brooded over us, and reveals to us the destiny which is before us? that which answers the craving want of the human heart, and so speaks to the spirit of the Creator, which slumbers there, that starting from the confines of its mortal chamber, it springs forth to meet its God, and returns to its home laden with his blessing?

Be the estimate which man may put upon this revelation what it may, whether it be welcomed or be crucified, it is coming—coming in the panoply of the Infinite Father—coming with healing on its wings to redeem man from his wanderings, and enable him to stand erect in the presence of his God redeemed by his freedom.

J. W. EDMONDS.

New York, *December* 17, 1854.

P. S.—In the Appendix to our former volume was inserted a letter from Governor Tallmadge, to the *National Intelligencer* newspaper, in which the name of Lord Brougham was mentioned in these words : " Recent accounts inform us that Lord Brougham and Dr. Ashburner, of England, and others of highest rank and intellect, have become converts to it, and that it has engaged the earnest attention of the most eminent German philosophers. And when we hear of such ' aged grandmothers,' such ' youthful patrons of the band-box, and worshipers of lace and ribbons,' and such ' weak-minded excuses for manhood,' with ' an ass's appendage to their heads,' as Lord Brougham and Dr. Ashburner of England, and Judge Edmonds and others of the highest order of intellect in this country becoming converts to it," etc.

It seems that Lord B. is dissatisfied with the mention of his name in this connection, and I publish the following correspondence as the most effectual mode I can adopt to remove the impression of which he complains :

WASHINGTON, *Jan. 20th*, 1854.

DEAR SIR—I received by the last steamer a letter from Lord Brougham, which it seems to be his wish should be communicated to you.

I accordingly inclose you a copy, and I remain respectfully yours,

EDWARD EVERETT.

JUDGE EDMONDS.

CANNES, *Dec.* 22, 1853.

MY DEAR MR. E.—Will you excuse me if I give you a little trouble ? A friend in England, on whose accuracy I can rely—not having myself seen the work—informs me that Judge Edmonds has mentioned me among those whom he gives as believers in what are called the " spiritual manifestations," and I am desirous that he should be set right, as some one has misinformed him on the subject. There is not the least foundation for the statement. From all I have heard of the Judge, I have great respect for his learning, his abilities, and his character; but not having the honor of his acquaintance, I must beg of you to set him right for me. I have no title to pronounce any opinion upon the point in dispute, but only to state the fact, that I am not among those who have given, or who have formed an opinion in the affirmative.

Believe me, sincerely yours,

[Signed]   H. BROUGHAM.

NEW YORK, *Jan.* 28, 1854.

HON. E. EVERETT, U. S. Senate :

Sir—I do not at all know to what Lord Brougham alludes, for I am not conscious that his name is anywhere mentioned in my book, nor could I permit myself to use any gentleman's name, in the manner he supposes I have used it, without his consent.

Still, as the book is the work of several hands, and others besides myself examined the proof, it may be that his name has crept in without my knowing it.

I have not had time since the receipt of your note to read the book, to see if I can find his name, nor shall I have time for several weeks to come. I will, however, avail myself of my earliest leisure for that purpose, and if I find it, I will hasten to make the amende honorable, and protect him as far as lies in my power from the disastrous consequences of his being identified against his will with a cause which is unpopular only with those who refuse to examine it.

Very respectfully your obedient servant,

J. W. EDMONDS

INTRODUCTION OF DR. DEXTER.

ONE of the strongest impressions which rests upon the reflecting mind, when man surveys himself, the world on which he exists, and the countless changes which are continually taking place, relates to the imperfection of human knowledge. But as the human mind is constituted for progress, and can find no rest in the past, but is ever striving to discover from the evidences of the present what are the realities of the future, it is not singular that reasonable and earnest inquiry should be made to understand those subjects about which nature and revelation are apparently silent. It is uniformly assumed by philosophers and divines, and perhaps by civilized nations everywhere, that the worth, the dignity, the importance of man lie in his rational immortal nature, and that though death is everywhere, man can not die. He exists forever, and therefore he must think; and because he is capable of originating thought, and exercising it in the investigation of the realities of universal nature and of his own selfhood, the knowledge which he thus acquires encourages him to extend his inquiries beyond the limits of material life, and to ask what is the life hereafter? If we are forced to admit the imperfection of human wisdom in all that relates to those principles which regulate and control the material world, how much more limited has been our knowledge of that world which we are taught by our own innate consciousness and by revelation will be the abode of that immortal spirit after it shall have left the body!

But from that period, comparatively recent, when man began by new and more certain methods to explain and understand the manifestations of the Divine intelligence, and, inspired by the noble purposes opening before him, to speculate on the phenomena which he everywhere witnessed, humbly and diligently seeking to unravel the mysteries both of material and spiritual life, thus to catch a glimpse, however dim and distant, of their glorious Author, how great has been the change in his views and ideas! Instead of barren generalities—of vague classifications—of propositions promising every thing to the ear, but performing comparatively little to the senses—of maxims based on pure assumption, and argument taking its stand on the basis of our presumed ignorance, we find that it has been practicable for human faculties to attain to a knowledge of truths based on a foundation co-extensive with the universe, and yet applicable to the realities of the material and spiritual world.

On the ordinary grounds of contemplation, it may well be accounted strange that this great result of human research and comparison has not satisfied every rational mind of the intimate connection of the spiritual with the material. · The evidence of such a connection confronts man at all points of his consciousness and his experience. It meets him on every path of science, of history, and of social and individual life. It is blended with every utterance which reaches the human mind, and continually new testimony is arising which even now is speaking in a voice of deep and awful intensity, proclaiming the glorious and yet joyful revelation, not alone of the Divine intervention in the affairs of human beings, but that the spirits of our departed friends can come back to earth and hold positive and direct communion with those whom they have there loved. However conclusive the testimony on which this revelation has been founded, and the support which it has received from direct and collateral manifestations in all ages of the world, it has none the less been opposed for its supposed inconsistencies and untruth. But the minds of the vast body of mankind rejecting at first any idea apparently contravening established opinions, will, after careful and earnest examination, ultimately yield to the evidence of facts. In respect of science, of history, of social life, this is true—and why may it not be true in respect to the disclosures of Spiritualism? Simply regarding it as the communication of certain realities otherwise unknown, why, confirmed and commended as it has been by wonders so numerous and impressive, may it not ere long be universally received as the great induction from which a complete knowledge of all that belongs to man's life on earth, and his spirit's existence in the spheres, may be derived?

It is not my intention at present to press upon the reader's mind the proofs that have convinced me of the reality of spiritual intercourse. I leave its proofs to the inquirer's own observation, for the reason that I am well aware that no mere argument in support of its truthfulness ever convinced any man. I might state with all fairness the history of the many circumstances and revelations I have witnessed and received, but no inquiring mind ought to accept as proof the evidence which has satisfied my mind. The opportunities for elaborate investigation are so numerous, and the advantages for every kind of manifestation so ready at hand, that there is no excuse for any one's taking the " say so" of any individual as truth. Equally at the present day, as in times past, " He who runs may read." The evidence which I might present as having convinced my reason, would perhaps be rejected by other minds pursuing the same investigation. To satisfy the vague desire which at times agitates the soul to know what there is of reality in that world which is sealed up by death from the examination of the physical senses, requires something more positive and definitive than those proofs which have satisfied other minds. To SEE IS TO KNOW. No man has ever adopted this motto from the promptings of a mere external policy. It is instinctively recognized both by the physical and spiritual existences, as embracing the only absolutely safe rule of guidance, and as such it claims individual satisfaction from all suspense or doubt. My reasons, therefore, for declining the consideration of this portion of my subject will, I trust, be understood.

I may here incidentally remark, however, that no reasonable man can refuse to credit the multitude of facts supported by the testimony of as many creditable witnesses, upon which the belief of present spiritual intercourse is now based. It can not be denied that there are an immense number of persons, educated and enlightened, receiving these communications and believing them to be true, after such careful and earnest investigation as has scarcely been bestowed on the evidences of Christianity since its eternal truths were first given to the world—and it is not irrelevant to ask, in view of the unexampled spread of this belief, and comparing its progress with the growth and increase of the religion of Christ, what length of time is necessary to test its truth, and what is at the present time the condition of this subject in the face of all the means, ordinary and extraordinary, which have been opposed to it? I do not offer these remarks as an argument to convince any one of the truth of Spiritualism, but as a suggestion for its sincere examination; for, to my mind, he who is content, without investigation, to regard the evidences that a new revelation has been made to man, as a fallacy, not only assumes to himself the ability to decide that about which he is entirely ignorant, but he denies in this assumption all the evidences on which are founded the Christian religion and the belief in the immortality of the soul.

With this preliminary generalization, I come to the more specific object now before me, which is to consider the constantly recurring question, "What good and useful purposes are being accomplished by the wonderful manifestations now attracting public attention, even admitting them to be of spiritual origin?"

In one view of the subject it seems strange, but in another it is not strange, that this question should be so frequently asked. It seems strange that, in an age like this, when the intellectual tendencies of mankind are almost uniformly toward materialism, and when faith in a hereafter state of the soul is fast losing its vitality and its practical influence upon mankind, any one should fail to perceive that a positive demonstration of the reality of a spirit-world, and its presence with, and influence upon, this world, must necessarily be attended with immense consequences, either for good or for evil, and that upon the whole the results could scarcely be of the latter character. Yet, when we consider that it is a prominent and really noble tendency of the properly conservative and cautious mind to admit innovations only upon the definite and specific proofs of their utility, we can not wonder that minds of this character should require the distinct and demonstrative *specifications* of the good results following, or which are to follow, this new spiritual unfolding. A few such specifications, therefore, will now be offered to the consideration of the candid reader.

I will not here stop to dwell upon the blessings of a liberation from the gloomy fears of future nonentity, and the joys of the absolute assurance of the continued existence, affection, and watch-.

ful presence of beloved ones departed from the visible form, which this new unfolding has brought to thousands and tens of thousands who were previously enveloped in the gloom of skepticism. These; in their social intercourse with the world, are daily and hourly telling their own eloquent story of the benefits which they have derived from Spiritualism. O could we but realize at one grasp of the *conceptive* faculties, the tears that have been dried, the sighs that have been hushed, the anxieties that have been soothed, and the heartfelt gratitude that has been made to ascend up to God by this new outpouring of spiritual light, and by the blessed assurances it has brought of the continued love of our departed friends, of the love of the angels, and above all, of the love of our heavenly Father, we would all be abundantly satisfied with the " good" which this new dispensation has brought to the world, even without inquiring for further proofs of its beneficent influence ; but leaving the full perception of these unspeakable blessings to the true instincts of the human heart, we proceed to consider the " good" resulting from these modern manifestations in a few other points of view.

And one world-wide and all-important use which they are evidently accomplishing is that of *conserving and reëstablishing the spirituality and religion of the race.* An intelligible conception of the bearings and importance of this proposition will be facilitated by a brief survey of the spiritual history of the world. It will be proved by such a survey, that spirituality is a natural and indispensable element of the human mind and of the race—in former times unquestioned, but in these latter days fast tending to decay, and requiring some new unfolding from the supernal spheres to preserve it from utter extinction.

With a few exceptional and temporary cases, the most prominent of which are found in the mental history of recent times, mankind have, in every age and in every nation, recognized the reality of existing spiritual intercourse in some form, and from this idea have derived their highest individual, social, and national impulses. According to the Biblical history of the Garden of Eden, and the coincident heathen traditions of a golden age, this intercourse was enjoyed by the first human beings that dwelt upon the earth. Thence it is traceable through the history of Cain and Abel, of Enoch, of Noah, of Abraham, Isaac, and Jacob, of Joseph, of Moses,

of Samuel, of Saul, of David, and thence through the long line of
the Jewish prophets, seers, priests, and other interiorly minded
persons of the same nation.   Nay, its light had not died out
among the Jews before, and in the days of Jesus, as the vision
Zacharias, the dreams of Joseph, the angelic annunciation to the
shepherds concerning the birth of the infant Messiah, etc., fully
testify.   Nor need we look to the history of the Jewish nation
alone for examples of spiritual communication ; for, indeed, the
Bible itself directs us to several cases of the same in the experience of heathen men.   Among these are the dreams of Pharaoh,
the prophetical impressions of Balaam, the visions of Nebuchad-
nezzar, and the evidently spiritual guidance which brought the
wise men, or magi, from the East to visit the infant Jesus.

More numerous still are the testimonies of similar import which
we find on opening the pages of general history.   We find that a
connection with spiritual sources of power and intelligence was
claimed by the gymnosophists of India, the magi of Persia, the
wise men of Egypt, the prophets and diviners of Greece and
Rome, the druidical priests and bards of ancient Gaul and Britain,
the scalds of Scandinavia, etc.   We find such a connection
evinced in the true prophetic dreams and visions of Mandane, of
Cyrus the Great, of Cambyses, of Darius, and others of the ancient
Median and Persian kings and nobles. · We find it proved by the
utterances of the oracles of Butos, of Jupiter Ammon, of Colophon,
of Dodona, of Trophonius, and by the sublime prophetic and didactic utterances of the Delphic Pythia, which, as the dictates of the
god Apollo, were for ages implicitly followed by kings, armies, and
nations.   Spiritualism, indeed, forms a fundamental feature of all
ancient, historical, and poetic literature, and the spiritual element
of this could not be taken away without essentially marring the
structure and consistency of the whole.

But all the valuable spiritual light and power which in previous
times had been vouchsafed both to the Jewish and the various heathen
nations, was purified and brought to a climax of perfection in Jesus
Christ and his apostles.   The partialisms, inconsistencies, and
moral imperfections which had often been apparent in the previous
demonstrations of a guiding spiritual intelligence were, by the
spiritualism of Jesus, supplanted by the most broad and genial
views of the universal love of God, the universal brotherhood of

man, and the universal harmony of truth. Under these recognized and practically illustrated principles, the inflowings of spiritual light and love were clear, self-demonstrative, and irresistibly powerful; and those who, submitting to the influence and guidance of the heavenly Teacher, experienced the opening of their interior faculties, dwelt in the sweetest and most sensible communion with each other, with the angels, and with God. Demonstrations from the spiritual world were, among them, frequent and universally recognized; and by a constant renewal of these demonstrations in some of their diversified forms, their faith was kept constantly active, unwavering, and so intensely lively as to exercise an absolute government over the outer lives and conduct of its possessors. If by a suspension of the interior gifts of the spirit providentially ordered for purposes of trial and humiliation, the votary of the new faith was immersed in temporary darkness and doubt, it was only necessary for him to institute a stricter discipline over his interior affections, and to appeal with more earnest prayer to the Great Source of spiritual light and joy, in order to have a renewal of those unmistakable evidences, interior and exterior, on which his profession of faith was based. It was not necessary to say to those persons, "Know ye the Lord and his truths," for all had this knowledge, from the least to the greatest, having the witness of its reality within themselves, and in the wonderful sayings and doings of their prophets, prophetesses, and other *mediums* for the spiritual afflatus.

These spiritual gifts and their outer manifestations continued to exist and to be universally recognized for some two or three centuries after the crucifixion of Jesus—indeed, so long as professed Christians remained sufficiently faithful to the heavenly light; and it is presumable that they never would have ceased had it not been for the moral decadence of the professed receivers of the Christian faith. But as the pure waters of spiritual truth and life flowed out from their fount in Jesus and his apostles, among the nations of the earth, and thence down through the subsequent ages and generations of mankind, they became more and more commingled with the sensualisms and corruptions of man, until in these latter ages they have become comparatively lost; and those whose sacred office it should be to administer them to a thirsting world are now, alas, found denying their very existence, except as confined to the deep and almost inaccessible wells of traditional antiquity. They would have us go to the New Testament records, and to them alone, for evidences of the outpouring of the spirit of God and of the reality of an immortal state of existence beyond the grave, discouraging all ideas of a present and direct intercourse with the spiritual world as necessarily savoring of infidelity! How strange that the professed conservators of the spirituality of the world should ignore the present existence of that apparent Divine law by which, according to the most reliable history, spiritual influx was kept perpetual from the earliest ages to comparatively recent times, and that they should suppose, in the absence of all scriptural and philosophical proof, that that law was entirely and for ever suspended when it came to the climax of its development in Christianity!

It is freely admitted that to those who are already sufficiently spiritualized to appreciate the facts and philosophy of the New Testament records, these may, in some degree, serve as a satisfactory source of proof in respect to the doctrine of immortality, and the reality of ancient revelations from the superior world; but to the countless and increasing multitudes who constitutionally and habitually depend for convictions of truth upon the exterior and tangible facts of the present, rather than upon the (to them) apparently mystical relations of the past, this source of evidence has, by actual experiment, *proved* to be totally inadequate. Hence within the last two centuries each succeeding year had added to the number of deniers of all spiritual existences and spiritual and divine revelations. Professors and teachers of Christianity have endeavored to arrest this wide-spread defection from spiritual and religious faith, by all the means which they have deemed legitimate to employ. Not recognizing *present* spiritual demonstrations, however, and finding the simple presentation of Scripture testimonies inadequate to produce the desired conviction, they have, in too many instances, become impatient and resorted to dogmatic and dictatorial methods of enforcing them. By these means the weak-minded have been crushed into an unreasoning assent to the *dicta* of their teachers; and with this exclusion of their rational powers from all participancy in the formation of their religious convictions, they have been made the willing slaves of whatever forms of superstition an ambitious and bigoted priesthood chose to impose upon them.

While one class of mankind have thus been led to divorce re-

ligion, in a great measure, from rationality, and become the de-
votees of an imperious dogmatism, alike unfavorable to their own
spiritual growth and restrictive of the religious and intellectual
progress of the race, another class, provoked by the tyranny of
church and priest, have not only been confirmed in previous skepticism, but have engaged in a methodical opposition to every form
of religion and spirituality. They denounce all these as unfound-
ed figments of a superstitious fancy, or cunningly devised fables,
invented to subserve a priestly domination. In a tone of free
inquiry, recognized as legitimate in every other department of
thought (and which the world can not much longer be convinced
is out of place when applied even to *this* subject), they have asked, " Where is the evidence of your spirit-world, of your God, and
of your religion ?" And as this class of minds for the most part
are unfortunately closed against the light of Bible testimony, their
queries have been left without satisfactory answers, and the quer-
ists have thus been left without any spiritually-redeeming power,
except it arise outside of the Church and even outside of the Bible.

Moreover, under the influence of this general denial of present
intercourse between the mundane and the spiritual spheres, it is
not to be wondered that the faith even of the *Church itself* has
grown cold and languid, and that its moral power has become as
nothing in comparison to what it was in its primitive ages, when
the gifts of the spirit were everywhere recognized. Facts known
and seen of all men render it daily more obvious that the functions
of the Christian ministry are falling into a mere mechanical round
of ceremonies, performed mainly from the impulse of time-honored
custom, and that all the existing forms of religious worship are
fast degenerating into meaningless mummery from which all spiritual life and power have departed. The really religious, the really
spiritually-minded (of which we are happy to say there are still a
few in the Church), see and acknowledge this, and are constantly
sending forth their lamentations from pulpit and press and in the
conference-room, at this great decline of spirituality among those
who should be the world's spiritual exemplars and teachers. This
moribund condition of spirituality in the Church is becoming more
and more conspicuous, and the hope of its being remedied from
resources within itself is constantly diminishing.

Such, then, is the tendency to an utter extinction of all spiritual faith both out of the Church and in it; and it would seem that nothing can arrest this tendency short of a renewed and tangible interposition of power and intelligence from the spiritual world. It would seem that for every evidence of an interposition of this kind, the true mind—he who seeks the unfoldings of Divine wisdom and love rather than to sustain the barren creeds of men— would spontaneously thank God from the depths of his soul, instead of opposing and denouncing it as a delusion or device of the devil.

We, then, feel warranted in the assertion, that all the evils of a supercilious and reason-crushing dogmatism, and of consequent spiritual slavery and sectarian intolerance, on the one hand, and of a weakened or totally annihilated faith concerning a spiritual world, a God, and his divine revelation, on the other hand, are the legitimate concomitants of that mistaken idea of sectarian religionists, whereby the great doctrine of immortality and of spiritual manifestations has been put forth in the form of a *mere theory*, resting only upon the evidence of alleged facts occurring in a remote and obscure age of the world. Had the professedly Christian fraternity remained in that moral simplicity and spiritual devoutness which would have secured to it a continuance of its original spiritual gifts, and had it constantly pointed the world to the *facts of its own* celestial-communings as the demonstrations of its professions of faith, there would now have been but little room for a crushing spiritual dogmatism and its resultant evils ; and the word " infidelity" would have scarcely retained a place in .our vocabularies. But since the " salt" of the Church has, in respect to these matters, " lost its savor, and is henceforth good for nothing but to be cast out and trodden under foot of men," it hath pleased Divine Providence to develop this conserving element of which we have spoken, in the form of what is now termed " SPIRITUALISM."

Let us now direct our attention more specially to the subject just named, and ascertain, if possible, precisely what it is, and what it is calculated to accomplish for mankind.

It is not denied that in this infantile stage of its unfolding, Spiritualism has exhibited many erratic, and some unpropitious, features. Appealing, as it has done, to people of every diversity of character and mental development, and being necessitated to adapt itself to their different capacities of reception, its specific manifestations have assumed all possible grades of dignity from lowest to highest. Its didactic and philosophic utterances, moreover, coming as they do from the spirits of men of all grades of moral and intellectual culture, exhibit all degrees and admixtures of truthfulness and error, and the elements of the new spiritual creation are thus far (speaking in general terms) somewhat in the state of the elements of the *physical* world in the first period of creation, and before the spirit of the Lord God moved upon the face of the waters to reduce all things to form and order. Yet notwithstanding this fact, we think that these modern demonstrations, when studied in all their variety, exhibit to the honest skeptic every requisite illustration and presumptive proof of the spiritual phenomena, revelations, and resultant moral precepts, found in the true history and the traditions of all ages, the Bible records included. Nay, we think they even furnish new and brilliant illustrations of the profound interior significance of many of the ancient revelations, and throw a light upon the future destiny of man, which prophets and sages of old ardently sought but found not; and at the same time they seem to put an end to the long-existing conflict between material science and spiritual faith, and make the former the handmaid of the latter.

To show that such are really their bearings and tendencies, and that, when properly contemplated, they will thus supply to the whole world an element of spiritual life which the sectarian churches and their creeds have notoriously ceased to afford, we will here institute a few comparisons between the ancient and alleged modern spiritual phenomena, with their respective modes, conditions, and subsidiary instrumentalities, and show that both are classifiable under the same general head, and that they hence mutually establish and confirm each other.

The recorded facts of the appearance of the spirits of Moses and Elias to the Saviour and three of his disciples (Mark ix. 2–8), of the appearance of the spirit of one of the old prophets to John the Revelator (Rev. xxii. 9), and the declaration of Paul that one office of Christianity was to bring its disciples into communion with " an innumerable company of angels, and with the spirits of just men made perfect" (Heb. xii. 22, 23), have their illustrative facts and philosophy exhibited in this modern unfolding too conspicuously to require any further remark. The same may be said concerning the appearance of the spirit of Jesus to Saul while on his way to Damascus, and of numerous recorded instances of the appearance of angels and spirits as found in the Bible and other ancient records, together with the various communications and physical manifestations which they made. These relations of ancient fact, which have long been subjects of skeptical ridicule, are completely rationalized and triumphantly defended by the parallel occurrences of this modern unfolding.

No less conspicuous are the coincidences and mutually confirmatory parallelisms between the *unseen influences* and their effects as described in the ancient records and those which modernly occur. Even the scene which is said to have taken place with the disciples of Jesus on the day of Pentecost has had its modern parallelisms sufficiently marked to prove the possibility and probability of the account concerning it, even in its most marvelous particulars. That impressible persons have in these days been often spontaneously drawn together into circles not previously appointed or contemplated, as the apostles appear to have been drawn together on the day of Pentecost; that in such associate relations they have been subjected to the most unmistakable outpourings of an invisible, spiritual power; that the receptacles of this influence have often uttered things wholly transcending their knowledge and capacities while in the normal state, and that they have in frequent and most satisfactorily attested cases even spoken in languages which they had never learned, might here be proved by citations of testimonies overwhelming to all rational skepticism; but, as before intimated, it is not my present object to prove the reality of existing spiritual intercourse, but to leave this question to be decided by the personal investigation of such of my skeptical readers as may wish to be satisfied upon the point.

The general *modus* of the recorded ancient spiritual communings, and of those which purport to occur at this day, exhibit marks of identity equally recognizable. Thus, in the tenth chapter of Daniel (4–10), we find the description of a scene which has been frequently reproduced, in all its essential phenomena, in the modern manifestations claimed to be spiritual. We see in Daniel's fasting and praying, as there recorded, what is now recognized as the preliminary self-discipline requisite to the unfolding of a good "medium;" we see in the "quakings" of Daniel's companions the ungovernable muscular contractions now known to occur to partially susceptible person's when brought under spiritual influence; we see in his vision of the person of the angel a phenomenon of spiritual clairvoyance which is now frequent; we see in his "deep sleep," and in the fact of his being strengthened by a spirit-hand which touched him, the now common spiritual magnetic trance, and the manner in which strength is imparted or withdrawn in such cases; and whoever, therefore, admits the constantly demonstrated realities of the modern phenomena, can not reasonably withhold assent from this and the like ancient occurrences, nor from any of the logical corollaries as to the reliability of the moral and spiritual teachings thence originating.

The intelligent reader will further pursue this line of comparison for himself, and as he proceeds, the evidence of the identity of the general laws governing those ancient and these modern unfoldings will accumulate at each step. This glance at the prominent features of the two, however, justifies us in the following assertions: If the alleged ultra-mundane developments of this time, more or less of which have already been exhibited in every third or fourth family in many of our cities and country localities, assuming every shape suited to the exigencies of an existing, universal, and deeply rooted skepticism—if these, I say, can not be trusted as of really spiritual origin, as they uniformly purport to be, then the comparatively few accounts of *precisely similar* occurrences, which we have derived from a remote and obscure age, must, in all consistency, be rejected as still less worthy of credence; and the whole phenomenal history of the Christian revelation itself must be written down as a fable. If, on the other hand, *modern* Spiritualism is admitted as a reality, and the tens of thousands of intelligent persons who, from personal observation, assert its facts, are *not* positively insane, then the Spiritualism of all ages and nations, which exhibits an identity of phenomena, and comes under the same general laws, stands established by a force of presumptive evidence which it would be the height of folly to discredit.

But if the phenomena alleged to have subserved the original development of Christianity are thus allowed to be established by the force of living parallelisms in this day, then all the religious principles and moral precepts of the Christian scheme will assume a freshness, and may be urged home upon the human conscience with a power, unknown in the ministrations of the professing

Christian teachers of this day ; and what is more, the same spiritual gifts which sanctified the lives and gave such a divine and
irresistible power to the reformatory labors of the early Christian
disciples, will again be objects of aspiration to all zealous and
pure-minded believers, and will be enjoyed by multitudes as fully
as they were ever enjoyed by the prophets, seers, and *energumens*
of the ancient times.

It is in this way that modern Spiritualism, when properly contemplated and developed, tends to conserve and bring forth in all
the fervent and brilliant glow of a living reality the normal spirituality and religion of the race, which otherwise is unquestionably
fast tending to decay and utter extinction ; and having thus disposed of this point, we proceed to consider briefly, but in more
specific points of view, the practical influences of these new manifestations upon individual and social life, and upon the higher
interests of humanity at large.

We hazard little in asserting that it is impossible for a substan-
tial knowledge of the existence of a spiritual world, and that it is
the constant source and medium of influences from spirits, from
angels, and from God, should be established in the mind of man
without producing a salutary effect both upon his inner affections
and outer life. It tends to raise him completely out of the sphere
of mere brute nature, and imparts to him all the dignity of an immortal, whose endlessly unfolding destiny will necessarily partake
of the qualities of his endlessly unfolding aspirations. Whatever
of mere groveling earthiness there may be in the thoughts and life
of the so-called infidel, must necessarily, in some degree, receive
a softening, subduing, and humanizing influence from the inflowing
of that light which shows him his intimate relations to a world of
angels, and to the God of all ; and he with whom the doctrine of
immortality is involved in *any* degree of doubt, however slight,
must be correspondingly benefited in precisely the degree in which
his faith or assurance upon this point can be increased. The light
which modern Spiritualism sheds upon the minds of all such, must,
therefore, even in this general way, tend to fecundate and stimu-
late in them the growth of all that is noble, genial, and divine.

But the influence of these spiritual disclosures operates in a still
more specific way. They teach us that however secret may be
our acts and our very thoughts, to persons in the flesh, they are all

seen and known to the inhabitants of the spirit-world as clearly as *we* can discern objects through the most transparent glass. He, therefore, who would hesitate to do an unworthy deed, cherish an impure thought, or conceive an unholy intention within the knowledge of a pure-minded sister, or brother, or other friend in this world who might be grieved or shocked by the same, will, if he is a true Spiritualist, be made cautious as to the regulation of his thoughts and the government of acts by the knowledge that such are exposed to the clear and constant gaze of some beloved friend in the spirit-world, and who can not but look upon his impurities and derelictions with grief. What firmly-persuaded Spiritualist has not felt a salutary check placed, by this consideration, upon the evils of his own heart, strengthening him in his struggles with temptations, and encouraging his aspiration for that purity of soul in which he can stand naked before the whole universe and not be ashamed!

Besides, with the absolute knowledge of spiritual beings sympathizing with ourselves, which these modern manifestations bring, there is naturally engendered a desire to *commune* with these beings, and receive their constant, superior guidance. In this way our susceptibility to their influence is cultivated and increased, and we are brought to act, in our daily lives, more and more under the inspirations of their wisdom and love, of whatever degrees or qualities these may be. And though it is not pretended that their promptings may be safely followed in all cases, or even in any case, without reference to the guidance of a Power superior to all spirits and angels, it is believed that with the safeguards against misleadings which the judgment and moral instincts of mankind in general will lead them to employ, the good that will be secured and appropriated from these channels of inspiration will, upon the whole, vastly preponderate over the evil, and that the evil itself will be finally made to work out its own destruction. Still the admitted danger of open intercourse with the spirit-world—danger of having our own errors of opinion and practice reflected back upon us and confirmed by sympathizing spirits who are in similar errors—is such as to require this caution—that no one should seek such intercourse without an humble desire to know the truth irrespective of previous impressions, and a prayerful looking to God for his divine guidance.

Such being the genial influence which Spiritualism, as a general fact, exerts upon the thoughts, affections, and life of the individual man, it is easy to perceive that it tends also to change and improve the whole relations existing between man and his fellows. Its influence in spiritualizing individuals certainly prepares them for a more spiritual consociation with each other. By imparting a deep sense of the eternal existence in which all the temporary distinctions of this life will be swallowed up and lost, it tends to impress each with the equal value of all souls. It thus tends to destroy personal pride, aristocracy, and all feelings of exclusiveness, and to fuse the high and low together in common interests and common sympathies. That such have been its effectsal ready to a marked extent, will not be denied by those who have been most observant of its practical workings; and it is believed that this tendency will be increased as the unfolding becomes more perfect, and its moral and religious features become more developed.

For reasons closely allied to the above, Spiritualism is necessarily at war with all mere sectarianism, with its restrictive influences, its discords, and its animosities. The facts and principles of this new development, by their own force and spirit, discountenance the idea of a monopoly of Divine favor by any class or party of people. They proclaim unbounded freedom of thought and investigation as the birthright of every human being, and thus dissolve the bonds of mere human creeds and conventional dogmas by which the human mind has been so long enslaved and its powers repressed. Spiritualism thus labors to bring each human being to the dignity of a true man, responsible to God alone for the just improvement of his faculties, and to diffuse among all men the spirit of mutual forbearance with each other's errors, or diversities of thought on the same subjects, attributing these to diversities of constitution or mental development, and expecting them to disappear as the general mind becomes more fully and more harmoniously unfolded. If in the contention for these principles there have been some cases of extravagance, extremeism, and violent denunciation of things really true and sacred, the fault must be laid to the charge of *Spiritualists*, and not to Spiritualism itself in its true and properly understood character; for *that* seeks and appropriates what is true and good in all sects and parties, and rejects only their falsities and evils, while it seeks light also from beyond all sectarian spheres of thought. We may add, that if Spiritualism accomplishes no other practical result than that of emancipating the human mind from the restrictive dogmas of the past, and placing it in the path of individual progress, the future generations of mankind will even then have cause to be thankful that it ever appeared upon the earth.

Finally, it is no less evident to the interior contemplator of these developments, that as they themselves progress and are perfected, they will necessarily tend to fraternize, elevate, and harmonize the whole human race, and to reconcile and unite mankind eternally to the Divine Author and Ruler of all. To the superficial observer of the apparent effects of Spiritualism in its present incipient stage, I am aware that this assertion may seem somewhat paradoxical, inasmuch as spiritual teachings, in their present state, are confessedly not entirely free from dividing and antagonizing elements. It not unfrequently happens that the teachings received by one spiritual circle essentially differ from those received by another, and that each claims to possess the truth, and the only truth, on the subjects treated of, and pronounces all opposing communications erroneous almost as a matter of course. It may be frankly admitted, too, that many spirits whose influence is now prominent in this unfolding, are not of the highest order as to intelligence and religious character, and that their influence, taken by itself, is by no means to be trusted by those who would seek safety in their moral and religious guides; but it should be observed that these are only among the exceptional and incidental facts of the great *general* unfolding, in estimating the influence of which latter the following remarks are applicable:

While destitute of a lively, realizing faith in the soul's transmundane existence (as most of people in and out of the Church now are, unless positively reassured on the subject by modern Spiritualism), the thoughts and affections of man necessarily tend earthward and selfward. He will know of few enjoyments which rise above the gratification of the senses and those cold intellectualisms which are immediately dependent upon sensuous perception. While in this state his motto naturally is, " Get and enjoy all you can while in this life, for beyond this life we know of neither enjoyment nor existence;" and thus he is apt to assume the character of a mere absorbent, appropriating all things to self and disregarding the common rights and interests of others, except as he perceives that an attention to them will in some way benefit himself beyond the extent of his sacrifices. The general lack of a lively spiritual faith makes this feeling correspondingly general among mankind; and the existing tendency to a cold, selfish, un-brotherly, unloving, and hence disintegrated and conflicting state of humanity, are the natural consequences as now observable in the whole spirit and tone of human society.

But the modern spiritual manifestations, by furnishing such positive proofs of a spiritual existence as appeal to and convince even those who are on the lowest plane of sensualism, present to all men the absolute *knowledge* of a higher and more enduring *sphere of attraction* than what belongs to this earth and its sensuous pleasures; and thus, whereas the thoughts and affections were previously turned earth-ward and self-ward, they are, with this accession of faith, immediately turned upward and heaven-ward, and an impulse to subserve the *eternal* and *spiritual* uses of man's being is immediately supplied where none existed before. As Spiritualism, therefore, progresses in the world, mankind will begin to live for *something higher* than what this world affords, and the selfishness and antagonism inseparable from the now prevailing worldliness will, in the same degree, be mitigated and supplanted by higher impulses and by aspirations having a common center in the great Fountain of eternal and spiritual existence, to which all things will then be felt to be subordinate.

Besides, although all possible gradations of spiritual communications, from highest to lowest, are being exemplified in the present developments, and although the inferior ones would generally, as it is confessed, have a corrupting influence if received and obeyed by *higher* minds than those to whom they are almost exclusively addressed, it will generally be observed that these, as well as all communications superior to them, are a *little above* the moral and intellectual *status* of the *particular persons* who receive them. According to this law of adaptation, the believers in spiritual manifestations are being instructed in *detail*, and as a mass consisting of details, all are being thus raised up to a higher plane. And that the *general* influence of these spirit-teachings has even already been exemplified in making mankind more unselfish, more just, more orderly, more free and loving, more progressive, and more harmonious, can not be denied by those who have taken an enlarged view of their practical effects, even though some isolated cases apparently to the contrary may be pointed out. Fraternity, progression, and harmony are, indeed, the constant burdens of the exhortations coming from the invisible realms, and the means and efforts for their realization are constant themes of contemplation among Spiritualists at their conferences and other public assemblages.

Moreover, as these wonderful manifestations from the spiritual world are contemplated in respect to their various and constantly multiplying phases adapted to the exigencies of an existing skepticism—in respect to their power of everywhere thwarting opposition, and in respect to the rapidity with which they are extending themselves throughout the civilized world, no deeply discerning mind can fail to be impressed with a grand *unitary plan* and *method* as governing them, which plan and method must necessarily have originated in a Power and Wisdom *higher* than the spirits themselves! In this light of the subject, the thoughts of all its contemplators are carried upward to an overruling and divine Providence, to whom the glory and honor of the whole unfolding should be ascribed, and who is using it all for the purposes of His own infinite Love and Wisdom in the redemption of mankind. In the progression of processes looking to the accomplishment of this glorious end, there will be observed the order of " first the blade, then the corn, then the full corn in the ear." The world now presents every diversity of human condition, from the lowest to the highest, and these are characterized by every shade of faith and unfaith. From the same Divine Hand influences are now sent down which diverge as they approach the divergent conditions of men, and, according to their adaptations, extend equally to those whose diversities of moral and spiritual state have attained their utmost limits. By these influences mankind are now being gently drawn upward as by ten thousand silken cords, and as they ascend toward the Source of the divine attraction, they will correspondingly approach each other, until at the apex of the mighty cone of celestial influences they will center in one grand fraternal and universal unity, in which God will be all in all.

But besides these modifications which Spiritualism is now producing, and will effect in the opinions of individuals and in the general manifestations of society, it may be that this new *pro-vision* (which may be called supplementary to the original) was meant to be introductory to the final consequences which the advent of our Saviour was to produce on man in every condition and position of existence. In view of the great decline in the moral appreciation of the truths uttered by Christ, in what method and form, or by what arrangement human beings could move on in this life, so as to be prepared for a higher and better state of existence in the next, if these present revelations had not been introduced as conclusive proof of spiritual communication in all ages of the world, and of the grand design in the appearance and teachings of our Saviour, we are unable to say. To us Spiritualism, either old or new, whether manifest in the earlier periods of the world, in the time of Christ, or under the various phases and aspects which it has assumed from that time to the present, completes an entire and thorough change in the externalism of the human path, modifies the circumstances of human progress throughout, in new forms and conditions, and fits them perfectly to fulfill the purposes of a *restorative discipline.* The entire but gradual change which takes place among men by the effective influence of this spirit-association, realizes the demand of the original scheme of creation, which scheme is apparent in the whole history of God's dealings with man, by his laws and by his special spiritual directions, and which evidences the best possible method for the happiness, security, and advancement of all the race. Thus to our view is the perpetual superintendence of His *messengers* manifested, who are distinguished by an earnest endeavor to bring men under the control of these influences, which will enlighten them as to the true laws of their existence, and strengthen them also to a just conformity to their effects, by public and impressive manifestations of His power and goodness.

The prevalent idea of man's duties in respect to himself and others, the principles on which the civil code of all nations has been founded, and the necessary qualifications which will insure to him progressive happiness in the other life, can be traced through every age of the world as resulting from direct and special spiritual intelligence and communication. It is not therefore singular, that while all the expedients for repairing the material delinquencies of man are gradually being brought into effective operation, something more was necessary to be accomplished in his behalf. The general declaration of God, through the agency of his spiritual instrumentality is, that every member of the human family is capable of advancing from this life, and through an endless eternity, toward a condition of entire restoration—that the voluntary power of each will be so strengthened that it will be enabled to control and direct the faculties and affections, and as if by a new *generation*, the human spirit will be capable of working efficiently amid those remedial circumstances which constitute the new economy designed for its renovation ; and all authentic teachings respecting the progression scheme speak of it as furnished to *restore* the original efficacy of those powers and attributes which have been displaced and impaired by an improper application or voluntary perversion. If we consider the whole moral and physical nature of man as a *structure* perfectly adapted by its conformation and its association, both material and spiritual, to effect its purposes in its appointed path, on which it auspiciously moved at the outset, but from which it was impelled by its disregard of its higher impulses and aspirations, we gain, in our view, an accurate idea of the influence and effect of Spiritualism, by regarding it as the means to restore the original condition of its functions, and to renew the suspended relations between the spirits of the just made perfect, and its purer desires and hopes, and to secure to man the gradual consummation of his progress and improvement.

If the results of this new revelation be commensurate with the effects which are now being produced on man and society, it will establish, beyond all controversy, the existence of that spiritual principle which we contend has exercised such incessant influence through all ages of time on the present and ultimate destiny of man. This opinion may ripen into established truth, and aspects of man's moral and physical nature, unexampled in their glorious brightness and purity, may be presented on this earth at no distant period. Humanity in its completeness has not yet been seen by any of us, but may it not be revealed when there is no obstacle to the free and uninterrupted intercourse of the spiritual with the material ? When ennobled with elevated conceptions of the might and grandeur of his Maker, and filled with sentiments of pure enjoyment in the contemplation of His administration, man regards this life as the means of understanding the true design and purposes of those laws, moral and physical, which govern existence everywhere, the effects of which will impel him to accomplish the ends of that existence, in bringing his spirit into harmony with all the manifestations of his Creator! Thus reason becomes religion, because it is enlightened by a knowledge of those truths which unfold to man the harmonic relations between life and immortality, and that the purest sentiments of his material nature spring from the higher affections of his spiritual, and the union of these is the source from which he derives his purest and serenest happiness. Then would the universe bear witness that the kingdom of God has come nigh unto all men ; for man in harmony with himself, with his fellow-man, and in intimate association with the spirits of the other world, would manifest the distinct and proper attributes of a nature so transcendently elevated and perfect, that he might indeed call God his father, and claim to be his child.

Is there, then, no hope for this state of progress and happiness for man, either under the dispensations of the old revelations or the promises and prospects of this new disclosure ? For eighteen hundred years the world has waited for the coming of that day when man should live in harmony with his brother and in fellow-ship with God. Prophets and priests have foretold its advent, and predicted the millennium by the positive promises which have been made by spirits of the other world. And may it not be that the shades of that long night are now shimmering into newborn day, the dawn of which colors the shadows of ages with its own bright tints of hope and promise ! Even now the prayer ascends from millions of happy hearts, disenthralled and redeemed from death to life by the power of those truths which Spiritualism has revealed—that the time may soon come when peace shall reign on earth, and good will to man be manifest in the earnest endeavor of all to assist each other to increase their own excellence, and the purity and happiness of the whole race.

If such results may flow from the effects which Spiritualism may produce on the material and spiritual powers of man either here or hereafter, what is there to justify an intelligent mind in rejecting its claims or refusing it a fair and unbiased examination ? It is true we can not cast off from us at once the opinions which we have cherished for years, but we all can grant even to new ideas that consideration which the extent and importance of their claims seem to demand. The doctrines we advocate demand no more. The whole subject of our religion, and the proofs which support it, can not be learned at a glance. All then we ask is, that we may not be opposed with presumptuous ignorance upon this subject, which we regard as sacred and holy ; for, perhaps, its truths may burst upon the unprepared mind with all the terrible certainty which will make its application individual. The first victory which truth gains should be over our own hearts ; for then, whether we remain on earth or are summoned to our eternal home, we are prepared for all exigencies. Calm in the prospect of that which is before us, we shall feel, when we leave this earth, that we are only going a journey into another country, where the loved and loving wait to receive us, and where our joys, our hopes, and our aspirations are centered for ever.

GEO. T. DEXTER

December 1, 1854.

Section One.

Saturday, July 30th, 1853.

This evening, the Doctor was in my library, and after conversing some time, I uttered the wish to hear from Lord Bacon.

He soon wrote :

WELL, my friend, though I am always with you, still I can not make myself visible or talk with you without the Doctor's aid. I love to talk with you, and were the Doctor and yourself differently situated, I should probably occupy more of your time than perhaps would be pleasant. Have you any thing to ask ? If so, let me hear it, and I will answer. BACON.

I said : No, nothing in particular ; but after such an effort as that of the last two or three days, I missed the company and sympathy to which, through my wife, I had become accustomed so many years, and I longed for some substitute.

It was answered :

Yes, and you want to know if you have acted rightly. This feeling is a consequent of the long and affectionate intercourse between yourself and wife. I can never fill that void, for these feelings, predicated on the young, fresh, and pure sentiments of your heart, unimpressed with the image of any other spirit, can realize at this time of life no other substitute which will fill that want, now a want indeed of the soul.

I look at you, and feel for you as a man, proud of you in the position you occupy, and striving to assist you in the efforts to accomplish what is before you. I can joy with your joy, and sorrow with your sorrow, take delight in all that interests you, and act with you in carrying out your plans and purposes.

But when the spirit turns back upon itself, and seeks from itself that response which met it at every point of life; when looking at its own yearnings and motives, it finds reflected the same aspirations of another spirit so closely assimilated that it becomes a part of his own, then there can be no sharing, no participation outside of that congeniality, but the spirit's which has taken up its resting-place in your own.

Dear Judge, in the sentiments of your heart, in every good motive, in every act in which you have conquered the propensities of self and the idiosyncrasies of your nature, you have acted out, through yourself, the very spirit-action of your wife. It is thus she claims the prerogative of your wife still. It is thus she manifests the love which, growing brighter and purer, will, at last, bring you together, when as one forever you will exhibit the same feelings, the same progression, till you develop all the attributes of goodness and perfection in that state of existence where there is no change, no separation for eternity.

Section Two.

Sunday, July 31*st,* 1853.

The circle met this evening at Dr. Dexter's. Among other things I read to them a letter which I had been preparing for publication. After doing so, the Doctor was influenced, and wrote as follows:

Now let there be silence, and let your minds picture the spirits surrounding you, influencing the medium, and assisting to carry out the intent of this meeting.

My dear friends, for a long time have I and other spirits visited your circle, and endeavored to teach, through the Doctor, the circumstances connected with our spiritual life. We have carefully abstained from advancing any thing opposed to the great laws established by God, and have as carefully adhered to the truth as it is known to us, that we might direct your minds to the investigation of those great principles on which is based every act of material life and every phenomenon belonging to the spheres. It has rarely been my fortune to meet so long with a circle whose individual members have so sincerely desired the explanation of Spiritualism, unmixed with any personal motive, unmingled with any preconceived doctrine or opinion. We have, therefore, refrained from special teachings or communications, and have considered the great whole of our subject as the important object to be accomplished. But there are circumstances which would justify us in directing our communications to one or more individuals, as in giving certain advice or in answer to special and particular inquiries, or in giving some direction as to their coöperation in the mighty purpose in which we are all interested. But there may be another aspect in which a special communication would be proper, and that is, when the course of procedure of any one of our circle may not be plain and distinct to his mind, and he requires our aid in opening to him the effect of certain action; or when, too, one of our friends may demand explanation when our teachings have been ambiguous and obscure. To-night it becomes my duty to communicate to two of this circle personally; to one in reference to his position as a believer in the communication of spirits with the living, and also to give him our advice in reference to its effect on himself as a man, and on the world, to whom he owes proper respect in consequence of the high position he occupies, emanating from that world to whose opinions he is bound to show proper respect. To the other individual I am to speak in reference to the effect of certain causes on his mind, and the consequent evil or good which may grow out of this effect as influencing the great duty before him, and the cause with which he is now identified either for good too or evil.

Having said this much, I now commence with you, Judge Edmonds. Every individual, whether of high or low degree, is possessed of certain inherent prerogatives aside from those on which are founded his civil or political rights. Every person of sound mind and of sufficient education is bound to serve the community in which he resides in such capacity as will most conduce to its best interests and advance the common good of all.

All persons are not fit for every position in the gift of a free people, but a man accepting office from the independent suffrages of any community, pledges himself, in so doing, that he will not only perform the duties of that office to the best of his ability, but he tacitly consents, under this contract, to explain to his constituents any great change which may take place in his opinion on any subject, apparently or positively, affecting the duties or influences of his office, or the received and acknowledged ideas on which the whole of their religion may be based; that religion, we mean, which is the common belief of this people, and that on which its laws and its government are based. No free people can demand that its governors, its judges, or any one of its officers shall, as a qualification, avow that he believes in the same denominational creed as any one of its people profess to believe; but they can demand and should require a pure and devotional belief in one God, and that any candidate for or incumbent of office should exhibit by his daily life and conversation that he shows proper respect to the laws which that God has established in relation to the natural world and his fellow-creatures.

Therefore, when any great or fundamental change takes place in the opinion of any individual holding a high office, upon the objects involving an entire revolution in the developments of the common religion, or in those subjects which are supposed to be but little understood and but partially revealed by the great God who rules our creation, I say he is bound to show the reason of his belief and the causes which induced it, as well as the moral effects which he supposes will arise from it, and the good that may result to him, to his office, and to the people themselves.

The reasons for this compliance are sufficiently obvious. Elected to office with the understanding that he recognizes the religious doctrines of the church which he has attended with his parents, or acknowledging the obligations admitted by the whole Christian world, he actually admits that he accepts as his belief the principles on which the laws he administers are built. Thus the civil laws are based on the moral law, "Do unto others," etc., and no difference in the specific application of any statute (or no law, however apparently individual in its effects) can be viewed in any other aspect than as based on this axiom, emanating, as understood and accepted, from a divine source. The violation of a law does not suppose a consequent punishment because the law itself has been transgressed, but that in violating the law you break the image of its principles, and that is the obligation which it imposes on every man to do unto his neighbor as he requires that neighbor to do unto him.

Now, if you, Judge Edmonds, have accepted the office you now hold, you did so publicly pledging yourself to administer justice predicated on the principle expressed above. You said, "I understand the laws of my country and state, and to the best of my ability will I see them executed;" but at the same time you said, "I believe as the whole Christian world believe—I am a Christian, although I do not conform to the doctrines of any church or sect."

You now have seen sufficient reasons to change the fundamental principles of that belief. You do not believe as the whole Christian world believes, and, in this view of the case, you are bound to set right the public mind in regard to the difference existing between your conclusions, derived from careful and protracted investigation, and those doctrines from which you have the right to differ. Why so? Because you disabuse the public mind of any erroneous notions of the character of that belief—you remove all the obscurity with which your silence would invest your opinion, and you show to the world, that while you do not deny either God or his laws, you, on the contrary, are now more observant of the moral obligations those laws impose, and that your duties to your fellow-men are made more imperious in your action toward them. You show them, that instead of denying the great principle of all religion, you accept it as even more obligatory than under the religion you formerly believed, and that without calling on the aid of those from whom you could receive counsel and assistance, your mind, renewing, as it were, its inherent and acquired attributes, develops new powers by the omnipotent might of progression. You exemplify by your daily acts that your intercourse with your race is of a more elevated charater, void of selfishness, and devoted to their absolute advance in all knowledge and goodness, both in your world and in the world to come. Aside from official position and·influence, you come nearer to the innate necessities of their nature, and you develop all of good of which that nature is capable. You contract no power, no resource, no ability; but the whole boundless universe is unlocked, and they are ushered into a liberty of action so glorious, that the soul is satisfied that it is to its own rights these things are vouchsafed. Men believe, because there is no happiness without it.

These things it was necessary you should know, as the views of spirits in reference to yourself; and now one word more. In the article which you have prepared,* explaining your views on the subject of Spiritualism, you have done all that we could desire; and, although we are no prophets, we feel confident that its effect will be to give you more stability. as an officer and. more true regard as a man.　　　　　　　　SWEEDENBORG AND OTHERS.

Section Three.

Sunday, Aug. 7th, 1853.

This evening, at the circle at Dr. Dexter's (it being the next day after my letter had appeared), it was written:

My children, let your minds imagine a sphere, or, rather, a locality, exquisitely beautiful, diversified with every variety of scenery, with lofty mountains stretching out far in the distance, and broad valleys teeming with vegetation of most luxuriant growth, with noble rivers flowing through

---

* Alluding to my letter to the public of the date of 1st August, 1853.

these valleys, and deep forests skirting the sides of these
mountains; imagine plains and undulating surfaces laid
out in fields and gardens, with flowers of every hue and
odor, and here and there beautiful residences scattered over
the whole territory; imagine, in fact, a world most beautiful in its harmonious blending of the practical with the
artistic, and in the divine order with which every arrangement has been made for the pleasure and profit of those
beings who were to inhabit it. Then imagine this world
filled with an almost untold number of intelligent spirits,
whose thoughts are constantly directed to those subjects
which will conduce most to the development of mind, which
will elicit most of good from every thing around, and which
will contribute most to the advancement of one another
resident in that locality, and their same race on your earth.
Imagine, too, that these beings are interested in every thing
which tends to the advancement of truth, and to the re·
moval of every impediment which may obstruct the recip-
rocal action of that truth in its upward progress from earth
toward heaven, and then imagine the deep, the fervent,
the enthusiastic, and the abiding interest with which these
beings have considered the wisdom or the practicability of
the publication of Judge Edmonds' letter, and the effect
which that letter has had on the public mind, now that the
press has given utterance to the sentiments it contains.
Words can convey no adequate conception of the absorbing desire which animates every individual to see for himself
or herself what its influence may be, not only on the minds
of their friends, but also on the feelings of those persons
who have opposed spirit-revelation from the beginning to
the present time. There are gatherings here and there.
Under the shade of some majestic tree you will picture a
party of men and women discussing, in terms of no common interest, this letter. In some house, where there may
be friends visiting, and from other localities (whose affinities correspond), you will see the delight, the anxiety, the
confidence, the hope and the faith which are expressed in

the countenances of both the friends and their visitors. In the depths of the forest, and amid the silence of nature, you may imagine spirits meeting spirits, and the first salutation is, "The Judge's letter is out." In the conferences on subjects belonging to the government, of neighborhoods or communities, the business is deferred, and the talk is about this letter. Spirits traversing the air, and meeting in space with other spirits, stop and accost one another, and, while floating on the transparent medium, they ask, What will be the influence of this first direct onset on the ancient superstition and errors of the world?

We are satisfied; and we trust that what of pain there may be in this effort, the good it may do will compensate for all anxiety and care, and afford a joy so pure and lasting that it shall satisfy the soul that it can really feel the links of that chain which cements it with these spheres and eternity.

Oh! when a duty has been done, and the spirit which has shrunk and hesitated has at last boldly dared to do and acknowledge truth, how its responses tell to the vibrating feelings of the soul, "I am indeed forever, and I know that I am ascending; I know that I am of God."

SWEEDENBORG.

I said I should like to know if they had a copy of the letter there, and if not, how they knew so well what was its purport?

Mr. Warren replied, that he had no doubt they had copies of it there, etc.

I answered, I did not want to speculate on the subject. I wanted to know.

It was written :

Why, you must speculate. Do you suppose that the millions of spirits who were in attendance on their friends in your world, and heard the letter read, heard the comments made, and heard the expressions uttered between individuals who had not read the letter, but who knew of the publication, did not know of it? and then, do you not suppose that the sentiments of that letter were made known by the spirits who attended your circle, and each individual to the thousands with whom they came in contact? And can you then ask how these things are?

Now for the proper subjects of our meeting.

At our last meeting, when I made a communication, I said there were two individuals to whom some things were to be said for a specific purpose. To one I have said all that was necessary, and to-night I am to address the Doctor, for the reason that the condition of his mind, while it produces its own unhappiness, does in some measure influence the communications through him, and retard the full and ready flow of that connecting current whose uninterrupted circulation is so important to the circle and the spirits who attend it.

It is now over two years, Doctor, I believe, since your mind was first directed to the phenomenon of spirit-manifestations. Your mind, naturally conservative, rejected this new subject with more than its ordinary prejudice, as opposed to every thing natural and divine. But after you had consented to an investigation, you did not admit as positive proof what you could attribute neither to collusion nor nature's laws, or what you could neither explain nor ascribe to any individual concurrence or participation. For a long time you were influenced by two different sets of feelings; at one time almost believing from the force of the evidence, and at another rejecting all evidence, and especially that which came from individual experience, and not direct to yourself from the spirits. From the very first I knew you could be made a powerful instrument for the advancement of our cause, and also an almost all-powerful instrument in disseminating truth and goodness through the world.

Knowing this, and analyzing your feelings, studying the action of your mind and character, I have since that time been constantly at work to present the subject to your understanding in such an aspect as would remove all opposition and convince you of the truth and of the divine nature of its revelations. But there was a time when I almost despaired of ever bringing your mind to a calm considera- tion of the subject, and eliciting a desire to know more than you already had learned. Still, satisfied and under the urgent coöperation of other spirits, and of the influ. ence of great plans and important movements in connection with the subject, I strove with you, and at last, more by the action of your own mind on itself and the deep affec tion which you entertain for your wife, you suddenly de- termined to go on in your inquiries and arrive at the truth, if that truth was to be reached.

Thus you commenced; and immediately seizing the op- portunity, in concert with others, we also commenced the teachings with a specific purpose, which was, to give to the world, what I two years since avowed to you I would do, my true religious sentiments, through you. In selecting you as the medium of communicating to the world my doc- trines, and also an account of the life and occupation of the spirits, I did so, feeling that through you I could give that which was a true and just account, without any inter- mingling of your own thoughts with the subject, and be- cause I knew that the innate and cultivated powers of your mind were just what I desired, to enable me to fashion my teachings into proper shape and substance.

To you, therefore, did I say two years ago, "I will write a new Heaven and Hell through your hand, Dr. Dexter, and it shall be given to the world as a correction of what I had written while in the form."

You may justly conclude, therefore, that while I selected you for the ease with which I could impress you, there were other circumstances which rendered your coöperation of great importance, and made you of as much value to me as my teachings would be to the world.

But it was to the mind I looked for that assistance; it was on its clear comprehension, its love of truth, its dis- tinctness and its perception, its calmness and serenity, and its cheerfulness, that I relied and expected to assist me in my arduous task of writing through you a work of so much importance, and which, to give it its first and proper effect on the world, must be continued until two more volumes shall have been written; for you have only had the door opened—you have just looked within the curtain. The revelations which will be continued in the second volume will afford you more light than your mind can conceive. Thus in carrying out my specified design individually, and the whole plan in connection with others, I relied on your maintaining that condition of mind which would enable me to give graphically the more important truths which were to come. At the same time, on your mind, myself and other spirits relied to assist with others in carrying out the great plans which have been shadowed to you.

Doctor, there is one thing certain : our work, your work, is of more importance than you can at present realize. Spirits of higher position than any with whom you have had intercourse are to teach you through me, and also personally to influence your hand, and write out what takes place in the localities in which they reside; to give descriptions of places, the customs, habits, laws, and government of each locality ascending; to give the history of the progression of spirit from sphere to sphere; the passage from one to another; the history, too, of the surface of the earth, or, rather, the spheres; the vegetation, such as the flowers, fruits, trees, and all those vegetables which are cultivated for the use of the spirit; the animals found there; the spirit-communion and power; in fine, every thing in connection with life in the spheres in the ascending scale as far upward as it is possible to have any distinct and tangible communication. If this is so, and I here proclaim it to be the truth, of how much importance, of what vast interest is it to us and to Spiritualists, yes, to the whole world, that your mind should not be disturbed with anxious cares and perplexities. I need not say, call wisdom to your aid, for I daily see your struggles, and I heard your prayer to-night for strength and assistance. But, dear Doctor, both yourself and the Judge know what has been said; you have in manuscript now what has been written, of what is before you. Your own mind has reflected on this matter; you have carefully digested and compared every statement made to you and to others, and you have just as carefully considered your own connection with these p.a.s as you have what else has been taught to you. Boundless as is the field, then, still there must be proper seed sown, and proper men to work it. Much depends, both to the cause and those engaged in it, that the teachings should be of such a nature as to convince the common sense of those who desire to learn. It is not every mind that can comprehend what is necessary to effect our purpose; it is not every mind through whom we could commune. There are very few persons in the world through whom these teachings could have been made. You ask, why so? I reply, if so, they would have been made long ago, if it were possible. Men of more profound learning than yourself have been tried, and of more absolute powers of mind, but they could not be molded to the great purpose we had to accomplish.

Can you not therefore understand the necessity of your being free from anxiety, that your mind should be like a spirited horse, fiery, bold, proud in its own consciousness of strength, able and powerful, but still easily influenced by the gentle means we exert?

As on you the whole of this matter depends, you must reflect seriously what must be done for yourself to enable you to continue that condition of mind which has allowed spirits so remarkably to communicate through you. It becomes of too grave import to defer longer, for as soon as the manuscript written is corrected, we design to commence the preparatory steps of the new volume.

Dear Doctor, I have written enough. I can not say, "Do so or thus;" I can only point out to you the importance of having your mind in an easy, passive state, and the great injury it would be to the cause of Spiritualism now,

if by any means you should be prevented from going on
with your work, or that our influence should be disturbed
or weakened, or that any thing should interrupt the mighty
plans laid out and partially revealed to you, from being
essentially and positively completed.

I have said enough. Good-night.   SWEEDENBORG.

Section Four.

Sunday, Sept. 4th, 1853.

This evening, at Dr. Dexter's, the whole circle being present, the first
manifestation was by a female, who was unfamiliar with our language.
Her first effort seemed to be to get possession of the medium.

We were then reminded of the course proposed the other evening, and
of the subject of the teaching—namely, PROGRESSION, from inanimate
matter up to man.

It was written:

WE accept it. But understand, our teachings are for
popular reading, and we shall reject all that is obscure or
technical, and try and elucidate the subject, so that all
who run may read.

We also wish you to understand, that we shall not give
you any high-sounding names to clothe our teachings with
their sanction. What will be given will come from men
developed and progressed, who are pure and wise, but have
only simple names and pure lives to guarantee what they
teach.   BACON.

Then it was added:

Let the circle remain quiet and silent. Judge Edmonds,
if you are willing, the first of our manifestations shall be
through you.

Then came the manifestation through me, which is annexed in a separate paper.

After it was concluded, some remarks were made as to whether what I saw was a picture or the reality ?

And it was written :

Now this first teaching or vision of fact is the continuation of our second volume, and in it will be given more of life, actual life of spirits, than ever before—their occupations, habits, connections, dress, conversation, pleasures, amusements, business, and, in fine, all that could or should interest you as belonging to the spheres.

You see distinctly what is absolutely going on in the life as it is, and the particular circumstances which occupy spirits at the time you see them. And you look at them as through a window at the real scenes of earthly life before you, and the persons acting therein. Now these things are given to your spirit, which is lifted upward, and gifted with the faculty of really seeing what is described.

This vision will continue several nights, and illustrate many things not before dreamed of in your philosophy.

The teachings now will assume the particular details of real life, and what is given is the reality of life as it is. You may suppose many things your own imagination, but it is really the absolute reality of living fact.

BACON.

I remarked with some surprise, that at the close of the vision I had seen horses and carriages there.

It was written :

That is not strange. You will have the whole of the vision and the explanation by-and-by. There is nothing out of common sense and truth in what will be given.

It was added :

You shall see the passage of a spirit from sphere to sphere.

Some remark was made by one of the circle as to the time that would elapse before passing to the higher spheres.

It was written:

Why, it takes an eternity to reach the celestial spheres. I mean, ages on ages shall roll away, before progression can develop attributes to entitle us to a residence in heaven.

Mr. Warren remarked it would seem short.

It was written:

True, true, Mr. W., it is but a day, a brief hour. If every aspiration is upward, as the soul yearns for progress, so shall that progress be.

Mr. W. asked into what sphere that spirit would pass?

It was answered:

They are not marked by lines, but affinities.

I inquired if she would pass into his sphere, or one above or below his?

It was answered:

No; my affinities are not distinctly given, for all my thought is on earth, as my duty is there; but she will pass beyond your thought.

Mr. W. and Mrs. Dexter remarked they did not understand that.

It was written:

It is easily understood. She will go to those globes where man's thought has not reached, where human intellect has never explored, and where all is as bright as it is harmonious.

Mr. W. made some remark about distance being no criterion of a superior sphere.

It was written:

Mr. W., the nearest to this solar system is the greatest amount of materiality. The farther off and upward, the less grossness. Of all the things that God has created, this world and its connections are the most material. God's manifestations must be more distinct somewhere. Therefore the nearer this point, the greater the ethereality.

Then the paper was signed in several different handwritings:

> " BACON.
> SWEEDENBORG.
> ALTA.
> JEAN.
> SAMUEL, AND OTHERS."

We asked who Samuel was? the prophet we read of in the Bible? It was answered:

He is one whose memory is lost in the ages which have passed since he left the earth.

Jean is a Frenchman.

Alta is a Druidess, and has by the force of her aspirations risen to the bright spheres. She was sacrificed on a stone altar by the priests. The times and scenes which signalized her earthly life, and the whole of her career while in the spheres will be given you.

VISION.

I was carried rapidly up to the temple where I had been twice before. So rapid was the transit, that I noticed nothing by the way, nor until I found myself inside the temple, and on the platform where the Presiding Spirit had sat. There was no assemblage of any great numbers there. I saw occasionally one or two passing along the galleries or across the area, as if going along in the transaction of their business. On the platform six or seven spirits were standing, grouped together, and discussing how they could get a person as material as I was, up to the higher spheres. One of them remarked, " That it was a good deal to get me as far as they had!" Another said, " Yes, but we can take him still farther." This was all I noticed particularly of their conversation, though I perceived what its general purport was.

I was standing alone by myself, on the left corner of the platform nearest the area. On my left there was an opening in the side of the temple, which enabled me to notice the scene which lay in that direction. Close to the temple arose a steep, rocky, rugged hill, very difficult to ascend. It was enveloped in a hazy atmosphere, which rendered objects somewhat indistinct, and which was very unlike the clear, transparent air that was found inside the temple. I examined the side hill very closely, and saw that it could not be ascended, except by climbing on my hands and knees, and clinging to the rocks and roots with my fingers and toes. The question arose in my mind, Was I willing to climb it? It would be a hard job to do so, and dangerous. See how far it ascends, how rough and rugged are the rocks, and the least step would dash me to atoms below!

After looking at it for some time, I said to myself, "I'll try it, at any rate." While this was going on in my mind, the group of spirits were observing me intently, and when I had come to a decision, they resumed their conversation, saying to each other, "He can make it out."

I looked again to see the undertaking that was before me, and to examine it still more closely. Then, upon looking to see how I could get to the side hill, I discovered there was an immense gulf between me and the hill, which descended, dark and gloomy, far down below where my eye could reach. I could discover but one way of crossing it, and that was by descending a very steep precipice to a point where the rocks jutted out from both sides, and where a tree had been felled across the chasm, presenting a slippery and precarious bridge of a single round log. It was evident that I could cross that only by creeping, and certain destruction would follow the least slip in crossing. As I was looking at it, with a swelling in the throat, as I have sometimes felt at the approach of imminent danger in my earthly life, I discovered another difficulty of no slight character, and that was a number of dark and malignant spirits concealed under the projecting rocks, lying in wait to interrupt my passage. At the head of them was the dark spirit whom I saw at the circle on Wednesday last.* What

---

* To explain this remark, I must mention that it had then lately happened that I had been developed to see the spirits that were around and near me. The first time this had occurred to me was in July, on a visit to Ohio, where I attended a circle, all of whom were strangers to me, except two. Soon after we were seated, I perceived what was so new and unexpected to me, that I thought it the effect of my imagination. I saw what seemed to me to be the spirits who were in attendance on each one present, and I resorted to several devices to determine whether I was actually seeing them or merely imagining it. One thing among others which satisfied me was, that being requested to ascertain the name of one of the spirits whom I described, I had seen it write with its finger in the air the word "Lucretia." I inquired if any one present recognized the name? No one did, and then on my request for the residue of the name, it wrote with its finger, " Charlotte L. De Verde," a name which those present recognized as that of a spirit who had been long communing with them, but which I had never heard of before.

Shortly after my return home from my visit to the West, one evening while the Doctor and I were sitting in my room conversing with the spirits, I saw near me the spirit of an acquaintance who had died in this city six or eight years ago. The third time I saw them was a few days afterward, when I was attending a circle in my own neighborhood. The medium became entranced, and it seemed to me that I saw very distinctly three spirits, who were at work upon him to bring him into that condition, and I saw that when he arose to speak, he but repeated the language which one of them was uttering to him. I was unaccustomed to this phase of the manifestation, and I again resorted to various plans to determine whether I actually saw or only imagined. Among other things, I left the room and sat for some time in an adjoining apartment, but there I could not see them, though the moment I returned to the room where the circle was, I saw them again, but with an addition. The medium had changed his position during my absence to the other side of the room. I now saw behind him the same three spirits, but I saw also a dark spirit standing directly behind him, and frequently whispering in his ear. The medium ceased to speak, and listened to this whispering. The effort evidently was to get the medium to speak the words that dark spirit was whispering to him, but in vain. This continued for at least ten minutes, until I arose, and placing myself in the precise position where he stood, I laid my hand on the medium's shoulder, and told him to say to us what the spirits said to him. He immediately arose and finished the teachings of the brighter spirits which the whispering of the darker one had interrupted. When he finished, I returned to my seat and saw that dark spirit had resumed his place and his whisperings, but now he was unable to awaken the attention of the medium at all. He would no longer listen to him. After repeated attempts he turned to me with a fiendish expression of hatred and rage, and, raising his finger, threatened me. He soon after left, but his appearance made so strong an impression upon me, that I had no difficulty in recognizing him again on the occasion mentioned in the text.

hate and mischief there was in his look! "Why does he hate me so? I never knew him here. But never mind," I said, "I'll make the passage, if I have to fight for it." And it seemed to me that the spirits were allowing me thus to see all the difficulties of the way, that I might realize them, and be prepared to meet them.

At this moment the Doctor was called out of the room, at which I was a good deal disturbed, and somewhat irritated. The whole scene was instantly distorted as if broken into fragments, and it was a long time before I could recall it. In the mean time I became conscious that the dark spirit had seized like lightning upon the irate state of my mind to produce this confusion, and it was almost impossible for me to shake off the influence. After a while I saw him returning to his lurking-place under the rocks, and he gave me a malignant look, saying, "See what I have done with your picture. Now bring it back, if you can." And he further said, " What is the use of your waiting for those spirits to get through with their consultation; if you are as brave as you pretend, why not try it yourself?" I was almost tempted to do so, goaded by his reproaches; but on looking at the group of bright spirits, I saw that they were not at all disturbed, and had full confidence that I would wait until they should tell me it was proper to cross. This restored my self-possession, and in a little while the scene all came back again.

I wanted to pass from where I was to those spirits, to consult with them about the journey, but there suddenly seemed to be an opening in the floor of the platform between me and them, as if it had been violently torn asunder, and the ends of the broken timber projected out in different places. Beneath the opening there was a dark vault, into which it would have been dangerous to have fallen. It seemed to me that this obstruction was not real, but only a deceptive appearance, and so I approached to walk over it; but as I came near the edge, the sense of its reality was so great, that I did not dare to go any farther. Determined not to be thwarted, I decided to leap the chasm, though the distance was very great. So with all my energies concentrated, I made the leap, and alighted on the end of one of the broken timbers on the opposite side. As I struck it, it gave way under my weight, and I was falling over backward into the dark abyss. I made one more desperate leap, and landed on the solid platform near the group of spirits. Finding myself safe, I turned to look at the danger I had escaped, and lo! there was no chasm there. The platform was whole and smooth, and the whole difficulty had been of my own creation only. What a lesson!

I approached the group of spirits, and there the dark influence was on me again; for that part of the platform on which they stood seemed falling from under them, and off on my right, where on former occasions I had seen that beautiful garden, with its transparent leaves, now I saw only an earthly scene, dark, rocky, and repulsive; after a little struggle that also passed away, and the former scene returned.

I turned to the spirits, and they showed me another path by which I could ascend to those higher regions, and avoid the gulf where the dark spirits were lying in wait. I rejoiced exceedingly at the prospect, and braced myself to the task of ascending. The path was long and narrow, and rugged and steep, and wound around spirally upward. I found it, however, much less difficult than I anticipated; and I was very soon at the entrance to a scene far surpassing in loveliness and beauty any thing I had yet beheld. I want language to describe it, so as even to give a faint idea of its surpassing beauty. The light that rested on the whole scene was of itself infinitely lovely—it was of a lake color, and very, very soft. What pleasure it must be to live ever basking in such a light as that!

I observed this light as I approached this country, and its effects on the entrance to it; that entrance was by a flight of steps, with heavy balustrades and massive posts. It was the scene represented in Wolcott's frontispiece; but where he has strips of grass, there were flower-beds, and the flowers, where touched by this light, sparkled like innumerable diamonds, presenting a scene more brilliant than imagination can conceive. If my sight had not

in a measure become wonted to such scenes, the dazzling
splendor would have been too much for me. Every thing
around me glowed and sparkled in this brilliant and gorgeous light.

Here came again that dark influence, and presented to my view, directly
in the midst of that delightful country, a deep and dark ravine, bounded
on both sides by rude and misshapen earthly hills. I spoke of it, and
the spirits, through Dr. Dexter, wrote :

Wait for a few moments, till we drive them away, and
give your mind full sway.   BACON.

I accordingly paused for a few moments, and was relieved for the rest
of the sitting.

The beautiful scene returned upon me again, and it
seemed as if I could stand for hours in one spot and see
ever, new beauties around me. On my left was a border of
stately trees; how gorgeous they looked in that glowing
light! On my right and before me, as far as the eye could
reach, was spread out a magnificent landscape, the face
of the country gently undulating, and covered with trees
and flowers, and running water, and smooth paths, and interspersed with pleasant mansions of a beautiful order of
architecture, and most pleasantly located. What a home
for a man after his weary pilgrimage here!

Off at my right the land rose gently into sloping terraces,
one above another, and pure streams of water were tumbling down the slopes, adding their hoarse murmur to the
repose of the scene.

The trees were so majestic! One I observed in particular
was immense; it drooped like the willow, with a leaf like
the oak, and shaped like the elm; its foliage was very
dense, and it cast a shade large enough to cover the whole
of one of our parks.

Under its shade, nestling snugly beneath its wide-spread-
ing branches, was a log-hut, like those I have seen among
the backwoodsmen on our frontiers. The man who built it

had chosen that spot and all its surroundings, because it brought back to his recollection his earthly life. He had been fond of nature, and was wont to select such romantic spots in which to reside; and thus he continues to enjoy what on earth was so beautiful to him. He can here enjoy every thing that is beautiful. He belonged to no church; he was of no sect, but he looked from nature up to Nature's God. He could not read the Bible, but he read of God in every leaf that trembled in the breeze. An Indian lived with him; how they loved one another! he was an old man, and the Indian was younger.

As he sat at the door of his hut, he heard the footsteps of his companion approaching; he immediately asked himself what he could do to make the Indian more happy? And so the Indian, as he approached, was thinking what he could do to contribute to the old man's comfort. Thus, forgetting self, they thought only of each other's happiness.

I saw, much to my surprise, they had their dogs and guns with them. The old man was sitting on a bench, made of a slab, with four legs thrust rudely into holes bored at each end. Scattered around the ground were the rude implements common in a frontier lodge.

I suspected they did not use it to sleep in, and I soon found it was not indeed their home, but had been erected by them as a reminiscence of their former life, to recall to mind their earthly hunting-grounds. They were exquisite lovers of nature. Behind their hut was a large rock, higher than the building; growing out of its crevices were trees, and flowers, and creeping plants; at its base gurgled up a spring of pure water running near the end of the hut, and there forming a little pond. They had excavated the earth just behind one of the large roots of the tree, and thus the pond was formed, the water falling over the root as over a dam, adding its gentle sound to the pleasure of the scene. Behind them, stretching far off in the distance, was an earthly scene, consisting of dense woods and mountains, among which was a beautiful lake, which

"Its lone bosom expanded to the sky."

It seemed to be ten or twelve miles long and two or three wide, and meandered up among the hills. It was an earthly hunting-ground, and recalled to them again the life which their love of nature had made so pleasant.

As they sat at the door of their hut, on one side they could behold those hunting-grounds, and on the other that beautiful country with its heavenly light. Far as their eyes could reach the scene was so beautiful!—presenting every variety of form, and colored with the tint of this gorgeous ruby light, so clear, so soft, so grateful, and re-flected from every thing around, from every leaf and flow-er, as if from ten thousand sparkling mirrors.

And thus they conjoined their life on earth and life in the spheres, and enjoyed at the same moment the beauties of both.

And it was because while here they enjoyed the beau-ties which God had scattered around them, and had learned of them the lesson they taught of Him; the lesson taught as well by nature as by revelation, to love the Great Crea-tor and one another—this they did when here, and hence the happiness they now enjoyed.

Section Five.

Thursday, September 8, 1853.

This evening the circle met at Dr. Dexter's, and it was written through him:

BEFORE we proceed to the legitimate business of our circle, and as I shall not write much, if any, for a few evenings, I take this opportunity to express my love, my faith, and my earnest desire, that while we approach the subject, to you and the world of so much importance, we should realize, that what we now teach is different from that ever given to man before—that the ideas given need examination and analyzation, and it becomes your duty to ask questions on any part you do not properly understand; for the world will examine and criticise, and it is left to you to get at the gist of the ideas we inculcate for your benefit and theirs. This you will understand.

After the Doctor has written for a time, the vision will be continued, as there is much to be done, and we can not let one evening pass without accomplishing something. I greet you all. SWEEDENBORG.

Then it was written in the other handwriting:

As I have more command of the English language, the spirits delegate me to write what they say. Now assist us by turning your minds to the time when there was nothing created in this system by God, and imagine what that condition must be. BACON.

Get the Bible, and read verse for verse, the first chapter of Genesis.

I read as follows:

"In the beginning God created the heaven and the earth."

I received instructions, when at a signal to be given through Dr. Dexter's hand, I was to resume or to stop reading.

Then the signal to stop was given, and it was written:

We will suppose that the writer of that historical sketch of the creation understood the beginning of all things to refer only to the creation of this system, denominated by the learned, the solar system, belonging to your earth, or in which your earth is included. But if our ideas of God are correct, and as he must have been at the time he fashioned this solar system as omnipotent as he is now, it follows, that there were worlds created before even the germ of either your world or any of the other planets existed; that if there were worlds created before your world, the Creator must have had an object in thus manifesting his creative power, and that he formed worlds for the beings whom he also fashioned to live upon them. Now, therefore, instead of saying, in the beginning, I shall say, God created this world, and the whole system of worlds with which it is connected, when the space in which they now move was one vast chaotic darkness; when not one living thing moved or had its being in the illimitable ocean of darkness, space, and almost eternal silence which were spread out there, as if God himself had not recognized it as a portion of the vast territories he was calling into life and existence. But it lay there dark, silent, and motionless. No life, no air even, moved over this vast space. Silent, without motion, dark and fathomless, it was creation *without a God*, for the spirit of the great Source had not moved on its surface, neither had it permitted one spark of life or light to penetrate its boundless domain. There was no form, no sides, no extent, for it filled the whole immensity far beyond the telescope's range, and even beyond the point to which man's imagination has reached. It was void, void of every thing which could generate life, void even of the presence of God.

Here, at the proper signal, I read: " And the earth was without form and void, and darkness was upon the face of the deep, and the spirit of God moved upon the face of the waters."

Then it was written:

Dark as the mind which denies God, and as impenetrable as the place where the spirit of God is most manifest, for years untold, for generations incalculable, ages and time beyond all imagination it had laid spread out from space to space like some huge monster. Yes. Imagine that at this time there were worlds on worlds sparkling in the glory of creation, replete with life, and reflecting the almighty power of the Great First Cause, in which were direct sentient spirits, developing the peculiar faculties and attributes of progressive beings, with suns, and moons, and stars shining in the dazzling brilliancy of life and light; and here, where now the sun shines and dispenses light and heat to so many worlds; here, where the stars send their sparkling rays to give brilliancy to their motion; here, where the moon sheds her reflected beams to afford to you the light at night; here, where your earth revolves and turns as one of this vast existence; here, where you have worlds and suns, and stars and planets, with their brilliant belts and many moons; here, where the hand of God has marked the impress of his power and might, there was no sound, no motion, no light, no life. What was there here? What distinguished this gloomy space? Can the mind conceive? Can human imagination realize? No. There was nothing here, and throughout this vast abyss there was no point on which the mind could rest. No thought could fathom its confines, no imagination could conjure up substance, shape, or form. It was distinguished by darkness so intense that the human mind fails to conceive of how it can be described. Motionless, dark, and silent it laid, not even a ripple on its illimitable surface, and to its extremest depths 'twas all alike. But the spirit of God moved over this silent lake of nothingness, and called from out its dark abysmal depths order, life, and a thousand worlds.

Mr. Warren made some remarks explanatory of his understanding of the teaching, and

It was answered:

Suffice it to say, that you have been told some time ago that this world was one of the latest creations of God; and that there were worlds created before your earth, admits of demonstrative proof, when men shall have invented a telescope of sufficient power to explore the worlds beyond the attractive influence of your sun.

Mr. W. asked about the idea of some astronomers, that there was a common center around which our solar system revolved?

It was answered:

That center is where the spirit of God is most manifest; and as the land, on its descent toward the ocean, seems to incline obeisance toward it, so the whole creation of untold worlds revolve around this central point in dumb, yet intelligent, obeisance to the Power which created them.

I asked, in order, as I said, to learn to discriminate between their teachings and the workings of my own mind, whether my ascending the hill the first time, and pausing on the way to address the crowd, was a reality or an allegorical representation merely?

It was answered:

It was the reality.

What? I asked—that I really did address that immense crowd, and detail to them my spiritual experience?

"Yes," was answered.

Then followed the manifestation through me, which I related and Mr. Warren recorded at the time, as follows:

VISION.

I found myself in the same place where I was on Sunday last. Then I had turned off to the right, to see that hunter and his Indian companion. Now I proceeded directly forward in the path which led from the entrance.

On my left, between the path where I was walking and the row of trees, were beds, full of flowers in bloom. At the end of the beds I observed a very singular plant. It grew four or five feet high, and was shaped like the wild pine-apple, a species of cactus which I saw in Central America. Its leaves were long and pointed, were green and white, tinged on the edges with scarlet.

Just beyond this plant, the row of trees and the flower beds terminated ; and there, off at my left, as far as my eye could reach, I saw a country stretching out before me which was one immense garden. A mist seemed to rest upon some parts of it, and at the farther end of the land-scape was a vast mountain, shaped like an ant-hill, its summits enveloped in clouds, and rendered misty and in-distinct by the distance.

At the spot where I was standing, a balustrade had been erected on the edge of the precipice. It was heavy, mas-sive, and beautifully proportioned. As I leaned upon it and looked abroad, I saw that that country was far below me, and down there I saw the temple which I had several times visited, and I noticed that the precipice before me was that which I had examined from the temple, and amid whose caverns I had seen the dark spirits lurking.

As I stood there, I saw three spirits approaching me. I asked if I dare trust myself to believe who they were? They were evidently my wife and children. They came down from the rising ground on my right by one of the side paths, entered the main walk, and turned toward me. I was too much overcome with emotion for some time to be able to see very distinctly, or describe clearly what was before me. I could see my children very plainly in their spirit-form and countenance, but my wife bore her earthly countenance. This was that I might identify her. With my children that was unnecessary, because they had died in infancy and had now grown to maturity. But, as it were, through the earthly countenance of my wife, I saw glimpses of her spiritual visage. I tried hard to see it in full, that I might afterward recognize it, but in vain. It seemed to be changing and flitting before me.

Through the Doctor it was written

[That is merely shifting the scenes ; only keep your mind calm and intent and it will come. You are to write the totality of every thing as you go on.]

She told me that since I had first visited the spirit-world, she had ascended from the plain where I saw her to this higher one, to which our children belonged, and now she had them with her all the time, but then only occasionally.

I noticed particularly their garb. Their dresses were all in the same fashion. They wore under-garments of pure white reaching to the ankles, and over them a loose frock, open in front, and fastened by a belt around the waist. Their sleeves were loose, flowing, and reached only a little below the elbows, leaving the hands and wrists and about half of the forearm bare. The belt which bound my wife's garment was purple, the collar and cuffs, and two strips down in front, were crimson. The children's garments were ornamented with pale straw-colored cuffs and belt. Around their persons, and to the distance of a few inches, there floated a transparent atmos-phere of blue, like an outer garment of gauze ; but it was constantly changing its hue, which, while it was emblematical of truth and purity, was indescribably grateful. On my wife's head was a chaplet of green leaves sparkling wondrously.

How beautiful my children looked ! I never saw so clear and lovely a complexion. My daughter's hair was of a pale yellow, and hung in large ringlets and loose down to her waist. They were both shy and diffident in approaching me, my daughter in particular. They have known as yet so little of me !

While I was standing with them, I noticed, off at my right, on the sloping bank, and only a short distance from me, a cottage, completely covered with some large trees growing at each end of it, and having in front a beautiful flower-garden, extending quite down to the main path where I was.

What a magnificent prospect there must be from its front portico! I had a wish to see it nearer, and I was instantly transported to the front of the house, leaving my wife and children below.

Directly in front of the house was a jet of pure water, falling back into a large circular reservoir, which was some twenty feet in diameter and some ten or twelve feet deep, and was filled with gold and silver and blue fishes, and among them were eels, colored like the gold-fish.

Around the reservoir was a smooth path six or eight feet wide, and covered with small sea-shells. Outside this path, and extending around the circle, though with four openings in it, was a border, its sides of close-shaven, fine velvet-like grass, and its center, about a foot wide, filled with a singular plant. It was about two feet high, shaped like our Indian corn, and bearing very profusely a double-leaved flower, shaped like the tulip, large as the balsam, and beautifully variegated with pink and white. Outside of this border were four triangular-shaped beds, to fill up the square. They, also, were full of flowers and shrubbery. In each corner of the triangular beds was a small tree like a dwarf cedar or *arbor vitæ.*

But while I was examining these new and strange things, it suddenly occurred to me, that I had deserted my companions for the pleasure of my explorations, and so I immediately returned to them. My wife then took me by the arm to lead me about and show me the country I was in.

As I walked along with her, I observed that the inhabitants of the various residences in sight of us—and there were a good many—came out and were gazing at us, wondering, and very much interested; for they knew I was a mortal, and no mortal had been there before. They looked upon my wife, who had so recently become a resident among them as to be only partially known to them, as possessed of some wondrous power which could thus raise a "mortal to the skies," as well as " bring an angel down." They asked each other what it was, and became aware that it was the strong love there was between us, which had, even when I was thus mortal, borne me along with her to those higher spheres. They looked upon us with admiration, for they had never conceived that the power of love was so strong, and they became conscious that the object of it all was, that I might return to earth and inform my fellow-mortals how glorious is the condition which they may attain, and how they may attain it. And they immediately asked themselves what they could do to help the great object in view ?

These things I noticed as my wife led me off the main path up that by which she had descended. I noticed also, as I walked along, the peculiarities in the pathway. All the paths seemed to me at first covered with a fine, clean gravel, but, on looking closely, I discovered they were covered with very small, delicate, and infinitely variegated sea-shells. They would have been crushed to dust under the heavy tread of mortals, but the light step of sublimated spirits did them no injury.

The path, as it ascended the slope, was terraced off by stone steps, made of a yellow, beautifully variegated sort of soapstone, not as hard as marble, but polished as highly, and shining with innumerable sparkling atoms. I could have paused for hours merely in enjoying the beauties of the path. Every thing around me was beautiful. There was nothing to mar the scene. The air, the light, the objects around, all were beautiful; and then the people seemed so happy—a sober, calm happiness which filled the heart too full for utterance. Then so calm a silence rested upon the scene, interrupted only by the chirping of insects and the song of birds, and off from the distance came floating on the ear the sound of vocal music, exquisitely soft and touching. And thus alone was the peaceful silence broken.

On each side of the path which I was ascending were posts and chains fencing in the grounds. They were for ornament merely. The posts were no larger than my wrists, and of highly-polished black marble, variegated with yellow and white streaks; they were low and exquisitely proportioned, and the chains hung in graceful festoons.

As we approached the level of the cottage whose fountain I had examined, the inhabitants came out to their gateway to greet us. Three females and a male thus came out, and three others, who were visitors of theirs, remained behind. The three females were a mother and her two daughters. The male was the father. She seemed about forty-five years' of age, and the two daughters eighteen and twenty.

As we were passing, the mother spoke to my wife, "Love one another? Yes, that is to do as God commands, and to enjoy his happiness." She said this calmly, yet her countenance showed the depth of her emotion. She could scarcely speak, she was so filled with love and admiration. She was strongly attracted to my wife, and her daughters, who stood behind her, wanted to clap their hands with joy. They were a very happy family, and it was many, very many years since they had left the earth. Their dresses were fashioned like the others, but were ornamented with green, and they, too, were surrounded with that gauze-like atmosphere of blue. One of the daughters wore pink sandals and no stockings. Their complexions were very soft and brilliant. No child's more soft and pure. Their hair hung gracefully down their backs.

In answer to a question put by some of the circle, I said the mother's hair was a dark brown, the daughters' a little lighter. It was parted in the middle and hung gracefully down on each side.

On the other side of the path was a cottage which had no shade-trees around it. The trees were not necessary to keep off the heat, and each one had them or not as taste dictated. It was of a brown color, and I remarked that I saw no house with more than one story to it. They were not obliged to ascend into the air with their residences, they might extend out upon the ground as far as necessary.

I paused at this house to examine it.

Its inhabitants came out and conversed with my companions, while I entered the inclosure and examined it alone and at my leisure. This man had a gate at the entrance to his grounds, not because it was necessary, but because he fancied it. And while I was examining inside, he and my companions remained standing by the gate.

The first thing I noticed was the gable-end of his house, which was next the path. ˙ It had at its ridge what looked like a chimney, but was not—it was a turret for ornament only. Immediately below it was a circular hole to allow the air to circulate beneath the roof, and below that was a window.

I was asked if I saw any glass in these openings? and replied, that in the upper one there certainly was not; how it was in the lower one I could not then tell, but I would look at another time and say.

I saw vines running over and covering this gable-end. At one corner the vine bore transparent blue flowers, bell-shaped, and large as a goblet, which sparkled most beautifully as the light shone through them. At the other corner was a running rose, bearing profusely a flower, pink color, streaked with scarlet. The two vines met together, twined around the turret, and hung drooping down mingling their flowers.

Next the house, and between it and the path, was a walk covered with sea-shells, and extending in a half circle into the space between the house and the path, thus forming a bed which was filled with singular flowers. Its border seemed first to be of box, but on closer examination I found it to consist of dwarf trees about six inches high, and shaped like the yew tree. They were so perfect and uniform in shape, and so diminutive, that I almost expected to see some of Swift's Lilliputians walking in the shade. · At each end of this bed were very beautiful tulips of every imaginable color. One of the plants sprawled out upon the ground; the leaves were shaped like snakes, and wound around like a serpent in motion. The end of the leaves raised up from the ground like a snake's head, and the upper side of the leaf had the appearance of scales. This plant bore flowers in clusters, on stalks springing up from its center. They were cup-shaped, and were white, sprinkled with fine crimson spots ingrained in the leaf of the flower.

While I was thus examining these flowers, I perceived the conversation that was going on between my wife and the man who resided there. They did not speak vocally, but perceived each other's thoughts, and so I perceived their conversation. My wife laughingly said, it had been just so here, that when I got into my garden, there was no getting me out of it, and she hardly expected I would reach her house this time. I, however, went on with my examination, for I felt that that was what I was there for, and not to indulge my personal feelings.

I saw another singular plant in that bed. It also clung close to the ground. Its leaves were long and pointed, their backs resting on the ground and their sides turning up. They were very numerous, and were piled on each other, and were of the deepest crimson color. The plant bore a small, pale-blue flower. It sparkled all over like the morning dew, and loved the shade, for it nestled under some of the larger shrubbery.

After examining each plant thus minutely, I stepped toward the house to have a view of the *tout ensemble*, and it was, indeed, very beautiful. While standing there, I discovered, just back of the house, a rude rock eight or ten feet high, of a slaty formation. I could not at first see it very distinctly, but the man in whose inclosure it was, observing that I was looking at it, threw his own light upon it, and I instantly saw all its beauties. Between the layers of stone were thin veins of gold and silver, and the face of the rock was interspersed with diamonds, rubies, and sapphires.

The whole sparkled most brilliantly in that pure light. The precious metals and stones were of no use in that country but to adorn nature, and so the face of the rock had not been injured by attempts to extract them.

At the base of the rock a pure spring of water gushed up, in which were swimming innumerable transparent little fish. The whole—spring, water, and animals—seemed very joyous, and as if alive and full of happiness.

The summit of the rock was covered with green moss and creeping vines, which hung down over its face, and gave me views of its beauty amid the leaves.

On each side of the spring was a long, rustic seat, and the whole scene was so full of calm, quiet happiness that I threw myself into one of the seats, desiring to be alone, that I might be able, without interruption, to drink it all in and enjoy it. I observed that my wife, who knew my propensities in this respect, was intently regarding me, and hushing the conversation around her so that I might not be disturbed.

While sitting there, I observed the rear of the house; that over the door and windows hung ornamental sheds of wood-work, constructed so gracefully that they seemed to hang down like drapery ; and all around the house running vines and shrubbery were profusely growing.

Upon the high ground, behind the house, was a rustic summer-house, from whence might be seen the whole country below, and whence I saw the people in various directions watching to see what effect the scene produced on me.

But I saw no children there, and I remarked how much little children would add to the beauty of the scene.

It was here added, through Dr. Dexter:

[When their affinities are so strong that they become a desire, little children respond and visit them.]

I again returned to that rustic seat by the spring, and on the opposite seat I perceived Lord Bacon was sitting. I did not get a view of his countenance to describe it, but I perceived an atmosphere of blue playing between us, and throwing out innumerable blue meteors, as it were, indicative of the truth there was in the communion between us.

At this moment it was written through Dr. Dexter, " Judge, please stop, for Mrs. D. is too much fatigued to remain longer. You will excuse me, as she is in my charge."

I then turned to pass down the walk and out of these grounds. By this time I had become familiar enough with the place, to be less shy than I had been of showing my true feelings. So, as I passed along I threw my left arm around my wife's waist, and her arm rested on my left shoulder. My son and daughter were on the other side of me ; she thrust her hand in mine, and thus we passed along until we reached the parapet, when I left them, and plunged suddenly down to earth again.

But before I close, I remark that the light of that scene around me had changed from a lake color to a pale straw color, and was very soft and pleasant.

8

Section Six.

Friday, Sept. 9, 1853.

The whole circle met this evening in my library.

The first thing that occurred was, that it was written:

THE Doctor remarked last night, after the Judge left, that he had been impressed with the idea (whether by spirits, or not, he could not say, and if it were by them, they would tell us to-night), that the materiality of spirits was confirmed by the whole teachings of the Bible from beginning to end. It is true that this idea was impressed on his mind, for the reason that we wished to note this idea for reference at the circle at the library.*

---

* During the revision of the MSS. for the press, I was directed to insert the following extract as a note to this passage.

" Scarcely any truth seems more clearly taught in the Bible than the future resurrection of the body; yet this doctrine has always been met by a most formidable objection. It is said that the body, laid in the grave, is, ere long, decomposed into its elements, which are scattered over the face of the earth, and enter into new combinations, even forming a part of other human bodies. Hence not even Omnipotence can raise from the grave the identical body laid there, because the particles may enter successively into a multitude of other human bodies. I am not aware that any successful reply has ever been given to this objection, until chemistry and natural history taught us the true nature of bodily identity, and until recently the objector has felt sure that he had triumphed ; but these sciences teach us that the identity of the body consists, not in a sameness of particles, but in the same kinds of elementary matter, combined in the same proportion, and having the same form and structure. Hence it is not necessary that the resurrection-body should contain a single particle of the matter laid in the grave, in order to be the same body —which it will be if it consist of the same kinds of matter combined in the same proportion, and has the same form and structure; for the particles of our bodies are often totally changed during our lives, yet no one imagines that the old man has not the same body as in infancy. What but the

But only on one point will we make any remarks, and in tracing the confirmation of spirit-teaching through the Old and New Testaments, we are particularly struck with the material nature of heaven, and in all the instrumentalities belonging both to God and his spirits, those who with golden harps surround the eternal throne, and those whom he sent on missions of love, mercy, or justice to earth; and when at last we arrive at the consummation of the Christ's life on earth, we are told that to satisfy one who was a doubter, the Christ bade him thrust his hand into the material wounds, made in his material body; and this, when he did so, satisfied him, and he doubted no more. Now the body and spirit of Christ had risen, and· Christ, according to the apostle, had ascended to heaven. I have only to say, if spirits were any thing but material combination, how could the body of Christ, material as it was, exist where no material thing could have being or life, according to the accepted idea of the orthodox? Thus we find that even the history of that pure being on whom the eternal hopes of half the world are centered, supports our teaching by his own, and substantiates· by his acts after death the doctrine we avow, that God does not manifest himself but through his works and matter.

BACON.

It will, we think, be well for Mrs. S. to be influenced

---

principles of science could have thus vindicated a precious doctrine of revelation?

"In the description which Paul gives of the spiritual body, a naturalist—and I fancy no one but a naturalist—will discover its specific identity. By this I mean that it will possess peculiarities that distinguish it from every thing else, but which are so closely related to the characteristics of the natural body in this world, from which it was derived, that one acquainted with the latter would recognize the former. Hence the Christian's friends in another world may be recognized by him from their external character, just as we identify the plants and animals of spring with those that seemed to perish in the preceding autumn."—" *The Religion of Geology*," by *Edward Hitchcock, D. D., LL. D., President of Amherst College, and Professor of Natural Theology and Geology.*

first for a short time ; then yourself, Judge, for a short
time also ; then Mr. W., and then the Doctor in continuation, if time permit.

Then for a short time I was impressed, and saw the following

VISION.

I found myself at the same spot I left last evening, seated on that rustic chair, with Lord Bacon sitting opposite
to me, enveloped in a grateful blue atmosphere.

On the side-hill, behind the house, I saw a large and
beautifully-shaped vase, six or eight feet diameter, and
made of brown stone.

It was standing directly under a projecting rock, from
which a small stream of water poured into the vase and
dropped over its sides.

I saw two children, about six years old, at the vase ; they
stood on one of the projections of its base, and were playing with the water, spatting it with their hands, and sprinkling it into each other's faces with great glee. They had
on no clothing but a scarf over the shoulder and around the
waist, and every once in a while they would look to see if
I observed them.

Off in the distance, beyond the house, and standing on
the brow of the precipice, I saw a monument, bright and
sparkling. The base of it was a large square block of
granite; on that was a smaller square block, of the same
color with the shaft, and from that towered high into the
air an obelisk. Out of its apex issued a crimson flame,
burning gently, and not very bright, but wavering and
flickering in the breeze. It was meant for a beacon to the
country below, to show them the existence of a higher
sphere. The sides of the monument did not seem to be entirely finished, yet they reflected a sparkling light in all
directions. Where did that light come from ? Now I

see ; it is the fire which is burning within which creates that light, and it casts a golden color on the surrounding scenery.

While I was looking at that, and wanting to approach those children and to go into the summer-house, Bacon laughingly said to me, "You have so many things to see, you know not where to turn first." That was so ; and the spirit, in whose grounds I was, left my wife, with whom he had been conversing, and approached me, saying, "Go with me, and I will show you something." I arose and followed him to the front of his house, and so down through his garden.

As I passed through this garden I observed a singular bed, of a circular form, which I paused a moment to examine. The edge of the bed was formed of a plant whose leaves all turned from the inside of the bed outward. They were of dark green, and lay one upon another, six or eight inches high. The border was about a foot wide, and was very unique and handsome. In the center of the bed grew a plant four or five feet high, with only trunk and limbs ; it had no leaves ; it was ice, and its buds were flakes of snow, and the whole thing sparkled intensely in the light.

I however went on with my host until we stood on the edge of the precipice, and there he showed me he had been at work, cutting out of the solid rock a stairway leading down to the country below. At one place he had tunneled a projecting rock, and it seemed that his task was almost done, though he had been many years engaged in it. From his residence he had discovered that many of the inhabitants of the country below were unconscious that there was a higher country to which they might attain ; and even they who did discover it found the way difficult, either up the precipice, and across the gulf where those dark spirits lurked, or through the temple and along the narrow and circuitous path which I had traveled ; and he had aimed, by his own unaided efforts, to remove the diffi-

culties.   It was to him a labor of love, and in its performance he had found happiness.

His intention was, as soon as his stairway was finished,
to give free vent to the fire within his monument.

Its flames would then shoot high into the heavens, and
its sides reflect that dazzling, golden light which would
show to the country below far, far in the distance, not only
that there was a higher and brighter country for them, but
where the pathway was by which they could most easily
ascend.

He called my attention to the fact, that in that lower
country there were many hills and projections from the
surface ; some of them steep and high, shaped like a sugar-
loaf ; some flatter and broader, shaped like an ant-hill ;
and some of them rough and jagged, like beetling rocks.
He told me that they, as well as that immense mountain
which I saw in the far distance, were all inhabited by persons whose aspirations had led them to select their residences there, and who were generally satisfied with their
condition, because unaware that it could be bettered.

They thought, indeed, that they had ascended as high as
they could, and their happiness consisted mainly in con-
trasting their condition with that of those below them, and
congratulating themselves that they were better off than
them.

He had had them in view in his labors, and he hoped,
when his beacon should be fired, that their curiosity would
be excited, and thence would be awakened within them an
aspiration to enter at length upon the ascent, to which there
was no end but the bosom of the Most High.

As I stood by his side, I noticed some of the inhabitants
below were toiling up the steep path that led to an eminence.

I observed that they were some of those who had started
on their journey after my address to them from the side
hill.   One in particular attracted my attention ; he was
an old man, with long, white hair and beard ; he had a

staff in his hand, and though he had the appearance of age, his step was alert and active, his eye quick and bright, and he looked ever upward. It was thus he discovered me, as I was standing on the edge of the precipice, high above him. He recognized me, and, pausing a moment, inquired of me whether he was in the right road? I nodded an assent, and pointed to the path a little turning to his right, which unhappily was not trodden enough to be very plain to a stranger. With a cheering smile he turned and breasted the ascent. I watched his progress. Not far above him I saw a bright and youthful spirit sitting by the wayside, evidently waiting for him. The old man saw him too, and recognized him as one he had known and loved on earth; so he pressed forward with still more alacrity, and soon came up with him. They embraced; and the young spirit, fondly throwing his arm around the old man's waist, lifted him from the path, and bore him gently upward, until they entered within the porch of the temple, and were lost to my view.

At this moment my companion reminded me that it was time for me to return to Earth again, and I did so at once

Section Seven.

Saturday, Sept. 10, 1853.

This evening, at my library, all the circle being present, it was first written through the Doctor:

IT will not be necessary that you remain entirely silent, though your conversation should not interrupt the communications. Therefore sit at ease, and occasionally talk, always recollecting that animated talk will retard full and free manifestations. There are many spirits here, and they are all anxious to say something, but I shall occupy all the time proper, and then give way to the rest.

Now, in the name of Our Father, we bless you. In the spirit of love we meet you, and we earnestly hope that our teachings will profit you, the world, and ourselves, and assist us to consummate the great end of our existence, Progression.   BACON.

Before we proceed to the subject of our proper teaching, it may be well to say that it is important that you should understand the character and attributes of God, that in the manifestations of his power, whether in his material or spiritual works, your minds may be disabused of the idea that there is any speciality in whatever emanates from him, or that he works by miracle.

When the thought is thrown back on the ages which have passed since this world was created, and calls up in review God's connection with the whole of the natural creation, we are, in spite of our opinions derived from our education, struck with the fact that every act of God in reference to the works of his hands has been predicated on certain immutable and unchangeable laws. Look at the earth. Not even the minutest thing exists or has its being, decays or dies, develops life or its kind, or in its connection with life and matter around it, but is subject to laws which have their proper influence on the same things situated either at the poles or the equator. Certain principles, equal and exact in their operation, govern every constituent entering into the formation of matter in every part of creation. And where by the combination of several constituents a new result is obtained, this also comes under the regulation of laws which remain precisely the same in their operation on the same substance, wherever it may be found. This probably will be admitted to be true by almost every person as applying to inert matter. But when we advance a step in creation, we find God's manifestations the same. The vegetable world is governed by laws which do not vary in their application or effect in any climate, in any soil, whether at that altitude where vegetation stops, or in the deepest valley where vegetation grows. But let us progress one step further, and select the lowest form of animal life known to man. Is there here any miraculous creation? Is life, or growth, or decay, or death dependent on any special providence of God? or does this class of animals come under the influence of certain laws, which exert the same characteristic power in all that concerns their life or death wherever they may be or are found?

What is a miracle? What use has God with a miraculous dispensation? To me, it seems detracting from the omnipotence of the Almighty, that he should find it necessary to change the order of his instituted laws by any out-of-the-way exhibition of his power. Admitting the great Source of all things to be a principle, and acknowledging his omnipotence and omnipresence, your minds can comprehend that there can be no special manifestation of his wisdom, his love, his power, or his glory. For were it admitted that God was a personage, it would not appear incompatible that he should have his preferences, or that he should show more of his love to one being than another, that he should possess all those feelings ascribed to him by certain writers called divine or inspired, who describe God as a being or spirit possessing most, if not all, the passions and feelings of man. Thus, when one of the creatures whom he has created should act in violation of his commands, we should not be surprised if he were to inflict condign punishment; or if another creature had acted nobly, and fulfilled his commandments, we should expect that the Great Spirit would reward him accordingly.

But let us follow this subject still further. Leaving the lowest order of animals, we approach the class which the learned call Mammalia, and to this class, under the same arrangement, belongs man. Now we find that the animals belonging to this order, genera, class, or species are always confined to the same kinds of food, when the animal is domesticated, prepared by man, and when in the wild state, always feeding on food of the same nature, and the effect of which is exactly the same. Not only in this particular of their organization do the laws instituted for their government apply, but we find that the same process of gestation obtains, and they nurse their young under all circumstances alike. I refer you to the simplest circumstances in their history, that you may the more readily follow me and understand my argument. But one step still onward. It has been said that certain animals were created for the assistance and use of man, and that he can tame them to his hand, so that they will perform the greatest and most severe labor at his command. In noticing this peculiarity, we are impressed with the apparent fact, that in the domestication of animals, the spirit of man acts through the material surroundings on earth, and makes itself felt outside its own organization.

And yet still forward: We find there are only certain species of animals that can be tamed, and that others refuse to obey the commands of man, and can not be compelled to work. The most ferocious beasts can, to be sure, be confined in a cage, and by blows and the most violent treatment be made to fear man. But even then, when removed from the influence they fear, they will manifest their ferocious and sanguinary natures. This is ever and always the same.

Nature in all her workings acts under the control of law, and she is a law-obeying subject. For thousands of years the seasons have passed and repassed in their order, yielding to man fruits and flowers, and the sources of all his sustenance, and much of his happiness. She has never rebelled. Penetrate the earth's depths, and the law holds its power intact. Scale the battlements of heaven, and there the law is paramount. On earth among men the law is still obeyed, perverted though it may be by their own desires and passions; but still any infraction is followed by a consequent punishment, not direct from God, but the penalty attached to its violation when that law was instituted. Is it not so in every department of nature over which man has no control? And when you leave the earth, and seek for confirmation in the skies, do you see any change? Do the planets wander in eccentric orbits? Do the stars fail to shed their light? Or has the moon vailed its face other than in obeisance of law? Has the sun ceased to shine, and has light and heat departed?

You ask, if this be so, what follows? I reply, that God, acting by laws which he has instituted, has invariably exhibited their effects through matter, and that the mind can not appreciate the consistency of creating one condition of life in connection with matter, and separating that connection when the spirit leaves the earth. And as every manifestation of the Creator, whether on this earth or in the thousand worlds he has fashioned, has been and is through materiality, we can not understand why his laws, so harmoniously working throughout the whole of his creation, will not still continue when the spirit shall have left this earth.

Here I will stop, and continue the subject in connection with the progress of creation to-morrow night.

Then through me this vision was related :

VISION.

I was again standing on the edge of the precipice by the side of him who had shown me that stairway. He called my attention to the fact that many of the hills and prominences I had spoken of were dim and misty, not seen plainly even by us, and it was still more difficult for their inhabitants to see at a distance. He at the same time called my attention to several points in the valley. It looked like an earthly scene when the sky is partly overcast with clouds, and the sun shines partially through them, lighting up different places, while others are in the shade. So here, though there was no sun to shed its light, yet various places in the country below were lighted up, some near and some far distant, by that large mountain. In some places it was a light bronze color, some places blue, then a claret color, and in some green.

I here inquired what the green color denoted, and it was answered through the Doctor :

" Developed affinities."

The light at different places was of different degrees of brilliancy. All denoted that the inhabitants of those places had begun to progress, and had aspirations for something higher in a greater or less degree : in some places induced by affection ; some by the love of truth ; some by desire to progress ; and some by developed affinities.

I observed that while these places were thus lighted up, on others a cold, misty cloud seemed to rest, obscuring them partially from view. The contrast was very great; and all this light was produced by the inhabitants themselves. It was of their own creation.

This varied light added greatly to the beauty of the scene, and besides, it enabled those who should stand where I did to see the advance of progression among the inhabitants below.

On that far distant mountain I saw a streak of golden light flowing down one of its sides, like burning lava. That told the story, that some of its inhabitants, impelled by affection, had begun to aspire higher, and were descending, in order to get into the way, and their path was thus marked.

At the bottom of the mountain it seemed to spread out, and denoted that the inhabitants who had come down were waiting for others, and seeking to learn which way to go. They did not know, and I noticed a majestic spirit clothed all in white, but invisible to them, was floating in the air over their heads, and pointing toward where I stood. He was trying to impress them. His hair was golden, and he wore a scarf of blue.

I noticed among them a young man sixteen or seventeen years of age, who had just come down the mountain. He was modest and unassuming, but his vision was more open than theirs. He told them he saw the way, that he saw the monument on the hill and the temple below, and he pointed out the way to them. He told them this with such an air of truth that it convinced them, and they chose him for their leader. But he said first of all he must take care of his mother, who had come down the mountain with him. She was aged and infirm, and so they made a bier for her, and took turns in bearing her along on their shoulders. He walked by her side, and was indeed a fit leader for them, for he thought never of himself, but always of his mother, whom he loved, and of others.

He led them away from the hills and eminences in their path, but through the valleys where those lights shone, where he and his party were ever welcomed and entertained, and where his band was constantly augmented by others joining them. They soon traveled more rapidly. His

mother gathered strength enough as she progressed to relieve her bearers and go alone.

I turned from this sight to join my companions, and I
observed three persons on horseback approaching, two
females and a male. All seemed young, and were superbly mounted. The horses were beautifully formed, like
coursers of the purest Arabian blood. One was white, one
a chestnut, and the other a light bay. The females wore
long, graceful riding-dresses of purple velvet; the male
a short jacket and cap of crimson velvet, trimmed with
gold cord. They had two dogs with them; one was a
shaggy poodle dog, and the other a small, delicate grayhound, black, with a few white spots, and fawn-colored
breast and legs. The whole appearance of the cavalcade
was very beautiful. They lived far in the interior, and
hearing of my visit, had come down to see. They were
conversing with my dear S. as I approached the gate.
One of the females, after looking at me as I was advancing, asked her if she did not wish I was there for good
and all? She replied: "No. His time is not yet. He is
yet to do much good to man before he comes."

On my arrival at the gate they reined their horses back,
and accompanied us on my passage out of that country.
This time I felt impelled to return by the circuitous path
by which I had first ascended. They all accompanied me
to the steps, and, taking leave, I began my descent. I
had not proceeded far, before I saw some one ascending
toward me. It was the old man whom I had seen approaching toward the temple. He was moving with a very
alert and lively gait, and, with his head still erect, was
twirling his staff around his head with a very joyous motion. I noticed that though he had the same white hair
and beard, the wrinkles had left his face, and he seemed
to be both young and old.

As he was advancing, I asked myself, What will he do in
this new country entirely among strangers? And I turned
around to recommend him to the care of those who had

accompanied me to the entrance. But I saw my interference was quite unnecessary. He had been discovered by
them also. They had sent the word abroad, and spirits
were flocking down in great numbers to welcome him. By
this time he had come up to me, and stopped to speak to
me. I pointed him to the group that were waiting for him
with looks of cheerful welcome. His emotions were too
great to enable him to speak. And with deep humility he
resumed his way, and so I parted with him.

I hurried down the path and into the temple. I was impressed I had a duty to perform there, but I saw no one in
all that vast building. I went again to the corner of the
platform whence I had surveyed the steep hill, and there
I saw the dark spirits still lurking under the rocks. They
were still lying in wait for me, and were unconscious that
I had already repeatedly made the ascent by another path.

I said this to them. They gnashed their teeth with rage,
and with " a vengeful hollo" plunged down far beneath my
sight, and so I returned to earth again.

'Section Eight.

Sunday, Sept. 11, 1853.

This evening, at Doctor Dexter's, it was written :

In compliance with the directions of the higher spirits, we wish to utter a prayer always before we commence the duties of the evening; and if it conforms with your feelings, one will be written to repeat every evening.

BACON.

We all expressed our assent, and it was written :

Oh, thou universal Spirit! by whose laws every thing was created, and by whose love every thing exists! we look to thee, and we regard thee as our Father, for thou hast taught us that in loving thee we approach in spirit the attributes which are thy characteristics. We pray to thee that our feelings may be elevated to a just perception of what is good, what is true, and what should belong to us in connection with others. Enable us to live consistently, and to develop those feelings of our nature which are innate and coeval with thee. Enable us to control ourselves—to feel the high obligations of beings destined to live forever. Enable us to improve the faculties of our spirit, as well as material being, and enable our desires for the true, the good, the just, and the beautiful, to develop with our days, and harmonize with all that we see of thee in thy works. Let us feel, let us see, let us know that in us are the germs of everlasting knowledge and happiness; and when at last we lay down this body, let our spirits rise in their new birth, active and earnest in the all-impelling desire to progress toward those spheres where thy glory and power, thy love and wisdom, are most manifest. Amen.*

Then it was further written:

Now, while our hearts are full, and we realize the presence of those bright and beautiful beings who are with us, let us resume the consideration of our proper subject. Last night I attempted to illustrate the attributes and characteristics of God by referring to certain facts which substantiate our position, apparent through the first volume, that laws established by God had their full influence now as in the beginning.

And in again reflecting upon the past, and turning back on creation, and all things which live, move, and have their being on its broad surface, we recognize one particular fact, and that is, that while insects and animals, vegetables and minerals, come under the control of and are governed by certain laws in all circumstances and conditions; that while the whole of their manifestations are obedient to principles which are now and have been unchangeable, they transmit nothing to the same species which follow after them. Remaining the same, they continue so from age to age, and their properties and characters, their attributes and action, appear the same in the same kind from one age to another; and yet the developments of feeling or instinct in animals would lead us to suppose that there might or could be a change in their nature, differing from the condition in which they might be situated at a different period of time. But does the horse of to-day differ in instinct or properties from the horse in the days of Moses? When we notice the small insect called the ant, and watch the wondrous workings of its remarkable instinct, we are struck with its sagacity and ingenuity. It constructs dwellings, contrived with so much

---

* Now while I am revising these papers for the press, it is written to me by Bacon, through Doctor Dexter, "This prayer will have greater solemnity and beauty when you understand it was composed and written by your wife."

wisdom, that even man can hardly imitate. It resolves into communities, and selects from its numbers some one as chief or head. It raises armies, and sends them forth on enterprises where much sagacity and absolute knowledge is required for success. It forces from others of a different sphere the strongest and hardiest, and compels them to serve as slaves and to perform all the drudgery of household or field labor. In fine, it manifests intelligence which astonishes the learned and perplexes the wise. But do the insects of to-day differ from those who were noticed a thousand years ago ? Why should their attributes remain the same, if God acted specially ? But enough of this.

I remark, that if God were a person*—were his acts directed by any special manifestation, there would not, there could not, be any dependence on the established laws of nature. What to-day would be noticed as arranged for the planets, might to-morrow be changed for some other institute, totally altering the whole order and appearance of the planets. The seasons would not follow in course. Where now are peace, and plenty, and order, and regularity, all might in a moment, in the twinkling of an eye, be transformed into a wilderness where no plant would grow, and where desolation would reign supreme.†

---

* While revising, it is written to me in explanation, " A person according to the expressed biblical idea."

† While thus revising (August, 1854), it is written by Bacon through the Doctor :

" In saying that he is a principle, we do not mean that there is no identity. If spirit possesses form, the source from which it springs should of course have form. The great Source of all, though manifest in every created thing, is not there in person, but represented by his law. As when a man has directed the erection of a house, he doesnot find it necessary to be there in person; his plans are executed by his workmen, and his idea is carried out in their performance of his laws.

" Thus with God. He is a principle ; for he is the source, the head, the germ of all creation ; for every thing has its origin in and from him. The laws he has established are the evidences of his existence, and the execution of those laws exhibit his impartiality and love. The various forms and phases of creation show his ideas of beauty and harmony, and the radiance and glory

Again; it is necessary for the perpetuation of all creation, that God should act by laws which are unchangeable;
for were it not so there would not, there could not, be any
development, any progression. Every thing that God
created shows emphatically that he intended development.
Suppose for one moment that any special providence should
influence man, what would be the effect? If man were, under the providence of God, successful in every thing that
belonged to earth, the consequences of any change would
so disturb his social connections and relations, that society
would become an anarchy, and instead of progressing in
all those characteristics which mark him as man possessing
a spirit, he would retrograde to the same level with the
brutes, and become so identified with them that he could
transmit none of those glorious discoveries, none of those
vast contrivances, which now so plainly show his origin
and destiny.

I remarked a few evenings since that even Christ's last
act on earth, even after he had ascended to heaven, was
proof of the materiality of the soul. I said this that you
might observe the connection and influence of laws acting
on matter here, with the same laws in their full effect
after the spirit has passed from the earth to the spheres;
and, that you might comprehend the force 'of that great
principle which I am trying to illustrate, *that an instituted
system of unchangeable laws, whose effects are apparent in
and through matter everywhere, must be perpetuated immuta-
bly through all time, as well for the harmonious action of
all created things, as for the development and progression of
the soul;* and that it was impossible for even God himself
to maintain the order and harmonious relation of the creation he has fashioned from chaos, if he were to change or

---

with which he has clothed the earth demonstrate his delight in that which
gives dignity and glory to his works.

"Thus, though the very God is a principle, yet he is and must be a person.
May not—oh! will not the form be developed to us, when we shall have
arrived at that state of holiness when we can see eye to eye and face to face?"

alter his laws or their action one jot or tittle. Thus much, and now for Progression. Read what is written, and I will continue.

I did so, and it was written:

We have brought our minds to the consideration of space as it was, when God had not called the principles of life and motion into action, or, rather, when the usual constituents existing through all space had not felt the impelling force of development, and could not, therefore, form or fashion themselves into organized matter.

Here, at the appointed signal, I read the 3d verse of the 1st chapter of Genesis: "And God said, Let there be light, and there was light."

"And God said, Let there be light." And now the time had arrived when, through the impelling power of development, the constituents or atomic particles lying dormant in that chaos were drawn by the operation of attraction toward one another. Thus was manifest the first evidence of creative power in motion. Then from every part of that vast space, from point to point, from limit to limit, over the whole of its vast surface, and even to its illimitable depths, the atoms or particles moving toward each other, obedient to the great law which governed their action— particles so small that they could not be discovered even with a powerful glass—now united with others, and then with others, until each new combination resolved itself into a still larger, and at each union the force and motion were increased, vast bodies of a gaseous nature were formed, the velocity and motion of which were so great, that, acting on the atmosphere which was generated by this revolution and combination of the atomic particles, light and heat were developed by the friction.

Here I read the 4th verse, as follows: "And God saw the light that it was good, and God divided the light from the darkness."

"And God saw the light that it was good."

To expect that I, the spirit of Lord Bacon, should be

able to penetrate the arcana of nature, and explain how God created every thing, would be assuming I was as intelligent as my Creator. I do no such thing. I give you opinions, and facts when I can do so. Much of what I now write is opinion. Take it for what it is worth, and glean what instruction and good you can from it.

Each globe was governed, as to its size, by the influence of the attractive power which gathered the particles together. Thus some were larger and some smaller, and all of them in their localities possessed peculiar properties differing from each other.

But it was not the ignition of the gases by friction that created the light that was separated, as it is to our earth by night and day; though we can imagine the glorious and transcendent appearance these vast bodies would make, lighted up by their own fires, and moving and flashing in what was before an eternal darkness; and we must recollect that each body was governed by laws, and that the development of no one of all the innumerable bodies now visible to your eye in the vast firmament above, was instantaneous with another. The body called the sun undoubtedly gave the light which illumined this profound darkness.

The mind is fired with its own imagining when it pictures the sun shining forth and dissipating the dark pall which shrouded this gloomy chaos. Now, indeed, did God say, "Let there be light;" for when that body had arrived at that state of development that it could send forth its bright rays, the deepest profundity of this eternal gloom was lighted up with its glorious beams.

Then flashed across its surface the golden light; then from its gloomy recesses were reflected the gold, the violet, the red, and the thousand sparkling rays that garnished that vast area as if with jewels of inestimable price. Then, for the first time, the clouds floating in space gave back the varied colors of the rainbow. Then did the eternal distance, incomprehensible to man, yield its heavenly blue to cheer and comfort him, instead of darkness more profound than night. Then waked to a new birth the flashing identities which give beauty to creation, and when the light from the sun first shone into those depths of gloom, it clothed every thing in the proper colors of its nature. Then did the Great First Cause see that the light was to his new creation beautiful, for it waked up from nature's eternal gloom the rays reflecting heaven's own brightness. Oh! it was a glorious sight to see nature thus unfolded, as if a dark mantle had been removed from its face, when to our earth it showed forth the glorious beauties of its surface, and sent such a glad shout of joy from every thing which lived, that its echoes have not yet died away in the distant limits of creation, but the murmur still travels on and will eternally travel. And when we all are in the spheres, and our spirits filled with the glory and power of God, perhaps we shall be viewing together the beauty of some planet beyond; then shall come to us, trembling and indistinct, this murmur in the distance, waking our spirits to a consciousness of nature's response, when God said, Let there be light.　　　　　　BACON.

VISION.

Then commenced the manifestation through me, which I related as follows:

I saw the old man whom I had met in the path, when he ascended the steps of this new country and mingled with the spirits there awaiting him. They had assembled in great numbers to welcome him, and they were profuse in their offers to him of a home with any of them, until he should erect one for himself.

I noticed that the color of the light, which was pale yellow when I descended the steps, had changed to that brilliant lake color which I had observed to prevail when I first entered there. And I learned that that was always so when a new spirit came among them, and it signified their joy at his advent.

The old man moved along the path, surrounded with this throng of joyous and affectionate spirits. And though his heart was full at the warmth of his welcome, I saw that his mind was also occupied with another thought. At length he gave utterance to it by asking why I had left the country, and whether I would not return? They told him I was a mortal yet, and could not remain; that I came there to see that country, that I might describe it to my fellow-mortals, and had been drawn there by the strong affection of my wife and children, and the great duty which had been opened to me. He immediately, and with great alertness, asked if they were there? They answered by pointing them out to him in the crowd on his left hand, at a little distance. He immediately left the crowd and moved up to them. He approached them with great respect and affection, and after a few words with my wife, he turned to the surrounding spirits and said, "I will take up my residence with this family. It is to him I owe my redemption, and I will serve those he loves so well till he comes." The spirits, with one accord, clapped their hands in approval of a course of conduct so consonant to the prevailing sentiment of the place. The surrounding spirits then left and retired to their respective residences, and that old man, with my wife and children, turned off the main path and ascended that where I had accompanied them before, and proceeded to their residence, a far distance up that path.

Thus far I had seen while the Doctor was writing, and it was a representation of what had occurred the day before after I had left. Now, when I gave myself up to the influence, I found

I was walking up that same path accompanied by them, and was just leaving the place where I had been shown the stairway. On both sides of me were beautiful residences standing back from the road.

One I noticed in particular, because it was surrounded by trees and shrubbery, as I had sometimes seen among the natives in Central America. The trees grew close together, and intermingled their dense foliage overhead, producing a very soft shade all around their trunks. They were trimmed up as far as the arm could reach, and the ground around their base was leveled very smooth, entirely free from grass, and kept very clean, so that it was a cool and delightful promenade. This grove was at the side and behind the west end of the house, and extended off, I observed, some distance in that direction. The whole place was very attractive to me, and I had a wish to examine it more closely. My companions immediately turned with me into the inclosure.

I noticed that the ground in front of the house, and between it and the path, were not, as at the other places I had seen, ornamented with flowers, but they were used as a vegetable garden, and it was in very perfect order, and growing very luxuriantly. I saw growing there Indian corn, potatoes, beets, and lettuce. There were other varieties, but I did not particularly notice them. But there seemed to be nothing there merely for ornament. All was for use, but all was in order. As I approached the house, I saw at my left some out-houses near the edge of the trees, as if for animals.

I became at once impressed that that was the farm establishment for that community, and he who lived there had been a farmer on earth, and now superintended it for the common welfare.

I saw no one around the place. The house was an old-fashioned farm-house, one and a half story high, with a wide portico in front, with seats in it. My companions stopped there, but I proceeded around the house into the grove.

There, back of the grove, I saw a large field of wheat growing very thrifty, and nearly ripe. It seemed to be stirred by a gentle breeze, and waved gracefully and peacefully, as I have often seen it here in midsummer. The grove of trees, and the clean, smooth walk under the shade, continued all around the field, and it was the only fence it had. Many of the trees bore flowers to their very top branches, and up some of them flowering vines twined to their very summit, mingling together, in an enormous bouquet, the golden flowers of the trees.with the pale purple flowers of the vines. The perfume that ever and anon was wafted in my face was most exquisite, sometimes almost too strong for my endurance. Along, back of the field and through the woods, a small stream of water meandered quietly, and on its banks and within the grove were many rustic seats. It was a scene of delightful repose and enjoyment.

Behind that field of grain was another, skirted in like manner by a grove of trees and a running brook; and behind that still another. West of these grain fields I saw several orchards of fruit trees, separated in like manner from each other by groves of trees which were much smaller than the others, so as not to cast too much shade; and amid those groves also there were the same running brooks. In those groves I noticed a tree shaped like an umbrella, not running up high but spreading out broad, with very dense foliage of dark green leaves, like the leaf of the lemon tree. From its lower limbs there hung down a species of moss, which was an air-plant, and dropped its festoons down nearly to the ground very gracefully.

I saw four of these orchards, one behind the other, and parallel with the grain fields.

I noticed that in one there were peaches, in another plums, very large and yellow, blue, and pale green. I did not observe what were in the others.

As I passed through the orchards and into the same kind of grove beyond, I observed that there was a considerable stream of water which approached from the west, and, as it reached the orchards, had been branched off into four or five smaller streams, which were conducted through the several groves and around the various fields, so as to irrigate them, and at the same time add to the beauty of the scene and its quiet repose.

. I had noticed as I passed, that the out-houses which I saw were for the mules which were used on the farm, but thus far I had seen no animals nor man. But now I noticed, beyond the orchard, a dense forest of enormous trees, and in it there was a water-fall and a saw-mill, and now I saw the man whose place I was on. He was at work at the saw-mill with four or five assistants. He was dressed in shirt and trowsers, and his sleeves were rolled up. He and his companions seemed very cheerful and happy at their work. It seemed as if they were toiling for the pleasure of it, and were evidently enjoying it. They were singing and laughing, telling stories and cracking jokes upon each other.

The saw-mill was at work with four saws agoing; but I did not see around it any of the litter which I have been accustomed to here: no loose piles of slab, no heaps of sawdust, no decaying logs, but every thing was neat and orderly. The logs were piled up in heaps, and so arranged as to look very handsome. They were arranged in piles. I counted the base. It consisted of eight logs, then above that layer seven, and then six, and so on up to a point.

All their rubbish and dirt, I observed, were carried off by a sewer dug under ground, and terminating at the preci- pice which I have already mentioned. By means of a waste-weir all the rubbish was carried off that way, and the water passed clear and pure down through the farm. When I approached, they were sawing a large log with the whole four saws. It was a singular kind of wood, some- thing like the bird's-eye maple, but the spots were larger, and the wood susceptible of a higher polish.

Each board, as it came from the saw, was finely polished and smooth, and I examined to see how that was done. The back of each saw was as thick as its front edge, and so constructed that it smoothed off and polished, as it went along, the roughness which the teeth made.

The mill itself was a beautiful structure. It was a Doric temple, with two rows of columns, open entirely at the sides,.

and a roof that projected over both at the ends and the sides. He had had time enough to build it, and had taken care to ornament it.

Just beyond this mill I saw a pasture in which horses and cows were grazing, and through it ran that stream of water.

Beyond this pasture was a woody grove, full of poultry, turkeys, geese, ducks, and chickens. It was a great aviary. I saw peacocks, macaws, the bird of paradise, doves, fantailed pigeons, canary birds, etc. It was a delightful music that was heard from this grove, and its feathered inhabitants seemed the very picture of merriment and happiness.

Beyond this aviary was an extensive forest, extending far back in the distance, and looked very much like the oak openings in the far West. The trees were far enough apart for one to drive a coach-and-four among them, and the under limbs and branches had been browzed off about eight or ten feet high. Occasionally, and more particularly near the creek, there were spots entirely free from trees, where there was a rich pasture. In these woods and in the pastures I saw many animals. I noticed particularly only rabbits and deers, of different ages, from the huge antlered stag to the young fawn.

My attention was attracted to a noise in the woods, and I saw a stag with large horns branching out, running toward me at full speed, closely pursued by a large grayhound. It was an exciting scene, and I asked myself, Do they hunt here? But I soon saw that it was only sport between those animals. As they approached the bank of the stream, the stag stopped and turned around. The hound stopped also, and began to gambol around the stag, apparently enticing him to chase in turn. The stag trotted with a stately gait toward the dog, who fled from him, and thus playing I left them, and returned to the house.

My return was instantaneous, as if I had been borne through the air at my wish, while my passage out had been a very leisurely walk.

On my return to the house I found my companions still seated in the piazza. A female of mature age, who seemed to be the mistress of the mansion, was standing in the door-way, leaning against the door-post talking to my wife. A younger female, apparently her daughter, was leaning out of the window of the front room conversing with my son and daughter. The younger female had a red collar to her garments, while those of the other female were trimmed with pale green belt, and purple cuffs and colors. Her hair was done up in a knot behind, but how it was fastened up I could not be certain, but it seemed as if by a silver arrow thrust through it. This was her working-dress, and she seemed to be as industrious as her husband.

I saw through the hall out back of the house a large churn as large as a barrel, of white wood with brass hoops, and very clean.

Observing what attracted my attention, she invited me to walk out back and examine for myself. I did so, and she accompanied me.

I found out there a very wide piazza on which the most of her work was done. At one end of it I saw many tin pans hanging up against the wall, and under them was a table, fastened to the building by hinges, and capable of being lifted up or let down at pleasure. On that she told me she made her bread.

I had not yet seen any glass windows. On this piazza there were openings for windows, but I saw no sashes or glass. Standing against these openings was a long, narrow table with drawers in it.

The floor seemed to be of stone, sloping from the house outward, and terminating in a gutter which ended in a sewer under ground, and thus all refuse water was carried off.

The water from the brook was carried into the piazza, and fell from a penstock in a small stream into a basin, elevated about four feet from the floor. It ran over the sides of that basin into a larger one on the floor whence it escaped into the sewer.

I observed that parts of the floor of the piazza were so constructed, that by moving an upright stick standing back against the side of the house, a lattice-work could be opened and let the air pass up. This was done to give ventilation, and I observed that the slats of the lattice-work were so constructed as not to let the water through, but to carry it off into the gutter.

While in this piazza, I observed back of the house several orange trees full of fruits and flowers, and monkeys playing in their branches. Here, for the first time, I saw a cat; she was playing with the monkeys, and chasing them up the trees. I saw also, at a little distance to the right, a large, old-fashioned barn for storing grain, and between it and the house was a large field of Indian corn. The barn was standing near the stream of water, and had contrivances by which all its rubbish and dirt would be carried off by it. And here I observed that the stream of water tended north, and became at a short distance again united with the others into a large creek.

In passing from the back to the front of the house, I observed the hall had upon it what had the appearance of an old-fashioned rag carpet. The female, reading my surprise at that, told me they had been farmers on earth, and had taken a great deal of pleasure in their way of living, and had purposely surrounded themselves with the comforts to which they had been accustomed.

The boards of the hall floor were so clean and polished that they shone.

I saw also in the hall an old-fashioned stairway leading to upper rooms.

Some one of the circle here inquired, If they thus worked for the whole community as a matter of duty enjoined upon them, or did it voluntarily? The female answered—

"We do it voluntarily. We take pleasure in it. When we want help we say so to those around, and they come of

their own accord." The daughter, laughing, added, " I
don't have much work to do, so many come and offer to
work, and when they come we have merry times. We tell
stories, laugh, and are full of fun."

I observed that their house was not large, and the family consisted of only three persons, the man, his wife, and
daughter. They were originally from Germany. They
had been in the spirit-world many years, and there had
been many new inventions to facilitate farm labor since
they left the earth, which they had learned and adopted.
Among other things, the woman showed me a pair of
heavy wooden shoes, the soles at least two inches thick,
and told me that she used to wear them, and then she
showed me the light leather shoes she now wore, and
laughingly compared them together.

Some one of the circle asked me to inquire how many years she had
been in the spirit-world?

She answered she could not tell by years, only by
events ; but it was before the Crusades. She added, she
remained only a few years in the lower plane, when all
three were united and ascended together.

I inquired of the daughter if she had never been married? She answered she supposed I would call it mar-
riage. There was one to whom she was much attached,
and they loved each other's society, and they were a
good deal together. He was now at work at the saw-mill.
And she said he would come in from the saw-mill, not at
all tired with his work, and would kick up his heels and go
to dancing. " Yes," added her mother, " and you join him
in doing so." She showed me a guitar and a flute, and
said they played and sang together. She said her father
sang, but her mother never found time to sing.

The young girl seemed full of frolic, and fun, and joy ;
she could hardly keep still. As she and my daughter sat
close together, I could not help noticing the difference.
My daughter was still and quiet, and apparently very intellectual. She was not without emotions, but she repressed

them, and I saw her once in a while lay her hand on her heart, as if to hush all within. She had a very heavenly expression of countenance. Her forehead was high, and seemed to be transparent, so that every thought could be read. The other girl had red cheeks and a round face, and was so full of frolic! My son stood at a little distance, leaning against the side of the house, in an attitude quite common with me; it is one which my wife always liked, and she had taught it to him.

I saw some company coming toward the house; they were three young females and a young man; they were very merry. The young man walked behind with one of the girls, and the other two were walking before them; he had been telling them something which amused them, and one of the girls—the one directly before him—laughed so loud and merry that it rang out clear and joyful, making every thing glad around. The young girl in the house went out to meet them; and when she met them she told them I was there; they had been told of my being in the country, but had not seen me, and had not expected to meet me there. They became silent at once, and showed the same emotion I had witnessed in others, love and admiration, and a wish at once to know what they could do to help the matter along.

The young girl of the house took her guitar and repaired to the grove at the end of the house, where she played, and the four new-comers danced; it seemed to be a sort of cotillion they danced, and ended with a waltz. The player amused herself occasionally by changing the time faster or slower, and then laughed at the manner she affected their motion so heartily that she could at times hardly play at all.

Then one of the females danced alone. She was exquisitely graceful; and hers was the very poetry of motion. She evidently was very fond of it, and her grace and motion were very beautiful. The player on the guitar was now very careful about her music, for she was as much enraptured at the dancing as the rest were. At length the dancer stopped, saying, " There, I have danced long enough for your amusement, now you dance for mine." She was tall and slender, yet round and healthy. Her hair was a silky chestnut color, and was tied behind with a blue ribbon. One of the other females had a head of thick, black hair, curling down her shoulders, and occasionally, while dancing, she would raise her hand and push it out of her eyes. The young gentleman had a light beard and mustaches; he wore a skull-cap, with a single feather in it; he wore it jauntily on one side of his head. He had large benevolence, but only a medium intellect. He was ever thinking what he could do for others, and never thinking of himself. The old man, however, who had chosen to reside with my family, had large intellect and great energy and decision of character; he had a sparkling black eye, and a very benevolent countenance.*

We turned to take our leave, for it was time for me to go. The matron invited me to call on her again, and she would, she said, give me a drink of buttermilk.

As we returned we found a narrow, paved path inside of the posts and railing, and we went along that, my wife hanging on my arm. The paving was of square stones, very highly polished, and full of the most beautiful petrifactions. Its ground-work was yellow, and presented an infinite variety.

That pathway led to the most stately mansion I had yet seen; it was a double house, two stories high, and painted white. It had no trees around it, but abundance of shrubbery and flowers. The grounds on which it stood were inclosed with a border of shrubbery, growing about four feet high; and I observed that when it led back from the path it zigzagged like a pair of stairs, until it met from both sides at a bridge over the creek back of the house. The bridge led across to a beautiful grove, at the edge of which stood a summer-house of open lattice-work, but with the

---

* Months afterward I learned he was Abner Kneeland.

most graceful roof to it that I ever saw. It was covered with flowering and fragrant vines, bearing white, pink, and scarlet flowers, variegated beautifully. One of the vines bore a flower, shaped and colored like a small, ripe pear. By one side of its neck it hung to the vine, and the other opened to receive the dew into the cup of the flower. Another of the vines bore a flower about six inches long and half an inch thick, shaped like the spirea, and covered with bell-shaped cups of ice, which sparkled in the light very vividly.

I returned toward the rear of the house, and on my way saw some of their implements; one was a hoe, its blade triangular shaped, the point of the triangle first striking into the ground. Another implement had a handle of wood, about four feet long, with an iron sickle-shaped blade at one end.

I passed through the basement of the house out in front; there I found a piazza, about sixteen feet wide, leading into a wide hall running through the house. In this hall were two flights of steps, which turned and united in one near the upper landing; I ascended the stairs, and found why that building was so large; its second floor was devoted to the purpose of holding the meetings of the community. I was surprised at the plainness with which it was finished and furnished. Along the sides of the room were raised seats, and extending across the room were wooden settees, or long chairs.

At one end of the room was a platform, raised two steps from the floor, on which, behind a sort of pulpit, the presiding spirit was accustomed to sit. On each side of that was a desk, raised one step above the floor. It was very much indeed like an earthly scene.

Over the center platform, and on the yellow ground of the wall, was a graceful scroll, on which, on a purple ground sparkling and bright, were in letters of gold the words, " God is Love."

Below this scroll I saw something which so much surprised me that I was persuaded it must be my imagination, and I said so.

Through Dr. Dexter it was immediately written: "If this is your mind, all the vision is, and all that you have ever heard. Pshaw!"

What I saw there was my own private seal emblazoned; it was one that I. had very lately adopted (within a week or two). It was a shield, having on its face a naked arm, with a ferule in it, and beneath it a scroll having on it the words, "The Truth against the World."

In answer to a question, I asked whether that had been put there before or since I had used it? It was said, "Before."

I then left that building, and passed down the path more rapidly. As I passed the house where I had seen the stairway in the rocks, the man came out and asked me to stop there the next time, as he had something else to show me.

We arrived at the balustrade from which I had several times descended, and, just as I was leaving, my wife pressed her lips to mine, and so I left.

Section Nine.

Monday, September 12th, 1853.

This evening, in my library, the Doctor and I present, it was written:

Now ask your questions, as I don't intend to write much to-night.　　　　BACON.

I then spoke of my finding my seal* on that wall, and said it was inexplicable to me; because I knew I had not owed the idea to any in-

---

* To understand these allusions, I ought to explain what my seal is, and the origin of it. The seal itself is shown in the vignette on the title-page. The origin of it was this: I had received a note from a gentleman, with a seal, containing emblems on the shield, and beneath it a scroll with the words, "The Truth against the World." This reminded me of a vision I once had, and I immediately formed the idea of making a seal for myself, combining that vision and the scroll.

That vision is recorded in my notes under date of February 10, 1852, in these words:

"I saw a naked female hand and arm holding toward me something dark, like a ferule, but what it was I could not discover. Nor did I perceive what was intended to be taught. The arm and hand were very distinct amid the intense black darkness which enveloped it."

On the 16th of February, 1852, it is recorded in my notes, that in answer to some explanations asked, it had been said:

"That picture represented the arm of Truth thrust through the blackness of error, and seen distinctly amid it; no shade from the error even coloring or obscuring the clear brightness of the truth. It had in its hand a mystery, dark-colored to be sure, but differing in hue from the blackness of error. That mystery was yet to be explained to me, and when it was, I must cherish and preserve it until the world was ready to receive it, and then give it to the world. The arm alone appearing, without the body to which it was attached, was intended to signify, that to us only a small portion of truth—one only of its members had as yet penetrated the blackness of the error which surrounds mankind in their present condition. At both ends of the arm there was yet room for investigation; at one end to solve the mystery contained in the hand, and at the other to develop to view the whole form and body of Truth in its beauty and brightness."

ternal promptings, but had derived it from the seal on a note from a gentleman, which I had lately received, and from that and a vision which I had had long ago, I had made it up, and now I had been told that it had been placed in that room before I had used it. I asked how that was?

It was answered:

Why, as soon as the idea was embodied by you, the seal was made and placed there before yours was received from the engraver. It was because the sentiment and idea were worthy being put in a conspicuous place, and also because of the affinities existing between you and the spirit-world, and also because of the great aid rendered us by Mrs. E.

I asked, It was then through your instrumentality it was placed there?

It was answered:

Dear Judge, you are surrounded by many spirits besides myself, and spirits who estimate you as I do.

I remarked how touching the incident was, and how the hearts of my children and wife must swell every time they entered that hall and saw that reminiscence of me there!

It was written:

It is, indeed, the seal of their mother's virtues and their father's faith and courage.

I then remarked that every time I had entered the spirit-world, I had found persons and things in the precise condition in which I had left them the day before. If it was a picture or an allegory I was seeing, I could understand how this could be, but if it was a reality I did not see.

It was written:

Certainly the commencement of every thing is arranged, and the circumstances coming afterward are entirely natural in their occurrence. You will understand these visions are real teachings, intended to illustrate certain facts in relation to spirit-life, and consequently we arrange the preliminaries, and let the after-facts take place of their own accord.

I asked some questions in reference to something I had seen.

And it was written:

No explanations out of school. Every thing will be explained as you go along.

The Doctor asked why this restriction?
It was answered:

I can tell you, Doctor; it is because we want the Judge's mind to be free entirely in re₀ard to both fact and its translation, and thus that every thing shall explain itself.

I remarked that he had said something just now about courage? It was not worth talking about, for every thing I had endured and dared had been more than paid for in the exquisite happiness I enjoyed.
It was written:

Well, Judge, you and I and the Doctor will talk this over together in places where all feeling can be rightly estimated. We won't say now whether it be true courage to brave the sneers, the contumely, and the sarcasms of a prejudiced world, because it pays, but we will leave that to the time, when, in coin that passes current in eternity, we all shall be paid for what we are, not for what we have been.

I inquired if the last teaching through Mrs. Sweet and others of that kind were allegories or the reality?
It was answered:

Allegorical teaching is one of the most pertinent methods of illustrating principles by spirits. She is impressed by the spirit who acts through her.

I said that I supposed that was the way Bunyan wrote his "Pilgrim's Progress."
He assented, and added:

At least I suppose so. I never saw Bunyan, but I should like to see him. His was a mind which, if it had not been bound to one idea, would have moved the world in another and better cause.

I said I wished I could commune with Voltaire.
He answered:

You can through Mrs. S.   Voltaire was entirely **misun**-derstood by the world in his own time and since.

I said Yes, and that had been done by the priests.
It was written:

It has been their policy to fetter mind in all ages.

Section Ten.

Tuesday, Sept. 13, 1853.

This evening, at my house, the circle met.   Mr. and Mrs. S. were absent, and two gentlemen from Hudson were present.
It was first written:

As some of the spirits from whom the teachings through the Doctor are derived have not yet arrived, we propose, first, to influence you, Judge, if you are willing.

BACON.

I expressed my assent, and after remaining silent for awhile, I re-marked that there was so much to see, I hardly knew where to begin. But, I said—

I had ascended the rising ground on which the terraces were, and there had opened to my view the most magnifi-cent landscape that I could conceive of.   An immense plain was spread out before me; and far in the distance, dim, and partly indistinct, was an immense mountain, from whose summit, which towered high in the heavens, there shone a most brilliant golden light, slightly bronzed.   By that light I saw there were beyond still higher prominences arising one above another, without end, until they faded from view in the immense distance.   What a contrast it was to the scene below!   There the inhabitants occupied solitary eminences, beyond which there was no ascension. Here it was progression onward, upward, as far as the imagination could reach.

Between me and that shining mountain a wide scene was spread out which seemed to be one vast garden. I could give no description of the gorgeousness of its appearance, of its light, of its rivers, its groves, its cultivation. I saw occasionally, off at my left, which was spread out a little below (while at my right the ground gently ascended), single hills, and elevations, lakes, and ponds of water. Among other things I noticed a huge, beetling, and rugged rock standing up high in the scene. What that meant, I could not say.

I was accompanied in my ascent up the path by my former companions, and by an elderly gentleman in the garb of a farmer, who rode a sleek, fat, and very lazy horse, and was followed by a dog equally in good condition and lazy.

When I had surmounted the rise, and came in view of the scene which opened to my view, I knew not where to look first, or what to describe, there was so much before me.

I noticed however, in particular, as I walked along the path, which was here spread out wide, and was very smooth and even, a house on my right hand of two stories high, with piazza in front of both stories. The grounds around it were very beautiful. In them and on the lower piazza a few persons were assembled, but on the upper piazza were twenty or thirty, principally, if not all, females, very gorgeously dressed in many colors. They leaned over toward me, as I approached, and waved their handkerchiefs, as if in welcome. It was a beautiful sight, and was rendered the more so by the evident joy and happiness there was among them.

They wished me to ascend to their elevation, and from that position to take a view of the country. I wanted much to do so; but I saw ahead of me, a short distance, quite a large concourse, who were evidently awaiting me, and I did not venture to stop.

As I approached the group, I noticed the place where they were assembled as peculiar. The path in which I was moving led directly up to a large fountain, which threw its jets high up into the air, and fell back into a basin of some forty or fifty feet diameter. There was a center jet, with several smaller ones surrounding it, and occasionally there shot out from the stream a jet that mounted into the air like a rocket, and then turned into vapor, giving a cool and soft feeling to the atmosphere, and not returning to the earth in drops. A very clear, silver light shone on the fountain, and caused it to sparkle like a mound of diamonds. The basin was filled with many colored fishes, and with aquatic birds of various sizes and plumage, and it was surrounded by a narrow border of close-shaven grass. The path wound around both sides of the fountain, and trended into the country beyond, holding the same width.

In this circular path, and between me and the fountain, that assemblage stood. They were variously and beautifully dressed, and in front of them, toward me, three spirits were standing. The center one was tall and majestic, clothed simply in loose, white garments, extending to his feet, and holding under his left arm a book. His appearance and manner, and the expression of his countenance approached nearer to my ideas of Jesus of Nazareth than any delineation of him I ever had seen, but I ascertained at once that it was not him, but the presiding spirit of that community.

My companions and myself, as we approached him, were filled with emotions of love, of reverence, and of awe that would not let us speak. The spirits which stood, one on each side of him, wore mantles of dark-blue velvet, and on their heads chaplets, which were badges of office. I can not describe the countenance of that presiding spirit; he seemed to be filled to overflowing with happiness; he was of large, capacious mind, and full of love to all around him. There was a solemn stillness brooding over all the scene that seemed to hush even the pulse's beat.

There were conflicting feelings awakened in me: one prompted me to fall down and worship him; and the other repressed that, and told me he was a man as I was, and asked, Why can not you be like him?

When I arrived within a few paces of him he took the book from under his arm, and with outstretched hand pointed me to the heavens off at his left. And there, amid the hush of that scene, amid its glorious beauty, its soft and gentle light, and its balmy air, high up in the heavens, and far distant, I saw the cross of our Redeemer painted. Rough and unhewn itself, it was surrounded by a halo of golden light, and on one of its arms a majestic spirit, clad in dark-colored and rich garments, stood leaning. High over it all flashed, in rays of sparkling silver light, "GOD IS LOVE." Directly over the summit of the cross was a scroll which seemed to spread abroad a feeling of solemn awe. On it was inscribed "HE SAVED MANKIND BY LIVING, NOT BY DYING." Below the transverse piece was a small scroll, on which was written, "DO THOU LIKE-WISE."

And then, amid the awful stillness of that scene, and its solemn impress, the picture faded slowly away, leaving behind it a lesson oh! how full of nature and of truth!

I perceived that none of those present, except that presiding spirit and myself, saw the picture—why, I could not tell, but I supposed the reason was that it was intended mainly for earthly man through me.

After that had passed away, I had an opportunity to look around and examine some portions of the scene. Off to my right I saw a large building built of yellow stone, three or four stories high, and with five gables fronting the path, of different sizes, and of Gothic construction. The whole exterior was severely simple, though justly proportioned and elegant. It was situated on ground that was a little elevated from the path, and some distance back from it. It was approached by a path, on each side of which were flower-beds and fountains, the great body of the lawn in front being covered with a dense shrubbery, growing irregularly, and full of flowers. I found it was their instruction hall, in which they had lectures, and where were deposited their books, their philosophical apparatus, their collections of natural history, etc., etc.

I observed that its entrance was by a flight of steps, leading into a wide and stately hall extending through the building. The gables projected from the main body of the building a short distance, and the door-way in the central gable was chastely yet richly ornamented with carved columns and arches.

I observed, also, that the spirits who formed that assemblage entertained the same feelings apparent in others— love and admiration, namely, at the strength of that affection which had worked the strange phenomenon of bringing among them a mortal yet in the flesh.

I observed that their garments were very alike in form and fashion, being the same I have so often described, but varied in color—some light and some dark—not somber, but rich. They were of different shades of blue and red and yellow, and presented altogether an appearance that would dazzle our vision here by its brightness.

I saw also many women in the crowd, and some few of them held little children by the hand, who nestled close to their sides, seemingly full of wonder at the scene. The females were standing in various positions of affection toward each other, some leaning on each other's shoulder, some with their arms around their waists, etc.

I saw approaching toward us from the right a very old and decrepit woman, bent over and feeble with age. She had on a common calico frock, and the dress of one in limited circumstances on earth. The old man who was attached to my family instantly recognized her as his grandmother, who had died when he was a child, and who now assumed that appearance, in order to make herself known to him. He stepped forward toward her, with a sense of duty that it was to her, rather than to my family, that he owed his services. As he approached her, she changed to a tall and beautiful spirit, clad all in white, and with a very intellectual and lofty expression of countenance, and with her right hand she pointed him to that burning mountain high in the distance, and said to him, "Onward." And she told him his services were already properly dedicated, and to make no alteration. Around her I observed that cloudy gauze-like garment of blue which I had seen around others, and learned that she was severely just to herself.

While noticing these things, a party approached from the west on horseback. It consisted of twenty or thirty persons of both sexes, and they were superbly mounted. I noticed particularly a jet-black pacer ridden by a female. He was a superb animal. They came from a distant community to invite me to visit them.

The presiding spirit called my attention to the shining mountain, and I saw that its summit was approached by a broad, winding stairway, with heavy balustrades and numerous landing-places, and terminated at the summit under an arch, through which streamed that golden light, casting its rays far down the mountain, lighting up the stairway to my vision, and throwing its reflection of golden and crimson light upon houses and land and water, and beautifying the scene wonderfully. And he told me that light was the product of the concentrated love of all the inhabitants, which thus shed abroad, upon all that surrounded it, its warm and grateful influence. I saw birds of song and of gay plumage flying into its rays, as they shot forth in various directions, and the animals confined to the lower plane sought the spot where it struck, that they might bask in it. Elephants and lions and other wild animals I thus saw, but they were savage no longer under its mild influence. I even saw the crocodile crawl from his watery bed, and as he reached the light his dingy somber hue changed to a lively green.

In the distance I saw a body of water, which seemed to be the end of a lake or large inland sea. On it were vessels with sails, most of them small, as if chiefly for pleasure, and one large steamboat, as large as one of our sea steamers. From all this I inferred that this was a bay only of a large inland sea which was hidden from me by the intermediate land.

And I saw, too, rivers meandering through the country, on which vessels were plying and over which bridges spanned, and lakes of various sizes in different parts of the country.

It was indeed a beautiful country to live in, amid its soft and grateful air, and its glowing but mild light.

I was, however, obliged to leave it, for my time was up, and I returned to earth.

Then came the teaching through the Doctor, and it was written:

We have now traced creation in the whole, from the time when all was darkness and chaos to the time when, fashioned according to certain laws, the whole of this vast assemblage of globes and planets and worlds were marshaled in their several positions and confined to certain limits, where they have rolled their ceaseless way ever since.

But let us trace still farther in detail the progressive development of earth and the spheres above, and explain by what process these mighty events took place.

The thousand orbs which traverse the vast space assigned them, and which show forth the might and glory of their Creator, were created from the smallest atomic particles the human mind can imagine. When the whole immense space now occupied by them lay silent, dark, and in almost eternal solitude, these principles which now develop life, and which now generate matter in its infinite variety of form and substance were dormant, for development had not brought their several causes to that point where action could possibly take place. This part of creation was indeed a blank, but when this point was reached then, as before mentioned, the first evidence of progression was motion. Then that subtile agent, that which neither spirits nor man yet understand, first exerted its almost omnipotent forces, and these particles were drawn toward each other, thus forming large bodies, and thus instituting motion. But if we carefully watch this process, we observe that when two of these minute atoms were joined together, the attractive force of the twain was in the ratio of their size, and also that their momentum was increased by the same cause.

Now, when this is understood, we are struck with the harmony which prevails under this law, which is everywhere observable in every department of creation to which man's mind can have access. When, therefore, the power was increased by the union of two particles, it gave additional attraction to draw toward the two in one, another body, and as the motion increased its circulation was over a wide portion of space. As the particles by this union increased in size and motion, some being above and others below, there was of necessity in situation, a separation, as it were, of the limits of their action; thus when the central body, which is the nucleus of the orb or globe, revolved in a certain part of this space, its attractive force could only extend so far as its momentum permitted it to go, and by this means it left to the influence of the same law, the other nuclea in other parts of space. But as the atoms were attracted to the nucleus, and were united with it, they abstracted from the void around certain properties which formed their constituents, and left the space a new media or a new development. It is undoubtedly from this cause that the atmosphere surrounding the planets, stars, and other bodies was formed. Now these bodies, increasing in size and velocity, developed new properties in themselves, and when they had attained that size that their friction was violent and rapid against the atmosphere, generated as I have described, the heavy, thick gases of which they were constituted ignited with this friction, and thus a new process of development took place. The result of the combustion of these gases developed dense matter, and this dense matter now being acted upon by the atmosphere, again developed new properties in that. But it must be understood that the density of the matter increased its ability to extract from the atomic particles, even now as ever floating in space, a greater number, thus surrounding the dense center with a cloudy halo; and when, by the force of its momentum, these additions were ignited, it gave to the whole of the thousand worlds, thus floating in space, the appearance of comets. The revolution and onward motion acting upon the atmosphere caused the gases to trail behind, thus giving to their aspect the tails with which comets are usually connected. Every addition generated new properties, and these new properties others; and when the operations of these generic laws are exhausted in the matter found in the orbits in which they are nursed, a new change takes place, which we will describe at our next meeting.

Section Eleven.

Thursday, Sept. 15th, 1853.

This evening, at Dr. Dexter's, the circle met, and it was written:

I AM not going to detain you long to-night. The absence of some of the members of the circle has interrupted our plans, and we shall more fully carry them out when we are all together. As so much has been written and revealed, would it not be best to converse about it for awhile, before we begin to write about our proper subject?

BACON.

Mr. Warren then remarked about the effect of their teachings the other night, as to the collection of matter from space, that it would destroy the equilibrium.

It was answered:

No; if you examine the remark to which you refer, you will find you are mistaken. I said the gases when ignited, by the velocity with which the body moved, left a trail like a comet by the force with which it came against the atmosphere.

If the matter were equally diffused there could not be any confusion. There was no new matter created, only the various development of what already had existence.

Mr. Warren, you might as well say that there must be a want of equilibrium in the case of a desert, because one part of the same surface is covered with forests, and on the desert there is none. Now, how do you account for the clearing of half a hemisphere of its wood and dense forests if the removal of matter would cause any confusion in the motion of this world? You should make good the deficiency by adding to it the vegetable development in some other part of the world.

No. Matter existed. And if you were able to explore the other systems, revolving around a central point, you would see that their geological formation exhibits ages on ages of maturity, beyond this world, or any of the other bodies created at the same time. The center is maintained by that attractive force which equally balances every part.

One great virtue inculcated by God, his developments in nature, and the spirit too, is patience. Imagine how long the Almighty must have waited to see the fruits of his laws executed in every department of creation, and imagine how much it retards our manifestation in the intensity of its action, in the nature of the communication, and in the thought communicated, when by any cause the circle is in any way either disturbed or deranged.

Then after saying considerable as to the irregularity of the attendance at our circle, which it is not necessary to insert, it was added:

I can not permit the opportunity to pass without saying, that our teachings may not conform to the received notions of earthly science in every particular, but we give you what we have learnt and our opinions thereon, and you must take them for what they are worth.

I, then, giving myself up to the influence, saw as follows:

VISION.

I was passing up the same path to the group of spirits near the fountain, and when I arrived there I was accompanied by that presiding spirit, and some others, to a mansion at a short distance on the right side of the path. It was a brown house, two stories high, with a piazza in front, the precise picture of the house in the country which I occupied when my wife died. On ascending the piazza, I approached a window which opened to the floor, and there I saw the same room, with the same furniture, and placed in the same position, as when she breathed her last. It had thus been arranged by her, as a reminiscence of earthly life, and she stood by my side as I was looking at it, carefully watching its effect on me, not without some apprehension as to what it might be; I carefully suppressed all signs of emotion, and calmly beheld the scene, and there and then was presented to me the picture of her death—not its mortal, but its spiritual aspect.* There was no group of mourners around the bed. The room was vacant of mortals; but floating in the air, over the bed in which the body lay, were two bright spirits, apparently young. They were our two children. Her spiritual body was also floating in the air directly under them. It was evidently unconscious when I first saw it. At length she opened her eyes, and extended her arms toward her two children. At the same time, she felt the strong attraction of the love she bore to those she had left behind. She turned to look at them. They were in another room in the house, yet she saw them. She seemed somewhat bewildered. She was aware she had died, yet the scene around was precisely the same to which she had been accustomed. Death was so different from what she had supposed it to be! It was but a continuance of life. She saw our sorrow. She was reluctant to leave us, and wanted to return to comfort us, yet she felt attracted upward. She arose to an erect posture, and felt so buoyant as if she could not help rising. She saw other spirits in the distance, some of them her old acquaintances on earth. As she arose she saw, opening to her view, a very glorious country, and she was accompanied by a great number of spirits, who were rejoicing at her advent. Among them were spirits from other planets, some from Mars in particular. It was a very joyous welcome they gave her. Still she thought of those she had left behind, and often turned her looks back to them, while borne aloft in the arms of her children, and welcomed by glad shouts all around her.

And as the scene passed from my view, the spirits who

See Appendix B.

surrounded me, said to me, "Such is the death of the pure and the good, who have subdued all selfishness, and culti- vated a love for others."   •

The awakening of the spirit to consciousness must have been some time after the breath had left her, for her body had been laid out in its grave-clothes, and the room was alone.

At the end of the house, next that room, I saw the same garden which she and I had so much enjoyed during the last summer of her life here. Besides, however, its walks, and bowers, and beds of flowers, it was covered with large trees, beneath whose shades the plants grew apparently uninjured by it, and beyond it was a dense grove of trees. I saw also another addition, and that was a statute as large as life of "the Guardian Angel," like that which now orna- ments one of my bookcases, and has so often reminded me of her. It stood in the midst of the circular bed, and around it was my frame for the cypress vine, covered pro- fusely with leaves and flowers, through which the statue was seen.

So, too, the piazza was a little different from ours. The green blinds, which with us excluded the afternoon sun, were removed, and the scene on which I looked was not the Hudson River and the Palisades as it had been here, but was the glorious spirit-country, with its infinite va- riety of beauty; and directly in front of us was a group of spirits very harmonious, beautiful, and happy. In the dis- tance, and prominent to view, was that jagged rock, whose meaning I do not yet understand.

Some of the spirits were examining the flowers in the front garden, some in groups conversing, and all were so joyous. In one corner of the garden was a statue of Peni- tence, with its hands and head bowed in deep humiliation. In the other a statue of Hope, with its hands clasped in front, and its looks elevated upward. The yard in front was small. I was surprised at that, and thought it argued want of taste. Off at the right was a dense wood, standing on the brow and side of a deep declivity, and amid its foliage I saw the same arbor which she and I so well remembered here.

It seemed that she had taken great pains to recall many of the scenes and things of earth which were associated with me and with pleasing remembrances ; even her old rocking-chair, in which she had nursed all our children, and whose screaking they yet remember so well, and her work-table, which was one of the first articles of furniture I ever got her. Seeing me smile while I looked at them, she affectionately took my arm in both her hands, and whispered in my ear, "It's good yet," thus alluding to an anecdote which often amused us almost from our first acquaintance.

So she called my attention to my military sash, gloves, and spurs, which she had hanging by the head of her bed, thus recalling scenes of my young days, in which we both then took great pleasure.

Thus I found myself surrounded with pleasant reminiscences of scenes and events which had occurred at different places, and during a period of thirty years that we were united here.

While I was looking at these things, a carriage and four horses drove up; they immediately attracted my attention, for one of my youthful follies had been a great penchant for driving tandem and four-in-hand ; and she, whose girlhood had been accustomed to the quiet, sober driving of her Quaker father, had soon learned to dash "fast and furiously" through the country with me. It was a beautiful turn-out. The carriage was light and tasty, with a high seat for the driver, and one seat behind for two persons. It was painted yellow, and on its panels was my seal! The harness was light and airy, and the horses were superb animals, of the true Arabian breed, with long, sleek bodies, clean limbs, and a springing motion to every step. They were well groomed, high-spirited, and well broke, and of different colors, being matched rather for quality than looks.

The presiding spirit and my wife entered the carriage, while I ascended the driver's seat and took the reins from the coachman.

We started for a ride. We descended a hill and crossed a bridge, driving westerly toward the shining mountain. It was very exhilarating: the jingle of the harness, the rattling of the wheels, the clear, ringing tread of the horses, as we sped rapidly along, reminded me of many a youthful frolic; but here the pleasure was much enhanced by the beautiful country through which we were passing, and the many and delightful residences that lined both sides of the way, as also by the thoughts which the scene and the associations suggested.

As we passed rapidly along, I ever and anon turned to speak to my companions of the beauties around me; and he who sat beside my wife seemed a little uneasy, as if I was not attending as I should to my driving. My wife reassured him, and told him she was used to it, and he might rely upon it, that I was at home where I was, and knew what I was about.

And now, how can I describe the scene through which we passed? It seemed almost an earthly one, but more sublimated, more refined, more beautiful and joyous, and so free; no trammels of conventionalism to mar the enjoyment. It was a beautiful landscape, interspersed with cottages and gardens, which had in very many instances carried out the idea of recalling earthly scenes. Thus there was the farm-house, the log-hut, the stately palace, the little garden, and the wide-sweeping lawn, the waterfall and the quiet pond, the towering forest and the lowly shrub, the smooth grass and the beds of flowers—all, as each one's propensity dictated, but rendering the *tout ensemble* infinitely various and charming.

Off at our left, I saw, surrounded by ragged rocks, a great spring of water, twenty or thirty feet in diameter, in which the water was not merely welling, but boiling up. Its main outlet was westerly, where it tumbled down the bank amid the rocks, and covered by overhanging bushes, amid whose dark shade it roared and gamboled along, giving great joyousness to the scene.

A small portion of the water escaped on the east side of the spring, and found its way down behind a log-hut, meandering quietly among the fields. It was crossed by a single slab, cut rudely out of a log, and its banks were lined with flowering shrubs and plants.

In the distance I saw some very stately mansions; one was castellated and spacious. It was surrounded by a large park, and was approached by a smooth road, which wound around pleasantly among the trees. It was built on an eminence, at the bottom of which the outlet of the spring passed, and was here dammed up so as to make a large pond and a water-fall. The lawn was clean and close-shaven, and descended to the water's edge; and all around it were cottages, retired and beautiful.

And I observed that though some of the grounds were fenced by rows of trees and bushes, there were always openings left for a free passage in all directions and through all parts.

As I drove along I came to quite a steep hill, which re quired some skill to descend. As we came to the bottom I let the horses out into a rapid gait; one of the leaders broke into a canter, and we sped swiftly and merrily along a level piece of road, on both sides of which a stream of water ran over a clear, gravelly bottom. On one side of the road was a row of trees like the weeping willow, but bearing a great abundance of light-purple flowers, six or eight inches long, interspersed with a pineapple-shaped cluster of crimson flowers. After a while the stream on the right crossed the road and united with the other and turned off, wandering through the fields till it was lost to my view. Here I saw a Virginia rail-fence, on what seemed to be a farm, in whose pastures sheep and cows and horses were feeding. I noticed particularly a mare, with a colt by her side; she was a beautiful animal. As she raised her head to look at us, her thick, long mane and tail blew forward, and her whole form and attitude were very graceful; she was a bright bay, with some white on the nose, with two white feet, and with white spots on her breast and flank. Beyond these pastures was a farm-house, with no trees near it. It was situated upon a little knoll, and was surrounded by fields of grain, farming utensils, and out-houses. I saw men at work, apparently unloading hay into one of the barns.

After passing that place, we ascended a gentle rise in the road, and came to a house by the wayside, which seemed like an inn, but was certainly a common stopping-place. The man who lived there, his wife and two daughters, came to the door; and here again was manifested the same emotions I have so often witnessed.

They who sat in the carriage talked with them a moment, but my attention was occupied with a stately building that stood near. It seemed to be a church, and presented its Gothic gable, in which was a beautiful rose window, to the road.

In front of the inn was a water-trough, into which a stream of clear water ran from a rudely-constructed penstock.

I turned to go back, and as I did so I observed how beautifully the golden light from the mountain lighted up the whole scene. It seemed to be shining through, and softened by a thin cloud, of a mingled purple and violet hue. The golden light seemed to roll down the sides of the mountain like burning lava through this thin cloud.

One luxury they had in abundance, and that was clear, pure water in every possible form.

As I was returning I observed that the houses on both sides of me were enveloped in different colored lights—some red, some blue, some green, some orange, and the like, which, while it added immensely to the beauties of the scene, served to indicate the prevailing characteristics

of the occupants. There was such indescribable loveliness, repose, and happiness in the scene, that I was
filled with emotions of solemn awe too full to speak. I
gave up the reins to the driver who sat by my side, and,
folding my arms, surrendered myself to silent contemplation.

The distant hills were surrounded by a purple haze, and
the general aspect of the intermediate landscape was of
a soft, rose-colored hue. It was their twilight. As I returned to my wife's mansion, I observed it was surrounded
by a pale, soft light of gold and blue, distinct from each
other, yet mingled.

I assisted my wife to dismount from the carriage, and
she stopped at her gate, swinging her hat around her
fingers; and thus I took my leave of her, and, with her
aged servitor, passed rapidly on my return.

As I went along, many told me they had something to
show me; but my time was up, and I could not tarry. So
as I passed the residence of him who had built the stairway, I paused a moment to say that I must defer my visit
to him to another occasion, and then I left the country.

Section Twelve.

The circle met in my library.

After a manifestation through Mrs. S., Dr. D. was influenced, and the following was written:

THIS is a proper opportunity for me to make a few remarks, and as the teaching through Mrs. Sweet* is intended to represent a spirit's entrance to the spheres who has lived entirely for his own pleasures, and who has not improved any opportunities which had been offered him by his connections and wealth, it was well said that his mind was a blank, and in this remark you have as perfect an exemplification of the soul's condition in some persons, as could possibly be given you, for it is the absolute law which obtains in all God's works, that every thing he has created must progress to develop its full and positive characteristics.

Now, when a child is born into your world, his mind is a blank. He neither thinks, nor is capable of communicating thought, and the first manifestation he makes is his desire to obtain food, which is purely a material attribute. But when in process of time that child's body develops, so does his brain become capable of receiving from the outward world those impressions which it can now convey to his spirit. There is a proportional growth of spirit as well as body. Now, the spirit in its growth, as well as the body, displays certain peculiarities, that evidently can not be derived from the impressions made on the material part

---

* See Appendix C.

of his organization; and those peculiarities may distinguish it throughout its whole life.

Suppose for a moment, that a child should die! can it be compatible with what we see of the works of God everywhere, that the spirit of that child should always remain in the same state in which it was placed on earth? that it should never develop the spirit-attributes, and forever be a blank? Or, suppose that, when arrived at manhood, with all the peculiarities developed by material impressions, association, education, and the spirit's own characteristics, it dies! Can the mind contemplate that soul after death remaining in the same condition, mentally and spiritually? God, even in the smallest thing, displays the divine principles by which his own existence is governed, as well as all creation; and from the first of the germ to the full and perfect insect he inducts it into several processes of existence until the perfect thing is formed, lives, and dies.

But even in the characteristics of this insignificant insect there is always a commensurate display of progress in all that concerns its life, as there is in man. And in each living thing, from the most minute to the highest of all, this same law is observed to exist, and may be called indubitably, the law of progression.

But when a man dies, as this man described to-night, with no view of the obligations binding him to his race, and who lived and died for himself alone, can you realize how all that God has taught you by the evidences in yourself and in all nature around you, that he intended his spirit to live forever in a condition created by this selfishness here? Were this so, and the soul maintained its own peculiarities manifested in the form, after death, what is called Heaven would be a perfect Hell, unfit for the residence of intelligent beings, and more especially unfit for the residence of a God. No; each one would carry into that place the same peculiarities of feelings which marked his spirit here, modified of course by the change which might have taken place either morally or otherwise. Still, if the law of progression was not in full effect, the soul would not, could not, increase in goodness, but would positively retrograde, as there is no such thing as a stationary condition either in the spheres or on earth.

The soul confined to this place, with its peculiarities distinct and unqualified, would, if there were no progression, develop the same properties which characterized it here, only that for want of new impressions, good or not, the development would necessarily be in the ratio of the want of the attributes which distinguish intelligence everywhere. I mean, if there could be no impressions after death, for want of new ideas, the soul must, and would, act on the old ones which its residence on earth produced. Many spirits, when entering the spheres, have a mind as much a blank in reference to all that concerns existence, as if they were just ushered into a life on earth, and it becomes as much under the education of other spirits in its own progress in what is good and true, as if, too, it were taught the precepts of righteousness by earthly teachers in your world, only the perception of the true and good is not in every case as instantaneous as was represented to-night.

Every man, no matter how good he may appear on earth, can not enter eternity spotless and pure. There must be many sins concealed from the world, and which he rolled like a sweet morsel under his tongue, that find him out here, and the change in his material condition facilitates this display. Now the spirit, if it were immediately ushered into heaven after death, could not assimilate with its new locality, and the thousands on thousands of spirits found there. They would be perfect, or would be so far in advance of the new spirit, that it would find itself positively out of place, and instead of being happy, it would be miserable. Though it desires to be good, and it has lived a good life on earth, the change from earth to heaven does not divest the mind of all the impurities its earthly residence has ingrafted on the soul. It therefore can not unite with the principle existing there, which is positive, entire, and absolute purity. Now, how can the soul become pure so suddenly? Can it become wicked at once, even when surrounded by all that can make a man wicked on earth? Does not the soul reject evil when first presented to its view? And does not a man who has never mingled with the impure and evil, shudder when he contemplates their doings? But when the mind becomes accustomed to its contemplation, it gradually yields to its influence, and at last unites with the wicked, and is itself impure. Can this effect be changed when the soul retains all its spiritual properties after death? No; when we contemplate the soul of man ushered into a new existence, under the full influence of the law of progression, we feel assured, then, that there is laid up for us a treasure in heaven, but that we must earn it ourselves. We then can understand the teachings of Christ, where he says, " Work out your own salvation with fear and trembling." Yes, the soul, recognizing its independence, trusts to the law under which its existence was vouchsafed to it. It feels, then, that evil is the certain result of an adherence to evils in design or act, and it acknowledges that the law will find him out, whether on earth or in the spheres.

It is to be remembered that any violation of a natural law brings its own punishment. And the same effect will be observed in the violation of a moral law. Then the similarity of the effect shows us that the spirit of God acts both materially and spiritually, and that his manifestation through the material adds to the force of the spiritual ; and when we also consider that any disregard of the material brings also a moral acknowledgment of wrong, we at once see that they are individually united in the spheres forever.

Entering into the spheres as a child, it is taught all that it will receive, and if it rejects, it remains the same in the exhibitions of the same passions and feelings, the same incentives and motives which on earth characterized the body and the spirit.

But if it does receive and seek for it, it puts on a new garment of righteousness, and takes its place in that house where there are many mansions, where the full opportunity is offered of receiving from the Father, through his instituted laws, all that belongs to it, as the son and heir of a glorious eternity. SWEEDENBORG.

Section Thirteen.

Monday, Sept. 18, 1853.

This evening the whole circle were present at Dr. Dexter's, and after some personal matters were written, I was impressed, and saw as follows:

I WAS again in that country near the fountain, but there were only two or three spirits there.

My attention was called to the steps leading up the shining mountain. In the full blaze of the light I saw an old man going up, with a staff in one hand and a book in the other. He moved slowly, but the ascent did not seem toilsome. Nor was that his first visit. He belonged there, and had been absent on some mission. Though he was at a great distance from me, I saw him very distinctly, and he saw me. As he approached the arch which terminated the ascent, he nodded to me in a friendly manner, and pointed up, as if saying to me, " Enter here, too." He then passed through the arch beyond my sight.

As I stood looking upon the ground and reflecting upon the incident, the presiding spirit, who stood near me, told me that that was Luke. He wore a sort of palmer's dress. His outer garment was a dark purple, bound around his waist by a cord. His inner garment was white.

I then saw, as if suddenly lighted up, one of the prominences beyond, and above that shining mountain. The
light was generated by this eminence itself, and seemed to
issue from the surface in numberless streaks of crimson
and blue light mingled, yet distinct from each other. It
showed me the path which led from the shining mountain
to it. It was a suspension-bridge, elevated at one end
much higher than the other.

On the summit of this eminence was a vast building.
surmounted by minarets, domes, castellated towers, and
pointed arches—a singular mixture, but very beautiful.
It was built of stones veined with blue, brown, white,
purple, and red colors. In the center of the building was
a large flat dome, from which arose a flag-staff in the shape
of the cross. From the staff hung in easy folds, gently
stirred by the breeze, a white banner with a border of
blue and black fringe. On the banner was this inscription:

In hoc signo vinces
Sed non *per* illud."*

There were four small flags flying from other parts of
the building, of different colors; but I was too distant to
distinguish what they were precisely, or the devices on
them.

Beyond this eminence I saw a passage leading from it to
one still higher. It was the span of an immense arch, the
farther end of which was lost to my view in the distance.

From the crown of the arch a pathway lay up, which
was supported by several tiers of arches, one above another.
The end of that path also was lost to view in the distance.
It seemed to terminate in a still greater eminence, which
was entirely enveloped and hidden from my sight by an
immense column of blue flame, tipped in a thousand places
with a slight tinge of gold. In the mountain with the

* " *In* this sign you conquer, but not *by* it."

shining golden light Love predominated, but here it was
Wisdom. I saw spirits, though not in great numbers, coming from the distance, and plunging out of my sight into
the blue column. Some seemed very small to me, as if
they were at a great distance, and I observed that all had
their heads encircled by a halo of light, not entirely circular as is often painted, but in a pyramidal shape, highest
in the center. This column of blue and gold, I observed,
terminated high above, in a bright silver light which
threw its bright rays far into the distance, illuminating
space far beyond where my eye could reach. The light
of Love and Wisdom thus terminated in Truth, and illumined creation around.

When I had observed these things, the presiding spirit
took me by the arm and led me into their Hall of Instruction and on to its roof. We ascended from the main hall
by a very singular flight of steps. They were shaped like
several X's placed one on another. As they came to the
different floors, platforms extended out. It was some time
before I could understand how they could be ascended;
but I saw that it was very plain and simple, as well as
ingenious. It was, in fact, a double stairway. They were
self-sustaining, and very easy of ascent.

The roof was built very substantially, of heavy massive
stone, strong enough to hold a battery of cannon. But it
was armed, not with instruments of destruction, but of
knowledge, and that was a number of telescopes of various
sizes. One of them was very enormous, far beyond any
thing ever attained on earth, and the machinery by which
it was moved and guided was very simple. I wanted at
once to go to that one and look, but its end was immediately depressed so low that I could not, and on looking
around, I observed they were all so, save the smallest, and
that was at the proper elevation. I accordingly approached it, and began my observations. I saw a single star that
had been invisible to my naked eye. It appeared now to
me about two inches in diameter, and was merely a flame

of fire revolving with amazing velocity. It was the nucleus of another world rolling out of the immensity of space, and forming itself in obedience to the great laws of creation which are ever at work. Its center seemed like a red-hot ball, somewhat more solid than its exterior, and thinning off into what may be called a fiery vapor. It consisted of particles of matter set on fire by the velocity of its motion, not yet amalgamated but attracted, and tending gradually toward a solid mass. It had been ages in progressing thus far, and ages yet must pass before it can be so far developed as to give birth to animal life. Thus said the spirit by my side.

I passed then to the next telescope, which was larger; and when it had been properly adjusted I saw another star, which appeared somewhat larger than the other. It looked like a red-hot cannon-ball, and was surrounded by a luminous vapor of about one eighth of the diameter of the solid part. This body did not move as rapidly as the other. Off from it, at various distances in the space, were smaller irregular pieces of burning matter, revolving in the same direction with the main body, and keeping up with it in velocity. These, I was told, were parts of the main body, which had been cast off in the process of its formation. They were now too far distant for its attractive power ever to be able to draw them to itself, yet so near as to keep them revolving nigh it, and preventing them from flying off into illimitable space. They, too, in time, when ages shall have passed, will be formed into regular bodies fitted for animal life, and revolve around the main globe as its satellites, at once giving and imparting light, and adding to the beauty and variety of the scene.

While I was looking, I saw that the red-hot nucleus of the main globe had diminished in size, and by becoming more solid had decreased in its dimensions, but the surrounding fiery vapor had not, and I plainly saw an opening between it and the globe. And it seemed to me that this vacancy must, for awhile at least, be augmented as the distance weakened the attractive power of the globe over this attendant vapor, until it also should become solid in the form of a ring, and be retained by the power of attraction in its position around the globe, the power being too weak, by means of the distance, ever to draw it back to the globe, while it would be strong enough to keep it from shooting off into space.

I then passed to the next telescope, which was still larger, and there I saw a globe, apparently six inches in diameter. It was white, and while the others were red, and shone by their own light, this one shone by a borrowed light. It had passed the state of ignition in which they were, and had formed a solid body; yet it must have been rough and misshapen on its surface, for I saw that the light which was reflected from it was uneven—in some places bright and in some darker, like the appearance of the moon to us, and for the same reason that its surface had not yet been smoothed down by the hand of time, but was filled with deep caverns and rugged prominences.

It was yet too rude and wild for the habitation of animal life, and ages must pass before it could become so. It must be an awful desert waste, with no life and no vegetation. I saw no satellites around it—no luminous belts; but I observed a narrow streak of atmosphere, as I conceived it to be; for I saw a star near it, and noticed when it passed behind this planet; and, by the change in its light, I discovered that there was an atmosphere, though very faintly developed as yet. The motion of this body was slower still than either of the others, and was singular in this respect, that its axis was at right-angles with the plane of its orbit, so that instead of rolling like a wheel it was turning like a top. Its motion caused it to be oval-shaped.

Through the next glass which I approached, I saw a globe, larger than either of the others, shining with a borrowed silver light, and surrounded by several smaller ones revolving around it. It had what seemed to be streaks of light around it. I at first supposed them to be of solid matter, like the body of the globe, though perhaps less dense; but I discovered that this was not so, but it was owing to the condition of the atmosphere belonging to that globe, which was of different degrees of density at different places, and so refracted the light differently, both in passing to and being reflected from it; and thus those streaks or belts were formed. The atmosphere which produced that effect was being refined and sublimated for the support of a higher order of sentient beings, and during its progress had this varying density.

The next telescope was still larger, and through it I saw the whole of a planetary system, with its glowing center, its planets receiving light from it, and attended by their satellites. They revolved nearly on the same plane. At the point from which I viewed it, the divergence was scarcely perceptible. I saw comets also passing across their orbits, going toward and returning from the center, some with tails, some with a nucleus, and some without. They are collections of matter undergoing the process of forming into a world; and as they pass immense distances through space, they collect more matter in those far-distant regions, and return with it, absorbing it within themselves by the power of their attraction. In some parts through which they move they find no matter in a proper condition to be absorbed; and as they become more dense, their orbits become less elliptical. They proceed to a less distance, and move only through the space where there is no matter fit for them to absorb; and the matter thus taken up, first in the tail, is finally absorbed into the nucleus, and contributes, in the process of time, to the formation of a new world.

A question was here asked by one of the circle, whether our sun was a mere luminous body, or an opaque body surrounded by a luminous atmosphere, and inhabited?

It was answered: "The latter."

I then passed to the last and largest telescope, and lan-

guage fails me to give an adequate idea of the scene which
opened to my view, even in the limited field of vision of
that glass, not one thousandth part of the arch above me.
Yet in that small field of vision were millions and millions
of shining worlds, of all variety of color, and rolling in
orbits more various than the imagination can conceive.
These numberless and unnumbered worlds are filled with
sentient beings, with souls destined, like ours, to people
eternity. The drops in the ocean; the grains of sand on
the sea-shore, multiplied by millions upon millions, would
give but a faint idea of the numbers.

Seeing the vastness of this creation—the infinite power
and wisdom it displays, I asked myself what must be the
Creator? Can the mortal mind grasp the thought or conceive the might and majesty of his existence? And what
is this Earth, in this vast and boundless universe, that for
it his eternal and immutable laws should be suspended?
And is it for man that it should be done? for man, destined, from his undeveloped state, to wander for ages in
the process of progression before he can be pure enough to
reach the Godhead? before he can throw off the impurity
which binds him down to this material existence, and begin to rise to those realms where the glory of God becomes
manifest? Is he of consequence enough in the universe to
impel the great Creator to surrender his omnipotence and
omniscience to his wayward fancy, to his overweening
vanity? Such were the thoughts which pressed upon my
mind as I surveyed that scene, and that presiding spirit
said to me, in his soft and solemn tones, "Stand here, now,
with your foot on this high sphere, your hand upon this
instrument of penetrating far into the hidden glories of
creation—your eye embracing only a portion of its vastness, and your mind, with all its expansion, scarce able to
comprehend its verge only; and think, if you can, of that
great Creator as one who can be angry at, or take vengeance upon, the inhabitants of one of the merest worlds
of his creation? Think of him rather as one who in his

love, as well as his might, has created this countless universe; who by his love as well as his wisdom controls and governs it, and who by his love pervading all created things, diffused abroad through all matter and all spirit, attracts and binds it together in unbroken harmony. Think of him as one whose power and wisdom are never exerted unaccompanied by his love.

"He is love; and to be like him, to be able to approach toward him, we must be love. Think of these things; and when you bow in humble adoration before him, let his love fill your hearts, and remember that you have no evil to fear of his creation, but only that which yourselves produce.

"And oh! when your minds dwell on the Great I Am, think of him, not as one clothed with the perversions of your animal nature, but as one whose love is too powerful to be overcome—too vast to be exhausted.

"Bow then the heart, and not the knee, before him; enjoy his love; profit by his wisdom, and fear not his vengeance."

Here he closed his remarks, and, after leaving me silent for a few moments, he conducted me out of the building, where I took leave of him on my return.

As I was passing down I saw around the entrance that lake-colored light, which denoted the approach of other and new inhabitants of this happy land. I paused long enough to discover that they were the van of the multitude whom I had addressed from the path up the mountain; but I could not tarry longer, and so returned to Earth again.

Section Fourteen.

Thursday, Sept. 22d, 1853.

This evening, at my library, the circle met. Present also Mrs. F., a medium from Maumee, Ohio.

It was written:

WE feel gratified to-night at having present at our circle meeting one of whom we have heard by our brother-spirit Bacon, and we propose that an attempt be made to impress her by some of the spirits present who desire to do so. If this suits all present, you can wait silent for a few moments and watch the result.

Cordially and in love, with our feelings all attuned to the love of God, everywhere manifest in his created works, we greet you, and we impress you to love another in the spirit, to feel that in every human heart are the seeds of eternal and divine love. Be constant in your efforts to act as well as feel, for while our God and our Creator feels the unity of himself with all parts of his creation, he still unceasingly acts to manifest that incomprehensible love which prompted him out of chaos to form an infinity of worlds for the abiding-place of man and his progressive development. SWEEDENBORG.

Mrs. F. remarked that she suspected the spirits would not be able to influence her, and it was written:

It is only necessary that she should hold her mind as it were in abeyance, to forget herself and the presence of others, and she can be carried to the inner condition and see us all. BACON.

She was then influenced, and saw the spirits that surrounded us. The only thing requiring particular notice was, that she saw a dark spirit also in attendance, who was striving to obtain possession of her, but who was prevented by the brighter ones.

Then it was written:

For fifteen minutes we will influence the Judge, but he is quite unwell, and only for this time will the impress be continued, and then go home. This picture will not be the continuation of the usual visions, but a new picture entirely.

I then saw as follows:

I was in a dark and gloomy country, all a dead level, whose soil was a fine black sand, parched and very dry. There was no water, no trees or shrubbery, but all was bleak and barren. In a distant part of the scene I saw a conical-shaped mountain, towering darkly among the clouds, and intervening were roads and dwellings.

It looked as if the air was full of that black sand, and a smoke, as if from bituminous coal, was over it all.

In front of one of the houses I saw two men fighting. Out of its window a man was looking and laughing at the affray. It was a dirty-looking hovel, and all around it was foul, neglected, and in confusion. How cruel that fight was! They were a large and a small man who were engaged. The larger held the smaller one fast and beat him in the face with his fist, long after he ceased to resist. Some of the passers-by regarded the scene with indifference, while some enjoyed it, and applauded and encouraged the large one to keep on.

Among those who passed, I was particularly struck with two who were engaged in deep and private conversation. One of them was a man whose forte was cunning, and whose penchant was to circumvent. He was never true, sincere, or straightforward. He was disclosing some plan he had devised to cheat some one, and, on raising his fist at his companion, he said: "Damn you, if you betray me." His companion seemed to be entirely under his control. He was weak, and admired the cunning of the other. He seemed to love to aid others in committing crimes, but not to have mind enough to devise any himself.

On the opposite side of the way, I observed what seemed to be a full-grown boy, had caught a dog, had split open his tail and put a stick in it, merely to enjoy the sport of seeing his suffering. He then turned the dog loose, and stood enjoying the scene. The attention of the owner of the dog was drawn to his cries, and, discovering the cause, he beat the boy, who, being as cowardly as he was cruel, fled, but was pursued, and beaten and kicked far up the road.

As my eye followed them thus into their country, I observed how dark and gloomy and forbidding every thing seemed! The people were of different shades of a dirt color. The light seemed to be an eternal twilight, or that of a dark, murky, cloudy day. The air they breathed was full of the impalpable dust from the dry, black sand, and all around showed privation and neglect.

At the door of one of the hovels, that stood a little back from the road, I saw a female who seemed to be about twenty-six years old. She was round and full in appearance—was a dark brunette with painted cheeks. Her whole appearance, garb, and manner were meretricious, and she had taken up her position there to entice some one to enter her dwelling. At length a man in passing turned aside, under the influence of passions which had marked his earthly career, and with her entered her house. I saw they were both influenced by the same passions, but were incapable of gratifying them. The woman became furious. She raved wildly, and in her insensate rage she dashed the things around her to pieces. The man enjoyed her anger, and she raged at him for laughing at her. She seized a chair and aimed a blow at him. He evaded it, and with his fist knocked her down. He struck her in the neck just below the chin, and when she fell, he gnashed his teeth in his rage, and stamped with his foot on her breast. He kicked her in the side several times, and rushed from the house.

. Here, as I was describing the scene, it was written through the Doctor:

"Does she not suffer pain? Watch and see, now. Examine her organization, and see its grossness. The vision is given you by a spirit who has been to that sphere. It is the only place in eternity where there is an approximation to physical pain."

I resumed my account as follows:

She did seem to suffer pain, but she can not die. She partly recovered her consciousness, for she had been rendered insensible by the violence, and she moaned as if in pain. She put her hand upon her breast, as if in great distress. She breathed with difficulty, and seemed to suffer in the throat where the blow hit. But the injury on her breast caused her the most suffering.

She was very coarse and gross in her organism. Her legs were large, her ankles coarse and ugly. She was very full behind the ears, bull-necked as it were. Her lower jaw was large and gross, and her lips and mouth like a negro's. She was rotten with the disease she had carried with her to the grave. There were large holes eaten by it in her groins and in her thigh. Ah! what a disgusting sight this was!

After awhile she arose from the floor and seated herself on the side of a bed. While she did so, I noticed the furniture and appearance of the room. It was in all respects an earthly scene, and amid its poverty and wretchedness she had bedizened her bed with curtains! As she sat moaning, she deeply felt her misery. She seemed to be aware that there was no end, no alleviation to it—nothing to change the intensity of her suffering—no pleasure that she could enjoy. She sought in her mind for some means of enjoyment, and found it only in the deep spirit of revenge which was awakened, and which she had a burning desire to vent upon him who had thus maltreated her. What awful torment she suffered while thus alone she brooded o'er her wrongs! worse by far she felt than the hell she had heard of while on earth, and she was persuaded there was no end to it. Ask her, and she would say that hell was eternal.

While she thus sat and suffered, a little girl entered the
hut; her manner and garb were those of the most hardened
of the street-beggars of our large cities. Her black eyes
glowed like coals of fire, and she seemed precocious in all
that was evil. She taunted the woman with her condition,
and laughed at her. The woman hurled something at her
head, which she dodged, and repeated her taunts, and then
fled from the house laughing.

What a horrible scene of human degradation, seen amid
that dark and gloomy atmosphere! I could scarcely
breathe myself; it distressed me, and I, too, left the house.
Its outside appearance was in keeping with all else. In
front of the door lay a couple of rough slabs as steps, and
the yard between the house and the road looked so dreary;
nothing but that barren black sand, with here and there a
sickly plant of stramonium and a few stunted plants of
chick-weed; and laying here and there, thrown carelessly
aside, various household implements, in various stages of
decay. All was poverty and filth, and amid it all, to contemplate her dress, bedizened off so as to render her person attractive! It was indeed a painted sepulcher—a festering carcass in a ball dress—revolting corruption be-
decked in flaunting colors. Then through it all, her
low forehead, her sinister eyes, her vacant look, her high
cheek bones! Pagh! I turned and hurried from the
scene.

As I got out into the street I saw a crowd tearing madly
along toward me.

They seemed to be dragging something by a rope, which
evidently gave them great pleasure.

Their shouts and yells made me think I had met a fire-
company running at the sound of the alarm-bell; but as
they passed me, I saw it was a living man whom they were
dragging by the ankle along the ground. He was suffering much, and screaming in his agony; but they only rejoiced the more, and I noticed, among those who run along
by his side, a struggle to see which could get nearest to

him, so as most completely to enjoy the scene, and lose not a bit of it.

They passed me, and I moved on. · Soon I came to a small collection of people who were acting the scene of hanging a man on the gallows. There was the scaffold, which had fallen, and a man was hanging by the neck in the death-struggle. His eyes protruded; his tongue was thrust out of his mouth; his face was flushed; he struggled and writhed, but he could not die. No welcome death could come to put an end to his misery. No voice of pity nor murmur of compassion arose to greet his ear, but only shouts and laughter, rendered louder and more furious the more severely he struggled and suffered, and accompanied by the beating of a drum—for they had made quite a military parade of it—and the gallows was surrounded by many in grotesque military uniforms, and armed with sticks and broom-handles.

Passing this scene, I came to one where a man was hanging in chains; he was closed in an iron net fastened to a cross-piece on two upright posts, some twenty feet from the ground. There was no one around this gallows; no attention seemed to be paid to it, except as the poor sufferer would hail the passers-by and beg for a drop of water. Thus I noticed a sailor pass, to whom he cried for help, and from whom he got the answer, " Help yourself, and be damned to you!"

Next I saw a party who were burning a man at the stake. He was fastened to the stake by cords so tight that he could not move a limb; and thus they roasted him by a slow fire.

Then I saw enacted a scene with which the history of the Inquisition has rendered us familiar. A man was undergoing the torture. There were only two or three persons around him, as if there was some exclusiveness in this enjoyment. His leg was in an iron case, and wedges were driven in to crush the bone and flesh together. How well they did it! how expert they were! and how they gloated over his yells of agony! It was to them a repetition of an earthly pleasure.

I next saw a tall, vicious-looking woman, of about fifty years of age. She was dressed in a spotted calico frock, very common and very dirty. Her hair was gray; her teeth were gone; her eyebrows were heavy, and under them glowed a snaky pair of eyes. She held by one hand a child four or five years old, who was squalid and ragged, but who seemed to be of a simple, pleasant, and affectionate disposition. The old woman was dragging the child along roughly, and beating it with a stick. Its legs, and arms, and breast were scarified.

How it made me weep to see that little sufferer! and how hard must be the heart, how dark the mind, that could thus delight in inflicting suffering on a child! Yet that too was, alas! but an earthly scene, enacted but too often in our very midst.

I next observed a well-dressed female sitting by the way-side, apparently in great distress. She had been driven out of his dwelling by the man for whom she had sinned on earth—for whose sake she had broken the ties of wife and mother—for whom she had retained, even in death, an insane attachment, and whose company she had sought as her only solace in the spheres. She had been brutally treated by him on earth, and as brutally driven from his side here. She sat alone by the wayside in that desolate scene, and amid that gloomy light, her face buried in her hands, and her whole frame quivering with the anguish she was enduring. No one pitied her. The passers-by sneered and went on, and she shrank within herself at the recollection of her past life. Her earthly career had dragged the gray hairs of her loving parents to the grave; she had deserted an affectionate husband, and brought infamy on her own children. All, all the past now arose vividly before her, and she saw no end to her misery. Oh! with what anguish did she pray for annihilation! how earnestly wish that she might cease to be! for oh! she withered at the idea of such a forever! The memory of the past was so vivid ever to her, and so horrible. It was her love of pleasure that had caused her fall. She had seen an actor on the stage in all the glare of his calling, and was dazzled; he was a coarse fellow; his success had been owing to his phisique; he was gross, sensual, and selfish, and he soon cast her off; he now hated her presence, and drove her instantly from his sight; and as she bent to the earth, she cried, "For this I sinned! for this I sinned!"

I approached near to her, yet she did not seem conscious of my presence. Indeed, I observed throughout this marked difference between this and the brighter spheres where I had been: here, no one seemed to be conscious of my presence, unless I made myself known; there, in the brighter spheres, all saw me.

I asked her if there was no end to her misery? She shook her head impatiently. I told her there was an end, if she would but only seek it. She looked up at me as I stood by her side, and became conscious of my presence, and that I was not of that place. I noticed a faint streak of light around her head—a fine, silver-like thread scarcely perceptible.

She asked me how she could find it? I replied, by penitence. She said she was so now. I asked if her sorrow was for her sin or for its consequences? If for sin, I could show her the way.

The expression of her countenance changed. A ray of hope seemed to enlighten it, and she looked as if she could have fallen down and worshiped me. She said she sought this place and that companion drawn by her love for him, and because she had nowhere else to go, but she had through it all felt shame and sorrow that her propensities had so attracted her there.

I then pointed her to that conical mountain, assured her that by ascending that she would have a view of a brighter and better country, and told her of the means of attaining it.

She said she was so feeble, so hungry, so sick, that she could not climb it.

I urged her to try, and assured her that every step would be easier; that she must work out her own salvation— she must toil for it. It was a long distance only to the base of the mountain, and a toilsome, painful ascent, and even when she had attained it she would but see in the distance a better country, to which still the journey was long and painful. Choose, then, I said, now your future— that long and toilsome travel to a happy land, or this for-ever, which now surrounds you.

I saw by her countenance that by nature she had been a kindly woman, and I told her that on her passage she would find the means of doing good to others, and she must help all she could; that every good deed, thus done, would aid her on her journey.

She arose from the ground, and, leaning upon the fence, she gazed intently at that distant mountain; and as she gazed, I saw the light around her head increased.

Amid all of her own sufferings she had observed those of that little child, and the thought occurred to her to take it with her. She immediately went to the old woman's hovel, where she saw the little one sitting huddled up in a corner, suppressing, from very fear, its moaning, while the old woman was scolding and abusing it. She begged the child of the old woman, and was instantly refused. She renewed her importunities, and finally the old woman told her if she would change garments with her she might have the child. She assented to it, and the change was made. The old woman was the taller of the two. The fine black silk dress she now put on left her coarse ankles and feet exposed to view; but that she heeded not, but, proud of her new and fashionable garments, she repaired to a piece of broken mirror that she had, and admired herself. In the mean time, the other female, clad in the long, coarse, and unbecoming garment she had now put on, took the child in her arms and left that hut. As she passed along, that little child put its arms around her neck, and, burying its little face in her bosom, gave free vent to the sobs which before it had been obliged to suppress. It was a touching sight. The child was dirty and ragged, yet its flaxen hair, its clear complexion, and its look of innocence awakened my compassion; and as it cried in its joy that it had some one to love, my tears also flowed in spite of me.

As the female proceeded on her way to the mountain, she became stronger and walked more erect. She finally ran, so as to get as soon as possible beyond the reach of her former companion, lest in his vileness he might attempt to interrupt her. The child, pleased with the motion, raised its head, and with one of its little hands patted her on the neck.

The female every moment felt stronger, and I noticed that a bright spirit now approached her from above. He was still at quite a distance from her, but he threw upon her a strong stream of light, whose influence cheered her on. He had discovered her efforts at redemption, and henceforth she would not be alone in her journey.

As she traveled along, she passed a bridge under which floated a sluggish stream of dirty water; some half-grown boys were bathing in it. One of them, a stupid, vicious boy, was the butt of the others, who were amusing themselves by holding his head under the water and trying to smother him. He struggled violently, but they were too strong for him. She paused a moment, and remonstrated with them. They quitted their play and pelted her with mud, and foremost among those who thus pelted her was him for whom she interfered. Some of the mud hit her on the side where the child was; she removed it to the other side, so as to interpose her own person between it and harm from their rudeness.*

---

* Now, in August, 1854, the spirits of the female and of that child have approached and spoken to me through a medium. She gave her name, and said she was a French woman, and lived in Paris during the reign of Louis

What a repulsive nature that boy is! A brutal countenance, with short hair, bull neck, and low forehead, he
hardly seemed fit to live. How many ages must pass before he can progress!

As she resumed her journey, I saw crossing the path directly before her a man that could not walk upright. He
had been ages there, and had lived on earth when man was so
little developed that he could not stand erect. He was one
of the lowest individualizations of man. He still moved
bent over, and used his arms frequently to help his locomotion. He was very strong in them, and by their aid
could jump a great ways.

As I turned to leave, I observed what an air of desolation and dilapidation rested upon the scene. Not a building anywhere in order, but every thing showing neglect
and confusion.

Thus ended this vision. After it closed, we all remarked on the sin-
gularity of that child's being there.

And it was written:

The child was there because it had been educated in
grossness, and died material in thought and sentiment, but
possessed the germs of goodness, which were developed
even there to add to the deep misery of the woman's suffering; and when the other woman expressed the desire to
progress, the opportunity was afforded to develop that
germ. She had been there but a short time. Good-night.

Philippe. She spoke of her parents, of her husband, and of her brothers and
sisters. She gave me some little account of the progress she had made, and
said she had not yet attained the base of the mountain toward which she was
traveling.

Section Fifteen.

Saturday, Sept. 24th, 1853.

Mrs. F., the medium from Ohio, has been spending a few days with me. On Thursday last she attended our circle, and while under the influence saw attending us, but standing a little distance off, a dark spirit, whose influence the brighter spirits who were with us were striving to drive off.

This evening she and I called on a friend. While there Mrs. F. was influenced by a dark spirit, who said he had a spite against me. I asked him what for? He answered: Because I frustrated his plans. I replied to him in a spirit of defiance, and told him we'd have a fair fight for it. Nothing else of interest occurred, and we left. On our return, we stopped a moment at a rapping medium's, and Mrs. F. got a communication through the rappings from her attendant spirit. I inquired if the dark spirit who had come was one in attendance on me? It was answered:

No; on some one else of the circle.

Late in the evening we returned home and sat alone in my parlor for some little time. I prepared to retire by fastening my house, and on returning to the room I found Mrs. F. very rigid, and evidently under the influence. I sat down to await the manifestation, and in the mean time took up a newspaper. She soon asked for a pencil. I got pencil and paper for her, and resumed my reading. After a while I looked up and saw she was very rigid, and that she had written something which she held down very tight on the table, and was pushing toward me. I read it. It was this:

You are afraid to trust your old friends, and think that we will not protect you. We will. If the Judge will sit on the other side, and touch your left hand, we will throw off opposing influence. Be quick.

I immediately did as directed, but as some delay had occurred from my attention being taken up with my reading, I was too late—the spirit had complete possession of the medium, and retained it for more than an hour.

At first we sat by the table very silent, and every muscle of her body was drawn to its tightest tension. I held her left hand in mine, and placed my right hand on her head, and continued to do so during the greater part of the interview. She frequently told me not to let go of her.

It was evident that the influence was an unhappy one, and that self-control and self-consciousness had left her. It was some time before the spirit said much, but the gesticulation was violent. He frequently looked in my face with a concentrated expression of spite, but I observed that his gaze was soon withdrawn under my steady look. His face was very much flushed. The eyes were open and protruded, and the cheeks swollen. Around the whole of the upper part of the neck, just below the chin and ears, was a white streak, as if there was no blood there, while below that the neck was so flushed that it was fairly purple.

The right hand was doubled into a fist, and he over and over again raised it to strike me. It seemed to tremble with passion and was very rigid and hard. I said to him several times, " Strike, if you want to." His eyes were generally fixed rigidly at some object on the table, and when I would say this he would turn and look at me, as if to see with what emotions I said it. Several times he raised his fist, and, shaking it at me, said, "Do you see that?" I said, "Yes," but I was not uneasy at any thing he could do, for God was over all, and in him I trusted.

This continued for ten or fifteen minutes, during which he got more complete control of the medium and talked easier. As soon as I saw he could understand me, I began to talk to him. I said I was sorry I had spoken to him as harshly as I had earlier in the evening. I was then a little combative, but now I told him I had no feelings toward him but compassion and a desire to do him good if I could. He gave me in return a sneer.

I can not give the details of the interview consecutively, for I took no notes. I must give it as I remember it, and in the order in which the events arise in my memory

Thus about this time he said to me, "I can tell you some things you don't know." I told him I was well aware of that, and hoped he would do so, for it would help me do good to the world. He replied to me, "Curse the world! I hate it." I asked him if his hatred and curses gave him happiness? For my part, I found that loving mankind, and desiring their good, made me most happy. He said,

"Did you ever have your damned neck broke on a gallows?" I said, No; that was a great misfortune, but could, if he pleased, be converted into the means of doing him great good. If he was one whom I had condemned, he might be assured that I had not done it without an aching heart. "No," was his reply, "it was not you, but he was an old fool." It was the world, he said, that had made him bad, and then hung him for it.

I did not wonder, I said, that he felt the degradation, but it need not be perpetual. I had in myself experienced the redeeming power that was available to him as it was to me.

"Ay! But did you ever murder?"

"No."

"Well, I have, and curse him! I'd do it again."

"You must be wretchedly unhappy in the place to which such feelings condemn you. Have you no aspirations for a better condition?"

I then asked if he hadn't a mother, or sister, or wife, or children in the spirit-world, with whom he would like to be reunited.

After a long pause he asked me if I knew Mary? Upon this hint I spoke, and dwelt often during our interview upon his reunion with her. I asked him if he had not loved her?

"Loved her!" was his answer; and then with a frantic gesture, as if inflicting a stab, he added, "and deeply was I revenged. I hate the world. Curse them! You don't know what wrongs I suffered!"

I told him it was not difficult for me to imagine, for I knew how much wrong man was every day inflicting upon his fellow. But still these feelings of hatred and revenge only kept his spirit-friends of a brighter state far from him. Much more like this I said to him until he was melted into tears. He nestled close up to me, and said he was happier than he had been for a long time. He asked me if I could help him, and if I would? But he would not credit my assurance that I could and would, and said, "I havn't confidence in any one."

I asked him what I could do to convince him of my sincerity? What object could I have in deceiving him? And if he didn't know what I had already dared and sacrificed for the cause of truth?

He said, Yes, he knew it, but he wanted a pledge, a sign from me.

I described to him my seal, and told him that in its words, "The Truth against the World," he would find my pledge.

He then said, " I shall suffer for this. Won't they torment me? Why, they taunt me and call me criminal, and tell me I was hung on the gallows;" and he asked me, " Do you know how many are here now?"

I told him I did not.

He said, " There are a good many. Your room is full of them. But they can't come near you. Twelve of them have formed a combination and chosen their leader, and are full of contrivances for mischief;" and then sinking his voice to a whisper, he said, " they are saying among ‚themselves you will take their companion away from them."

Then, after a pause, he said, " Curse them! Black devils! I don't want to be back among them."

I told him he need not, that all depended on himself. If he would earnestly desire to be lifted up from their association, he could be. Repeatedly during the conversation, and after he had shown signs of penitence, I asked him if he did not see a light dawning upon him in the distance. Once, after gazing very intently, he said he did.

Once he paused and listened, and said, " Do you hear that?"

I answered, Yes, I heard rappings where he pointed, and asked what it meant, but he gave me no answer.

At length I urged him to leave, for he could see how he was causing the medium to suffer.

He said he had found her on her way down to New York, and discovered that she was not afraid, and therefore he could influence her. But he was afraid that if he left her, he would not be permitted to speak through her again. I repeatedly assured him he should. I proposed he should come to our circle to-morrow night, and we would hear him.

He said he didn't want to expose his shame to the world. He wanted to talk to me privately.

I said it should be as he pleased. He then asked me to give him a written pledge that he might come.

I sat down to write one, and asked his name. He said he had a good many, but I might call him Misfortune.

I then wrote these words: "I promise Misfortune that he shall have a further opportunity to confer with me through Mrs. F."

He asked my name, and told me to sign it.

Then I asked, "What good will that do you? You can't take it away with you."

He answered, "Lay it on the table. They will see it, and I can't go back without some evidence that I have been here."

He said when he came again he would bring some one with him, for he was not alone in wishing to get out of that bad place. And if he found out what I said to be true, he would proclaim it so down among those people.

He then gave me instructions what to do with Mrs. F. when he left her. He told me not to let go her hand, and to keep one of my hands on her head all the time, and not be alarmed at her fainting, for she would not die.

Section Sixteen.

Sept. 25, 1853.

This morning, while I was sitting in my library, writing, Mrs. F. came in and stood up near me. She said she felt the influence upon her. I paid no particular attention to it, but went on with my writing. Looking up, after a while, I saw her eyes were closed, that tears were rolling down her cheeks, and that she was fully entranced and unconscious. I then gave attention to the manifestation.

ERE long, she said, " Can you wipe tears from the eyes?" I said " Yes, and from the heart also."

She asked, "Is there any hope?"

I told her indeed there was to those who truly repented and earnestly desired to be better and purer.

I asked if it was the same person who was here last night?

" No; but he sent me here." Then falling on her knees before me, she bowed her head, and in a low voice, said, " I will confess to you." After a brief pause, she added, " I murdered my own child."

She then asked if she could come again? I said she might, and she said she must leave, or she would injure Mrs. F.; and so she left.

Soon after, Dr. Dexter came in, and he was influenced to write as follows:

I can not permit the Doctor to remain here much longer; but as there are circumstances of importance to be understood, I shall instruct you for a moment, and then insist on his going.

In the first place, in regard to Mrs. F., the direction given by the spirit* should not be taken literally; for if

---

* In reference to her diet.

she entirely abstained from food, she would not be able to perform the duties before her.

It is not the absolute effect of food taken into the body necessary for its support that will interfere with the manifestations through her, but it is the grossness of the nutrition derived from that which in amount gratifies the taste, not the demands of the body. If there were not enough taken into the stomach to support the functions of the nervous as well as the muscular system, she could not be approached either by good or unprogressed spirits. The instruction should be understood as meaning that she should take just enough food to keep the several organs in proper action, and no more.

The intention of all that you have witnessed is of far more serious import than you now suppose. In all that you see, though it may appear singular, if you will cast reflection back to the teachings personally months ago, you will perceive that it was then told you that these things would be revealed sooner or later. But let your judgment be exercised in every thing. Let your analysis be complete, and let nothing interfere between clear comprehension and what you hope may be the effect. One thing is certain. In the revelations you will witness there are principles involved of which you have not even dreamed, and it requires from all of you the just exercise of all your mental powers rightly to refer to each separate effect the design and purpose thereof.

Let them be heard. If they come in crowds, give to each a hearing, and then decide on each individual case as it is presented.

BACON, AND ALL THE SPIRITS ATTENDING.

After he left, a spirit manifested herself through Mrs. F., who said:

She had been a female who had had great pride in life, and was ambitious of pomp and distinction; that she had sold her virtue to a villain for gold; had enticed her own daughter to sin, and then to murder her child to hide her shame, and who had herself committed suicide to avoid exposure.

She said the female who first came was her daughter, who had told her of this way's being opened to escape from the darkness in which she dwelt.

She once asked me, " Did you ever despair?" I inquired if she did? She answered, Yes, for she saw no end to her misery ; that she had been there many years, and was sinking lower and lower. She was now residing in horrible darkness, alone with her daughter. Her daughter, she said, was purer than she was, and would never again return down there ; and she could not bear to return alone to that darkness. Her crimes, she said, were her only companions ; the memory of them was ever with her. And " Oh !" she exclaimed, laying her hand on her heart, "how they burn, burn, forever burn here."

She said Jane told her that through us there was a way opened to escape from that horrible place. I inquired if no one ever came to teach them a way ? She said, " No ; only that man who was here last night came and told them of this way."

And now, she said, if she could not go away from that place, she could take some one down with her.

While we were conversing, she looked around and told me there were a good many others then present who wanted to talk to me, but some of them did not dare look at me ; she attempted to drive them away.

I told her those were the feelings that kept her down where she was ; that instead of desiring to take any one down there, she must wish to lift some one up ; that instead of driving them away from the road which was opened for her escape, she ought to labor to help others find it.

She said no light came where she was, but all was dark and lonely.

Once she told me to lay my hand on her head, as she was sinking down, and could not stay without my help.

She asked if she might come again, and gave me as her signal a pressure with the right hand, and her left hand on my head.

She complained of the light in my room as very oppressive, and I was compelled to darken it.

The next that came was a man. The first thing he said was to ask me if I ever got drunk? He said the cup had ruined him. He was the husband of the last woman, and he hated her bitterly. He said she ruined him and Jane, and she deserved to suffer. He thanked God, he said, he did not live away down where they were. He said murder, suicide, and drunkenness surrounded him while on earth. He did not murder nor commit suicide, but died of delirium tremens.

When I talked to him of repentance and atonement, and working out his own salvation, he asked me how? And I told him by doing good to others, and first and foremost, to his wife, by helping to elevate her. Thus he would not only aid her, but himself by subduing the feelings of hatred and revenge toward her, which bound him down to his present condition, and would ever bind him there.

His signal was three grasps of the hand.

The next that came seemed to be a sea-captain. His manner was rude and rough. He had been a cruel and drinking man. He had made the men stand round, he said, and used the cat-o'-nine-tails pretty freely. He asked me if I thought that fellow he kicked overboard was drowned! He said he was a mean fellow, anyhow. He asked me several times for something to drink. Inquired if I was pilot there? He had been told that through me he could find a way of getting out from where he was. I told him the way was by repentance and atonement. He asked what I meant by repentance?

"Why, did you never hear of that when here?"

"Yes, but I never paid any attention to it."

" Well then, you must bow your heart before God with true sorrow for your hardness and cruelty."

" I can't do that; I can't knock under. I must keep my flag at mast-head."

" What! in defiance of God? Then I can not pilot you."

" But what must I do?"

" Do good to your fellows. For every blow you have struck, do a good deed to some one else."

" Well, but what is a good deed?"

" Any thing that forgets self and seeks to benefit others. Go forth among your associates, tell them of the way that is opened to them, and help them in it."

" There is a hell of a stir down there now about it. I met Jack on the way. He said he had been here, and now he has left us."

" Well, you can leave too, if you will. But you must work for it yourself, and first by subduing the feelings which now you cherish."

He paused for some time and asked if he might come again?

I said, No—not unless he could bring me an account of some good he had done in the mean time.

" Suppose I bring a fellow with me, will that do?"

" Yes, if you will first explain to him all I've said to you."

He then gave me a signal by which I should know him, viz.: three slaps on the back of my hand, and he left.

The next that came was a young man who began by asking me if I was a father? He then told me, with tears in his eyes, that he had been a very, very disobedient son. That he was delicate, and had been tenderly nurtured. That his father never denied him any indulgence, until at the age of twenty he fell in love with a female who was purity itself, but was poor. And his father interfered to break up the attachment, and was going to bind him apprentice on board of a ship, and send him away. So in his wrath he cursed his father and ran away, and ere long died the death of a dog in a foreign land. He had loved his father, but his mother did not care much for him.

He said that when he died, his heart was full of a feeling of revenge toward his father, and he rejoiced at the sorrow which he knew his father would feel at his death. He had taken that same feeling with him into the spirit-world, which he had only lately entered, and had there cherished it and gloated over the idea of the tears his father shed at his loss. And with much bitterness he said, "I have had my revenge!"

He told me that ever since he had been in the spirit-world he had wandered alone over a bleak, desolate, and uninhabited country, where there was just light enough to see how gloomy and dreary it was. That he had heard that I could show him the way out, and he had come to see if I could. There were a great many others coming, and he was so heavy that he could not ascend up to me without help. He described his dreary life, wandering ever thus alone, brooding over the single thought of his revenge upon his father.

I asked him if he had never been taught the lesson of the saving power of love?

He said he had not, nor was he at all aware, till I told him, that it was this train of evil thought which he cherished which had caused all his suffering. I told him how all nature was bound together by the attractive power of love, and repelled necessarily by its opposite. That so long as he cherished that opposite, it was as inevitable that he must wander alone, as it was that he should burn his finger if he put it in the fire. That as soon as he would cherish a spirit of love, he would attract others to him and he would cease to be alone. And that if he wished to ascend from his condition of misery, he must be obedient to the law of love, and show it forth in subduing all selfishness and aiding others. That, first of all, he must revive his love for his father, and as soon as he could, approach him and breath upon him a soothing influence. In the mean time, he must begin his task by laboring for those who were around him in his world.

He asked me how he should do this, and where he should begin?

I answered that he must descend from his solitariness and mingle with others, even if their society was distasteful to him; and there he would, if he sought them, find opportunities enough to benefit others. He would find many poor wretches whom he could aid in a thousand ways, and he could at least go among them, repeat the lesson I had given him, show them the way to escape which he had found and thus become an apostle to teach the truth for the redemption of man even in these gloomy regions.

He said he would do so, that he did love his father, and began even to love me, and asked if he might come again?

I said, Yes, provided he would do some good to some of those around him.

He asked me if he should bring one with him the next time, and if that would not do?

I replied, Yes, that would be something toward it, but he must occupy himself so intensely in doing good to others as to forget himself and the evil thoughts over which he had brooded so long.

I inquired if there were many spirits from that dark country now present?

He said, Yes, a good many, but they could not come near me except through this channel.

I asked if they could'nt hear and be benefited by what I said to him and others?

· He looked around slowly and answered, some of them could, but some were so thick they could not.

He then gave me a signal by which I should know him, placing his hand on my heart as a token of affection, as he termed it.

I congratulated him on this early evidence of the presence of redeeming love with him, and he left us.

Section Seventeen.

Sunday, Sept. 25th, 1853.

The circle met at the Doctor's, and I became influenced.

I saw a large concourse of dark spirits assembled in front of a large building, which was misshapen and rude in form, and a good deal dilapidated. In front of it was an open lot, the soil of which was that dark, fine sand, and in it grew here and there a sickly weed. The whole scene bore an air of neglect. The building could be entered by a broad flight of rude steps. On the platform, at the top of the stairs, three spirits were seated in chairs, as if presiding. Around them, on the platform, were a number who seemed most intimate with them and occasionally talked with them.

It seemed that this was their judicatory, and they had been trying some of their number for violating their laws. The culprits had been condemned, and were then undergoing their punishment, directly in front of that building, where I saw quite a crowd was assembled.

In their midst an upright beam had been erected with two cross-pieces at its top making four arms, which revolved around the upright as their center. The arms were eight or ten feet long, and twelve or fourteen from the ground. At the end of each arm a human being was suspended by cords fastened to their wrists or their thumbs. The position of the poor wretches was of itself very painful, and they writhed and screamed in their agony. But the arms were made to revolve, and as the condemned were thus borne along just over the heads of the crowd, I saw that the spectators, amid shouts and laughter, tormented them as they passed, some by whipping them, some by piercing them with sharp instruments, and some by applying fire to different parts of their bodies. But I saw that no one there enjoyed the horrible scene more than did he who sat in the middle of the three judges, and seemed to be the presiding genius of the scene. He reclined easily back in his chair, and with a smile of great complacency chatted familiarly with those around him, who, it seemed to me, were like parasites, praising his judgment!

I passed away from the scene shuddering, and soon came to a high, abrupt precipice, on the summit of which I saw three females walking. Two of them approached the very edge of the precipice and looked down. The other remained some distance back, and remarked that she could never bear a dizzy height, it always made her so sick. Upon this hint the others acted. They approached her blandly, and as soon as they got near enough, they seized her and dragged her to the edge of the precipice. There they held her in defiance of her struggles and agony, just over the beetling edge, seeming to threaten to throw her off, and occasionally professing to relax their hold upon her. They enjoyed it heartily, and I observed that her screams of agony and theirs of laughter attracted the attention of the passers-by below them, who paused in their way, also enjoyed the scene, and applauded the actors in it.

I passed away from that scene also, and came near to a large concourse of dark spirits, who were very intently engaged in preparing something, which from their numbers I could not see. Everywhere thus far I had seen laughter and merriment, such as it was; but here I saw a serious, earnest, concentrated feeling, apparently of intense hate. There was no laughter, but a stern determination seemed to pervade them all. With all my efforts I could not discover exactly what they were doing, but I read their thoughts enough to perceive that they were engaged in some plan to interrupt, if possible, our operations through this spiritual intercourse with us. And I left the scene while they were thus engaged.

During the time that I was seeing this, I was conversing with Mr. Warren about a difficulty which he suggested of understanding what it was that impelled spirits thus to descend, even when they had a wish to stop short of that.

As soon as the Doctor could be influenced, it was written through him:

You ask why those spirits descend to those dark places? The reason is obvious. The great law of like attracting like obtains throughout the whole of the spheres. When a departed spirit enters into the spheres, he is at once attracted where he finds congeniality of place and persons. They could not be happy in the bright spheres. They could find no enjoyment where there is either virtue or goodness. Thus their first efforts are to locate themselves where the acquired attributes of mind in all its workings may be gratified. Their bodies are gross and their minds still grosser. Now there is in this condition of both body and mind a state which rejects magnetically all above, and they are compelled to return whence they came when they are by any means brought or force themselves into a place above them. As when on earth a mind gradually becomes perverse, it seeks, from the very attributes it has forced on itself, a correspondence with that state where its every feeling may be most manifest. They obey the law observable in all nature, that every thing seeks its kind and is compelled to retain that connection.

You have been taught that the good spirit, on its entrance into the spheres, enters a condition where its affinities may develop themselves. Now, if they are continually rising, they will seek spheres above them, but if they only maintain that state, they do not progress. But if they do not even maintain their first estate, they must seek a condition absolutely corresponding with the feelings which they have generated by their retrogression.

Compulsion arises from the equal action of the law of

affinity, and is manifest as much in the higher as in the lower spheres. Take, for instance, a man born, and without being permitted to go into the world, he is shut up in a dungeon, and while there is taught every thing wicked. Now this man dies. Where does his spirit seek for its residence? Why, exactly where his feelings may have the greatest chance of display.

Now, if by chance he rises to a spot where there is more of goodness than where he is, the force of his desires compels him to return, and though he may desire to stay there, he knows without he is incited by some development of new desires that he is forced back by the omnipotent influence of the old feelings.

The reasons are plain, and need no more explanation.

BACON.

One thing more: when a spirit returns to a sphere above him (a wicked spirit), he seeks in those with whom he has this new acquaintance the feelings in them which most correspond to his own. This is one reason why it is said the devil tempts you. It is only the correspondence of like with like, good or bad, which, like chemical affinities, mingle wherever they exist, without they are protected by some counteracting desire for good which thus overcomes the effects which the bad spirits wish to produce. No spirit can become bad all at once or good suddenly, and the law of progression and retrogression is in full force in both conditions of good or evil.

The teachings seemed to have ceased. I inquired about the manifestations during the day and the previous night.

It was written:

Yes, but you must learn that a *truly* evil spirit is a devil in subtilty and artifice.

I said I had not overlooked that, but I questioned as to what good had been done?

It was answered:

Why, neither you, nor I, nor others, can judge of the

effect yet. That you did right, no one doubts. The result
time will tell. I mean your method was good, and every
thing was done in such a manner as would do good, if good
could be done.

Then it was written:

Now, for the benefit of all, and especially the Judge, we
shall retire, but if possible, if the circle can meet to-morrow night, much can be done for good, and the manifestations will be more than usual through all the mediums.
I wish it could be, but you must not let Mrs. F. be influenced in the least till to-morrow night.

I said, But I had appointed the spirits who spake through her to meet
me to-morrow afternoon at four o'clock, and I did not want to break my
engagement.

It was written:

Dear Judge, you must know that those who have been
with you so long have privileges of knowing all circumstances perhaps in advance of most spirits. We have permitted many things to be said, but for yourself and for
others, we advise you to defer the meeting until night.

We agreed to that, and took our departure.

Section Eighteen.

Monday, Sept. 26th, 1853.

This evening all the circle met at my house.   Mrs. F. was also present.

We waited a little while for the Doctor, who was detained by a professional engagement.   While thus waiting, an unhappy influence came upon Mrs. F.   She resisted it, and with my aid she finally drove it off.   But it affected me almost as much as it did her, and it distressed me, both in body and mind, more than any spiritual influence I had ever felt.   It continued with me even after it had left her, and immediately after the Doctor came in I was impelled to go to the table and read the prayer.

My interior perceptions were then opened, and I was enabled to see the spirits which surrounded us.   Behind where I sat, and around that part of the circle, I perceived the bright light of the good spirits, but directly in front of me and behind the Doctor, who sat facing me, I saw a large concourse of dark spirits at a short distance off. That part of the circle was very dark.   The Doctor was entirely enveloped with the somber atmosphere, so much so that the brighter spirits, it seemed, could not approach him near enough to communicate through him.   The dark spirits were a very compact body, extending quite in the distance, so that with the darkness their rear was hidden from my view.   They were led by one person who seemed to have been chosen from his energy and decision of character. He was immediately attended by quite a number who seemed to be a sort of council for him, whose minds were inferior to his, but evidently superior to the great mass who were behind him.   The feelings with which they had approached our circle were very apparent, and now I plainly understood what they had been planning and arranging when I had seen them the previous evening. They were ignorant that I had thus seen them, yet my having done so had put me on my guard, had prevented my being surprised by so novel an exhibition, and enabled me to act understandingly.

It seemed that my utterance of the prayer, and the union of the minds of the circle upon it, had partially interrupted their advance. I saw, however, they soon rallied, and were preparing to force their way nearer to us, and I entreated the circle with one accord to fix their thoughts upon God, and our reliance on his power and mercy. The effect of their doing so was instantly apparent. That dark band was thrown into confusion. Its leader turned his back to us and harangued his associates with a great deal of vehemence. He stamped his foot, gnashed his teeth, and gesticulated violently. The order and regularity which I had observed among his companions were disturbed. The whole crowd, and particularly the front rank, were agitated, and they stirred among themselves as if debating what to do.

At this moment the Doctor's hand was influenced, and he wrote :

Read the prayer, and add this to it.

And oh ! our God ! enable us when we feel the manifestations of thy almighty power, that we may earnestly hope to subdue within us all that tends to retard its exhibition, and humbly to desire that by the innate properties of our connection with thee, we may realize that either in good or evil thou art with us.

I obeyed the direction, and again turned my attention to our unwelcome visitors. It seemed as if they could not advance any nearer, but had determined not to retire, but remain at hand ready to take advantage of any contingency. They were again quiet and orderly, and stood in dogged silence looking on, and casting abroad their influence as far as was in their power. It reached past the Doctor to me, and I was very much agitated and distressed. I now, for the first time, discovered that my own will was not strong enough to rid me of their presence, as it always before had been, and I buried my face in my hands and for the first time in my life earnestly, though silently, prayed to God for his aid and protection, for never before had I been made so conscious of needing it. I had relied upon myself and my own power, but now had fearful evidence how frail was my dependence.

Immediately after thus addressing the throne of Him, it was written through the Doctor:

For thee alone, Judge,

By the power of thy just intentions, by the good thou seekest to perform toward thy race, we, thy friends, direct thee to mentally command the absence of those spirits, whose presence is so annoying, in the name of God, and they will obey thy command.

This was signed with an unintelligible scrawl.

This direction also I obeyed, and for at least ten minutes I sat amid the entire silence of the circle, as sternly and as resolutely as I was able, commanding that band of dark spirits to retire. They reminded me that I had promised to have further interviews with some of them, and demanded the performance of my promise. I refused, however, to listen to such a consideration at that moment, and from them thus banded together, and insisted that they should depart.

All this was done mentally, and at length I began to perceive that they were departing. They faded gradually from my view, and seemed lost amid the somber cloud which had hung over them.

While I was becoming conscious of this, it was written through the Doctor:

What now, my friend? are they gone?

I replied they were, and then it was added

This is the first concentrated effort made by those spirits who, we told you some time ago, had organized together to prevent all good through your circle's efforts. They will not trouble you again without you admit them.

Now we will introduce a spirit truly anxious to rise. She will make gentle impressions on Mrs. F., and you will see the difference. Direct her to God!!!

Now I can sign my name, BACON.

Let not your hearts be troubled, for in love, in the glorious garb of truth we are arrayed, and no harm can come, for in the name of the most high God we are now with you.

Judge, for one moment be silent and see the dazzling glory which surrounds us. BACON.
SWEEDENBORG.

I then saw around the circle light clouds rolling gently and in easy, grateful forms, and of most brilliant colors. They were white, like banks of snow rolling one above another, and beautifully tinged and colored with rose, blue, crimson, and purple hues. Floating among them, and appearing and disappearing, were many bright and happy spirits, who seemed full of gladness and affection. They seemed to be rejoicing that they could again surround us. I observed, however, at the spot where those dark spirits had been, the light of the clouds was paler and more dim, as if their influence had left its taint behind them.

And I am now, as I write, reminded of one incident of the former scene which I forgot, and namely, that while I was sitting sternly regarding that dark band, and commanding them to begone, I saw a streak of very white light shooting its rays like the aurora borealis, that came from above and shot swiftly down, angularly, about midway between us and the dark spirits. I saw that it cast no refulgence beyond its own immediate limits, and even failed to light up the dark soil on which it struck; but it seemed to be a barrier like a wall of light between them and us, yet so transparent that I could easily see through it.

But to return.   After I had described that glorious scene to the circle, it was written:

"Now look at Sweedenborg in the glory of his sphere."

I looked, and saw amid those brilliant clouds a bright spirit standing.   There issued from him a bright light which surrounded his whole form with a halo of golden and silver colored rays that shot out from him in all directions for the space of three or four feet from his person. Outside this halo were many other spirits, less distinctly seen, who seemed to be attending on him.

Then it was written:

Describe his face and figure.

I did so, nearly, in these words:

He was tall and majestic, and was enveloped in a flowing garment of pure white which descended to and covered his feet. His hair was long, dark colored, and, parted on his forehead, flowed down in curls to his shoulders.   His forehead was broad and expanded, and was of a most dazzling whiteness, seemingly transparent. The top of his head was high, and he seemed to be distinguished for benevolence and capacity of intellect. His eyebrows were heavy and projecting, and his eyes were black and large and very glowing and bright.   All his features were prominent, particularly his nose and lower jaw. His upper lip easily trembled with emotion, but showed great firmness and self-control.   In his left hand he held a book.   On his breast was a metallic plate, like those which the Jewish high-priests wore, but I could not see what were its emblazonments.   He raised his right hand and pointed upward, with a look of great enthusiasm and devotion.

And thus the scene faded from my view.
Mrs. F. then became influenced, and it was written:

The Judge and Mrs. D. will take her hands.

We did so, and then had this manifestation:

She shed tears, and seemed greatly distressed, and at length, in a voice full of emotion, she cried, "Help!" I told her that help was at hand for those who earnestly sought it.

After a severe struggle she said, "I want my child."

I asked if her child was in our sphere?

She made me no reply; but after a while, with great agony, she said, "Would you tear out your own heart? Would you stab your own child?"

I told her that even for that there was forgiveness.

"Where shall I seek it?" she cried.

I answered, "Of God. You have but to kneel before him in true devotion, and ask with a contrite heart. None are so vile but they may be forgiven. Repent of the evil past, and atone for it. Mourn not for the consequences of crime, but for the sin itself, and a door will be open to you."

She asked, "Where?"

I answered, "In your own heart. Bury there the memory of past sin in the consciousness of present good. Blot out the memory of former wrongs by doing good now. Are there not many around you to whom you can yet do good—whom you yet can aid and relieve?"

Her only answer was, "Oh, help me!"

I answered, "I will help, but you must follow my instructions. Help yourself—labor for your own redemption —work out your own salvation yourself—purify your own heart by subduing all selfishness."

She cried, "Dare I to hope?"

I told her she might well hope, if devoutly and with a contrite heart she would humble herself before God and seek his aid.

She then knelt and cried, "God the Father! help!" Seeing her so overcome with emotion that she seemed unable to form her own prayer, I asked her to repeat after me, and then said, "Our Father, who art in Heaven."

She interrupted me. "Oh, not mine! not mine!"

I told her yes; hers, if she but earnestly desired it.

Then, with a shudder, and looking behind her, she whispered to me, " That evil spirit !"

I told her to fear not: they could not disturb her while she was with us; that we were surrounded by good spirits, who would be glad to approach her and aid her more than we could; that they were kept away from her only by herself; and in proportion as she should ardently desire their aid, would they be able to come near her and take her by the hand.

While I was speaking, she seemed to be listening, as it were, to a distant voice, and at length said, " Whisper it again."

I bid her be of good cheer; they were drawing nigh.

" Oh!" she cried, " teach me to pray."

I told her the true way to pray was to feel the might, the mercy, and presence of God; to acknowledge in her heart her dependence on him; that every good deed was a prayer, and that she could not more earnestly pray than by doing good to others.

At length she said, " I see the light, do you know! I see the light; it is coming near. Do you not hear their voices ? Is that my mother's face ? It is! it is! She comes! she comes! Joy! joy! joy! Lift me up. I'm coming up! I'm free !"

I told her it was the truth had made her free.

She cried to me, " Hold me up; bind fast the cord around my arms, that you may lift me. Now, now my feet are established. I take hold on eternal life."

And then, while we were reflecting how soon His mercy comes to those who earnestly seek it, she left us.*

---

* While we were correcting our papers for the press, this same spirit manifested herself through one of the mediums, and said:

" I'm here. I am happier now; tell them so. After waiting so long in darkness, I begin to see the light, and am happier. I believe now He is my God, for I feel his love everywhere. Pardon me for coming thus; but my joy was beyond bounds that I had thus begun to advance."

Mrs. F. then sank back in her chair in a state of unconsciousness. It was then written :

She will revive in a moment perfectly restored. This is the effect of a true manifestation.

The intention of these manifestations was to enable you to judge of the true and false, and for this we permitted, what has never before been allowed, the admission of so many dark spirits into the pale of your circle ; and for this we have indeed fought and conquered.

BACON AND ALL.

I then made some remarks showing my suspicion that all the manifestations on Sunday had been from spirits evilly disposed, and for mischievous purposes ; and as I saw Mrs. F. was becoming influenced again, I advised efforts to resist it.

But it was written that it would be the influence of a bright spirit, that of Bacon himself.

In a little while he spoke through her these words :

Seekers after eternal truth ! Ye do well to analyze all that comes before your understanding, but judge not too harshly of the spirits. I see you will repel many who wish to come, and to whom it will be profitable to come. I come to open the way for them. You would have repelled them if I had not assumed this condition. Some are now here to whom you have promised an interview.

But I inquired, How can we tell that they are so ?
He answered :

If they present the signal truly, you will know them, and by their coming a second time.

Then he left her, and another spirit manifested himself through her.

As I sat by her side, I felt that it was the spirit who had been with us on Saturday night, and had called himself " Misfortune."

Some one asked her what she had been doing since her last visit to us ? She answered : " What have I been doing ? Rooting out of my heart the evil passions which bound me darkly below. I am lifted up, and am working my way to heaven. Adieu ! God's blessing on you all !"

I noticed that his right hand was clenched, and I remarked, "Your fist doubled again?"

He instantly opened his hand, and, baring his arm, raised it up before me, and said, "Do you know that sign?"

I told him, right well; and now I wanted also the word. He answered, "Truth."

He then added, "Do you know you have redeemed me?"

I told him how deeply I rejoiced to hear it, and reminded him that I had told him that such a result would give me happiness that would last for ages.

He then said, "I told you I'd bring another with me— Jane, Jane!"

Yes, I told him I knew he had sent her, and I had heard from others that he had, even down in his dark abode, in defiance of all opposition, proclaimed the glad news that a way was opened to them, and I had thus seen that he could indeed be redeemed.

He answered, "I am redeemed from the curse of sin by your aid. You have saved me."

Nay. I replied that it was the truth which had saved him; "the truth against the world."

He then said, "Do you know love's subduing power? I hope! now I hope? I can not tell you the joy it brings. Do you know what rest is to the weary, joy to the heart-broken? Then may you know the fullness of my joy. Do you know I am liberated from the bonds of sin and despair, and see before me the eternal light of pure blessedness?"

Then, after a pause, he added, "I told you I could tell you something. Listen. Do you know their weapons are prepared, their plans laid for your destruction? Be on your guard; they would be glad to drag you down to their own condition. But fear not, and look up, whence your strength comes. Man of God! labor faithfully in this sin-subduing work. It takes hold, even down in the dark regions where I have dwelt; it reaches far down there, and will bring up the fallen to realms of light through your action. Accept my thanks; my efforts will be used to restore those who are now so degraded." He added that he would visit me again, and keep me advised of their plans; and then he left.

After a little while another came, and began by laying his hand on my heart, and said it was in the name of " Affection." Do you know the signal? Did you ever instruct a disobedient child?"

I told him I recognized him, and hoped his wanderings had ceased.

He said, " Do you know that that unholy resentment toward my father does not burn in my heart now? I am changed through your kind aid. I now try to ascend. I look up to the bright light before me. You helped me. You guided an erring child back to his father's love. You have reclaimed a wanderer to be redeemed—awakened his heart to repentance—awakened a desire to lay hold on eternal life.

"You distrusted me; you doubted me?" I told him that was true. He said, "You were wrong; your doubts repelled me. Oh! could you but know the joy of a pardoned heart! Many others will come to visit you. The way is now opened. But take notice; there are two ways." I asked, "One for the true, and one for the false?" "Yes."

" How shall I know them apart?"

" A principle shall be awakened in your heart by which you shall know. To be lost and to be saved! Is not that joy! To see the kindly hand extended to lift you up! the love that lifts us up! You are my friend and my father. It is your kindness that has saved me. There are many there wanting to be enlightened as I have been; do not repel them. I am going slowly up that mountain; the light gradually increases, and as I am developed, I have a hope—I am incited to look forward to have my knowledge increased."

I told him that if he would but earnestly seek it he would have the aid of bright spirits to instruct him.

He answered, "I can see their footsteps now; but for you, I might have been left in darkness."

I asked him who first sent him to me?

He answered, he had met one who had told him I would help him.

He added, "Another channel will be opened by which they can approach you. Then I will come again. Now I must leave."

So he left, and the manifestations closed, except some private ones.

P. S. I have lately. several times in dreams and in waking thoughts, had presented to me the idea of a quarrel with my father, continuing for years, and affecting a whole life. I could not imagine why such unwelcome thoughts were intruded upon me; but now I see how well they prepared me for the task I was to perform with this unhappy young man.

Section Nineteen.

Thursday, Sept. 29, 1853.

The circle met at my house this evening. All were present.
It was written:

THE meeting of your circle is like the gathering of a company of soldiers after a battle: the officers look over the ranks, and, finding them all safe and without wound or bruise, rejoice with much joy. So to-night our hearts are moved with affection and love toward you all, friends, and we greet you in the name of God.   BACON.

Something seems to be necessary in explanation after the very remarkable manifestations which were made here a few nights ago, and the real intention and design of what was then represented should be explained, that you may understand what action to take in regard to them. That you, Judge, or either of you, are able to assist in your world the uneducated and degraded to learn and advance toward what is good and true, neither yourselves or others can doubt. There is a principle of the spirit's nature which is of itself able to generate noble aspirations in the spirit of the most illiterate and debased. There is, too, an innate desire away down under the mass of error and ignorance which impels the crudest mind to seek for that it does not understand or comprehend. But when to that mind is opened the broad avenues of truth and knowledge, it does not owe to its instructor the meed of praise for the principles inculcated. No. Its gratitude, its veneration, its affection may be poured out in gushing streams toward him who has showed the way, and he will look up and admire, but still the truth which has opened to his soul is heaven-born, and comes like the Holy Spirit we read of, direct from God. Direct from God? Yes, in the comprehension of his eternal laws,.in the realization of what is his own prerogative and what is his destiny!

I have made these remarks that you may understand that nothing of all that has been accomplished by the spirits, or what will be achieved by you, has or should be attributed to any thing else but the administration of the eternal laws of God.

Bright as may be the prospect before you, glorious as may be the idea of aiding an immortal soul to spring from darkness and degradation to the light of knowledge and progress, I pray you all to reflect, that to Him who has established and perfected the laws by which this change from mortality to immortality takes place, is to be ascribed all the glory and honor forever and ever. Amen.

I do not understand that in any thing which has taken place here you are instructed to admit to your circle every spirit, good or bad, who makes application. The design of many bad spirits is to gain admission by any contrivance possible, and to thus circumvent your plans by learning what they are and how they are to be accomplished. There is a deeply concerted scheme here to destroy all the good which may be done by your efforts, by instilling in your minds doubts, distrust of yourselves and others, and also by inciting certain passions and feelings to lead your mind away from the real objects before you, to that which will perplex, destroy, and break up the whole harmony of the plans in which you are engaged. Recollect that the truly good man is the easiest to be approached by the artful and wicked, for suspecting no evil himself, he suspects no evil in others, and thus he leaves the door wide open for all to enter, both good and evil. That there were some spirits deeply smitten with a sense of sin, and earnestly desirous to throw off their bundle like Christian of old, I have no doubt. But that there were and are spirits even here to-night who would like to come under the mask of repentance to gain a foothold in your platform *I know*. I need say no more, for you all will understand what I mean.

I remarked that I had been originally desirous of aiding all who came, and though I had not been without suspicion as to the sincerity of some of them, yet I did not like to repel any, lest I might drive away the sincere penitent. But from what he had said on Sunday, I had been induced to believe that the safest course was to refuse all, and now I knew not what to do, or how to tell the difference between them.

It was written :

What was said by the medium, when I manifested myself through her, had somewhat the color of her own mind in it. She entertained the same feeling in regard to the admission of spirits as she then expressed, long before she came to your city. I did not intend so to be understood. I meant this, that duty should be performed under all circumstances. To your enlightened minds that duty was plain, because you had already become acquainted with what was required of you, and that you were to judge of, when to permit a spirit to approach, when every circum-

stance in connection with what was seen, taught, and known
of him satisfied your minds that he was impelled to come by
a sense of his own degradation. To this, in the admission of
every spirit who claimed entrance by the strength of your
promise, Judge, your judgment certainly did not consent,
for it was shown to you what the design of crowds of spirits
was when they should have gained admission to this circle.
Answer me, all—For what purpose was that dark vision of
the evil spirits given to the Judge? Did we not so impress
his consciousness of the dire intent for which they were here,
that his soul realized their very plans, though in embryo?
Could it be possible that he should weep because he had
seen fifty dark spirits, when he has fought and triumphed
over his thousands, even in himself? Is it necessary for me
again to say that your judgment is to guide you in all that
you see and hear? When they come, consult those who are
always with you, those whom you trust, and they will tell
you what to do.

We were then told to ask our questions, if we had any.

Mr. Warren asked, Do the inhabitants of the various planets in the
solar system at death go to the same spheres with the people of earth?

Yes.

Are the spheres where you reside material globes, on the surface of
which are the same general manifestations of vegetable and animal life
as on earth?

Yes.

Do all the inhabitants of earth go to the same globe?

No.

In advancing, a grade, do you leave one globe and go to another?

Yes.

Do those spheres and globes possess gravitation, and do they revolve
around a central sun?

Yes.

What distance is it from us?—how situated? Is it visible to us, or not?

Calculate the distance from space to space unknown, and you have it. We can't tell, at least I can't, never having measured it. I can only say, when I want to go to any place, I am there.

The distance is only to be calculated when gross matter requires absolute and positive locomotion. I understand what you desire, Mr. W., and I really appreciate your intention. But you will not at present get any positive or approximate calculation of distance. Add the distance of the fixed stars four times and multiply by twice fifty thousand, and then you are as near it as before you commenced.

In answer to other questions it was said, that none of the globes where the spirits dwell are visible to us; that the spirits from other globes go to the same places with the inhabitants of earth; that many of them are not in advance of us; and that advance depends, not on distance or locality, but on purity.

Mr. Warren asked some questions about the sixth and seventh spheres. And it was written:

That is an arbitrary division. We make none such here. You can make this division if you please, but I can only say that the process of advance includes many, many gradations, and you will find there is not so much difference among spirits, between this and your world, as to lead to a separation of locality alone. Mind, purpose, and action constitute the division.

Mr. Sweet then called their attention to and asked an explanation of that part of the teaching about the creation which said that in chaos there was no motion. He had thought that motion was coeval with God, and that if any part of creation had not motion, the Spirit of God was not there, and consequently he was not infinite?

It was written:

I will just call Mr. S.'s attention to the time when this earth was unfit for the habitation of man, and ask him why it ever was in that condition? Why should it not have been ready fashioned? Why are there now wandering in space the nucleii of other worlds? Why not all progress at once? If the Divine Spirit pervaded every thing, of course there must have been the same degree of development in every part of creation. Thus animals could not have had any starting-point, but because the Divine Spirit pervaded the principle, all development must have assumed the same ratio or state of progress at one and the same time. But God's laws work from the germ to the full and perfect development. Thus, in the seed when planted, there is a time when the germinating process has not commenced. But when it does so, it goes through its whole progress till the perfect grain bursts forth. Do you suppose in all space there is now motion?

Every thing has a starting-point, and though God is infinite, he can not act in advance of the laws he has established, for, if he could, what is the use of his laws? Now that God created other worlds is proved by astronomy, for the central point of creation is detected by certain phenomena known to the scientific. But God was just as much acting when the space was without motion as he is now, for the very constituents out of which this world was formed were then at work to develop the proper state from which matter could be evolved. If motion were coeval with God you might realize him as motion too. Nothing was coeval with God but spirit, and it was this infinite spirit that created motion, matter, and the laws which control them.

Then, after a brief and unimportant communication through Mrs. S., the circle left.

Section Twenty.

Sunday, Oct. 2, 1853

The circle met at Dr. Dexter's.   All present.
It was written:

You will observe the influence of the spirits on other members of the circle than the Doctor, as it will be impossible to influence him much to-night, as he is really sick.   But what I have to say through him will be said now, for I find it very difficult to write.

Some time ago you were reminded that a careful examination of your hearts was one of the real tests of your progress toward purity and truth.   To-night it is proper, after all that some of the circle have seen and witnessed, that this examination should be made; and of others, too, the question should be asked, Have all the intentions of life been true?   Have we desired to conform to the principles that we acknowledge as our guides, and have we in every thing acted knowingly, as we ought to have done?   Have we entertained toward others any feelings but those which are consonant with love!   Do we regard God and his laws with true affection?   Have we progressed?

Friends, 'tis not alone that we believe, but do we act? Are there no secret purposes which may retard our progress toward immortal perfection?   The spirits surrounding you, and who are with you daily, are the witnesses of many noble, virtuous, and glorious aspirations for what is indeed the real purpose of life; and when we propose these questions, we do so because ye are indeed the chosen vessels in which the truth, as it is of God is to be distributed throughout the world.   Be ye perfect, even as God is perfect.

BACON.

Mrs. Sweet then asked the spirits if they would take care, while communicating through her, that she did not commit any error, or allow her own mind to mingle with their teachings.

It was answered:

My dear Mrs. Sweet: You, as all the rest of the world, are not yet perfect. That the spirits influencing you are aware of the peculiar feelings of your heart relative to the manifestations through you, is known to you, for you have been told so before now. Therefore, depend upon. it, and let it satisfy you to-night, forever and aye, that if you do not say what you are impressed to say, you shall be immediately stopped short, and shall not go on until you are brought under the full influence. This is enough for all you wish to know.

One word more: After Mrs. S. has spoken, then the Judge. will be influenced, and then the circle had better separate, as the Doctor needs rest.

I wrote what I did in the commencement, for these are thoughts that make their impress on the spheres. Oh! that our whole thought and acts were indeed measured by the standard of the vision on the cross—that it is not indeed in dying that Christ redeemed the world, but in living and exemplifying the glorious principles of God's truth in every act of his life.

The spirits then caused me to feel their influence, and after sitting in silence for some time, during which I saw much of what is hereafter recorded, I exclaimed,

Oh! what a fearful ordeal! What a day of judgment!

I had again ascended that path leading to the fountain, and there again approached that bright spirit who presided over that community, and by whose side I had on former occasions stood erect in the pride of my anticipation, that I could be like him. But now with what different feelings did I approach him!

Since I last met him I had seen what sin was—how fearfully dark and corrupt is the heart into which it has been permitted entrance! how loathsome in its daily life! how

15

terrible in its consequences, amid the despair that seemed
to have no end. I had seen the dark spirits in whose
breasts have raged, with undisputed sway, all the passions
of our material existence. I had seen how lasting on the
soul were its unhappy effects ; and how impossible it is,
when the soul is free from the material garment and its
aids to forgetfulness, to banish or suppress the memory of
aught of the past. And now, as I approached that bright
spirit, this lesson was uppermost in my mind, and it was in
deep humility, growing out of a burning recollection of my
evil past, that I approached one so pure and bright. How
unlike the proud aspect that once marked my approach to
him, was the deep humility which now bowed me almost
to his feet! He stood near me alone ; the other spirits
who had accompanied him when I first approached, had
seemed to be conscious of what was before me, and, unwilling to mortify me by their presence, had, with sorrowing and sympathizing countenances, retired. The expression of his countenance was different from what I had ever
seen it before. Its benevolent tone had now a sad and
mournful hue, and he seemed to feel as if he fully realized
the depth of my despondency, though he had never himself had so much cause to regret.

He kindly took me by the hand and led me toward the
house where my wife resided. As I approached it, I saw
her standing by its entrance with the same mournful, sym-
pathetic expression of countenance, yet beaming with hope
and encouragement. As I passed her she seized my hand,
and, by gently pressing it, assured me of her sympathy and
affection, at the same time that she thus awoke within me,
with terrible vividness, the recollection of all my wrongs
to her. My conductor led me to an inner apartment in
that house, and left me there, with the remark that it was
my residence ; and though by the preponderance of good
over evil in my life I had been able to ascend to that level,
and in some respects live with my wife and children, yet I
was not pure enough to associate fully with them, and, for

the present—at least, whenever I retired from the busy scene around me—that was my closet, and was to be occupied by me alone. Thus speaking, he retired, and I was left alone with the memory of the past.

The room was long and spacious, and had but few articles of furniture in it. A bed in one corner, a few chairs, and an altar standing in the middle of the floor, were the the chief. But I did not notice that much, for my attention was at once drawn to letters printed on the walls of the room, in colors of black, of red, of silver and of gold, and which covered all the walls all around the room. With those letters were thus recorded all the events of my life—the good, and the evil, and the mixed. Thus they stood out before me, and turn my eyes where I would, that record was present. I did not much observe the lighter letters, the darker ones seemed so much to preponderate— at least, at the earlier periods of life. I observed that some of the events had been obliterated by heavy, black lines drawn through them ; but then and thus were brought up before me many events of early life, which I had forgotten amid the bustle and stir of subsequent events.

It was a terrible ordeal, a fearful waiting for of judgment. I buried my face in my hands to hide, if possible, the sight from my view. But in vain ; for memory, painfully awakened by the record around me, was busy in its duty of retribution, and I prostrated myself before that altar, in deep humiliation at the sense of what I had been, and, with a torn and contrite heart, fervently prayed to God that that terrible memory might pass from me. While thus prostrate, my wife entered the room, and gently led me from it. No word was exchanged between us. My heart was too full to speak, and in silence I retired from a scene which had shaken my soul—of whose strength I had proudly boasted to myself—until its weakness had seemed that of infancy, and its dependence on something more than its own power was but too manifest.

As I came out of the building, I found the presiding spirit awaiting me.

He called my attention to a volcano in the distance that was throwing its fires high up into the heavens, and emitting from the summit of its flame a dense, black smoke. I observed that the top of the mountain, which had once towered high into the air, was now partly burned off. Its lava had, in times long past, run down its sides, and contributed to fill up and elevate the valleys, and now it was pouring forth ashes, which, falling in thick showers on the surrounding country, was creating and enriching the soil. I perceived also that its sides, or crusts, were burned very thin, and must soon, by the operation of those fires, be consumed and fall within the crater, and the rough places of earth be made smooth, and its barrenness be converted into land fit for human habitation and human wants. As I was regarding this, the spirit said to me, Thus in all nature, in man as well as matter, the same law obtains. As in this mount its center must be burned out by those raging flames before it can be made to beautify nature around, so must the human heart be purified by its internal fires—first throwing out its lava to fill up the deep hollows of its existence—casting off from its bosom its foul, black smoke, and fertilizing all around it by the consumption of its own impurities and the production of a material that is capable of enriching, beautifying, and leveling what remains.

As the rugged parts of material existence are softened and beautified by the never-ending operations of God's laws, so it is in man; and in proportion to the density and quantity of the contents of these material prominences, so must the fire that burns them out be more intense and more enduring.

Such, he said, is the law now operating in man. If the human soul had preserved its level, there would have been no lofty mount to consume; but if there be elevations, they must be destroyed. He bade me remember the lesson, for it was true, not alone in that instance, but every-where and in every thing. The law of progression was the same everywhere, operating in the same general manner always alike, and always in man or matter producing the same results.

And now, he added, take care that while the dark spirits may hail you—as some of them have done—as "Man of God," the brighter spirits may not have occasion to say to you, "Man of Sin;" for think how far you, who can be approached by those dark spirits, must be from those near whom they can not come. And beware, lest in reproaching the overweening self-conceit of others, you be not prompted by the influence of your own.

And now farewell, and forget not that the fire which burns, also enlightens.

Section Twenty-one.

Thursday, Oct. 6, 1853.

This evening the circle met at my library. It was written:

There are some parts of the Bible which evidence the profound knowledge which the spirits who dictated it had of human nature. One passage in particular is not only expressive, but it comes to the very doors of our hearts, and knocks for entrance. I refer to the passage where it is said, "Come now, and let us reason together." This is indeed an appeal to the higher attributes of mind. It suggests at once the ability to comprehend all that was designed we should know, and it also suggests the necessity that the ability to reason should also extend to examination.

In referring back to all that has been revealed to you in
spirit-intercourse, much, you will observe, has been said
on the subject of spirit-examination; and it has been
required of you, that you should not only ponder upon the
truths which have been taught you, but that the very principles laid down as the guides of opinion should also be
recognized as the rules of *action*. It was not the whole
design of either God, in the action under his laws, or of the
spirits as the instruments of their execution, that spirit-
intercourse should benefit man by what was revealed of
the condition of spirits after the death of the body, or that
man should derive happiness from the knowledge that he
would positively meet with the loved ones who had
journeyed on a little while before. But it was the intention to communicate to the world by this means the necessity that the spirit in the body should be under the same
laws as the spirit out of the body. It is certainly true that
to most of our race the absolute knowledge of the demands
of their spirit-nature is as unknown to themselves as if
they existed in the bodies of the brute creation around
them. They are unacquainted with either the form or the
complexion of that eternal principle which animates their
organization. They do not know whether it be black or
white, and yet they would fain believe that it is indeed
fair and beautiful.

Strange though it is, what to their consciousness should
be distinctly understood, is a sort of dim reality. They
feel an impulse, but they know not the source from which
it emanates.

To the spirits in the spheres the reflex of thought is met
at once. The thought stands distinct on the very countenance. The soul feels its own attributes, it receives its own
prerogatives, and it manifests its rights by an independent
manifestation of its powers to feel and act. What should
prevent man in the form from aiming at the same ability
to manifest the pure indications of his thoughts, desires,
aspirations, hopes, joys, sorrows, and all the phenomena

of spirit-action on its own matter? Why should it be the strongest effort of men to conceal their emotions, and thus to deceive others as to the true purpose? Let us reason.

To the merest child the thought is often suggested, What am I made for? What is the purpose of my creation? If this is a child's thought, it is one worth the careful consideration of developed man, what indeed is the design of our existence? Were our existence to terminate on earth, and the body, when it is given to the dust, was there to lie, and no principle to spring from it to live forever, it would seem to be the purpose of its creation that it was to live and enjoy all that this earth affords for pleasure or happiness; that its enjoyments should be entirely confined to earth, and that its thoughts should be limited by the surface and extent of that globe on which it lived. True it is, that if the body were created alone to live and die, that the life on earth should conform to the law of its existence, that its aspirations should be limited to the objects which impressed its senses, and that there should not be one manifestation beyond the material condition in which it is placed.

On the contrary, the spirit which exists in the body is not satisfied with its material connections. It sighs for a more extended communication; and the rudest savage, when he views the glorious orbs rolling in the space above, feels the longing of his soul to know something that shall give him proof of what they are. To him, the wind, as it passes, whispers thoughts of the world beyond, dark and shadowy though it be. The glorious sun dazzles his sight and reveals to his spirit the awful grandeur of the power which created it. The murmuring brook, as it gambols o'er its rocky bed, utters thoughts to his darkened mind which struggle to be comprehended. Ay! in the savage, wild as the very beast which he pursues for his sustenance, is a living evidence of the demands of spirit to make itself recognized. But to civilized man the question is already

answered.   He questions not the soul's existence, he
denies not that that soul is to live forever.   No.   The
savage struggling in the darkness of ignorance strives to
reconcile the demands of spirit to the evidences of his
existence.   But civilized man, recognizing what these
demands are, is striving to conceal the true properties of
that soul by a demonstration of every thing else but its
true attributes.

What, then, is the object of this teaching?

That man should not only " reason together," but reason
with himself, and demonstrate to himself the claims which
his spirit has, not only to the things of this world, but to
the things which are unseen, but recognized as true.

I have felt it my duty to say thus much to-night, for I
wish you to all understand than no man here can progress
either in the estimation of his fellow-man without he impresses the world with the sincerity and truth of his intentions, nor can progress hereafter without he carries his
soul in his hand, open to the inspection of all, spotless,
pure, and without blemish.   No man can see the awful
glories of the spheres, if he is not indeed without guile.

This lesson refers to your life as well as ours.

BACON.

Section Twenty-two.

Friday, Oct. 7, 1853.

Early this evening in my library, while the Doctor and I were talking, he was strongly influenced to write, and I judged from the vehemence of the manifestations that it was an unprogressed spirit; and I advised him to resist the influence, which he did successfully. I now inquired if there was any one, now present, who had been there? It was answered:

No; not one spirit.

I said, That was queer. It was written:

No; not queer, for we were all absent.

I remarked, that I surely could not have been left alone?
Then it was written:

Yes. One spirit just now says he was here, and that you were and are surrounded by a host of dark spirits contriving their nefarious designs to manifest themselves. That spirit was Voltaire; he says that in a few days he will confer with you through Mrs. S.

I inquired, Is there no way for me to get rid of this annoying influence?
It was answered:

You do not want to, for there is a design for good in all this.

I said, Then I am indeed becoming crucified.
It was written:

Yes, and fortified, too, Judge.

I remarked, that it made me suspicious, and took away from me my freedom and ease of action in regard to communing.
[Thus far the handwriting was that of Sweedenborg. Now, in Bacon's, it was written.].

Move just as before, my friend, for are we not all with you? Your own judgment is and must be the guide; for we design that out of this darkness you shall bring forth a marvelous light.

I said something about the wisdom with which the matter had been guided, for this manifestation of dark spirits was necessary to enable me to teach both sides of the question, and they had been withheld until I had been prepared and fitted to receive them.

It was written:

That is it exactly. Had it come before your internal was developed, you would have confounded the two kinds of manifestations.

Section Twenty-three.

Saturday, Oct. 8, 1853.

This evening, through Dr. Dexter, in my library, it was written:

THERE is something of higher interest connected with spirit-manifestation than the mere appearance of spirits, either through the raps or visions, or other methods of communication. To every living being there is innately a desire to be satisfied of the truth of the immortality of the soul. But this fact, once demonstrated to the mind, will not satisfy the desire still existent, or avail him, when he shall have entered the spheres, if with the knowledge that the soul shall live forever it is not prepared to live in purity and in the glorious garb of progressive truth. In this view, therefore, there is something more necessary for man than a mere belief in the validity of all he sees and hears from spirits.

There is something of far more importance than that he can relate to others, the very wonderful things he has witnessed—that the spirits have accomplished for his sake. This something is the positive realization of the truth of what spirits teach, and the positive belief that in his action under these teachings his welfare here, and his happiness hereafter, are to be enhanced.

A mere belief in any subject is of no consequence if it does not work out within ourselves a radical change in all the acts of our lives. Thus a man may believe that a part of his fellow-creatures are suffering from famine, but of what avail, if this belief does not prompt him to assist them by every means in his power? There is nothing strange in the communication of spirits with the world. You appreciate the manifestations of mind in an individual living in Europe, and you feel the truth of principles emanating from persons of whom you have had no previous knowledge ; and you admit that a grain of wheat can and will grow when placed in the ground, but why it does so you can not tell. Thus are you conscious that your spirit is impressed from other causes than those with which you come materially in contact.

How often have either of you realized thoughts when you could not trace the source from whence they emanated? Thus are you surrounded with many evidences of mystery in daily life for which you find it impossible to account. It is of no consequence how you explain the mind's action. You are not alone to judge of its action in that which is educated, but you are to take the innate promptings and yearnings of the spirit and the phenomena that come, as it were, without cause; for who has not, when sitting alone, felt positively that some one was present with him ; and who has not experienced, when impressed with a sense of some evil foreboding, that the evil has fallen on him in some form or shape, and that his spirit recognized the warning as coming from the other world? These are trite and simple illustrations, but they are nevertheless pertinent evidences that the soul holds intercourse with the spirit-world without the cognizance of the senses. Then why—if this should be so—should it appear so strange that matter can mingle with matter, and the senses recognize that spirits can communicate?

But, after all, what is the whole of this revelation? It is this: that there is a necessity that the heart and the desires, the thought and the act, should be purified by what is taught you.

Oh! my friends, could you but know all that is before you; could you see the effect of a life of sin in the flesh, when the spirit leaves the form, and takes up its abode here, then would you see that sin or evil enters, as it were, into the very constituents of the soul here; that it dims the luster of its original brightness, and that it prevents its onward aspirations. Are you to rest satisfied with believing that what is seen or heard is true? Are you Spiritualists? Spiritualists? Yes, indeed, your spirit is dissatisfied with a life of matter bound to earth by ties that change its heavenly nature, and mark it as unfit for the company of those who are bright, pure, and happy.

What are your thoughts? Do you love? Yes. Do you love not only on this earth, but do you send the affections in advance onward through the spheres and love what there is and will be? Are you cautious in injuring the feelings of others? Are you strong in adhering to your own opinions? For truth's sake, are you ready to crucify all that is unholy in your natures, and trust for a recompense in life and death?

Oh! I charge you, foster the affections, but be mindful that you are at all times liable to receive a wrong direction to those feelings—the noblest of your nature—by those who are constantly on the alert to deceive you.

If you are believers in spirits, believe that what they teach of truth and righteousness, a judgment to come, is as true as the very God who created you, and that the whole object of all that is given you is to elevate your natures, purify your hearts, and fit you for an inheritance where moth nor rust shall corrupt, and where thieves can not break through and steal.

Much has been said lately about self-examination, and the spirits feel that they could not do their duty without again asking you, What of your hearts? is it well with them? Is there no evil thought or purpose? God bless you all.   SWEEDENBORG

Section Twenty-four.

Sunday, Oct. 9, 1853.

The circle met at Dr. Dexter's. It was written:

I have mentioned several times lately that if any person present has questions to propose, to do so, and it seems that the object I had in making this suggestion is not understood. I say again to-night, if any one has any question to ask let him ask it now.   BACON.

Mr. Sweet asked a question about the existence of matter, and whether it was not coeval with God?
It was answered:

Matter being eternal does not prove that it was from the beginning with God. It exists eternally.

What idea have you of God? Is he a personage or a principle?
It was answered:

God is a principle, and also an identity. If God was from the beginning, and in him was all knowledge, power, and wisdom, it must have been through these attributes that every thing was created. To suppose that matter existed *ab initio*, would confer on an unconscious substance the same properties that belong to God, especially if he did not create it, or at least, existing at the same time with him, it would have had a creator antecedent to God who possessed more power than he did or does.

One remark is true, that God pervades every thing. But listen. ' Let the mind go back to that period when the Spirit of the First Cause sprang forth, self-created, and in all the glory of his might and majesty. Imagine, that standing alone amid the everlasting space, he looks around and sees nothing existent but an infinite nothing, and then suppose him creating from his own body the several properties which constitute matter, and from another principle developing spirit.

If the mind can grasp this idea, how much opposed to all the fundamental principles we have taught would it be! But when you realize the existence of a cause to which is known to belong all the requirements of matter, and all the laws which would develop it, you feel satisfied that in this principle of development you have a starting-ground or basis on which to predicate opinion.

There is no more difficulty to an enlightened mind in supposing God just as capable of developing the constituents of matter as he is of creating any new form out of the matter now existing. It is the self-same principle of progress; and it may not be amiss to inform you at this time, that among many spirits of high estate there are many who believe God himself the product of developed intelligence. How this may be *I* can not say, but this is the opinion of many here.

When I say that in the whole of my life, of near three hundred years in the spheres, I have never found one spirit who can explain what the principle God is, and how created and existing, or how he created matter, you will see at once how little is known on the subject here.

Then it was written to me:

If you have the courage we will show you the whole

object of the presence of the dark spirits. But you must be firm and strong and battle vigorously, for the sight will make you tremble when the host shall pass before you. Are you ready?

I answered that after what I had seen lately, I confess I was afraid. It was written:

Then I will give you strength and courage, and your wife will give you purity.

I said, " Then, very well, I am ready," and this is what I saw:

The bright spirits had left us, and the dark ones having discovered that, came in great numbers. Their leader stopped them, he feared that something concealed was intended. But he was reëncouraged by my mood of mind all day, which he had been conscious of, and neither he nor any of his companions seemed to be aware that I could see them. He issued his directions to them how to operate with different members of the circle. One of them came behind me and rapped on my shoulder, thinking that I was deceived as to who it was.

They were very cautious and stealthy in their approach, as if fearing to wake us from slumber.

They presented to my view first a female in the form of one whom I knew right well. She was bland, soft, pleasant in her manner. But I saw into her eyes, deep down into her head, and they seemed like burning coals of fire, in the black mass of the brain. The sight of those eyes was most revolting. She little thought I saw beneath the exterior, but I did, for I saw both her heart and brain. The former was like a boiling caldron of black poison, bubbling up from the fierce fires that were burning beneath it.

It was really a female, and a ruling spirit among them, and if ever there was a devil, surely she was one.

Finding that in this form she affected me not, she assumed that of a little child of two years old, with golden locks and of fair complexion. But amid it all were those eyes of fire, which, it seemed, could not be hidden from me. Imagine that lovely child, with its look of innocence, its soft and clear complexion, "like a rose leaf crushed on ivory," and those eyes of fire shining through it all!

She had studied my character well I saw, and had approached me in two of my weak spots already. I wondered where next her assault would be directed. It was to my love of splendor. For next she came in the form of a queen of stately mien, with her crown on her head, and dazzling in jewelry. She came in her chariot, drawn by four stately horses, and surrounded by her guards in glowing uniforms. She invited me to a seat by her side, to enjoy with her the splendor of the world which was all before me. But she was unaware that those infernal eyes shone out amid it all and warned me to beware. I could see in her a cool, concentrated hatred of me, but kept under her control, and as she thought, concealed from me.

She wondered I was so callous, so impervious to her assaults, as I had before yielded to them, and she became very much enraged at her failure.

When they first came near, they stationed some of their companions around off in the distance, to watch and give them warning of the first approach of the brighter spirits. And now this female, surprised at her defeat, and suspecting that some of the brighter spirits might be near influencing me, inquired of the sentries if they discovered any? and one after another they answered, No.

My attention was thus called to the outskirts, if I may so call it, of this circle of dark spirits, and I saw that there was hanging over them a dark cloud, like a heavy thundercloud in our atmosphere, with loose, jagged fragments hanging down, and a dark, lurid light thrown upon it of a dull, burning red—a horrible light, and very uncomfortable. I suppose they must feel as we do at times when a thunder shower is approaching, only ten times as intense, for there is no bursting of the cloud and clearing the air for them. How close and oppressive that air must be!

As I turned to look back, I saw that the female had descended from her carriage, the splendor of her garb was gone, and she wore now, instead, a dark-colored, close-fitting frock, which trailed upon the ground.

They seemed to be waiting for some one to come, and they were far more deliberate and cool in their actions than I fancied they would be. While they were consulting, a spirit came and said he had been with me all day, and he detailed to them the influence he had exerted over me, and had brought me to the point nearly of quarreling with the Doctor, but he said it was not too late yet.

One thing they said among themselves was, " He has been striving all his life long to win the good opinions of his fellow-men, and is very sensitive to every mark of disrespect. He boasts he can stand the withdrawal of their good opinion. Let him feel this neglect everywhere. Let the world put slights upon him. He is not as strong as he thinks he is ;" and, he added, with a fiendish laugh, "if we can not make him flinch, we can make him suffer."

I noticed on the right side of me some spirits who were conversing of the Doctor and me. One of them who took the lead in the conversation was tall and thin, with a hooked nose and large, prominent chin. I had seen him before, but I could not remember where. With what bitterness he hated the Doctor, and me, and all mankind. He had been very selfish in this world, and had been eminently successful in amassing wealth and power, but found now that all was in vain. He had lived in vain, for his wealth and power were gone, and he hated alike God and man, for it seemed to him that he was now destined to live forever in that dark society, without hope of amelioration or end to his sad life. He told his companions that he had been with the Doctor and me, and that we had been almost ready to quarrel. They must yet bring that about, but it must be done adroitly, for we had been forewarned, and were on our guard. One of that party, I perceived, had a personal hostility to the Doctor. I described his appearance, but the Doctor could not recognize him.

I soon perceived that their whole plan of operations had been concerted, and the task divided among them. One was to excite our irritability and embroil us, if possible, with each other and with others, to make us jealous, impatient, angry.

Each one's share of the task was distributed to him by a spirit of much activity, who floated around over the heads of the party telling each his part. I perceived that some of those spirits were influenced by a general feeling of hatred, and a desire to put a stop to that which they know will benefit mankind. Others were influenced by an emotion of jealousy toward those who believe this new doctrine, and who enjoy a privilege which had been denied to them. They saw no end to their condition. They thought that it was eternal, and they recognized no reason why we should have what they did not possess. Some of them I saw had the same personal feelings of enmity they had on earth, and some were angry because we had not been so easily moved by them as others had been.

The spirit who was passing around giving instructions came to a knot of five or six, who seemed from their garb and manner to have been priests. They were very much despised, even by that dark assemblage. They seemed to feel mean, degraded, and trodden upon, for all treated them with contempt. And it was no wonder, for they had been hypocrites on earth; mere sensuous men, very material in their nature, and did not believe the doctrines they taught, nor did they suppose that any one else believed them, and they thought that as some form of religion was necessary among men, theirs had been devised. They found, now, how sad a mistake they had made, but they knew no remedy. They were too much cowed and dispirited to act, and seemed too stupid to understand the instructions given them. They answered, by saying listlessly, "What can we do?" The directing spirit turned from them with undisguised contempt.

At this moment my attention was called to what was directly over my head, and which I had not before noticed. There I saw the devil, if there is one. Yet he, like the others, had lived as a mortal once on earth. He was floating directly over me, on the lower edge of that dark and lowering cloud. He was calm, composed, stern, and resolute. He was alone in his elevation, and looked down with contempt even upon those who were most slavishly carrying out his plans. There was great determination of character displayed in his face, yet his exterior was remarkably calm. He seemed to have a faint suspicion that I was seeing him, and he attempted to hide his eyes from my sight by shading them with his hand. He did not succeed, for I saw his eyes, and through them down into his brain, and while with all the others the eyes seemed to be two glowing coals of fire, his whole brain seemed to be a furiously raging furnace, filled with a blazing red flame. How that raging fire was ever tormenting him! yet he covered it with that calm exterior, like the fires of Ætna raging beneath its snow-capped summit. And while he calmly looked on the bustling, moving crowd below, formed plans for them, and superintended their execution, he rejoiced that in it all he could find pleasure—in the success of his plans by our suffering and fall, and in the failure of them by their rage and disappointment.

I saw in the crowd a spirit whom I had seen before. He was fantastic in his appearance and actions, yet filled with hate, and incessantly active. He was dressed to represent the devil as he is often painted by man. He wore a cap, which, close fitting to his head, was ornamented with what seemed two horns. His feet were so dressed that they seemed to be cloven, and he had appended to him the appearance of wings and a tail. He was very dark and somber, and around his mouth he had painted red streaks, so that when he opened it and thrust out his huge tongue his appearance was most disgusting. He seemed to be the harlequin of the group, yet never paused in his intense and bitter hate.

One of their plans was most horrible. It was to work upon one of my children till she should be made insane, and then throw her into a trance, so that fancying her dead, I might have her buried, and afterward discover that I had buried her alive! A plan so hellish and over which they gloated, made me shudder and grow sick.

I saw that the spirit who floated around giving orders returned again to the knot of priests, and told them they must influence their brother priests on earth to carry out their plans. They answered him, with a feeling of weakness and despondency, that "It was of no use, the clergy on earth would not dare to do it, for fear they might lose their situations." That directing spirit turned from them again, with utter scorn, exclaiming, "Miserable devils! incapable alike of Good or Evil." I saw that all the other spirits kept aloof from them, and that while all the others were actively engaged and conversing with each other, they stood silent, listless, useless, and desponding.

I saw that one of their plans was to affect our healths, which they boasted they could do, by means of their magnetism.

They subjected the whole company to a very rigid scrutiny, for they saw that their former plans had been betrayed to us by some one, and they denounced the severest vengeance against the one who did that. It was manifest to me, that they were not at all aware that I was seeing them.

Here it was written through the Doctor:

Let the circle now sit still and see the manner in which the bright spirits enter, and hear the explanation of all that has been revealed, and how it is to be thwarted.

Then I saw penetrating through that dark cloud a brilliant light come, driving it back and scattering those dark spirits in all directions. It came like a blazing, brilliant sun, in circles of light, their edges, blue, crimson, and purple, and floating in it were innumerable bright and happy spirits. In its center was Sweedenborg again, with his book and breastplate, and the room was filled with bright spirits.

And I was told that their fiendish plans can be defeated by our own purity, and that to our own efforts we must owe our purity and our protection.

Directly over Sweedenborg appeared two spirits, bearing a scroll on which was written: "The Truth against the World." Sweedenborg pointed up to it, and the scene slowly faded from my view.

Section Twenty-five.

Thursday, Oct. 13th, 1853.

This evening, at my library, all the circle were present, with the addition of General Bullard, of Waterford. It was suggested by Mr. Sweet that a particular course of manifestations, which he pointed out, should be pursued, and in answer it was written:

It is sometimes, when all the spirits are assembled here for the purpose of carrying out a certain plan, almost impossible to arrange the magnetic current so as to communicate freely, and it ought to be understood that when the higher spirits come to your circle, really to do good, the absence of any member positively interferes with the whole order of manifestation. Certainly, therefore, it is of importance that each member should be present, unless detained by sickness, and that no ordinary excuse should be given or received unless a high and noble duty prevents attendance.

Spirits come from afar, and leave their happy homes to visit you. They forego many pleasures to do you good, and they are invariably here. How much they are disappointed at finding the circle incomplete, we leave you to judge; but the fact must be told, that they can not communicate, and when the order of communication is established, to interfere in any way to break up the concerted plan, causes a desultory teaching to result instead of those for our second volume.

Let this, therefore, be rectified, and let every member feel obliged to be present, except sickness or some imperative duty prevents.   BACON.

If, therefore, any members of the circle can not attend, or will suffer slight circumstances to prevent attendance, make your arrangements without reference to them; as I am now directed to say, that in consequence of the non-attendance of members, from whom much was and is expected, some spirits have discontinued their visits to you, who would have given much that would have been of invaluable benefit to the whole world.

Friends, 'tis no slight matter to drive away a spirit, in fact, to grieve him so as to prevent his utterance of that which is of so much importance to know; and could you see the feeling which now disturbs the spirits to-night, you would feel that this duty was the most important of that which influences your whole life. Your circle must establish a ready and active current, so that all kinds of revelations may be made. You are standing still instead of progressing. Why is this so? Think and answer.

This morning many spirits met in this room to consult about the condition of this circle. Among the many things which have retarded the advance of the circle as a whole was what has been mentioned, but there are others, and I must say, that your own feelings have not been right and true. Let the circle individually ask the question of themselves, Have I, by my feelings, retarded my own and the circle's advance? and you will see what will be the answer. We feel grieved that there exists among those for whom we have striven to do so much, any feelings which ought not to be fostered or entertained.

What are our objects and purposes? Why are we here? Oh! if you wish to stand on the mountain's height and overlook the whole prospect of life here and hereafter, cherish no unkind feelings, thrust from your hearts thoughts which cloud the prospect and dim the brightness of the future. We know what you think; every feeling of your souls is open to our view, strive to conceal them as you may. But they stand out to our ken as distinct as though you gave them utterance. Do you think that in your acts you do not manifest feelings? And have your acts been characterized by that high principle of love you profess to believe and cherish? ·

It is no pleasant task to speak in this manner, but we chasten for your good and for the good of the cause. Let but one evil thought or purpose be entertained or executed, and the whole cause must suffer, and perhaps be retarded for years!

We desire that you may take our lesson as intended, for your good alone, and believe us that in your chastisement is our suffering. We want you to talk this matter up, and arrange some system that we may go on as before.

Imagine to yourselves some twenty spirits from the higher spheres whose magnetism differs from ours. They are here, and while here assist in establishing a current by which all who are designated can communicate. Now, when they find, night after night, the medium indisposed, or unwilling, or absent, their current is disturbed, and they can not teach.

On Sunday last the teaching was entirely different from that intended; the higher spirits wished to communicate, but the medium was not in condition, and another spirit took possession. Another thing, when some of you have staid a certain time you are impatient to go, and it is the case, that when the full circulation of the magnetism is perfectly established that the higher teaching can be given —thus it may be in the latter part of the evening that the most important teachings can come.

For all or for nothing; for every thing or for naught, should be your motto. You can not love God and the world, and in this cause you profess to love God and to carry out the truth as it is revealed by his instruments.

Now your consultations will be of service as they will arouse your thought to the importance of what we say, and you will act accordingly.

Thus far it was Bacon who wrote; now Sweedenborg wrote as follows, in reference to a remark made by one of us, that we hoped they would be patient with us, and let us try to restore the efficiency and usefulness of the circle:

Yes, we are patient. We watch like the stars, whose silvery light is still shedding its mild beams down on the darkened earth, though clouds do intervene and shadow their radiance. We watch the seed we have planted, though the thorns of life spring up and choke their growth. We watch you while engaged in the active business of life, or when your thoughts, turned inward and searching your own hearts, bring up to your own consciousness the truth that you are not perfect. We are patient, for we wait the time when you will develop all that is good and true in your natures. We wait for the ocean in its ceaseless motion to cast up on the shore the inestimable pearls which lie hid in its bosom. We ask you to bear and forbear, to temper your feelings to the condition of feelings as you find them in others. Oh! were not truth omnipotent; were not truth against the world worth waiting and watching for, what use would it be that the spirit waits so long for the golden gates to be opened that it should partake of those joys never, never to cease?

What is life but watching and waiting for that happiness always to come, but never to be found in your world?

Come, then. Let your hearts renew their efforts, and let your spirits unite with ours in a fresh attempt to achieve a victory over self. 'Tis in yourselves you will find the greatest cause for trial. In self is all that retards your progress here or hereafter. The time is not far distant when you will test the truths we have taught, for you will see and feel that in yourselves alone, and by your own efforts, can you work out your salvation.

SWEEDENBORG.

Then it was added by Lord Bacon:

Now, Judge, we will impress you for a few minutes, and give you a new view of spirit in the spheres.

I then saw as follows:

VISION.

Can it be possible that I am right? that I see correctly?

The lesson they are showing me is that the spirits are the instruments of God in controlling and governing the elements!

What I first saw was a comet careering through space with wonderful velocity. It was that velocity which created its light and heat. It was nebulous, composed of many distinct particles attracted to each other, but not yet united—some were left behind it in its rapid flight, and some were lost to its attraction and lagged behind in the immensity of space, losing their motion and light, and remaining inert in space, until again awakened by some exercise of the power of attraction.

The destiny of this nebulous mass is in time, and by the sure and gradual operation of immutable laws, to form a dense globe, and in it are all the elements of such a world as this, from the merest particle of inert matter to the form of man.

The process of its progress I saw was watched over, controlled, and directed by an innumerable host of spirits, that attended it in its course, and whose business it was to correct and restrain all aberrations of that matter from the laws constituted for its government. The very rarefied condition of this matter, with the extreme rapidity of its motion, were calculated to disturb the operation of those laws, and it was the business of the spirits to counteract that. They were the instruments of the Great Creator, charged with the duty and clothed with the power of executing those laws. Not miraculously, nor in contravention or by a suspension of them, but in conformity to them, as in tilling the ground and planting the seed we afford the opportunity for the law of its development to operate.

I saw the spirits performing this duty, some of them floating along outside the nucleus watching, and others inside exceedingly busy. I saw some in the very center of it very active as if something was out of order, and they were engaged in the task of putting it right. I saw, too, that occasionally they required help from others, and immediately received it from those who at the moment were not occupied.

I could not help reflecting what a magnificent fate it must be, thus to career through space and survey the myriads of worlds that filled it!

I was then taken near to this earth of ours, and there I saw—though not as distinctly—the same occupation of spirits in reference to this globe.

At this moment it was written through Dr. Dexter's hand: -

"If you desire, you will see that the spirits engaged in this occupation are such as on earth are occupied in investigating the great laws of nature there, and analyzing and inventing, and by their discoveries assisting the world to understand the laws of God and their action."

Then it was said to me by the spirits:

Do you doubt this? Do you wonder? Think a moment. If one spirit is strong enough to move the Doctor's arm against his will—if one could grip yours and hold it with an iron grasp, from which you could not escape—if a few of them can make the sounds you have heard, and move material bodies as you have witnessed, what must be the united power of the countless millions who, since creation began, have been rolling out into the regions of space from the innumerable storehouses of human life, for ages upon ages beyond the comprehension of man? And they said to me, "Recollect, that when you cast off your material trammels, your nervous power is vastly increased, and it will not be difficult for you to realize this idea as natural and probable." They told me they were intending to show me their operations over the elements here, and they wished it understood that their power was only to execute God's laws, not to create, and to execute according to law, not arbitrarily. Sometimes the execution of the duty was attended with much violence, and that was unavoidable, for they could not always control the elements as they wished. Hence there were tornadoes, hurricanes, etc., and such like disturbances in the elements. The equalization was constantly liable to be disturbed by the operation of other laws arising out of the unprogressed state of the earth—its high mountains, its deep valleys, its great inequalities of surface, and other manifestations of its unprogressed condition. These causes operate to produce these disturbances, and to restore the equilibrium must at times be unavoidably attended with other disturbances. Hence those convulsions, which were more frequent formerly than now, and will be less frequent as the earth progresses to its final development.

To illustrate this, they bore me to the moon, and I was directly over it where I could see its surface distinctly, its high prominences, its deep valleys, its great unevenness of surface, and they said to me, "Do you not see that if the moon had an atmosphere like that of your earth, with the rapidity of its three-fold motion, that atmosphere must be very much disturbed by this inequality of surface? and so too with water, which is but a denser element? Can you not perceive that if the surface of this globe were smooth and level and free from these inequalities, the elements would not be as much disturbed by the motion?" They alluded, they said, to all the elements which go to constitute an inhabitable globe, for all were subject to the same law.

I observed with much minuteness the surface of the moon. I saw no living thing there except a few plants. Sometimes in the crevices of the crumbling rocks, where some little soil had gathered, there were a few specimens of vegetation; but they were large, coarse, low, creeping weeds.

I saw many different colored rocks; some looked like hard slaty rocks—some streaks that seemed to be light-colored granite—some shining and sparkling in veins as if gold and silver—some very black and shining, like anthracite coal.

These things I saw in a vast basin, as it were, like the crater of a volcano, with huge, craggy rocks bounding it on all sides, and jutting far up. I saw no water. Some of the rocks had fallen from the sides and tumbled into the valleys, where they were crumbling. But every thing was dreary, desolate, silent, solitary. The spirit of life had not yet been developed.

I saw, however, that there were fires burning beneath its surface. In one place a dense black smoke ascended, occasionally illumed by a lurid flame that shot up amid the awful desolation of the scene.

They told me then to turn my eyes, and from where I was to view the earth. It seemed a monstrous ball of pale light, but quite different from the appearance of the moon to us, in this, that it did not show the great inequalities of surface of the moon, but more like Jupiter with its belts, occasioned by the workings of its atmosphere.

The size appeared so much larger than the moon does to us, that it seemed to me as if it were nearer.

As I noticed it, I saw spirits also accompanying it in its round, employed as they were on the comet. I saw, too, that our earth in its course left behind it a tail like the comet, but much more sublimated and almost invisible to me. That was the denser and more impure parts of our atmosphere, which were thrown off in its course. As each individual on earth is constantly imbibing from the atmosphere around him the element of vitality, and throwing off such portions of it as are not incorporated into his system, so the earth, in passing through space, is constantly imbibing the elements of vitality for its atmosphere, and throwing off such portions as are useless.

The same law operates throughout all creation, springing from and guided by the same Wisdom. And thus the space through which the earth moves is the great storehouse from which its atmosphere is constantly replenished, as in its turn our atmosphere, is the storehouse whence man's vitality is replenished.

I saw that the moon had some atmosphere, but too inconsiderable in amount to permit the existence of life, except a few of the lowest and least developed plants.

I saw, too, that our atmosphere was more dense near the earth, and more rarefied step by step, without any definite termination, though there was a point beyond which it could not be detected by mortal observation.

The spirits who floated in the outer and more rarefied portions seemed to me to be brighter and of a higher order than those who herded nearer the surface of the earth. The latter were darker and more heavy, more sluggish. Many of them seemed afflicted with a sort of listless indifference as if they had no purpose, no object in view. They seemed to be unhappy, and to wonder if they were created for that and nothing else. They looked upon the earth, as they floated with it along near its surface, with a strong attachment to it—with a burning desire to be again on it, but with a consciousness that that could not be, and that they were separated from it forever. Their condition was very unhappy—some were angry at it, some sorrowful, and they were quite unconscious of the nearness to them of those brighter spirits, for they could not see them any more than we can. I saw a marked contrast between the two classes. The brighter ones frequently clustered together, assisted one another, and were happy. The darker ones most commonly wandered alone, but would sometimes cluster together, and then quarrels and jarrings among themselves were ever there. Their feelings were very bad, and they vented them on each other. And I saw occasionally that a brighter spirit would dart, with the celerity of thought, through the denser parts of the atmosphere and the ever-wandering crowd of darker spirits, down to earth's surface to hold holy communion with man.

Section Twenty-six.

Sunday, Oct. 16*th*, 1853.

This evening the circle met at my library, and after a brief communication through Mrs. Sweet, in relation to our harmony, in which Mr. S. made some suggestions as to our mode of proceeding, it was written :

SINCE the formation of this circle there has been but one instance of a want of harmony, and this only for a few moments. It becomes those spirits who originally met with you to answer the suggestion made, and we do so plainly, because it is not that one, two, or three of you might be influenced, and thus affect the minds of others. For the truths we desire to teach, for the good we hope to accomplish, we wish the method we pursue should be understood and appreciated by all. You are all working for one object, and it matters not who is influenced if the teaching reaches the design we wish carried out.

If one of you is under influence, it does not and can not affect another magnetically; that is, it will not interrupt the exhibition through another; but if your minds are disturbed, the disturbance arises from yourselves, and can in no sense change the intent of the communication going on.

We can not lay down any given plan of action at the commencement of a meeting; for though the great principles are laid out and we act on them, yet to say that we will do so and so, might place us in an awkward condition, as we might not be able to fulfill what we say we will do. The very best teachings and visions through the Doctor, Judge, and Mrs. S. were given, as it were, impromptu; and though there are many bright spirits here from the higher spheres who purpose to reveal through all of you, yet we find that sometimes one spirit can influence, and then another, and then another, and so on. We commence working on you from the moment you are seated till you leave, and it often requires hours to place you in such a state as we can freely communicate with you. Thus, again, the bright spirits may not be able to come here till late, and then we must use the means we have till they come. You see, therefore, how we are situated, and you will remember that we shall not disturb you by any thing we do if you will not allow your own minds to operate and disturb yourselves. We, on the whole, will judge what to do, and we will direct you properly; therefore leave to us the arrangement, and you shall be directed right, etc., etc.

BACON.

There are spirits here who wish to give the Judge a vision, and it will be the brightest and most gorgeous he has ever witnessed. Therefore, for a few moments, talk and relieve yourselves, and then hear the vision. We shall allow you forty minutes, and you must talk right up to the matter seen without prolixity, as we mean to go the rounds.

Then came this

VISION.

Away off in the regions of space, as if in the midst of the starry firmament, I saw a bright and majestic spirit sitting in a sort of throne, which was placed on a fleecy, white cloud. A few feet above his head reposed a wreath of flowers, from whence flowed rays of light to his head, forming, as it were, a crown of light and flowers. He had on a loose garment, beautifully variegated with blue and pink, and ornamented with purple velvet, which sparkled as with diamonds. His left hand rested on a globe, on the arm of his seat, from which radiated a golden light, indicative of affection. On the right arm of his chair was a similar globe, radiating a silver light, indicating wisdom. His right arm was raised, and he pointed me to a distant view. He was evidently of a higher command, in the execution of God's laws, than any I had yet seen. Far beneath him were innumerable stars of all sizes careering through space, and apparently gamboling in the exuberance of their joy. At first the scene seemed to me one of great disorder; but as I gazed, I saw how all was order and harmony. I saw many spirits coming to and going from him, as if with messages—coming as from the distant stars, and vanishing in space with inconceivable rapidity.

While I gazed, I saw a very bright light, most gorgeous, like a blazing sun, approaching him from behind, and forming a background to him. The rays of it were ever shooting out from its center various hues, yet it seemed formed of numberless concentric rings of different colors. I can convey no adequate idea of its glorious splendor.

That light was the central sun of all those systems of worlds I saw beneath his feet, and he was the high and holy intelligence that governed their action in obedience to the laws of God.

He arose from his seat, and leaning on it with one arm, he pointed me with the other off to his right. There I saw a bright and dazzling spirit with no clothing upon him, but shining like burnished silver. He was floating in the blue ethereal, and seemed a great storehouse of dazzling light, which he was scattering from him in all directions.

I saw that he was superior to the other spirit, yet I felt as if there was a sense of solitude about him, and that he had no companions. He replied to my thought by spreading out his hands and saying, "These worlds are my companions; my solitude is peopled by myriads of shining intelligences."

He pointed me to other systems of worlds far off in the illimitable distance, and immense in number. He seemed to be the apex of a cone; spreading out and beneath him were the worlds which he governed, whose guide and director he was. He pointed me to one still higher than himself, his superior in power and wisdom. Of that one I saw only the head.

The great lesson taught by these scenes is the occupation of the spirits, one above another, in their career of progression—each greater than the other, and executing God's laws on a larger scale and in a higher sphere.

Through the Doctor's hand it was here written:

"This is one process of development. Watch and see his form rising from that brilliant cloud of lambent flame. This personifies truth as developed to minds prepared to receive it. You never, perhaps, may see any thing so brilliant and gorgeous again. Let the circle be particularly silent, and let their minds turn to this subject."

The vision proceeded:

There arose up from beneath this bodiless spirit a beautiful rose-colored, flame-like cloud, in the center of which appeared a magnificent temple enveloped in this rose-colored light.   It was indeed a glorious sight, which language is inadequate to describe.

The temple was surrounded by a great number of spirits, with musical instruments in their hands, and from them arose a flood of music, far surpassing any thing ever heard by mortal ears.   The building had a Doric roof, and stood high up from its base.   It was ascended by a flight of many steps, extending across the whole front.   There were three rows of columns on each side, of infinite variety of colors; they were not Doric in form, but tall and slender, and somewhat of the Ionic order.   This temple was open at its sides, and its pavement and columns shone with a brilliant, sparkling gleam amid that rose-colored atmosphere.

On each side of the building was a glorious garden, variegated with water, shrubbery, and flowers, equally dazzling in their brilliancy.   The leaves of the flowers and plants were transparent, yet shone with a glitter like the ice-plant, or as if covered with frost in the morning sun. The water was now a calm and placid pool, now a bubbling stream, now a jet, and anon a tumbling fall.   The flowers were of all possible colors, and I could see their perfume arise from them and mingle with the atmosphere. At the same I could see the plants drinking in, through their leaves, the life-principle from the atmosphere, and giving it out sublimated and refined as perfume.   Those plants were in all stages of development, so that it seemed as if spring and summer, conjoined, reigned there forever. There was every variety of foliage and shady trees, now dense, dark and cool, and now sparse and transparent.   The water was full of fishes, gamboling in the joyousness of life in such pure waters, and the air was full of birds, rendering it beautiful with their plumage, and vocal with their song.   One bird I noticed in particular; he was brown and plain in look, and as he reposed on a limb of one of the trees, he sent up his joyous song, ringing clear over all other sounds—its notes like the softest flute, expressive of happiness, and imparting a feeling of gladness to all around.

The basement of the temple, I saw, was prepared and fitted up for a room in which public meetings were to be held. At one end of it was the seat of the presiding spirit. It was the precise, tomb-like monument of myself that I had seen once before, on which was recorded my age when I died. Back of that, on the wall, was a picture of that cross in the sky, which I had seen with its attendant spirit and its scrolls. Beneath that picture was my new seal painted, and on each side two other seals; they consisted of shields with emblazonry. One had a cross-bar running diagonally, above which was the scene of the good Samaritan; and below a bright spirit, who was lifting a slave from the ground and knocking off his chains. The scroll beneath the shield contained these words: "Love conquers all things." This was Doctor Dexter's coat of arms; the other was Mr. Warren's. It was quartered by bars crossing each other at right-angles. In one quarter was a shepherd surrounded by his flock; he was reclining under a tree, and examining the starry firmament. In the second quarter was a man far down in a deep pit, and examining the formation of the rock and earth. In the third, a man reading; and in the fourth, one with crucibles, and other chemical apparatus. The inscription here was, " Knowledge is Progressive."

That end of the room was gorgeous and beautiful. Between the shields were columns of just proportions, and richly carved; and between the columns hung full and flowing drapery of various colors, tastefully blended, hanging in festoons very light and graceful.

Along the sides of the room were suspended many banners of various colors, with blazonry on them; one feature was that they were not dusty or dingy, as they are apt to be with us.

On the other side of the building the garden had a deeper shade and a more dense foliage than in that part which I have already described, and it terminated in a gentle slope, from the summit of which was exposed to view a landscape exquisitely lovely and very extensive. It was variegated by towers and palaces, and stately mansions, by water, deep groves, and green fields, and all seen by that soft, rosy light, and seeming to be full to overflowing with joy and gladness.

In the garden were statues, and grottoes, and summer bowers, and rustic seats. In one place was a gigantic bronze statue, with a lofty, benevolent countenance; one hand was outstretched, pointing upward, and with the other it was raising up a dark-colored mortal who was groveling in the dust, and was rising, yet reluctant.

In a lovely and deeply-shaded bower was a group of white statuary, with the dark-green foliage for a background. It represented a female lying on a bed, and dying. She was old, and ragged, and haggard; all the surroundings denoted destitution and want. Her clothes were tattered, her hair disheveled, and her countenance showed much bodily suffering, yet it had a lofty and elevated expression, as if her mind was rising above, and was unconscious of her suffering. By her side stood a female holding one of her hands, and pointing upward with a look of hope and love that was inexpressibly touching.

This I learned was the residence of that spirit whose head alone I saw; now I was able to see its whole form; it was that of a female, and was so light and ethereal that it was transparent.

I returned back from this scene, and approached again the spirit with the silver light, and there I saw its home; it was like a Saracenic temple, and was enveloped in a mingled light of silver hue and pure blue. It had points to its several gables, but its arches were circular, and there were small pinnacled towers at each corner. In the rear of the building was a battlemented tower, from which floated to the breeze the ample folds of a white flag, having on it a red cross.

Section Twenty-seven.

Thursday, Oct. 20*th*, 1853.

The circle met this evening. There was no manifestation through Dr. Dexter, and through Mrs. Sweet there was a brief one, which was of moment only as it foreshadowed her development.

Almost as soon as we got seated, I began to feel the influence, and saw the spirits that surrounded the circle. After a while the cordon of spirits opened at one spot and showed me in the distance a great number of them, who were attracted to us, some by curiosity, some to learn, and some to communicate and teach.

I was soon taken up that opening and passed away some distance, until I seemed very small. Here I was required to stop and look back on the world I had left, and behold how insignificant were its joys compared with those of my spirit-companions! how dark and gloomy its life compared with the light and happiness which surrounded them! and it was said to me, "Think not then of man's unkindness, but be thankful that you have admittance to a world where your purposes can be understood, the good you aim at be appreciated, and any sacrifices you may be required to make, will meet their reward."

It was a bright and beautiful spirit who said this to me. His garb was a beautiful crimson gown, long, loose, and loating. It had a belt, cuffs, collar, and hems of embroidered gold-work, and over it all was a thin, gossamer-like garment, as if it was an atmosphere of a pale-blue color, which was transparent and ever moving like living flame. He had long, gray hair, falling in curls to his shoulders. His countenance was very intellectual and evinced great firmness, as if he could stand unmoved amid a conflict of worlds.

His affectionate manner toward me was very touching. It was like a mother drawing close up to her her child to protect it from harm. He was surrounded by many bright spirits, who regarded him with great reverence. He was a very benevolent man. I had never seen him before, and was impressed that it was Washington.

He said to me, "'Tis for man's emancipation you strive, and it will be attained; in the knowledge that it has been attained, and in some degree by your instrumentality, you will find your reward; and when hereafter the incense of the grateful hearts of millions of redeemed spirits shall ascend before you, you will appreciate what my joy is in being hailed by an immense nation of freemen as the Father of His Country."

He said, "Though it is long since I spoke to you, I have been often with you, and have not been unmindful of your progress or your action. And, oh! heed not the hostility of weak or wicked men; for as the freedom of our country was achieved through many difficulties and many dark and gloomy trials, so through similar discomfitures will this work be completed, in the redemption of our country from the thralldom of the bigotry and superstition which the darkened ages of the past have transmitted to the present as its inheritance. Then fear not, falter not, but onward! Be calm, be dispassionate, be firm, and rely upon it, that the sun of righteousness, while it will quicken into life the seeds of truth which you may sow while living, will brighten with verdure the grave where you'll sleep."

While this was said to me, I seemed to be at such a distance from the earth that it seemed to be a partly luminous ball of two or three miles in diameter.

By the side of this spirit I saw those of La Fayette and Tecumseh.

I returned slowly to earth through the dense ranks of

spirits who lined my path on both sides. .They gave me, as I passed, many smiles of cheering encouragement. Among them I recognized many acquaintances. One was my mother, who blessed me as I paused before her, and reminded me of her dying moments, that she had said to me, as I sat by her side, "John, I am dying," and I had answered, "Yes, mother, you are going to reap the reward of a life well spent."

I then returned to the circle.

Section Twenty-eight.

Thursday, Oct. 27th, 1853.

The circle met this evening at my library. There were three persons present as visitors.

Through the Doctor's hand it was written:

WE wish to try an experiment, that is, to impress both you and Mrs. Sweet together, and to teach by a dialogue.

BACON.

The spirits will be Voltaire by Mrs. S. and Cardinal Woolsey by the Judge.

After a little while—

VOLTAIRE said: What a vast revolution has taken place in the opinions of men since I was a resident of earth!

WOOLSEY.—Yes, the infidelity with which you were charged while here has since then grown immensely among men. It is not now so pretentious as it was then, but it is deeper and wider spread, and, unless arrested, will sink mankind into deeper materialism than has been known for ages.

VOLTAIRE.—Infidelity to what and to whom? to the law

of man or of God? Dost thou pretend to censure the infidelity of my soul which could not bow to the narrow creeds and sectarian prejudices of the minds around me? Dost thou say I was an infidel, because I dared to speak the immortal truth which beamed in upon my soul, darkened as it was with gross materiality? But still it was immortal truth, and possessed the very essence of the Godlike divinity. My soul required a larger, a more extended plane of thought, a more unbounded field of knowledge than the teaching of man could supply. Yea, my darkened soul hungered for light.

WOOLSEY.—I spoke of the infidelity with which you were *charged*, and, alas! you know the charge yet lives in many minds. But I meant not to censure, but only to lament; for with minds like yours, such unbelief as yours in the teachings of the day, material as they were, and of man's invention, might work no injury; but the same cause which operated on your mind operated on others too weak and feeble to see the great results at which you arrived. And while with you infidelity may have been but a disbelief in the dogmas of man, in others it was a disbelief in the existence of a God and the eternal existence of man; and it is that which has spread with such alarming prevalence throughout the world, that a vast majority of the civilized part of it, disgusted with the teachings which you repelled, have learned to doubt that there was any existence for man but on this earth. And these dogmas have, day by day, been sinking man deeper and deeper into the love of this world alone, and hence have been engendered selfishness and strife among men, until they are, indeed, unlike what they were designed to be by their great Creator. The cause—the cause of this is the great inquiry? for when that shall be ascertained, the remedy will be comparatively easy. What say you—for you know—is that cause?

VOLTAIRE.—My opinions, as given to the world during my lifetime, are, indeed, tinctured with a spirit of bitterness and controversy; but, while giving those opinions, please to remember, that my mind was tortured, as it were, by an internal warfare. I looked upon mankind as being beneath me in intellect and discernment. I looked upon them as puppets who might be led by any strong mind that might please to control them, and the spirit of combativeness was aroused within me that such elements should exist in the mind of man, and he still be called an immortal being. What! such man a part of the divinity destined to exist forever? and yet how puny he seemed when compared with the great First Cause from which he pretended to have sprung!

I grant, my opinions may have done some injury in some cases, but I am convinced they did much more good. They aroused the souls of many men from their cringing, low position. They broke the trammels and let loose upon the wing of thought many an aspiring soul. But my soul in its range became lost also. Instead of making the nice distinction which I might have done if the spirit part of my nature had been developed as well as the material, I mixed them indiscriminately, and thus lost sight of the object I had in view, and thought in my battle with the world that there was no hereafter, while I wished only to be convinced that there surely was. But the spirit in which I pursued my researches sent me back empty hand- ed and more strongly girded about with the infidelity of which you speak. And my life was spent, not so much in striving to defeat the good which might be done by the Christian religion, as in battling their foolish opinions and blind credulity. Even I, with all my infidelity, could, upon the basis of my belief, mount far above them, ay, beyond their very vision, and see the glorious world re- vealed in the face of nature, and the wonderful revolutions of the earth. And I could be filled with a sense of awe and a feeling of unbounded liberty which they never ex- perienced in their dark and cringing position.

I confess I do not regret the spread of my works, for I see far greater causes of evil, and baleful effects flowing from those causes, had there been no opposing principles to work in the great mass of mankind. They would not all bow. They would not all be slaves, and if that which I advocated gave them one exalted thought and enabled them to penetrate into the realms of knowledge, did it not open their eyes to see their true position? No, I do not regret to see my teachings, but I do regret that I lived so long on earth and became so little aware of what I might have been, of what I might have done, if I had been blessed with the light of Spiritualism, which has now dawned on the mind of man.

Unbelieving and uncertain I entered the spirit-world, repelling with my very presence every approach of light which might have shone on my darkened vision. It was the material part of my nature which was developed on earth. My spirit part was lost in my wanderings for light. It was shut up in the material part as in an iron cage. Defiant and proud I entered the spirit-world, not knowing, not caring to know, the hereafter I had so strenuously fought against while in the body. But let me make this confession. There was ever in my soul a still, small voice which would come from its deepest recesses and would pierce away beyond the bounds of space and ask for light, and return dissatisfied and weary. It was a constant striving of the desire to know and the determination not to know. So my entrance there could not have been gladsome. Had not the opinions which I had spent my whole intellect and energies in propagating all come to naught as regards man's immortality? And I plainly saw if the soul was immortal there must be a God, an immortal spirit, who ruled this vast and illimitable space which surrounded me.

How I traveled—incessantly traveled—and strove to convince myself that it was still a material world I lived on! How my spirit wrestled with the truth which was crushing me with such force! and I could not realize myself as a spirit, that I had left my mortal abode. There was none with whom I could claim companionship, for had I not denied every one of them's being immortal? There was no resting-place for me. I was ever restless, ever wandering and unsatisfied. My soul was dark and bitter within me, and I was as a maniac without power to work out any design my mind might plan.

I say I entered the portals of the spirit-world proud and defiant. I was led away from the habitations of spirits and was taken into mighty space. I was permitted to gaze on the wonderful works of the spirits' abodes. To me they seemed indeed wonderful, and I was carried about with resistless force, and made to gaze until my soul became so filled with the sense of the magnificence and power which controlled these mighty wonders, that I fain would have hid myself away in the clefts of the rocks, but I could not do so. I yearned for companionship and longed to tell some one how I had been misled, not by others, but by my own wild imaginings. I began to realize how insignificant I was in that great world of immortal spirits, and, finally, having become so weary, so humiliated, my proud spirit thoroughly humbled, I was allowed to associate with some of the inhabitants. And now I began to realize the position I had occupied on earth, and to see that which I should occupy in the spirit-world. And it was not a pleasant one, my friend.

A complete revolution, an entire change in my spirit-organization, took place, and I became a delighted learner. My ideas being already expansive, how I progressed! My soul felt the warm and glowing love of God to light it up, to help its immortal graspings, and rapidly I became associated with the great and the good and the developed in wisdom in the spirit-world. I saw how great had been my mistake, and I felt how great must be the reparation which I must make to atone for all which I have said or done or lived, which would lead men's minds away from the right path. Glorious with the light of celestial wisdom and beauty are the lessons which I have learned, and far beyond all my soul could ever have conceived in this world has been the unfolding of the boundless storehouse of wisdom and knowledge.

I have lived to look upon my earthly existence as a bitter warfare with the world and with my own spiritnature. I have deeply regretted the opinions which I advocated, which were the means of leading any astray, but I also feel deeply and fervently grateful to the all-wise Creator that I was made an instrument even of controversy in the Christian world, that thus men's minds might be opened to a spirit of inquiry and progression.

The effects have not been so bad as the world believed them to be, but the causes which led to the many contentions and discussions will still exist until man's spirit has worked him out of the thralldom of blind opinion and blinder prejudice and unprogressive religion. The cause of Christianity must become infidel to its present opinions before the world can arrive at that state of free and enlightened wisdom which shall make every man a law unto himself.

WOOLSEY.—I wonder not at your contempt of mankind as they were when you lived on earth, for they and their mental condition were the legitimate product of more than a thousand years of religious domination, and the extreme to which you were led, though not unnatural, was to be lamented, and it is that extreme which now so widely pervades the whole civilized world.

But the cause of it lies deeper than you have mentioned. I saw it among the religionists with whom I associated ; I saw it in the cloister and in the desk, and most among those whose minds were most enlarged by education and culture. It was this. The dogmas taught as religion were at war with the aspirations of our own souls, and with the workings of the laws of God as we saw them all around us. If we sent a searching thought deep into the recesses of our own souls, we found there—innate and existent— what shall I call it? an aspiration, a belief, an instinctive feeling as it were, at war with that which we were taught as religion. If we sent our minds abroad, searching through the external universe, it returned to us laden with the conviction, that the operations and the laws of the Great First Cause were equally in conflict with it. And in proportion as we were able to make this internal or external search, as the mind by culture· increased in the capacity to examine itself and the laws of nature, and to understand them, we recognized, we felt the overpowering influence of the teachings thence derived, that the religion taught us could not, in many respects, be true. However earnestly we might have tried to believe, however obstinately we might have resolved that we would believe, however successful we might have thought ourselves in deceiving ourselves into the idea that we did believe, there was still lingering down deep in the inmost recesses of our souls the conviction that it was not so.

While that was the condition of the cultivated and the educated in your day and mine, so now it is the condition of vastly greater numbers, because now knowledge is more generally diffused among men, and with that knowledge has come now, as it came then, the extreme into which you fell—the denial of a God and a future existence for man. How welcome to us would have been the revelations now making to man! How welcome ought it now to be to man, for it guards him against that extreme, lifts him from the deep degradation of such unbelief, raises him from the mire of a material existence only, and opens to him a knowledge which will make indeed a new heaven and a new earth : a new heaven, because spirits fitted for it will enter there—a new earth, because man, while upon it, will learn and execute the great purpose of his existence there. With that knowledge, his existence there will not be as it was with us, in vain in reference to the future.

It is indeed a happy day for mankind that is now dawning upon them, for they will be taught to feel and will feel, as you now do, the law of love, which has, to be sure, been often on the lips, but has found the heart too closely surrounded by materialism to be able to penetrate it. That barrier is now being destroyed. The great law of love will enter there, and will show itself forth in greater regard for the happiness of each other, in the suppression of that selfishness which has so long cast its dark pall over man's life on earth, and will teach men, by the best of all possible lessons, that of experience, to know how much he will add to his happiness even on earth, as well as his happiness hereafter. It will be no longer to him a mere sentiment written on the sand of the sea-shore, to be obliterated by the first wave which the storm of human passion may excite, but will be written on the heart in letters of fire, and will be indelible, because written with the finger of an Almighty hand.

We see this—we, who have lived on earth when it was darker and more selfish than now, because more ignorant of the high purposes of our creation; but the years that have rolled on have brought to us the knowledge that this is indeed a great reality—that there is a God, and that we are destined to live with him forever.

Oh! how our hearts have yearned to teach mankind the lesson, the want of which we so deeply felt—the absence of which made our entrance here so sad, and left its impress for eternity, because it arrested the progress which is our destiny! How our hearts have yearned to open to them the reality of the holy communion of spirits, for we know that thus they too shall be elevated to a nearer approach to us, and through us to a nearer approach to their Creator! How our hearts now yearn to enable them to see the light which is now pouring in such glorious floods upon the world, to dispel the darkness which has so long brooded o'er the minds of men, and to light them to a way to a life eternal in its duration and its happiness.

After these teachings were given, and a part of them read over, we conversed upon them for a few moments, when it was written:

How beautifully a thought which is founded on truth

impresses the mind prepared to receive it! This is so, not only in regard to sentiments of the mind, but also in reference to all the revealed works of God, when the principle on which they are based is understood and appreciated. The whole universe of God teems with the beauty of divine thought, and the radiance of this celestial beauty is perceived when the spirit of man is in harmony with the Great First Cause. It is not strange, therefore, that you admire thoughts which are the revelation of the inner sentiments of the spirits who once were as you are, living and acting in your world. Were your minds opposed to the truths they teach, how dark and gloomy would be the ideas they inculcate, how distasteful! The great principles of love would become the cause of discord and opposition. But the truth which opens the mind to feel, to see, to know, enlarges your view and brings you at once into a divine existence. But it is not only in the happiness you derive from a correspondence with our views that you are to base your life while in life. It is not only from the glow of honest joy that you are to learn what there is for you to do. You are not to be confined to thought alone, or the thoughts of other men and spirits. You are to develop your own happiness in yourself, in the progress which your spirit makes in sending its search through all creation, material and immaterial. If you can judge of God by his works, and learn that he is a Spirit full of love and mercy, and that you partake of the glorious attributes of his Spirit, how much does it behoove you to act as well as think—act in relation to·what you *know* is your duty. The flower tinted with the variegated colors which adorn it with beauty, may attract the eye and may grace a garden, but the humble shrub, from which we extract those agents which conduce to the good of man, though it may hide itself in the deep shade of some forest, is sought for and prized as an instrument for good indeed. It is prized, not for its beauty, but for the innate virtues it possesses.

Your relation with this world must bring you in daily

contact with those for whom you may work for good. You may develop in the humblest mind those instrumentalities which shall add to your own happiness as well as the eternal interests of itself.

While therefore you admire, FEEL—feel that your part is to act, to work, to live an example of what you profess, and thus to excite the earnest inquiry of all men—Are these things indeed true ?   SWEEDENBORG.

Section Twenty-nine.

Friday, Oct. 28th, 1853.

This evening the Bishop of ———, and Doctor ———, of Kentucky, were in my library, with the Doctor and myself. The Bishop was investigating, and avowed himself a believer in spiritual intercourse; but he betrayed an ignorance of the nature of spirit and the life after death, that showed he had thought little on the subject, and that was marvelous to me in a high dignitary of the Church. After they had gone, Lord Bacon wrote :

I WAS somewhat inclined to answer the Bishop cavalierly when he asked me to write the Apostles' Creed in Latin. I have forgot both the apostles and the creed long ago, and hope I shall not again be subjected to the indignity of learning it. But, Judge, how little the secrets of the priesthood are understood, and how little their avocation is understood ! How powerful a hold have they on the minds of the world, and how little good really have they accomplished !

They claim that they are the advanced guard of civilization, and that they have hung out the banner of truth on the outer wall of human progress. Alas ! for human nature, which has suffered them to triumphantly dictate to its ignorance what their reason feared to investigate! Alas! for the world which would submit to the dictation of men, who, proclaiming that they understand the laws of God, are inculcating the errors of their creed or sect.

Priests of God? Holy men? They are but the drones of society—the very worms of life which prey on the finest feelings of man's nature—the instincts of his soul. They priests? Yes, the priests of ignorance—the very barriers of progressive inquiry; for they trammel thought, confine reason, and send the mis-born soul into the spirit-world without the least knowledge of his destiny.

Look abroad over the world, and ask yourselves who is it that has accomplished all that has stimulated man to search, investigate, and seek out from nature the secrets which advance his mind and give to his soul the first gleam of hope everlasting? Has it been the priesthood? Has it been the ministers of God? No; for they have tortured the chosen spirits of any age when they have differed from them in form or tenet. They have barred up all outlets of human enterprise and knowledge, unless it conformed to their dictum. They have sent their hirelings into every household, and have bound on the rack the good and true, the aged and young, when they have differed one iota from the severe laws they have laid down for the rule of man. Not content with driving man to despair in life, they have sent his spirit howling into the spheres, with their anathemas following him like an accursed spirit when he reached there. They pretend to minister to a mind diseased, but they have made the death-bed a dice-box, by which the everlasting happiness of some good man was cast on the hazard of their approval. Alas! for the priesthood! Alas! when they pretend to teach man the destiny of his soul!

But look again, and ask yourselves, what have they done? They have taken one book, called the Bible, and from this they have fashioned laws which limit all inquiry beyond this source. They pretend to assist all efforts for the good of man, but they confine that effort to the narrow circle of their creeds. Yes, they have sent their missionaries into all parts of the world, and have proclaimed a Saviour to all men, but they have taken care to have it well understood that no man can be saved unless he joins their particular church. Have they given to man the prerogatives of his nature? Have they opened to him the opportunities of free inquiry? No. They have established a religion, and have so connected the laws, civil and political, with it, that they have forced nations of men to contribute to its support, and have amassed, from the hard earnings of the poor, vast sums of money, which has added to their power and increased their ability to do evil.

Have they adhered to the very doctrines they profess to believe? No. They have cast out the good man for his independence, and they have crucified a thousand times again the Saviour, for they have made his mercy and love a mere mockery. Have they given one true idea of God? No. They have made him play a farce in the face of his whole creation, and they have made him—the Great First Cause—deny his own nature. Alas! alas! they are indeed priests, but the priests of unrighteousness. Verily, I say, they are the banes of society, and in good time they will be found out, and then for judgment!

Section Thirty.

Sunday, Oct. 30th, 1853.

The circle met in my library. Through Dr. Dexter, it was written :

Now before we begin on our proper subject, permit me, my friends, to make a few remarks applicable to all mediums. Placed before the world as they are, it becomes important that their minds and action should correspond with the great principles they profess to believe ; not only that they may impress the world with the truth of their belief, but that they may be able to convince themselves that the germ of action is that of truth itself. It is sometimes more difficult to convince ourselves that we are wrong than to assure the world that we are indeed believers in any doctrine we profess. And it is not only this public demonstration that mediums ought to make, but they must bring their hearts up to judgment, analyze the feelings of their souls, and find out if indeed they are predicated on the truth.

It is sometimes the case that when the mind is impressed with the truth of a new idea, it gives its thoughts free license, and acts on other principles than the new idea would justify. And much license may have been given to thought when you consider the whole of action founded on what has been called spirit-doctrines.

We have taught that God is a principle ; that he has established laws for the government of his creatures ; that man, under these laws, becomes either good or evil in this as well as the other world. We have inculcated virtuous lives, free thought, and the desire that every day and hour should add to your spiritual and intellectual progress here and in the spheres. We have revealed many things, of which before you were ignorant; and we have said that your thoughts were read and understood by us in reference to your moral as well as material reflections.

But the time has come when something more on this subject should be revealed, that all may know how they stand in relation to themselves as well as others.

Identified as the mediums are with the doctrines promulgated to the world, each in turn will be called on to aid the spirits in the great work which has just begun. But in reference to their action with and for us, it is proper that they should understand what is required of each, and what should be the moral condition of their spirits to render them able to execute what we shall prescribe for them to do. When, therefore, the spirits have for a long time had intercourse with man, when they have frequently and intimately visited him, they begin to study more intensely the inner workings of his spirit. Thus, then, we dive down into the secret recesses of his heart, and bring up to view the very feelings and sentiments he had hoped he was concealing even from himself. Studying before the general characteristics of his nature, they now investigate all the phenomena of his spirit; they trace the course of thought, of sentiment, of affection—the cause of every feeling which which has its seat in the sentient part of his being. They go further than this : they specially delegate spirits to perform this duty, whose charge it is, daily and hourly, to watch each thought in its inception and manifestation. They regard expression in the daily life, and expression where the thought is locked up within the heart and gives no utterance, except by those signs which indicate to similar thought in others that it is existent. But the spirits whose duty it is thus to take this espionage of the secret thoughts of men are high, bright, and pure spirits, who are so sublimated that they can penetrate the very being, and there behold all the wondrous workings of the mind.

Say you that this is indeed placing you under guard and

watch? Say you that this is indeed prying into that which no one ought to know? But, say I, you profess to believe spirits; you profess to an entire change of feeling in regard to life and its duties; you profess to live for progress, and to earnestly desire to shun and to root out every thing evil and impure in your action and thought. Can you not understand, then, that you are specially guarded? that that love which makes you the especial charge of holy spirits is for the purpose of enabling you to overcome evil for good by our aid and influence? Can you not realize that it is for some great and noble object that you are thus placed within the reach of those guides who shall direct you toward those glorious spheres where there shall be no evil, and where you shall be pure and holy?

But woe to them who are the instruments selected, if, indeed, they listen not to what we have said—who, in spite of all the means of progress, choose rather the evil than the good! Human mind never pictured to itself the degradation which will ensue here on earth, and the infinite misery hereafter.

My friends, deep is the faith of those who are engaged in this work—their love. Oh! words fail to express it. Their patience is like time, ever and continual, and their forgiveness beyond that of parent. You, what are you here for? What do you profess to believe? Earnestly strive with us. Earnestly desire to know what you are, and earnestly pray that you may so understand the operations of your own hearts, that you may be able to overcome evil with good, and on earth, as in the spheres, every day advance one step toward light and truth.

SWEEDENBORG.

We asked a personal application of these remarks, and it was answered:

If I exhaust much time on this subject, it will be of service to you all. You ask for an application in what I have said? Hear me, then, and realize, if you can, that every spirit present here to-night willingly suspends his labors that you may be instructed in that which shall enable you to know and to judge how you are to act, and when you are to cast off that which may be evil, and take on that which is good.

The day is dawning when the truth will gird up its loins and travel with speed through this world. You are its avant guards; you are its companions. In joy or sorrow, in prosperity and in adversity, you must go on; there is before you all much to do; the light is twinkling like a star dimly seen. Can you behold the glorious beams of the noonday sun? Then while we are moved for you, let your hearts drink up these sayings and listen.

Now, in the very midst of you, all the spirits kneel together, and are singing a song of love and praise. And while I am writing, there comes a flood of radiant light streaming into their circle, clothing them with a brilliance mortal eye can not behold. And a spirit from the higher spheres descends and stands in their midst, and, raising one hand toward heaven, says, "To me belongs this lesson—to me belongs the explanation, and through the mouth of the Judge will I utter it."

I give way, and with yourselves I listen, for from those glorious spheres both you and I can derive instruction.

SWEEDENBORG.

Then I was impressed, and said :

Servants of the Most High! have ye in your hearts no vain glory? Lingers not there the love of man's applause, which so often taints mortal life? And are your labors prompted only by a love of God and your fellow-creatures? Is there not lingering deep down in your souls the remains of those passions which have tinged your mortal career in times past? Speak! for ye know.

Is there no self in your motives, or in your actions, in the great cause of truth in which ye are enlisted? Deceive not yourselves. Vaunt not yourselves of the love, the admiration, the regards of bright and holy spirits; for little know ye how deep is the grief which ye may cause them by cherishing, still lingering around your hearts, the selfish passions which your material existence may have engendered.

Vaunt ye of your courage? What is it but that ye are not sunk as low as some? Pride ye yourselves on your knowledge? What is it but a fearful addition to your responsibility over those who yet slumber in ignorance? Regard ye yourselves as teachers? What are ye but infants, tottering with feeble steps over the threshold of knowledge?

Oh! mortals! weak and sinful mortals! Bow yourselves in the dust before that purity which has selected you as its instruments—purity of whose extent you can not conceive, and in whose presence ye are dark as midnight. Humble yourselves before that mighty Power whose servants ye are, and, looking abroad upon the boundless universe which has been unfolded to your view, think how insignificant ye are. Let your thoughts roam o'er the countless millions of holy spirits who people eternity, and ask yourselves what ye are? And remember, that as you have been favored with light and knowledge beyond your fellows, so shall the more abundant fruit thereof be demanded of you. As you have been the recipients of that love which purifies and elevates the heart, so will it be demanded of you the more, that ye should show it forth in your lives. And oh, beware! beware, for your own sake; beware, for the sake of those whose love for you now causes them to tremble for your future, how ye permit an entrance into your hearts of a single unkind feeling; and be assured that every indulgence thereof will be but heaping coals of fire on your own heads—a laying up for yourselves treasures of sorrow which will haunt your footsteps many a long and weary hour in your passage through eternity.

To you the kingdom of heaven has been opened beyond any thing ever yet known to mortal man. On you has been shed a holy light beyond that of your fellows. On you hopes are built—oh! how great, how fervent, how cheering! To you is committed a task—oh! how infinitely important! And on you, consequently, rests a responsibility and devolves a duty which naught but purity of life and action and thought can enable you to discharge.

Know, then, yourselves. Know, then, yourselves! Dive deep down into the recesses of your hearts, and bring up in stern review before your judgments, enlightened as they have been by the knowledge given you, your most secret motives and purposes, and by an unshrinking amputation cut off from yourselves the evil propensities which retard your progress and impair your usefulness.

Do this, and be happy. Do this, and ye will be able successfully to accomplish the great work before you. Do this, and in the glad shouts which will welcome your entrance into the spirit-land when your day of work is done, will you find your abundant reward; and as ye journey through eternity, the remembrance of the good ye have done will lighten your footsteps and cheer ye on the way to that Great Spirit in whose hands are all the corners of the earth, and from whom pours, on all whom he has made, a never-ending stream of love.

What matters it that the heart is pure and the purpose honest, if there is not strength to do right? What matters it that you profess to be servants of God, if you fear the censure of man? What matters it that you rejoice with exceeding joy at the revelations made to you of the marvelous works of God, if fear of man retard an upright avowal of them?

What matters it? I say much, indeed, does it matter, for ye can not at once serve God and Mammon. Ye can not at once be the recipients of his wondrous bounty, and yet worship the world by fearing its clamor.

The time will come when ye will hail with glad shouts, with hearts overflowing with joy, the hour when ye proclaimed yourselves to the world, regardless of its frowns, that indeed ye are the chosen servants of the Most High God.

What fear ye? It is the cause of God in which ye are engaged, and fear ye to acknowledge it? Oh, fear not! Fear not! Fear not man, fear only God, and remember that he who denies his Master may in his turn be himself denied. Buckle on, then, the whole armor of God, and be well assured that in his cause not a hair of your heads shall be injured. Measure not this great work by the miserable standard of man's applause, but by the metewand* of eternity.

Fight! Fight! But fight first yourselves. Conquer first yourselves. It is yourselves that most retard your progress, that most impair your usefulness, that most impede the development within you of powers innate there which could make you marvelous instruments of working God's wonders before men.

Oh! seek to know yourselves, seek it with humble, contrite hearts. Seek to bow before the throne of the great Creator your stubbornness, which prompts you to resist even his will. And forget not, that as your gifts are great, as the blessings bestowed on you are beyond those of others, so is more demanded of you; and that as the great principle, that we are judged by our opportunities, exists everywhere and forever, ye can not escape its influence on yourselves.

Think how great, how wonderful is the power that is given you—that of revealing to man the immortal life in the spheres, the power to open to his knowledge the very gates of death, the power to penetrate into the grave and dispel at once its darkness and its mystery—the power to open to him a glorious future, and to lead him to it—the power to enable him to shun an evil future, and the power to lead him back to the great purpose for which he was created.

---

* The old Saxon name of measure.

Such and so vast, so momentous is your power. Look
upon it. See its never-ending consequences to yourselves
and to mankind, and ask yourselves if it can be that in
the evils and adversities of this transitory existence ye
can find aught that may justly impair or impede it?
Ask yourselves this question now, for by-and-by it will
ask itself of ye, and, oh! beware in time that ye be prepared in eternity to answer it wisely and well.

With some the greatest difficulty is a pertinacious attachment to certain previous notions which imperfect
knowledge bestows. Honesty and sincerity are by this
cause shorn of their power to advance you as they otherwise would. Keep pace with the knowledge that now
flows in upon you. Measure it not by the standard of
preconceived opinions, but by that of nature in all her
works. Be not too tenacious of your own opinions, for
that tenacity hems your hearts around with a triple barrier
through which truth finds it hard to penetrate. Eschew
this, and believe that it is the clean and untarnished mirror alone which can reflect the eternal truths of God in all
their purity and brightness.

And now, dear friends all, could you see, could you feel,
oh! could we in the slightest degree make you sensible
of the deep, the abiding, the overflowing love which has
prompted us to deal out these admonitions to you; could
you but know the intense interest with which countless
numbers of pure and happy spirits regard your progress;
could you but understand the immense value to the cause
of truth that your purity and progress are; could you but
see how many thousand hearts are overflowing with love
of you, you would know and appreciate the motives which
have prompted us thus to chasten that we might purify—
thus to burn your gold in the furnace that it might be
brightened, and thus to warn that we may draw you nearer
to ourselves and bind the stronger the links that are to
connect you with us to eternity.

Section Thirty-one.

Thursday, Nov. 3d, 1853.

The circle met at my library. Mrs. Sweet being absent from illness, it was written:

It was proposed that the Judge should be impressed to-night, but as the teachings on Sunday night were changed for a special object, it might be as well to continue our teachings through the Doctor for a time on the proper matter of progress, and then afterward influence the Judge. If this is acceptable, we will do so.

BACON.

We assented, and it was written through the Doctor:

In prosecuting so great and profound a subject as the one on which we propose to enter, it is necessary that the medium's mind should be easily controlled and directed, as the course we have pursued for some time has naturally diverted his mind, so that we may not be able to write freely and connectedly at this first essay; but as time presses, and as we can not delay longer, we must make the attempt.

It was remarked in the last teaching on progress that a new principle was developed. This should be understood as taking place after the developments just before mentioned.

Thus when in the space around, latent with the constituents out of which were formed the atomic particles from which the nucleii were fashioned, there was then existent a sort of gaseous body which by its motion through the atmosphere became ignited. Now the combustion of this body developed a new body, and also gave off to the surrounding atmosphere the constituents which this combustion evolved. It would be impossible for me to trace each succeeding step in the process of this progress. It would fill many, many volumes. I can only give you the great principles, and leave you to fill up the rest.

As the external part of these bodies was burnt out, they no longer assumed the appearance of fire, but became as it were consolidated by this process. The external crust then became a dense substance, on which the atmosphere produced certain effects, and which also by its very change became the seat of other changes which in themselves developed others. This law obtains throughout all nature, that when by the apposition of any bodies certain effects are produced, these effects in themselves generate a new principle, which principle generates another, and so on *ad infinitum* forever.

Thus you can understand what I mean. Those bodies burning with the fire, the result of the combination of their constituents and motion, produced a new order of matter on their external part. Here there was a new principle, and this principle opened to the influences of causes a field for new results. Thus the external part became condensed, and this condensation produced an entirely different appearance, and also came under the operation of entirely different laws from their former gaseous condition.

Here, then, we have the commencement of the many and varied changes on the surface of your globe, and the thousand orbs which roll in space. How can mortal conceive of the remarkable phenomena which have taken place since the world assumed form and shape! I can not give you a better idea of this process than to refer you to the ideas advanced in detail in the work called, "Vestiges of Creation," for a minute description of what I believe to have taken place; for, as I have before remarked, my teachings are only the results of what I have learned here, and are not to be understood as any thing but an opinion. Leaving, then, the minute detail of all the steps of progress to be obtained from the work referred to, I pass to the consideration of that state of development which took place when the earth became fit for the habitation of man.

Now turn your minds back to that period when the world, after undergoing so many varied changes by the action of the intense fires, by the decomposition of the rock, by the displacement of the various strata, by the entire disappearance of the dense vegetation of a certain character, and by the destruction of continents and the relative change in the mountains, the disappearance of seas, and the appearance of rivers which flowed where immense forests before had their location, and imagine this whole earth now laid out with mountain and dale, rivers and seas, woodland and plain, with birds, and beasts, and flowers, and shrubs, all declaring the power of an Almighty God, but without a single human being yet existent on its broad surface. Imagine a summer morning—the sun rising and greeting the carol of the millions of winged songsters, whose joyous song made vocal these dark forests, whose dense shade concealed their depths from his golden rays. Picture to your mind the towering mountain rising in solitude to the clear, blue sky, and gilded with a golden crown of radiant light. Follow the course of this broad river, wending its way through these vast plains, blossoming as a garden of beautiful flowers, whose gorgeous and varied tints reflect the colors of the rainbow. Watch its sluggish current as its dark waters slowly course their way until, meeting with a mass of rock, it dashes foaming and bubbling through the rocky pass, and hurries on to the sea. Behold the whole of this earth glistening and sparkling in the mellow light of a summer morning. Nature everywhere alive— the birds giving forth their carol—the stately horse dashing across the plain and snuffing the morning air in his headlong course. There, amid that cluster of palm trees,

lying couchant, the magnificent lion, and near him sporting
the timid fawn. Yonder, with his glistening striped skin,
the sleeky tiger. How craftily he creeps under those low
bushes, but notices not the gentle calf that, bleating, follows its mother! The trees filled with fruit, the earth covered with its animals, the eternal sea smiling with the
sparkling light of this summer morning, singing out its
songs of praise as it sends its waves to the shore, and
shields in its bosom the varied tribes of fishes who make
its waters instinct with life. Thus is now perfected for man
the whole creation—every thing ready for his use, every
thing prepared for his sway who is to begin an existence
here, that is to end where?

Then it was written that the spirits would impress me, which they
did as follows, purporting to be by the Druidess:

VISION.

I had a view of a tall, rough, unhewn rock, like a
column, standing in the midst of a circle of similar rocks
not so high, very massive and rough. They stood on a
knoll looking off upon the sea and the rising sun. There
were rough, unhewn rafters reaching from the tall shaft to
the lower ones. The space between them was filled with
withes woven together, and that was covered with a kind
of long grass fastened down by willow bands, forming a
circular roof. That covering extended only over the top,
and the whole seemed a rude temple. Near that center
rock were four piles of wood, like the ancient funeral
pyres for burning sacrifices on. Inside I saw the priests
officiating, not in great numbers; but outside were many
people prostrate. On these four funeral piles were four
different sacrifices—fish, fowl, brute animal, and the human. The human sacrifices were of persons who had been
educated from early infancy to believe that to be a sacrifice
on those altars was the surest passport to happiness hereafter. They were chiefly of young persons near maturity.

There were more convulsions of nature in those days than now. Mankind, not understanding the laws which produced or governed them, looked upon them as indicating the anger of the great spirit who they felt governed them. They were hovering between a belief that the sun was that great spirit, and a sort of instinctive notion that it was not. It was a very indefinite notion. But to conciliate that spirit and deprecate his anger they thought nothing could be more acceptable than to offer that life which they valued so much; and it was not in reference to the future but to the present that they deprecated his anger. They were a very rude people. Their dresses were very simple, and of very coarse texture. It was a northern climate in which they lived, and to protect themselves from cold they wore fur under their clothes. I saw no covering on their heads; both males and females wore their hair flowing naturally. Their upper garment seemed to be made of two square pieces with openings for the head and for the arms, fastened around the waist by some sort of a band, and descending down to the middle of the thigh. The under garment was a sort of loose pantaloon, descending to the knees; from the knees down they had the skin of some animal fitting close. They wore a kind of sandal made of wood. They were poor; their dwellings were dug down in the ground five or six feet, with a roof over them like that over the temple.

' There was an opening at the top in the temple and in the houses for the smoke to escape, and the inside was blackened with soot.

I saw the priests approach the altars. One of the victims was a female. She lay upon her back on the altar, her hands bound to her sides, etc. All the victims were alive. The priests wore long garments that trailed on the ground, fastened at the neck, and on their backs were worked hieroglyphic characters. There were twelve or more at each altar, and facing from the crowd. They seemed to be bowing and chanting, with guttural sounds, in a sing-song tone. Outside of them, and inside the circle of stones, was a complete circle of men and women, two or three deep. Many of them had horns in their hands of goats or cows, or shells, to blow on. Some with a rude sort of drum, a hollow log with skin over it; others with flat pieces of wood which they beat together. Some of them had no instruments—they must have been singers. They stood immovable while the priests went through their ceremonies.

After a while the priests turned around, facing the outside of the circle and with their backs to the altars. As they did so, I saw the front of their garbs, which before I had not seen. The dress was the same as the others, except that the edges of their upper garments were bound with fur. They wore on their heads a singular sort of covering, like a skull-cap, fitting close to the head, with square projections on each side above the ears, and a loose piece hanging down over each ear to the shoulders. They wore bands on the neck, wrists, and ankles, which shone and seemed to be made of tin.

They raised their hands with one accord, as if blessing the people, and as they did so, the musicians began their discordant noise, and all the crowd outside, kneeling still and with their faces to the ground, shouted and clapped their hands over their heads. The instant the shouting began, some young persons, apparently attendants on the priests, rushed into the temple with blazing torches, and set fire to the altars. They caught instantly, and were at once enveloped in blaze and smoke. This was so rapid, that the suffering of the victims must have been very brief, and their cries were drowned amid the clamor of the musicians and the shouting multitude.

I could not imagine how such small altars could contain fuel enough to consume the victims, but I saw that the attendants were constantly bringing more fuel and heaping it on the victims until they were burned to ashes. The fuel had evidently been carefully prepared, and was so bituminous as to burn rapidly. I saw, during the process, the half-burned corpse amid the flames and ashes.

While the flames were raging, the crowd outside had arisen to their feet and were dancing to the sound of that discordant music. When the victims had been entirely consumed, the crowd outside and all the musicians prostrated themselves on the ground, and the priests, carefully gathering up all the ashes from the several altars, walked around among the people and scattered it over them.

Then the people retired from the temple to their respective homes.

It seemed to me that the priests were the rulers of the people, and that very many people looked with contempt on the whole ceremony, but dared not say so, for fear of their rulers. They were evidently prepared for some revolution in their religion.

That kind of sacrifice was not very frequent. It was a great and rare ceremony.

They were a very rude people, living chiefly by hunting and fishing, amid dense forests. They were a savage, fierce race. Their moral sentiments were very little developed. The tops of their heads were quite flat, but their intellectual faculties were quite prominent, forming, in these respects, a strong contrast with the Caribbean Indians whom I had seen in Central America, who were as kind and as gentle as they were ignorant and simple. They could not have felt much pain at the idea of a human sacrifice, nor could they, in their condition, have enjoyed much pleasure.

I next saw the entrance into the spirit-world of the spirit of the human victim.

Though she had been carefully educated in their secluded schools with much pains, to make her believe that her sacrifice would be beneficial to her, yet she dreaded death, for she was uncertain and uninstructed as to the future, and the world around her was very pleasant.

19

She awoke to consciousness in the spirit-life before the ceremonies were concluded. Her first emotions seemed to be but a continuation of the feelings which predominated in her at the moment of her death, and she could not realize that she had died. She saw the whole scene around her just as she had seen it while in life. The only difference she could discover was, that instead of being bound on the altar, she was now floating in the air, just above the rude temple, and viewing the scene through its roof. It puzzled her a good deal. She did not understand it. She before had no idea of such a thing! But as she gazed, she felt herself drawn upward and away from the scene, until it faded from her view. It was not till then she looked around to see what was thus drawing her up and where she was going.

On one side of her she saw a number of dark spirits, who approached quite near to her, and claimed that she should go with them. They were vociferous in insisting upon her doing so.

On the other side she saw a number of bright spirits, who were at a greater distance from her, and who spoke not, but gazed upon her with looks of kindness and affection.

She had been a pure and innocent girl, doing right according to her best knowledge, and she had intellect enough to understand at once that she had a choice where to go and what that choice ought to be.

She turned her back on those dark spirits, and reached out her hands imploringly to the brighter ones. They instantly approached her, took her affectionately in their arms, and with songs and rejoicing receded far in the distance and passed from my view.

During the vision I was impressed that the scene occurred in the north of Europe, and about two thousand years ago.

Section Thirty-two.

Sunday, Nov. 6th, 1853.

The circle met this evening. After some personal communications through Mrs. Sweet, it was written through Dr. Dexter:

THE influence on certain minds of causes presuming to emanate from the world of spirits produces peculiar, and, perhaps, unnatural emotions. Thus, in the individual who has entered on a new exploration of facts unconnected with the natural world (as is generally understood), the feelings of his mind resemble the commotion of the waters at Hurlgate; no two eddies or currents of thought are alike, and the new and varied impressions which agitate his mind resemble nothing before of the emotion or sentiment of mental action.

Thus it is to all of you that truth, in its nearness of presentation, elicits thoughts painful, from their magnitude and importance, and the mind is completely staggered in the contemplation of the great impressions which it recognizes.

Can it be understood, therefore, if the mind is swallowed up in the thought of spirit-intercourse in the form, that the emotions which influence it on its entrance into the spirit-world should almost confound it? That when the tangibility and reality of life forever is offered to the individual senses, that the first emotions should almost exhaust its capacity of realization?

To you, friends, the spirit-revelation is but new and limited. What will henceforth be revealed to you will so far exceed what you have realized, that you too will ask the question, Are these things so?

I make these remarks that you may be prepared for what is to take place.

Now, Judge, let your mind direct itself for a short time to our impressions, and we will afterward give a teaching through the Doctor on our proper subject.   BACON.

I was then impressed, and spoke as follows :

Far off in the distant regions of space—rolling orbs of light, of various sizes, in the background—located, as it were, in mid-heaven, is the scene which is presented to my view.

There is a clearness to the atmosphere far transcending all we ever see here, and the sky is a deeper blue. In this space, seated upon a globe or orb of light, on a sort of throne, is the most lofty and elevated spirit I have yet seen. The throne is very beautiful, and is surmounted with a canopy in the shape of a crown. Leaning lightly, with their arms on the projecting points of the crown, are several bright and pure spirits. And so by its side, and on its top, are many similar spirits. They are young, apparently from sixteen to twenty years of age ; and they cluster around that throne, with great affection for the person in it, like loving children around a fond parent. On both sides, and over it, are innumerable spirits, clad in beautiful and many-colored garments, and very lovely. They seem to be at leisure, and are very affectionate to each other. No one wishes to be alone. Their arms are twined around each other's waists. They gather in small groups, and seem to derive their happiness from each other.

He who sits there enthroned is clothed in a garment of the richest red, ornamented with gold and silver and sparkling gems ; even his sandals sparkle thus.

His countenance is indescribably bright. It is more dazzling than the noonday sun. Around his head is a halo of golden light, indicative of love, which is ever pouring its streams far into the distance, and illuminating all around him, mingling with the light emanating from the attending spirits, as we sometimes see the clouds of a summer eve blend together. He is the very Spirit of Love itself. His affection is an overflowing well, pouring its grateful waters on all around him. I have never seen any thing equal to it. No distrust of others—no unkind feelings can find entrance there. How dark does the recollection of this world seem, compared with the glowing love of that!

His countenance is transparent—clear as the finest alabaster, yet so soft, so sweet!

Raising one hand, and pointing upward, he says, "'A closer walk with God.'* 'Tis love alone that points the way; love for him—love for all the creatures he has made. What is the mighty power which has spoken into existence the countless worlds that roll before you, with their myriads of immortal souls, but the demonstration of his love?

"Think you He has peopled these worlds that thus roll for eternity through space, that they might be doomed to unhappiness, that through eternity they should be miserable? Oh! no! no! no! His love spoke them into being. His love is a part of the spirit he cast from himself as the germ of their existence. The worlds in which he has placed them are filled with the same undying spirit of love. The air, the ocean, and the earth are full of this divine attribute of his nature; and the natural longing of the human heart, wherever located, speaks of the same impress.

"We who roam far into the regions of space, amid countless worlds to you unknown, and far beyond the wildest flight of your imaginations, see everywhere His love. His might, his wisdom, his all-pervading presence are but evidences of his love, and manifestations of its domination. We who, for ages countless to you, have lived near unto his presence, as we have advanced step by step, from our material nature, to a closer walk with him, have seen only his love.

---

* Some allusion had been made, in our conversation, to the hymn beginning with those words.

"Oh! could we but make you receive our testimony! When we speak to you of His love, does there not rise from the deepest recesses of your hearts a voice that responds? And will you not listen to its pleadings? It is deep speaking unto deep, and will it not answer? It is the spirit of God speaking to itself, and are your hearts so darkened that it can get no reply?

"Through all His wondrous works the arm of his love is outstretched to you, and will you turn coldly away? Will you smother the divine influence that is working within you, and bury it amid the crumbling ruins of your material passions? Worms of the dust that ye are! groveling from your material nature upon the earth to which you are confined, will you spurn the hand that thus reaches out to lift you from your degradation, and enable you too to career on angels' wings through the illimitable space which is redolent of his love?

"Oh! bethink you in time! Clothe Him not with the vile attributes of your material existence. Defile not his holy love by enveloping it in the garb of your evil propensities. Deceive not yourselves by the crude and false notions of him which your blinded teachers have inculcated; for in that deception is your condemnation—in those false opinions are your darkness and unhappiness.

"And now, when the light of His love is flowing in overwhelming streams upon you, beware that the barriers of your selfishness do not shut it out from your hearts; for according to the light you receive will you be judged; according to the blessings bestowed upon you will be your accountability. Your future is in your own hands, and its darkness or brightness will be of yourselves.

"Go forth, then, all of you, among men. Go forth, with your own hearts answering to the call of His love. Go forth, aiming only at the redemption of your fellows. Go forth, regardless of the sacrifices which you may be called upon to make. Go forth as the ministers of his love, casting behind you the earth, its passions, and its cravings, and proclaim throughout all the corners of the earth that love which now yearns through all space, from him to us, and through us to you, to elevate you to a nearer approach to him. Go forth, then, as the servants of the Most High, strong in his power, and confident in his love, and redeem mankind; so that when your task is performed, you, like us, may bask in the love which fills our souls.

"And go back thou, oh! man of a stout heart and mighty faith, and in thy daily walk show that thy heart answers to the Spirit of God, which speaks to its dark recesses: purify thyself with fervent heat, for only thus canst thou be a useful servant of his purity."

Here his teachings ceased, and I seemed to return toward earth; and as I approached it, I shuddered at the contrast! I saw its darkness, its strife, the turmoil of its boiling passions, its gross impurity; and as with emotions of deep grief I paused and looked, a voice spoke to me, as from a far distance, "Go forth on thy mission, for even this barren wilderness shall yet blossom like the rose."

Section Thirty-three.

Thursday, Nov. 10, 1853.

The circle met this evening at my library, all present but the Doctor. I was soon influenced, and said:

I SAW the same scene I witnessed last Sunday evening, the same spirit shedding abroad that beautiful golden light and surrounded by that host of bright and loving spirits. But I was not as near to it as before, and, as I approached it, it seemed to recede from me. I was evidently advancing toward it, but it receded faster than I advanced, and so it diminished to a very small size in the far distance. It left behind it a beautiful rose-colored light, that diverged from it and radiated in all directions, until it was mingled and lost in the blue ethereal through which I was passing.

I could readily perceive that I was moving through space in the same direction. I felt myself supported and borne forward by many spirits who were with me, but the grossness of my nature retarded me, and a want of that purity which enabled them to go so easily. The spirits around me told me that if I could only attain to that rosy light, and fully feel its influence, I should become more ethereal and progress more rapidly. They continued to urge and help me forward, but I could only enter its outer edge, where it was so diffused as to be hardly perceptible. Still we struggled on, and amid our struggles, I heard a voice from that far distant spot of light, that fell upon my ear like soft, thrilling music, saying:

" Come! come to the home of the pure and good. Come to the land where reigns forever, and over all things, that love of which we have taught you. Come to the land where the light of God makes the soul free—free to learn his marvelous wisdom—free to enter his courts with praise —free to approach nigh unto him. Come and see what happiness, beyond your comprehension, the soul is capable of enjoying and imparting. Come where the heart is ever lifted up in songs of praise of his goodness, is ever filled with his love. Come and see what the soul of man is capable of being, of doing, and enjoying. Come! and, standing in our midst, and casting your eyes backward and forward into eternity, see how inconsiderable is the time in which you are enveloped in your material existence, and yet how its direction for good or ill makes its impress for eternity! Come! and with your understanding en- larged, your capacity to know increased, by the divine light that will be shed upon you, come and see what is the great Creator whom you are so fond of clothing with human attributes. Come, where, feeling his power and his love, you may worship him with a just appreciation of his nature, and may feel the ennobling and elevating influences of that appreciation. O come! for it is the power of love alone that can draw you up, and that power which can alone reward you for the struggle. Come, and forget the groveling worm of the dust, and think only of angels who may revel in the light of his love forever."

But, alas! I could not go. I felt the soft and soothing influences of that voice, which fell upon my ear like the mellow notes of the horn by distance made more sweet; but with all the aid of the spirits around me, I was left behind. But they bade me "Despair not. It can yet be done; and even that happy home of the good and the pure can yet be attained by every human soul—can be! but oh! through what toil! through what earnest labor! through what unceasing efforts! It is the home of the good and the pure alone, and naught can attain it but a life that is, in its whole, a life of goodness and purity. Plant firmly, then, in your material existence, the foundation of the ladder by which you may ascend, and know, that while it may be surrounded by angels, ascending and descending, you, too, may ascend the more rapidly onward and upward for ever."

After a brief pause, I added:

I was taken to that scene near the fountain, where I had so often been, and there I saw a large collection of spirits, some with musical instruments in their hands. They were singing, but oh! how softly, how sweetly the hymn:

> "There is a happy land
> Far, far away,
> Where saints in glory stand
> In bright array."

While they were yet singing, I was taken back to the balustrade, on the edge of the precipice, and my wife, who

was by my side, leaning on the railing, said to me: "Look
below, and behold the change which has been wrought in
so short time!" and I beheld that many places which were
once dark had become lightened, and there were more
bright spots in the scene. The light seemed shooting up
from the inhabitants themselves, penetrating and dispelling
the dark clouds which formerly brooded over them all. I
saw many more bright spirits hovering over them and
drawing nigher to them, and I beheld that the dark spirits
who once lingered there were repelled by that light. It
was a scene of great activity; the dark spirits, as they were
thrown off by the increasing light, were struggling to resist its influence and to retain their proximity, while innumerable bright ones were darting from place to place,
and aiding the people in their struggle for light.

As I beheld, she said to me, "Such is the effect which
the spirit-teachings have already produced in your darkened sphere, and will it not be a happy day when o'er all
that scene that light shall universally prevail, and the
light-spirits be allowed to draw so near you as to be daily
and hourly in communion with you? That time will surely
come. It may not be during your sojourn on earth, or
during that of any of you, who are now engaged in this
holy work; but when you all shall have passed from that
scene, and you can stand on the confines of the spirit-
world, and behold, each of you, the good you have done,
oh! how your hearts will swell with gratitude to him for
permitting you to be ministers of his holy will in the redemption of man! how full will be your hearts of that
happiness which can flow only from love to God and the
creatures he has made. And you, my husband! think not
of man's praise. Think only of the happiness which you
may earn by obeying his will."

Section Thirty-four.

Sunday, Nov. 13, 1853.

This evening I went up to the Doctor's.

The spirits after writing a few words of a private nature through the Doctor, gave the following teachings through me :

THE ultimate destiny of man ! So far beyond any thing that the most extravagant imagination has ever conceived !

Measuring that destiny by the standard of the powers manifested by man when in the form, and impeded and chained down by its material shackles, the mind has not imbibed even a distant conception of his future, either as to his happiness or his might. Happiness, compared with which the most joyous life on earth is dark despair; and might, that approximates man nigh unto the Godhead, and clothes him with many of its divine attributes : the attribute of diffusing happiness and dispensing justice among the countless millions that people space ; the attribute of executing His laws o'er all the vast universe of matter He has created, and the power to grasp and make his own—that knowledge which has no bounds but illimitable space, and no end but eternity.

The object of our material existence is to lay the foundation for this high destiny; not its only object, but a primary one, the progressive development from the womb to the grave being but means to this end. And as the ball falling from on high to the surface of the earth moves with constantly accelerating velocity, so the soul of man, starting on its race of progression, speeds in its progress with ever-increasing rapidity; and as the ball, if arrested in its course, loses a momentum it can never regain, so the soul,

having its progress arrested, must feel to eternity the loss
of that momentum it can never recover. I mean, though
the ball, though starting again after its fall has been arrested, may at a certain distance acquire the same momentum
it had obtained when it was stopped, yet at that distance
it can not have the augmented velocity it would have had
if its passage had been unimpeded, for it has lost it forever.
So it is with the soul in its advance in knowledge—that
knowledge, be it understood, whose foundation it was designed should be laid in the material existence.

No matter what the cause which arrests its flight,
whether from the want of light or the abuse of it when furnished, the effect is, more or less, the same. How vastly
important it is then to man, that he should not only understand his ultimate destiny, but the object of his primary or
material existence! Important, I mean, not only in reference to his advance in knowledge, but in reference to his
happiness also ; for you must at once perceive that that
law of his nature which demands of him that he progress
in knowledge, can not be violated without causing him unhappiness, and that unhappiness is, more or less, according
as the violation of that law is willful or accidental. Is it
not so with any law which applies to your material existence? If you thrust your hand into the flame, it causes
you pain, and that pain will be aggravated by the consciousness that you have of your own accord produced it.
The law applying to this simple act is that which governs
our whole existence in all its various and most minute parts
as in its totality.

Then, as to the effect on his progress in knowledge, first
or last, he must know—earlier or later, he must achieve
the knowledge which is to enable him to attain his high
destiny, and perform the sublime and mighty duties belonging to it : the duty of executing the will of the great
Creator in marshaling countless worlds in their orbits, in
gathering from the disjointed matter scattered throughout
space, new worlds upon new worlds, and developing from

that matter, when properly prepared, immortal spirits in their turn to people eternity. As hour by hour countless numbers of immortal spirits are ushered into a life that is to be eternal, so hour by hour are new worlds evolved, as fitting scenes on which to enact their part in the drama of existence, and to give play and scope to that germ from the Great First Cause which is speeding its way back to the source whence it emanated.

Briefly has this been said, but I pray you ponder on it well, for when your mind shall once have grasped the idea, a new field of existence will be open to its view—new sources of happiness be unfolded, and its eternal progress be begun.

Section Thirty-five.

Monday, Nov. 14, 1853.

This evening the circle met in my library, and through the Doctor it was written:

Our subject for this evening is in continuation of the legitimate matter for our book. We have rapidly traced creation's progress from the atomic particle up to man, and are now to consider the special development of this head of-the animal creation, or rather, give you our opinion of the manner in which this development took place.

But there is much to be considered before entering on the causes which generated from the whole of the created works of God this being, bound to earth by his organization, and yet connected with heaven by his birthright and his attributes. Man, specially or individually considered in reference to his physical organization, represents only a condition of existence at once adapted to place him at the head of animals. Not referring to the immeasurably greater amount of nervous matter which is so beautifully distributed throughout his system, and so arranged that every impression should be carried to a distinct point, where the result of that impression would produce the proper action, but in reference to the arrangement of his organs, their position, size, shape, etc., he is indeed qualified to stand, as he was designed, at the head of animated nature.

The various organs which compose his body resemble in their shape, and the position which they occupy, the same organs relatively situated in other animals, affording striking proof that as far as regards his physical conformation, he is the improvement on every other animal creation, and that he was therefore the latest creation. In reference to the powers and capacities of his organism, he does not possess the strength of the horse, but the arrangement and construction of his hands and arms enable him to move weights that the horse can not stir. He can not see in the night as some other animals can, but his eye is so situated that it can embrace a much larger scope of vision than that of any other animal created. He is not so fleet as the deer, but the muscles of his limbs enable him to run down the fleetest courser, by their strength and endurance.

Aside from the organization of his brain and the vast amount of cerebral substance which evidently denotes his susceptibility and powers of comprehension; aside from the action of his spirit-nature, which controls the action of all impressions and their effect on his brain, the whole fashion of his physical nature exhibits him as capable of enduring every vicissitude of climate and every condition of life, from the rudest savage life, where, isolated and solitary, he exists as a beast of prey, to that condition where, in large numbers, he is forced to provide for his physical wants in another and entirely different manner.

By the size and shape of his lungs, and the connection

of the vessels which convey the blood through them to all parts of his body, he manifests his ability to exist in the highest altitudes as well as in those locations where the atmosphere is humid or blended with a thousand ingredients deleterious to life. By the exquisite fashioning of his skin he can throw off what is obnoxious to health, and by the peculiar arrangement of its organization he can endure the most intense heat as well as the most severe cold.

His digestive organs can dispose of an immeasurable variety of food, taken separately or collectively; and, perhaps, there is no other animal that can so long exist without food or drink, without injury to his body, as man in his natural state. Take him in all the developments of his physical system, he exhibits, as a whole, a distinct class, in which certain characteristics are observed possessed by him alone, and yet so intimately blended with the peculiarities and physical attributes of so many of the other animals around him, that it appears as if in him were to be found something which exists in all the species, orders, genera, and classes of every created thing, that he might in his physical nature be able to conform to the same conditions and circumstances of life in which they are placed, and that his system might be able, under such circumstances, to develop the same properties and capacities which might be required if called on to act when so situated.

Thus you will perceive that I intend to describe man in his physical construction as representing the best characteristics of most of the other animals of which he stands at the head; and that from this conformation of his physical nature he would be able, were it necessary, without the coöperation of his spirit, to take the lead in every thing which belongs to mere material existence; that his organization would enable him to do just what every other animal does, and much that they, by their organization, could not possibly accomplish; that his very organization shows by its similarity to that of other animals, by the shape, size, and position of his bones, muscles, nerves, etc., etc.,

that he was formed after the separate genera of other animals were created, and that by this correspondence he was
an improvement on all and every other animal that preceded him.

Thus, when you compare man with the dog, horse, etc.,
etc., you find in him certain organs which resemble the
same organs in those animals, and so you may go through
the whole creation, and view the various organs in every
animal, and you will find some organ in man which will
correspond to some organ in them. I grant that a somewhat similar correspondence can be traced in the several
divisions of orders or classes of particular animals, but in
no one animal can this universal connection be found. As
if man alone, of all the created works of God, could claim
kindred with every part of that creation, of which, emphatically, he is the masterpiece.

And when we thus view him in his physical organization, as comprising all the various attributes of the separate
orders, species, etc., etc., of animals, all, as it were, concentrated into one body, we are prepared to comprehend
why, of all other animals, he should be selected to receive
that other part of his nature, which, while it places him
as the master of the world, likewise gives him preëminence
in eternity. His physical nature, were it deprived of its
soul, would, by its own peculiar organization, claim prece-
dence over every other animal, and he would have controlled them to minister to his wants; but when we view
him as possessed of a separate and distinct identity, we
can then conceive of how much importance his physical
nature was to creation, and for what purpose God breathed
into his nostrils the breath of life.

This reflection is worthy of some consideration, for it
opens to your minds the subject of man's creation in a different aspect than, perhaps, was ever before presented to
your minds.

On looking over creation you can trace each distinct
class of insects, birds, and animals from the germ to the

perfect development, commencing at one point and continuing in a direct connection in a determinate succession; but in every variety you can distinguish the source from which it sprung.

In every development you can detect the same properties manifest, in a greater or less degree, as in the parent source, and you are struck with the similarity of instinct, appetites, etc., etc., which characterize all the race from one variety to another. But were you to separate the spirit from the body of man, you would not, could not, trace that same manifestation in all the varieties of his species found on earth, for the reason I have given, that his material nature takes on so many of the various attributes of the animal creation, that his manifestations are universal, not special. And this view brings us to another part of our subject of much moment and importance.

If there were no spirit connected with man's material organization, would he have remained in the same state of existence his position placed him in, as have the other animals around him?

You ask how can this be answered? In reply, let me say, that in all the works of God, when he has instituted certain conditions of existence, the developments in that state or condition are always in exact relation to the very attributes that condition manifests, whether in animals or vegetables.

Thus the horse, under all circumstances, is a horse, the ox an ox, the apple is yet an apple. Each species may develop some new attribute as a species, but it always refers to the very nature it exhibits, from the germ to the development, and it can not transcend the position in the scale of existence in which it has been placed. As a horse, the breed may be improved, but the improvement can not go beyond the increase or development of its properties as a horse. It does not generate any new attribute which connects it with a class of animals above it, but is always connected with beauty of form, strength of body, fleetness, docility, etc., etc. So with all other animals. And in some, when under the fostering care of man they apparently develop something new in relation to this law, they often return to their old habits and nature whenever the influence is lessened or they are allowed the least degree of liberty.

But I will continue this subject at our next meeting.

In answer to a question asked by one of the circle, it was written:

Why, men are constantly surrounded, outside of a certain sphere, with dark spirits, who, when that sphere is opened, can always come in contact with certain gross parts of their organism, and thus influence their minds. They are not outside, but quite near, as they always attend the good spirits wherever they go on earth. Your physical nature is the means by which they influence your mind, and as the good spirits are in connection with your mind, they are in connection with your body. The former influence your spirit direct, the latter by exciting some of the propensities of your material nature, and thus reach the mind.

Section Thirty-six.

Tuesday, Nov. 22, 1853.

The Doctor being at my house, I inquired if I had received aright, the night before, an impression that an alteration had been made in the public room of the community where my wife resided? I asked the question in this general form; but the impression I alluded to was, that one expression used in my evening's lecture at Philadelphia, a few evenings since, had been inserted in a scroll under my seal.

My question was answered by giving me a minute account of the alterations which had been made in the public room alluded to. It had been much improved and beauti-

fied with windows descending to the floor, and between the
windows pictures of the most interesting acts of our efforts
in the cause. Over the commander's seat was a canopy,
in the center of which, and visible from all parts of the
hall, is the seal. In front of that seat are the three banners
I saw in the procession.

I do not give all the details, only the important items.

I said in reply, that was not the alteration I referred to,
and I supposed, therefore, I said, that it was my imagination which had given birth to the idea of the scroll.

It was answered:

"Why, Judge, this *is in* a room, but it is the room of
judgment, and you can see it in a moment."

And, sure enough, in a moment I was in the spirit-world
again, and walking rapidly up the broad avenue toward the
fountain; there I saw assembled a large crowd of spirits,
with very pleasant smiles of joy and welcome. My wife
was standing at the entrance of her garden, with her two
children and the old man, her attendant, by her side. The
presiding spirit waved his hand for me to pass on to my
wife, and I did so. I passed through her garden, toward
her mansion, she leaning on my arm, and saying to me,
"Is not this like old times, now?"

I entered the hall of her mansion, a wide and spacious
one, with pictures hanging on its walls. As I ascended the
stairs, I caught a glimpse of one of them. It was a portrait of me, at the age of about nineteen, in my military
dress—preserving very faithfully the likeness of me the
first time she ever saw me after my mere boyhood.

When we reached the head of the stairs (for this time
she ascended with me), I observed an inscription over the
entrance to my room, "Leave not Hope behind."* She

---

* This evidently referred to what I had once said to her when I was connected with the State Prison, that, unlike Dante's Infernal Regions, I wanted
to inscribe over its entrance, "Leave not Hope behind."

entered the room with me, and conducted me to a large easy-chair directly behind the altar, and while I was seated in it, she leaned on its back.

I turned my attention at once to the left-hand corner of the room, where, on the former occasion, I had seen that terrible dark record; and now, to my great joy, I observed that the letters had, many of them, faded so that I could not read them; some of them had been scraped off, as if to make room for something else; and she called my attention to one spot, and said, "See! that record is all gone." My answer was, "Yes, my love! but the memory of it has not.".

She called my attention to other things, and I saw from each end of the altar there sprang up a jet of soft, golden light, which diffused a mellow hue over all the room. She pointed to the end of the room at my right, and it was very beautiful.

There were two windows which descended to the floor, and opened out upon a balcony, from which was a view of her gardens, and the groves and water beyond them. There was a cornice across the end of the room, as if of crimson velvet, festooned up by golden cords, the tassels hanging just below it. There were curtains to the windows, reminding me of the cartoons of Raphael; but what was pictured on them, and whether by painting or embroidery, I could not tell, for they were drawn back and festooned up. Between the windows the groundwork of the panel was a dazzling crimson; on it was painted in blue luster my seal, the arm in bronze, tinged with crimson, and the letters on the scroll in gold. Below the seal were two spirits, holding in their hands a curtain of white satin, the shading and folds of it very perfectly painted, and on it were the words, "Dear companions of my toil and faith! Pause not! Faint not! Falter not!"—the expressions I had used in my lecture.

The letters seemed to be formed of a golden light, for they flickered as if a living flame, and they were seen through a thin, gauze-like screen of pale blue.

I saw, also, a statue in each corner of the room : one was of a man naked to his feet, around which hung his pantaloons. His arms were tied above his head to a ring in the wall, and his face was turned over his left shoulder with a mingled expression of terror and defiance. Behind him stood a large, burly man, with his right hand as if to strike, and holding in it a cat-o'-nine-tails. The remaining figure of the group had his back toward me, but his right arm was raised, as if saying, "Forbear." It represented a scene which once occurred in the State Prison.*

---

* It seems to me that I ought to tell the story which is here referred to— not merely that the allusion may be the better understood, but to convey more distinctly the idea how far our earthly actions penetrate into our spiritual life.

In our former volume I remarked that I was appointed President of the Board of Governors (Inspectors, as they were called) of one of the State prisons of New York. The mode of government which obtained was entirely that of force; the cat-o'-nine-tails was freely used, and horrible cruelties were daily perpetrated. I found this so engrafted on the whole system, that it was almost impossible to change it. I, however, contemplated a change, which was finally effected. In the mean time I felt that I ought to witness, personally, what this whipping with the cat-o'-nine-tails was, so that I might judge of it for myself; yet I found it difficult to force myself to do so, and time ran on without my screwing up my courage. At length, one day, passing through the main hall of the prison, I accidentally stumbled on the scene; I saw a group assembled around the whipping-ring, and a prisoner tied up to it, as represented in the statue. I approached them and found the flagellation had not yet begun, though all things were in readiness. I inquired of the officers what offense he had committed, and learned that he had been making a noise in his cell at night.

While I was speaking with them, his head was turned over his shoulder, as in the statue, and he was scanning my looks very intently, with a strong expression in his own of a hope that I would interfere. I did not, however, but moved back a few steps, as if to witness the scene. His countenance rapidly changed, and assumed a hardened, desperate look, and he said, " Whip away! It ain't the first time. It has never done me any good yet, and won't now."

I immediately said to the officers, " Then take him down. He knows best what will do him good. You don't whip for any thing else. Take him to his room, and in the mean time we'll think of something that will do him good." He was untied and directed to put on his clothes. He was very much surprised, and all the time he was dressing he was looking at me, as if asking what it all meant. As I turned to leave, he spoke to me in a very submissive, respectful tone, and requested permission to say a few words to me. I assent-

The group in the other corner was a statue of myself, holding in my hand a map, to which I was pointing the attention of a slave, who, seated on the ground at my feet, was intently gazing on it.

I could not see what was delineated on the wall of the room behind me; but the eradication of so much of that gloomy record awakened in me such feelings of gratitude, that I said to my wife, "Let us kneel together, for that we have never yet done, and give thanks to God!" She asked if she might not call in our children? I said, "Certainly." And as we four knelt around that altar, I uttered this prayer:

"O! thou great Jehovah! beneficent Father of all created things! shed abroad upon our hearts the impress of thy divine love, that we, aiming at thy purity, may revel in its mellow light forever."

We arose, and she, leaning on my arm, led me from the room. As we were leaving it, I turned to look at the other side of the room; she playfully checked me, saying, "Remember Lot's wife."

We then entered a room on the opposite side of the hall, which was the exact counterpart in all respects, in every little article of furniture even, of my library in the house where she died. It looked out, however, upon a different scene.

---

ed, and took him to my office, where I discovered that he was laboring under disease which was fast verging into insanity; that he had been unable to sleep during the night, and had asked the guard for some water. His request not being attended to, he had repeated it rather impatiently, and in too loud a tone, and that was his offense. I found from his story, and from inquiries of the officers, that he was an old offender, had been in prison two or three times before, and was one of the most turbulent and unruly among the eight or nine hundred prisoners there congregated.

I put him into the hospital, and kept him there about a fortnight. I frequently conversed with him, and finally returned him to his work. During the residue of his confinement in that prison he was one of the most orderly, submissive, and obedient men there; and in my efforts to reform the government of the prison, I frequently referred to his case as an instance of what might be done by judicious kindness instead of brute force.

She called me to the front window, and there I beheld a large collection of spirits, who, with musical instruments and with their voices, sang a song she used to sing to me so often. It was, "John Anderson, my Joe!"

My vision was now so improved, that whereas before I had seen only the blended light of the spirits who hovered in the air over the scene, now I saw each one separate and distinct. They were of all imaginable hues and colors, and presented a picture lovelier far than imagination ever conceived.

In the earlier part of the evening, when Lord Bacon had spoken of my son, I had wanted to inquire as to his characteristics. "Now," my wife said to me, "look at him, and judge for yourself if he is not all we would have him to be." I did so, and was not a little amused at the faithfulness of the copy of myself; but he had a good deal more modesty than his father.*

My wife also called my attention to the country below our elevation, and which at my last visit I had seen lighting up, as if improving spiritually, and which I had supposed was intended as an allegorical representation of our earth's condition. She, having noticed my error, now said to me, "No! that is an actual reality in the spirit-world, and shows you how intimate is the connection between yours and ours. As you rise in light, and knowledge, and purity, so does the world above you rise, for their affection for you keeps them down. As you elevate the pedestal the statue rises."

As I stood gazing, suddenly the tower, which was now completed, was lighted up, and threw its glowing light far over the scene below, showing the inhabitants below there was a brighter world above, and the way to it.

At length I turned to leave the library, and said to my son as I did so, "This, Master Sam, is where you pursue

---

* He died more than twenty-five years ago, in the third year of his age, and was now grown to manhood.

your studies till I come ?" He replied, "Yes, father, but I
do not study the same books you did. Yours had too much
of man in them; mine have more of God."

After we passed down the stairs, my wife led me through
her bedroom to the piazza. I pointed to my military
badges, and told her I must say to her as Bacon had once
said to me, "Don't remind me of my earthly absurdities."
"Yes," was her reply; "but the propensities which took
that form in your youth, now properly directed, enable
you to fight the battle of truth so well;" and she asked me
if I remembered the story of two brothers which many
years ago I had read to her? and said, "That is the difference between giving to our faculties a proper and an improper direction."

She left me at the entrance to her grounds, and the presiding spirit, taking me by the arm, walked down the path
with me, and said to me, "You now see how the consciousness of doing good can obliterate the record of evil. Go on
as you have begun, and perhaps even before you shall have
left the earthly form, that room may be fitted for the residence of a pure spirit. I am not unconscious of what you
have written to-day. Continue so. Forget ever yourself,
and think only of the cause, for in the cause is involved
the good of others. And now, farewell, till we meet again,
and that will be soon."

Section Thirty-seven.

Thursday, Nov. 24, 1853.

The circle met this evening. Mr. and Mrs. Sweet were absent, and two friends from the Shaker Society of New Lebanon were present.

After a few words of a private nature, it was written:

FOR a moment let me attempt to instruct you on certain matters in respect to which you seem not to have a perfectly clear opinion.

It certainly can not be the case that any member of this circle has professed such a belief in spiritual teachings, that what they have learned should in any way affect the existing relations of life, other than that they have afforded you a clear idea of your duties, and that they have inculcated a higher standard of love to God and to man.

For what purpose has God created man, organized his material part, and mingled with this organic creation an essence, a spirit-portion, which is to live after the primitive body shall have passed into the matter out of which it was fashioned?

The body of man is familiar to your senses, and the constituents out of which it is composed have been so analyzed by man, that even the most minute particle has been made as plain as the whole person.

But the soul still remains a mystery, notwithstanding all that has been taught you of its powers, its capacities, and its relationship with its Creator.

Can it be possible that I should be able to convey to your minds an adequate idea of what it is and the part which it is to perform in its ultimate existence? I know that what I am this night discussing has been the earnest thought of many of your circle, and I feel that it may be this earnest desire to penetrate still further into the mysteries of spirit that has induced me to take that for my subject to-night. Dimly as I shall be able to shadow to you the ideas which are my own, still I do hope that what I say may afford content at least to your minds for the present, if it does not present an entire solution of your inquiries.

The soul, then, as you have learned, is a part of the God himself, and it is not an arbitrary creation, but springs spontaneously forth to fill up that connection with one part of creation, as much as the whole cause is manifest in the universe itself. By this spontaneous emanation it receives and retains its individuality, and is more or less affected by the organization with which it is blended. The soul is a God of itself, for it possesses the power of generating thought, creating out of that thought the tangible evidences of its power. But not creating itself, it is under the laws instituted by the source from which it sprung. As it is an emanation from the God, it possesses much of its nature, and it is only its admixture with matter that prevents its manifesting the attributes which such an origin has conferred on it. Its present destiny is to assist in the development of itself in its combination, and also in the perfection of that matter with which it is combined; for as God, in his connection with the matter he has evolved from nothing, is continually speeding it to its development, so man's spirit, in his present relation with matter, is continually assisting the body to assume, under the laws of God, that condition which will enable that spirit to manifest its powers and faculties in a greater degree, and also to contribute, by this development of the perfect body of man, a true appreciation of all the influence of those laws, and thus to institute in this world a system of perfect harmony of material action.

I do not believe, strictly speaking, that this kind of teaching is of the most profitable kind for your minds, for, say what I might, there would be a mystery still surrounding the subject which can not be unfolded until your spirits see the dawning of that eternity, the sun of which is spirit, and whose countless constellations are spirit's spirit. But I wish to make a few suggestions only, that I may afford some idea which will content your minds to wait until the dawning of that glorious day shall afford to your spirits' view the positive demonstration of that reality, the imperfect idea alone of which you can now appreciate. Thus, then, in its material connection, the spirit assists in the establishing of a material harmony, by which creation will be advanced, and by which the spirit can better understand its true and ultimate destiny.

For when every material thing, and especially man's own material part, is in such exact harmonic relation and action that no impression on his senses is unjust or untrue, then he can better understand the moral laws of God, and can, by this harmony of action, the more perfectly develop those properties which will produce that state of existence where love will reign supreme and God be acknowledged over all.

Admitting this, what then is his destiny after the spirit's separation from matter? Were there no impediments, in consequence of the inharmonious action of the material body of man, the spirit, taking from earth but little, if any impurity, would, as soon as it leaves the body, assume that position in the spheres which it now reaches by a long course of progression and development. It would immediately assume those distinct duties which it is required now to perform only after years of study, thought, and a persistent adherence to those divine laws which develop its true nature and attributes. But now, as you well understand, its condition is one of progression, and it lingers by the way to rid itself of those evils which its association with the body has created.

The ultimate destiny of the soul is to assist God in the administration of his laws, and to people those worlds

rolling in space so far beyond the reach of man's comprehension that I could not describe them were I to attempt.
Its ultimate destiny is to arrive at that state of intellectual
power and greatness that it can aid in carrying on the
operations of the millions on millions of worlds, and to
teach the incalculable number of spirits, born and unborn
into the spirit-world, their own nature, and the position
which they too are to occupy.

This destiny comprehends every thing which you can
understand of truth, holiness, love, knowledge, and more,
much more, than I can tell you. I have merely stated
what I understand as fact, and I also understand that in
addition to what I here have stated, there is a degree of
happiness and glory and other duties which I am not yet
able to comprehend. But as the spirit arrives at that state
it occupied when thrown off from the Godhead, it then is
invested with certain attributes, of which no spirit here
can give you any knowledge.

But after all that I have said, no finite mind could comprehend the whole destiny of spirit, even if it were told it
in plain, distinct terms; for, if we can not comprehend
what that condition must be after the spirit has arrived at
the point at which it was disintegrated from the parent
source, how can you realize what that destiny can be? It
therefore may be sufficient for us all to know, that when
the soul is conscious that it has assisted an erring spirit to
progress; when it is conscious that it has contributed to
foster in the human heart that desire to progress which
will impel it onward to eternity and purity; when it is
conscious that it has sustained the sinking courage; when
it has sacrificed its own desires to aid another's aspirations;
and when it has yielded to the law of love, and for that
love forgiven all wrongs against itself, and has loved the
very hand or mind which has done that wrong; when it
has felt its own nature, like the God from whom it sprung,
impel it to clasp once again thè weak, the erring, the very
wicked of its kind and say, "Brother, go with me;" when

it shall, even if it costs it a pang, confer one happiness on
a human heart, then it may know, despite all reasoning,
despite all theories, despite all self-intentions, that it is indeed progressing toward that state, where its ultimate destiny will be to shed abroad on all around those very attributes of happiness which it so keenly appreciates, for he
who confers by love, happiness on others, can by that very
love enjoy above his kind that true happiness which comes
direct from God.   BACON.

I was then impressed, and had this

VISION.

I was in the scene where I had been so often, and was
approaching the fountain. As I did so, the presiding
spirit, taking me by the arm, said, "Now go with me, I
will lead you to new scenes. Are you capable," he said,
closely scanning me, " of bearing the sight? We will see."

So I passed with him, gliding rapidly to quite a distance
to the mountain with its golden light, which I have mentioned. Here we ascended a flight of steps cut in the
rock. It was a laborious, toilsome ascent, and as I arose,
I had a view of the plane which I had just left, and of the
second and third below it, each elevation that I attained
seeming to expand my view.

At the head of the steps was a gateway or entrance
flanked on the outer edge of the precipice with a round
tower, from whose summit hung in easy folds a flag.
From the entrance streamed far into the distance a flood
of golden light, as if the place was overflowing full of it,
and it was gushing out to light up all it could reach. We
began to come within its influence ere we gained the summit, but when we attained the entrance and became enveloped in it, it produced a singular feeling, which I experienced even physically while I was describing the scene,
and which thrilled me with love and happiness, and I exclaimed, " If this is a specimen, then there is indeed a happiness in the spirit-life of which we have had no concep-

tion. If such is the effect on me just entering there, what must it be on its residents?"

I can not describe the scene which opened to my view. It was filled as far as my eye could reach, with a mellow, golden light mingled and fringed with a rosy hue. Imagine the most gorgeous, and beautiful, and variegated garden ever pictured in Eastern fable; take the most beautiful scenic representation of our theaters, multiply them a million times, and you can scarcely conceive the reality that was before me. What happiness to be there! And yet I saw higher elevations still in the distance. It seemed to me impossible there could be higher conditions of beauty and happiness than the scene before me. Yet there were, for I saw them.

Every thing was so full of joy and gladness. Look where I might, I saw it; among birds, beasts, plants, man; all— all were full of it, overflowing with it. I saw innumerable spirits moving about; some in shady bowers, some sitting beside a murmuring brook, some reclining on beds of flowers, some floating as it were on the perfume and drinking it in, some sauntering around sparkling fountains whose waters were of different colors, some strolling in the smooth walks in pairs and in groups, lovingly clinging to each other. I saw no one alone. No sad recluse harbored there, but each one's happiness was in that of others. Interspersed amid the flowers and shrubbery were many statues. But I can not describe the infinite variety of beautiful objects before me. I stood and gazed with solemn awe.

Ever and anon as I gazed around me, I saw in the distance, his head shining like a blazing sun, but with a mellower light, the presiding spirit of that community, and I learned from my guide that all the spirits I saw around me, and many others not then there, had duties elsewhere, and here assembled only in the pauses of their toil. They were constantly coming and going, and this was their relaxation only.

The spirits around me perceived me, and saw my emotion. Some encouraged me, some smiled pleasantly at my embarrassment, and some beckoned me to enter, and at length I approached that presiding spirit. He was of gigantic proportions, and sat upon a throne which seemed to rest on banks of clouds. He was enveloped in a halo of that glorious mellow light, and sat in an erection something like a niche with its statute. The beauty of his throne I can not describe. It was enameled white, and ornamented with gold and blue. Great numbers of spirits were on each side, and behind and over him. In front of him it was vacant. I was led up to him—not directly in front, for I could not bear his dazzling brightness.

He said to me, " Is it difficult for you to conceive a condition of man so superior to your mortal existence? Know that we have only entered on the threshold of that eternity of love and happiness which is your destiny. The difference between you and the merest atom of inanimate matter from which you have been developed is but a step —though a step of ages—a feeble, halting, crippled step in that eternity. See to what you may attain! Is it not important you should understand how to attain it, so as to hasten your progress, and not retard it? That knowledge is now proffered you; are you prepared to receive it? It would have been in vain to have proffered it to inanimate matter, to the vegetable, to the unreasoning animal, or even to the reasoning animal, man, until in his progress he had attained the capacity to comprehend it. Are you yet at that point, or must the lesson so often attempted to be taught to man be again abandoned for a fitter season? Must they who can be used as the instruments of conveying that knowledge to man be again, as they so often have been, done to death for that cause? Is man ready yet again to strike the hand that is outstretched to lift him up, or will he grasp it with some appreciation of the infinite love it proffers? Is man yet so enveloped in his material garment, that the light of Heaven's love can not penetrate it?

Is his heart so hardened with self, that even Heaven's purity can not soften it? Is he so wedded to his animal propensities, that even angels' voices fall silent upon his ear? Is he like the earth from which he sprung, dead to the voice of that love with which heaven echoes now and forever?

"Oh! how.long! how anxiously! how lovingly have we waited to see him arrive at that condition when he could comprehend the love that was so ready to embrace him! Shall we wait yet longer? Are we doomed yet again to turn sadly away, frustrated in our efforts, disappointed in our hopes of his redemption? Must we yet behold him, like a worm, still grovel in the dust from which he sprung ¿

"O! bethink you! It is the Spirit of God himself which you thus by your evil propensities chain darkly to the earth. It is his Spirit of eternal life spoken into your being which you thus bury beneath the mountain load of your material passions. O! bethink you! It is the immortal spirit of love pervading all the universe which you thus smother in the dark atmosphere yourselves create.

"Rise, then, O man Lazarus! and come forth and step from the grave into which ignorance and bigotry have thrust you. Walk forth in the image of a living soul, brightened by the immortal spark which is from the eternal sun, and to him. Come forth from the dark tomb to which you have consigned yourself, and come to the arms of the bright and the pure, which are outstretched in love to embrace you.

"And oh! could you but know the thrill of glad joy which you could cast through heaven's vast mansions by your response—could you but hear the shouts of rejoicing that would hail your reply—could you but know the happiness you would confer on the countless multitudes above you, who have mourned your darkness, and who would hail your ascent from its gloom, you would not pause in your efforts to share it, or repel the Saviour which thus again comes to redeem you.

"Say this much, O mortal! to thy weak and erring fellows—speak to them with the trumpet-tongue of Truth—speak to them Heaven's own teachings, and thou wilt yet find deep buried in the darkest and hardest heart a voice that will answer, for it is the Spirit of God that slumbers there."

He leaned forward when he had said this, and pressed his lips to my forehead. "Go forth," he said, "with the seal of Heaven on thy brow, and beware that thou taint not its brightness by aught of earth's impurity, for of him to whom much is given, much shall be required."

Previous to his beginning to speak, the whole of that great crowd of spirits was moving about, talking, laughing, etc., but while he spoke there was a holy calm, a perfect silence resting on the scene. Joyhood ceased its laugh, the brook staid its murmur, and even the leaf which had rustled in the breeze was still. But when he ceased, there arose from that bright host a joyous shout saying, "O man! man! weak and erring man! know that thy Redeemer still liveth."

The sound of that shout floated softly on my ear, and seemed to bear me away on its wings, and so I departed.

21

Section Thirty-eight.

Monday, November 28th, 1853.

At the circle at the Doctor's, through him it was written:

WHEN, after a shower, the sun has broken forth from
the clouds, and every blossom and flower, every tree and
shrub, rejoice in the invigorating freshness of nature restored, there still lingers around the mountain's top the
mists which conceal it from view.

The broad earth, clad in its robe of green, laughs out in
its renewed strength its grateful praise; for the rich sustenance which comes from above, and the woods, which
clothe the high ascent to the mountain's summit, give forth
their rich incense of nature's perfume, their meed of thanks
for the boon bestowed. But there hang these dark clouds,
like a huge mantle, shrouding from below the gloomy
rocks and the jutting precipices, as if all indeed there was
storm and night. So, too, the world—so, too, man. When
to his mind, truth, like the grateful shower, comes laden
with the rich attributes of good, and every token is fraught
with love and happiness, there stands aloof, invested with
the cloudy darkness of prejudice or error, the stern and
unyielding determination of his will. When has there
been vouchsafed to human mind a greater lesson than nature everywhere presents? When has God's wisdom assumed a more benignant form than when he has offered to
his mind the simple analogy of his love and power in the
crudest work of his hands? It is not in those glorious
manifestations of his Almighty power, or in the terrific exhibitions of his awful grandeur, that man is to learn how

closely connected he is with him, the Infinite! the Incomprehensible! It is not when the ocean is lashed in fury in a storm, its huge billows upheaving their mighty crests, and answering back in their surge heaven's artillery, or in their maddened plunge sweeping away the works of man—ay! and of nature, too, or in the lightning's flash, shivering the rocks, or giving to the storm and the whirlwind the sublime and awful aspect of nature warring with herself, that we are to be convinced that God is mighty in power, inconceivable in majesty!

No; all these exhibitions of the terrible attributes by which God governs the world he has created, cause the soul to shrink within itself, and tremble in its utter helplessness; they terrify, they paralyze. But when the humble flower opens its purple leaves to the morning sun, and exhibits nature's jewels in the dew which glistens in its rays, the soul of man can realize the glory of the Deity, the love which fashioned it, and can, without fear, look through nature up to nature's God. My friends, 'tis the silent workings of the spirit which is the labor of progression. While heaven can not be taken by a *coup de main*, so the spirit can not be stormed into a belief. The mind, in search after truth, must be free to elect, must be independent in its choice; but it requires no force to precipitate it into goodness. Let, therefore, the eternal truths which we attempt to.teach you yield their rich influence in the effect which is perceptible in your acts, and learn that in the charitable considerations with which you view man in all his actions, is the seat of your progress. I rejoice once more to meet with you—to look around on your familiar faces, and to feel the chord of true affection vibrate in unison with my own spirit; and I am happy to say that I shall again have the pleasure of teaching you for some time to come; and I trust that even I shall have the great joy, when I shall meet you face to face in the spheres, when you shall know whether I have taught you truth or falsehood; and when wending our way together

toward the incomprehensible glories of the higher spheres,
my spirit shall see your spirits face to face. Then, yes,
oh! then may it be my great joy to say, "My son! my
daughter!" and to hear you respond, "My father!" "Yes,"
then shall I say, "your father am I—your spiritual guide
toward truth; but there is one greater than I who is the
truth, who is love—he is your Father and mine, for he is
God."   SWEEDENBORG.

Then, after a pause, it was further written:

The study of mind, in its various manifestations, is one
of the most curious and wondrous subjects of investigation
ever presented to the human intellect; and the phenomena
it offers, the remarkable phases it presents, are very like
the kaleidoscope, which, every turn it makes, represents
new combinations of colors and new forms of arrangement.

But the most interesting part of this inexplicable mystery is the effect of mental conclusion on action, and the
causes which induce conclusion, operating by its own force,
or arising from its prejudices.

That every mind arrives at the same result from the same
impression no one believes, or at least admits; but when
the mind, really desirous of arriving at truth, is so determined to act independently of that which in another mind
absolutely arrives at the same result, it is indeed as strange
as it is peculiar. There is something in the independent
action of mind searching for truth, and that kind of truth,
too, which brings permanent satisfaction, that inspires man
everywhere with respect. Regardless of the sarcasms and
censures of the world, it moves onward in its research, intent upon the object it has in view. There is a moral sublimity investing an individual resting on the consciousness
of his own purity when he breaks away from the trammels
of society and dares to think and act for himself. A mind
like this emulates the Creator, for it generates in itself its
principles of action, and is governed by causes of its own
creation. It is bound by no form or doctrine, and its ideas

are universal, for it sees in all things the universal application to all conditions of things and men a universality of action induced by a compliance with the laws of God.

Such a mind makes its impress whenever it comes in contact with mind, and gives an impetus to thought which is hindered by no barrier but its incapacity to think; but when this mind, free in every element of greatness and nobility of purpose, motive, and action, manifests its inability to grant to another mind the same privileges itself assumes, it exhibits the taint with which mind is encumbered when it is confined by its mortal connections.

Why should this mind open intuitively to the freedom which God has bestowed on the thought? Why should this mind, appreciating all that is good, pure, and holy, and acting in concert with these mighty principles, disregard the mind which claims affinity by its aspirations, and in its acts and prejudices assume that it can not comprehend the other? Why, by act, send the trembling hope back on itself and cloud the visions which that hope has called up? Why seek not to know the earnest efforts of the other to understand the way by which it has climbed to its elevated condition?

Why lavish on minds whose surface alone reflects the image of the deep emotions which move the very depth of the other? Why crush the dawning truths and pure aspirations which soon would lead sentiment to associate with sentiment, and establish a concord as harmonious as it will be lasting? Why say to itself, I can give to you my respect, but beyond this I can not go? Who has limited the longing desire itself has felt for truth? Who has barred up its own passage to a higher and better elevation? Who has said thou shalt not understand those laws which will bring peace and knowledge to your spirit, and who has dared to say thou shalt not understand thy connection with thy God? In all this it has felt the assistance of those mighty harmonies which have established laws and given birth to principles. Searching for light, it has penetrated the infinite darkness with which a thousand causes have shrouded mind, and has found light, at last, beaming upon itself in a flood of glorious radiance.

Beyond this world it has sought and found the same affinities which another mind now seeks to obtain, and it has had the freedom of unlimited converse with all God's laws, divine and physical, as the guerdon of its courage. But shall mind, thus enlightened by truth, refuse that same light to another? Shall the affections and sentiments be coldly looked on when the unutterable longing for companionship is manifest by the similarity of its desires? No. Whatever influences may thus mark the true efforts of its own researches here, the future will place together on one plane mind with mind that asks for, that desires truth. No unkind relatives shall then interrupt the harmonious flow of the same hopes and wishes for the good, the pure, the holy. No prejudices or impressions of years shall prevent these two spirits from being bound together by the same motives. No transient thought of what may be the beautiful, the sublime, the awful unfoldings of truth itself shall then interfere with the same pursuits and the same objects.

Mind, thus acted on and thus acting, is the same in the destiny which their desires will insure, and as one, yet independent, they will wend their way till the time when the fulfillment of their earthly struggles is accomplished.

BACON.

Section Thirty-nine.

Monday, Dec. 5, 1853.

The circle met at Dr. Dexter's. Through me this vision was given :

VISION.

I saw a spirit standing erect in a chariot, to which horses seemed to be harnessed. He was holding the reins in one hand and in the other brandishing a javelin. He was driving through the darkness of space. The chariot and horses were of a silver color, set out by the dark background. He was moving swiftly through space and leaving a train of light behind him. He was followed by a great number of spirits not quite as bright as he was. They, too, passed along with great velocity, apparently very intent on some object in the distance. Ere long I saw them arrive at the object of their pursuit.

It was a wonderful sight, and opened to me new views of the spirits' power. A vast nucleus of a new world had been formed, evolved out into the regions of space, and it had been set in motion in its appropriate orbit. It had moved in that orbit long enough to have a portion of its matter condensed in the center, but a vast amount of it still remained uncondensed.

It had been attended in its course by those spirits, whose duty it was to see to its proper development, and all had gone on well for ages, while a new world was thus being formed out of the disjointed matter scattered through space; but now it had met with some disturbing cause. The spirits attending it had tried to counteract the tendencies of that disturbance. They had occasionally succeeded in

checking it, but had not been able entirely to overcome it.
In spite of all their efforts it had gone on increasing its inharmonious action, so that when I approached it, it presented
the wonderful spectacle of a world raging, as it were, in
a furious passion, tearing itself to pieces, and it bid fair to
be scattered in broken fragments in all directions, for its
parts were moving with immense velocity but with great
irregularity.

The spirits attendant upon that world were very active.
I saw them moving from place to place seeking to overcome that discord, but seeing it increase upon them all
the time.

The spirit whom I saw in the chariot, with his long
train of attendants, had come to their aid. He stopped,
and paused to look upon the confusion before him. Two
or three of the spirits belonging to that world came out to
converse with him, apparently making a report to him.
They seemed very much excited, and well might they be!
Large masses, vast as our earth and our moon, were hurled
back and forth; some were dense and black, others luminous and lighted up by the burning mass. The whole were
revolving with frightful velocity, and every now and then
some vast mass would fly off from the center, thrown off
by the centrifugal power into the nebulous matter which
was more or less dense, which in like manner was disturbed by their passing through it, and thus the confusion was
constantly augmented. But the attractive power of the
dense center drew those masses back again, and they fell
back into the burning revolving center with a tremendous
crash.

This was frequently occurring with vast masses of the
dense matter, varying in size, in density, and in conditions
of ignition. The frightful velocity of the revolving motion
threw them off, and then their power of motion was resisted by the density of the nebulous matter through which
they were passing, and was finally overcome by the attractive power of the mass remaining in the center, thus

again forming a part of that center to be again thrown off, disturbing and deranging all the nebulous matter by their erratic wanderings, and bidding fair to resolve that forming world back into its original condition of disjointed matter wandering through space.

The spirits in attendance on that world were engaged in all parts of it, endeavoring to overcome these outbreaks and reduce its matter to an orderly obeisance to the laws which were developing it. Some, more venturous, were far down among the burning masses; and as I observed them, I saw one spot in the center unlike the burning masses which I had seen thus thrown off. It was of a red, flame-like color, and was continually moving up and down, like the pieces of dirt which a swiftly moving carriage-wheel will throw off from its rim. But the center was a bright white light, and did not partake of the confusion which pervaded the outer masses, though it was revolving on its axis with inconceivable velocity. That was the center of the nucleus, and its light was produced by the ignition caused by its velocity. The attendant masses of matter had not yet acquired the same velocity of revolution, though they revolved around the same center, and the consequence was, that though sometimes they were absorbed into the center and acquired its motion, at other times they were instantly thrown off, again to return to the center, drawn by its attractive power. The whole world thus revolving before me, and thus disturbed and deranged, was tens of thousands of miles in diameter, and thus was I permitted to see man's position as a ministering spirit of the Great First Cause, executing his laws amid the boundless realms of space, and performing his will in developing from disjointed matter new worlds, in their turn to be peopled by sentient and immortal beings.

I saw each spirit acting in his sphere, having a portion of the task to perform, some daringly penetrating even to that burning center, seeking there, at the very seat of the disorder, to overcome its destructive action; others at the extremity of the nebulous matter seeking there to prevent its being thrown beyond the redeeming power of the central attraction; and others, in great numbers, in various intermediate positions, essaying to enforce the law which aimed at the final amalgamation of this vast mass into a well-organized world, in its turn to roll on its course amid the countless worlds His almighty hand has fashioned. Each acting in his appropriate sphere had something to do.

I saw the directing spirit first order the spirits who were in and near the nucleus to withdraw to the outer edge of the nebulous matter. I saw them coming out in all directions, and as they became conscious of his presence and of the aid at hand, their excitement subsided. They felt that an adequate intelligence was with them, guiding all things.

He next directed the vast concourse that had accompanied him to join with and assist the others, and I saw them proceeding in all directions, far and near, to execute his bidding. They surrounded that immense mass of nebulous matter in vast numbers, and, at an appointed signal, with one accord pressed in toward the center. And I soon saw that it was rapidly decreasing in size, and its material was becoming condensed. This outward pressure I saw began to produce an effect on the center. One piece after another of the broken fragments which had been hurled off and were revolving irregularly around the common center, fell back upon and darkened its brightness; as they fell, some rebounded, but others were again forced down upon them, until they again became united to the mass of which they were once a part. And all this under the influence of the united pressure of that host of disembodied spirits, who had once tenanted mortal forms as we do.

What imagination could have conceived that this was a part of the destiny of man?

When that nebulous matter shall become a world, peopled as is this earth, and its inhabitants shall penetrate its interior, they will wonder at the disarrangement of its strata which they will discover, and speculate as to its causes. Yet how simple, how natural the laws which have caused it!

I perceived that the outer parts of the nucleus had a more rapid motion than the center, and the consequence was, that the darker masses, which had at length adhered together, became also ignited, and burned with a brighter light, their rapidity of motion causing the intense ignition, and I saw that at length order was issuing out of the chaos I had witnessed, and that all was coming to be well again.

While I was gazing on this scene, so full of sublimity, so novel, so grand, so instructive as to man's destiny here-after, the directing spirit said to me, "The same law whose action you have seen here, pervades the whole created uni-verse—man as well as matter, and matter in its smallest atom as in its vast aggregation in the largest world that rolls through space.

"To the intelligent mind there is no mystery in this. You, in your primary existence, at times see the elements breaking away from the domination of the laws established for their government. You, in a limited mode, with your feeble powers, can sometimes bring them back, and you do so often with rock, and earth, and water, and this which you have now witnessed is only a manifestation of the same law on a broader field. Know that every law gov-erning the universe operates as much in an atom as in a world, or a system of worlds, as much in your earth as in the countless multitudes of worlds that people the immen-sity of space. You here behold what is your duty and your destiny hereafter. You perceive what knowledge is necessary to enable you to perform your part hereafter. You now know that the knowledge of these laws, so ne-cessary for you, can be attained by you in your primary existence. Their great principles can be evolved by you from the earth you inhabit; and in your primary existence, by studying the laws of the nature which surrounds you, you can fit yourselves to be of His ministering spirits who wield this vast power throughout all space and to eternity. And recollect, those laws apply to man as well as matter, and that when you pass from one stage of existence to another you will find no law which you might not have learned in your primary condition. For the Great Creator governs the universe by immutable laws and has given to man the capacity to understand them.

"The means we have now used have been to give proper action and play to the primary law of creation, that which, when applied to matter you call attraction, and when applied to man you call love. That is the great principle which pervades the whole universe. Its action is sometimes disturbed in man as well as matter. Then the power of His ministering servants is employed to restore the due operation of the law.

"So it is now with man on the earth. The action of this law has been disturbed with him. Mankind, instead of being one harmonious whole, revolving duly and orderly in their eternal course, are disjointed and thrown from their proper position in broken fragments. The power of the spirit-world is brought to bear to remove the disturbing cause with you, and that power is to be exerted, not merely by the bright spirits who come from far-distant realms, but by you, too, who inhabit its broken and burning center. The spirits whose province it has been to attend upon your earth, and see to the due operation of its laws, have long struggled in vain against the disturbing causes which have made mankind a black, and burning, and disjointed mass.

"The Great Spirit of Love which rules all things has now sent to their aid the brighter intelligences, whose presence has hitherto been unknown to you. The task upon which they have entered will be performed, for it is easy compared with that which you have beheld.

"Fear not for the result. Go forth boldly in the work which you have begun, and in times long hence you will look upon mankind as I now look upon this world, lately so disjointed, moving truly on, obedient to that great law of attraction which will yet extract from the confused mass of your world immortal spirits, moving in harmony with and obedient to the laws of the Great Creator. To him be your thanks paid. To him lift up your grateful hearts, and while bowing in awe before his might, be ye sure that his love is almighty to save, all powerful to triumph over sin and death."

Section Forty.

Monday Evening, Dec. 12, 1853.

This evening, at Dr. Dexter's, the circle met, and through me a VISION was given.

I WAS in the darker regions where I had been before, but I had a much wider and more extended view, and saw a vast many spirits. They were uneasy, and wandering about from place to place, never content. The only relief there was to their monotony was the opportunity occasionally enjoyed of tormenting some one.

There was not the uniform somber look to the atmosphere that there had been. There was a faint light, like a cold watery sun, as we see sometimes on earth. It seemed as if a far-distant light began to penetrate here and there through the gloom.

I observed occasional efforts of some of the spirits to rise from the ground, like a young bird trying to fly for the first time. This was quite general with them; all seemed trying the experiment. They arose but a little distance, and some succeeded in floating along above the surface instead of walking as heretofore. They were disputing among themselves what it was, this new power.

It was a vast country that was before me. I saw to an immense distance. It was peopled by great numbers. Some parts were darker than others, and some of an ink-like blackness. They who lived in those dark places had no idea that there were any lighter places. It being too dark immediately around them to see abroad, they did not know of any brighter condition. There was a great variety of shade to the atmosphere, from a light gray to a black. I had seen the same variety in the happy spheres, only there it was a variety of light, here it was a variety of darkness.

I now approached one of those black spots, and there, in a miserable hovel, was a human being. He was ghastly thin, haggard, almost a skeleton. He knew no means of escape from that dark habitation, where he was all alone. The most violent of human passions were raging in him, and he was ever walking back and forth, like a chained tiger chafing in his cage.

There was a little light in that habitation of his, but it was an awful one. It was the red, flame-like light of his own eyes. They were open, and staring like burning coals, with a black spot in their center, and were constantly straining to see something, the darkness was so horrible to him! He had no companion but his own hatred and the memory of the evil past.

He paused once in a while in his walk, raising his clenched hand above his head, and cursed his Maker that ever he created him. He cursed also the false teachers who pretended to tell him the consequences of a life of sin, and yet knew so little of it themselves. They had told him of a hell of fire and brimstone only, and he knew that when he died, casting off his material garb, such a hell could have no effect upon him. He knew that such a hell was impossible. He therefore laughed the idea to scorn, and, dreaming of no other, he believed there was none. Now wakening to the reality of a hell far worse than had ever been painted to him, he cursed God and man that he had been left alone to dare its torments—that he had been left in ignorance of what must follow the indulgence of the material passions to which he had given up his whole life.

If you could have seen the agony that was painted on his face, the despair and hatred that spoke in every lineament, the desperate passion that swelled every muscle, and the horrible fear that stole over him of what further or worse might ensue from his daring defiance of his God, you would have shuddered and recoiled from the sight; and what aggravated all this suffering was his ignorance that there was any redemption for him, and the belief that it was forever!

When he was on earth, he felt always that he could fly to death as a refuge from earthly unhappiness, but he could find no death where he then was. He had never met yet the death that he expected, and he hoped to find it in his present existence. He had again and again, in every mode which his ingenuity could devise, attempted to slay himself, to put an end to his torment, but every attempt had only added to the conviction that it was without end.

He clasped his hands together over his head with a gesture of mute despair, and standing thus a few moments he cried, " Oh! for annihilation!"

If you could have heard the tone in which that imprecation was uttered, you could have formed some idea of the torments of the damned. He had worked himself into a frightful paroxysm of passion. He had thrown himself prostrate, and there, groveling in the dirt and writhing in agony, he howled like the most furious maniac that Bedlam's worst cell ever saw. At length, from sheer exhaustion, he was still. His physical powers could go no further, but the worm of his memory of the past which never dies, was but the more active because of the cessation of the ex-

ternal effort, and now, as he thus lay prostrate and exhausted, solitary and in utter darkness, all the evil deeds
of his life on earth chased each other through his memory,
sporting with his agony, and faithfully performing their
terrible duty of retribution.

Oh! how gladly he would have welcomed the insanity
of which he was reminded by his own wretched condition;
how he would have welcomed the surroundings of his material existence as appliances once again to help him forget! How he craved even physical pain and anguish, for
he believed that in them he might find some relief to the
mental agony which was so much worse! How he would
have welcomed some companion, no matter how degraded,
so that he could feel that he had some fellowship less horrible than with himself.

Section Forty-one.

Thursday, Dec. 15, 1853.

The circle met.   Through me it was said:

THAT remote light approaches, and amid it is seen a
spirit sitting on a throne, surrounded by great numbers
coming through space. A lovely voice comes from that
spirit, saying:

"Your grossness repelled—your increasing purity attracts us. The holy light of God's love in which we dwell
begins to surround you, and while it draws us down, it
lifts you up.

'It raises a mortal to the skies,
And brings an angel down.'"

The scene approaches quite near to me, so that I can recognize some of those who are standing near the throne. What a beautiful lesson it is!

"We come," says that spirit, "from the far-distant realms of the blest, to aid in the divine work of the redemption of man. We come, because the tidings have reached us in our bright abode that man may be redeemed; and we come, by His divine command, as your redeemer. Standing here by my side is the messenger who has triumphed over death and the grave, who has brought to us the glad tidings that the hour of your redemption is nigh. She comes, borne on the wings of that love which is of God; buoyed up by that purity which here is power, and in humble adoration of the Great Creator—in the child-like confidence—in the ever-enduring affection of the Heavenly Father, she has come, invoking to the task the power of the bright and the pure, who have long since passed from your sphere. It is the voice of God which speaks from her heart, and we obey it. It is the appeal of that affection which pervades all his creation which is the atmosphere in which we live, and which finds in our hearts a ready response. We come, then, in the might and love of our Heavenly Father, to dispel the darkness which ages of ignorance have cast around your footsteps—to overthrow that infidelity which has had its birth in the struggle between the ignorance which has mistaught and the knowledge which has confuted. We come to teach man that the great qualities which mark his existence, the attributes which he derives from the Great First Cause, and the exercise of which can alone bear him back to the source whence he springs, are knowledge and love—knowledge, in which alone is to be found the power to perform the great duty before you, and love, which attracts you to others, and others to you, and can alone give you strength to perform it. That love slumbers ever in the deepest recesses of your hearts; it is planted there by the hand of the Almighty. Bury it deep as you may beneath the mountain load of your material propensities, it must, it will yet spring forth to answer to the voice of God when it speaks to it.

"That knowledge! whence shall you derive it? From the voice of man? O how vain the hope! See how many centuries have rolled into eternity, while such has been the source whence you have drawn your knowledge, and see how far, in consequence of it, you are lagging behind your immortal destiny! Will you seek for it in the teachings of those whose whole material existence is enveloped in the selfish desire of building up sects? Will you seek it in the lessons which conflict with what you know, and see, and feel to be true in God's works around you? Will you seek it in the teachings which deaden the affections, which blight the divine love that is planted within you, and which forbid you to exercise your reason? Will you seek it in the teachings that war, day by day, and hour by hour, with the divine attributes of knowledge and love which are a part of your nature? Do you hope to find it in the awful struggle to which the human heart has been so long subjected, to receive a faith against which the instincts of your heart revolt, and which your God-like reason can not comprehend? Will you grope, thus darkly, amid the crumbling ruins which the past ages of ignorance have left in your path? With your God above you, will you still keep your eyes cast downward? Such has been the progress of the past, has it made man happy? Has it advanced him in the destiny that is before him? Has it not, on the other hand, filled your earth with strife, bloodshed, and misery? Can no lesson be drawn from the unhappy past? Will you still grope along, dead to the lessons which experience teaches? Will you still choose darkness rather than light, that your deeds may still be evil? and think you that the Great Creator has not revealed his laws so that you may understand them? Indeed, indeed he has. Through mortals and through nature—in his words and in his works alike—has he spoken to man. Read, learn, and be wise, but think not that in the great volume of nature

which he spreads out for your view he has omitted to write
his eternal and immutable laws, and has deigned to give
them only through the lips of weak and erring mortals like
yourselves. What are the countless worlds that sparkle
in the star-lit dome but pages in the great book of his
revelation? What are the innumerable hosts of sentient
beings, destined like you to inherit immortality, who inhabit those countless worlds, but parts of the great lesson
he is ever teaching?

"The grass that springs beneath your feet; the pebble
on which you tread; the brook, with its gentle murmur;
the cataract, with its hoarser roar; the ocean in its boundless majesty; the humble flower that blooms, unseen, amid
the depths of the forest; the lofty mountain, towering high
toward heaven; the cattle on a thousand hills; the dense
forest, redolent of life and joyous song; the soft and balmy
air; the storm that rages; the noonday sun, and the darkness of midnight; the aspirations of your own hearts; the
operation of the omnipotent thought that is placed within
you; the child nestling fondly in its mother's arms, and
old age tottering on the verge of the grave—all, all are
parts of the great lesson, He is teaching of his will and
his love. They are his revelations, and, unlike those which
man gives to man, to the honest inquirer they can not falsify
or deceive.

"Read, then, his word which he has thus written with
his own Almighty hand in the book thus open before you,
and see if there you can find one precept that conflicts with
the instincts of your immortal nature—which are ever,
'mid all your corruptions and darkness, teaching the abiding
truth that God is love, and that to be with him and of him,
love must be the breath of your nostrils, the life-blood of
your heart, the very spirit of your existence.

"This lesson we come to teach to weak and erring man,
to lift him from the degradation into which his material
propensities have sunk him, and draw him nigher unto
God.

"In that love, in man's capacity to understand and appreciate it, he will find at once his Redeemer and his Saviour. Whether it be spoken through mortal lips or through his vast creation, it is still full mighty to triumph over sin and death—all-powerful to save—all-conquering for man.

"This is the lesson which the bright hosts of heaven are pouring in such glorious streams of light on benighted man. The hour has come; the day of his redemption is nigh, and against its advent the powers of darkness can no longer prevail. Heaven, through its mighty mansions, rejoices in songs of praise to Him. Already has its joy visited your hearts, and soon shall it spread abroad, infusing into the hearts of mankind the knowledge of his love—that man, aiming at his purity, may bask in its glorious light forever and ever."

Section Forty-two.

Sunday, Dec. 18, 1853.

At a meeting of the circle, it was written, through Dr. Dexter:

OUR Father! thou who art the principle of truth, of good, and of purity, we pray that thou wilt teach us that when we seek for what is truth, we may begin from our own hearts, and upward progress to its source. That we may feel that no thought or act of ours can be measured by thy purity, unless it is in itself free from the propensities of our animal nature. That in regarding ourselves we may regard others, and learn to deal gently with their faults and errors—that we may become as little children before thee, tracing in the sunshine of thy love those glorious images

which should fill our minds—that we may forget all sins
against ourselves and learn to forgive as thou forgivest.
·We ask thee, O God, to send thy spirits to our aid in all
that becomes us as man and woman—and when at last we
lay our bodies in the grave, may we enter eternity without
one fear that our sins on earth shall then find us out.

SWEEDENBORG.

My friends, it has been so long since I have conversed
with you, that I am almost a stranger, but the love I bear
toward you all still burns as brightly when I am absent as
when I am present, and I wish for a moment that you would
listen to what I have to say.

It is well at proper times that I, who have assumed the
province of your spiritual teacher, should come to you and
teach you of those things it most behooves you to know,
that in the multiplicity of communications given to you by
other spirits, you may not forget the high and holy purpose for which these teachings were instituted.

It was not alone that the world should become edified
with the truths uttered by and to our circle, that we revealed them through your instrumentality. It was not to
prove by these means that a high order of intelligence was
capable of communicating through you the wonders of the
spheres. It was not that we might corroborate, by any
thing said or done at your circle, the sayings of spirits by
other mediums and to other circles. But there was a special object also in appealing to the individual character of
each member of your circle, to induce in each a new order
of thought, and by this means institute a new order of
action. It matters not what ideas are given you, or what
new revelations are made, and what the effect may be on
yourselves, so that you do but act in accordance with the
general principles established by our Creator.

I mean simply this, that all men are governed in their
feelings and acts by what impresses them as right. They
reason on what they receive, and what their mind decides

is truth. But there may be much error in this system of individual or independent thought; for the soul in its natural relations is influenced by what is obnoxious or that which is unpleasant. How much, therefore, may the spirit in its conclusions be biased by the unfavorable directions given to truth itself by the original and independent influences of the natural part. Conscious that we design to do well and live truthfully before God, the spirit assumes an original action which may have a strong foundation, but a superstructure that is weak and tottering.

My friends, the mind that can throw off the early affection it has acquired, except for evil, is indeed independent, but is it right? Can our affections, based on the gentle and true impulses of a nature whose material preponderances are but emphatically slight—can it set aside those ideas which come directly from the soul through less of grossness than in after-life, and be considered as other than erecting a superstructure weak and tottering? It may be that what are called reason and experience have changed ideas, but there is one great law which you are to understand, and that is, that as you grow older the material influences direct you so silently, so secretly, so unawares, that when you ascribe to the reason and progress of your understanding your change of thought, you may in fact obey this silent, secret, but all-powerful control of your material natures. Now this may appear strange. But when you consider that no spirit who enters on the progressive stage of eternity is made to understand the true position it is to occupy till it has cast off as a garment the selfish notions and ideas it cherished most when on earth, you can then indeed realize what I mean by what I have said.

Now, what I have to say further to you to-night, I have learned since I last communicated with you, and I wish your earnest attention and careful thought, for it is for your special instruction I reveal it; and for the good it may do your natures on earth and in the spheres. Listen, then, to what I say.

You have been taught that God is a principle—that he is the source of all goodness, love, and truth, and that in him are the attributes which, properly directed by his wisdom, impel man to progress toward the goodness, and truth, and love which he exhibits through his works.

This is true. God is indeed the first and last, the beginning and end. But God works by means; and as it is necessary that material connections should be established to convey certain influences that the harmony of creation may be kept up, and the relative relations be felt throughout all creation; so it becomes necessary that God, in the communication to man of his laws and the effects of his principles, should use those connections which are in the same state or condition, or, rather, in the same order of existing arrangement. Thus, when he has placed around your earth an atmosphere, he has made the union of the several ingredients which compose it the means by which he produces certain known and important effects. And also when he transmits through the earth the subtile and powerful agent, electricity, he has chosen certain organized substances by which it is most easily transmitted. Thus, also, when he intends to carry out any purpose under his laws, the means are always adapted to the end, and he chooses certain agents to consummate this purpose.

Spirits are chosen, or, rather, they are impelled, to undertake the execution of the laws of God, and under this law of their impulses they are selected to carry into execution certain acts in reference to 'individuals, and they, under this arrangement, are called guardian spirits. Each one of you has more or less guardian spirits. And they are constantly teaching you by the thoughts they engender in your minds, and the direction which they endeavor to give to thought. And to each of you there is being prepared a teaching that will probe your souls, and exhibit to your consciousness on what kind of a basis your life-action is founded.

It is hardly commensurate with the high aspirations of a

good spirit, that when so long and so intimately associated as I have been with you, that he should not inquire of you the use you have made of the jewels he has bestowed on you; and therefore when I say that your guardian spirits are to probe your hearts, I say, under this law, they are as much the instruments of God as are the agents which execute his daily laws. Bring then before him the secret feelings of your souls. Ask yourselves if you have prized the inestimable jewels you have received as you should? Ask, if to carry out your own purposes you have unknowingly retarded the progress of others? Ask, if what you consider truth may not be the determined influence of your will? Ask, if you have studied other hearts, and have understood them? Ask, if you have made your own inclinations yield to what before God is truth? Ask, if you have deceived yourselves, and in that deception have misled others? Ask, if your actions have not been simulated? Why do I suggest this critical scrutiny of your hearts?

Why dare I, the spirit of Sweedenborg, unseen to you, but seeing, oh! how clearly, ask you to call up in review all the thoughts and feelings of your hearts? Why do I reiterate these things? Why do I wish you to look up to the great Source of truth and love? Oh! it is that your souls may be so pure and white, that your natures may become so sublimated, your thoughts may harmonize so entirely with the glorious affinities of the upper spheres, that your very natures may reflect the God-like attributes of perfect truth—that you may stand as polished statues, pure, spotless, and radiant in the finish of an eternal progression begun on earth—to end only when you shall stand forever with your feet on evil, but your heads in the glorious light of everlasting goodness.

I am glad these thoughts have been called out by what has been said. Now you all know that the violation of a physical law is followed by a proper penalty. You know when you eat or drink in violation of law—when any thing is done contrary to the law of your physical existence, your bodies suffer sooner or later. Now is it possible that an entire isolation from the world is necessary to understand that God affixed a penalty to the violation of a material law, and that you should feel and know its punishment —that he would still more regard the law of his own moral nature, and in its violation inflict the punishment it demands? Have I taught so long to you that progression in the development of mind—in the observance of the relations existing between man—in the development of his intellect and the love of unmixed purity and truth, are the result of obeying these laws as unmixed happiness on earth also—for the truly good man regards not the ills of life, but looks to the end? Have I taught you so long, and yet you do not understand that when you do wrong, your natures, moral natures, suffer? No education can warp or mask the suffering of the spirit when it has committed a moral wrong. No; if there is a God, if there is a soul, that God as surely recognizes a moral wrong, and the soul as surely perceives it, as the mind knows there is a body. And we may reason and argue, but we must come back at last to the fundamental principles taught by Christ, that love to God—the yearning of the spirit to exist and dwell with God—and love to man, in the performance of all those duties established both by God and man, is the sure road to right and truth. When we go beyond what we are conscious we know, then are we mystified. But there is a simple and sure path which all may tread safely. 'Tis in regarding what we know in following what our consciences teach us we can comprehend.

Section Forty-three.

Monday, Dec. 19, 1853.

The circle met, and after some miscellaneous teachings, the following came through me :

I WAS in those darker spheres again. The object that now attracted my attention was a woman and a young child, sitting on a rude bench by the side of a hovel. They were all drawn up in a heap, sitting close to each other, as if attracted by a mingled feeling of fear and love toward a man who was walking rapidly backward and forward at a little distance from them. I did not get the precise relation they had occupied toward each other here, but I learned that the woman and child had been suddenly cut off from life, and were more attracted to him than to any one else in the spirit-world, because of the tie which had bound them to him here. They looked very wretched and unhappy ; and the man, as he walked back and forth in front of them, had them constantly in his mind, and was ever a witness of their misery. It would seem that he had been the cause of their death from some evil motive or other, and that they had thus haunted him, and when on earth thus tormented him by their presence, which they had been able to make palpable to him, and that the suffering which this had caused him he had been compelled to conceal from the world and keep entirely to himself, without daring to hint it to any one lest it should expose his crime. And that suffering had been so great, and had endured so long, that when death approached, he welcomed it as a relief from their presence. But the first sensation he had on waking to consciousness in the spirit-world, was their

presence more palpable, more near than ever before; and
from the time of his entrance to that world, which was long,
long ago, he had never for one moment been exempt from
their presence. He had resorted to various expedients to
get rid of it, but he found that one effect of death with
him had been to deprive him of means which on earth he
had often successfully used to rid himself of their presence.
He tried all those means in his present state of existence,
but in vain: his victims were ever near him, too near for
him to shake them off. He had fled from place to place,
in the hope of escaping them; he had rushed into crowds;
he had occupied himself with the most exciting pursuits
of spirit-life; he had plunged into solitude; he had entreated them and threatened them, but all in vain—he
could harm them no more—but at all times and under all
circumstances they were near him, performing ever their
melancholy task of retribution. At length, in utter despair of ever escaping them, he had ceased his efforts, and
retired alone to one of the darker portions of that country,
where he thought he could shut out from the world around
him the knowledge of his extraordinary sufferings. But
even here too he was disappointed. Though his darkness
of mind might have found a fitting residence in the deepest gloom of that unholy place, yet their superior elevation
ever lifted up the darkness which he craved, just so much
as to make him visible to all around him. The closing
part of his life on earth had been an enduring effort to
conceal from man the knowledge of his crime and his sufferings in consequence of it, and now, in the spirit-world,
there was the same enduring, and even more ardent desire
of concealment, with the conviction that he could not conceal. Thus, then, he lived, with no companions but the
victims of his evil passions, and no employment for his
mind, which on earth had been very active, and was now
even more so, but the recollection of his crimes; for one
crime with him had led to another, so that when now he
turned his thoughts from one offense they found refuge

only in the recollection of another. Thus he lived day by
day, year by year, ever engaged in that uneasy movement,
that unhappy mental irritation, which kept him ever traversing that limited path and moving backward and forward in presence of the living evidences of a life misspent.
If you could have seen the agony which was painted on
his face, which was portrayed in his gestures—which was
delineated in his fitful, uneasy gait, you would say that indeed "the way of the transgressor is hard."

Once in a while he would look at his victims with a feeling of concentrated hatred, as if he would tear them to
pieces, but his power over them was gone. Occasionally
as he passed them he turned his head away from them, in
the hope of driving them from his thoughts, but some motion or action of theirs recalled his attention to them. And
I saw him chafing his hands and holding them above his
head in the most horrible feeling of despair you can imagine. He beat his head with his hands and threw his arms
out. He paused once in a while, and looked up for some
means of escape. I saw him in utter despair seated on the
ground, covering his face with his hands. His whole
frame shook with emotion, and it seemed as if he would
have wept, but no tear would start. And as he thus sat,
his victims rose and approached him. The woman laid
her hand upon his shoulder, and the frightful agony with
which he started to his feet at that touch made me shudder. He resumed his walk more rapidly and more un-
easily. The woman and child returned to their seat, and
it seemed from his motions and gestures that his sufferings
and his despair were constantly on the increase.

"Oh! how gladly," he cried, "would I welcome the
death I dreamed of, rather than this state of existence!"
Death, though it should send him to the hell of which he
had heard, for even its pain would be a welcome refuge
from the eternal and ever-increasing torment he was now
enduring. That torment was vastly increased even in his
mind, by the consciousness that his victims were chained to

his life by and through himself. That his injury to them did not terminate with their homicide, but continues by their condemnation to his society. That condemnation was not owing so much to his act as to the lives themselves had led here and the attraction which had bound them together here, and which binds them together still, so that it was his love and his crime which alike chained him and his victims to the same condition of wretchedness, to which neither he nor they could conceive any end.

Section Forty-four.

Monday, Dec. 26, 1853.

The circle met. Through Dr. Dexter it was said:

WHEN the eye looks up to heaven and beholds the stars, and the light thereof strikes the nerve of that eye, the mind is conscious that there is a body through which that light is received. The ear takes note, and distinguishes the different sounds of music. The mouth distinguishes the various flavors of food and substances which are taken therein. The nose detects and separates the unpleasant from the pleasant odors; and we with our eyes shut can distinguish the form of various objects when pressed by our fingers.

The body has two conditions: one of reception, and the other of rejection. As the mind, the soul recognizes an idea distinct from any suggestive cause it shows a condition independent of surrounding influences or causes. Thus it stands alone, and is influenced in its isolated condition. It is this condition which enable us to approach you, aside from the material influences or causes which may impede or facilitate this connection and communication with you. The spirit must be in this independent, suggestive, or receptive condition before we can influence the mind to act of itself; I mean when we can take mind and use it to express our ideas; for the soul alone receives us as we come, and recognizes us within itself, or surrounding itself, and grants us that privilege of using your material nature to speak through you.

When we occupy or are identified with the soul, we become the motive power of the mind, we govern and control it; and having, as it were, usurped (by permission, for it is a recognized usurpation) the powers and faculties of the mind for our own purposes, we then, through the material instincts, govern every impression which is made upon the sentient extremities of the nerves. Thus we can control, in the receptive condition, the whole body, mind, and soul. There are cases of so complete spiritual control that the mind might be separated from the body and not feel it.

To show the difference that exists between this condition and its opposite—the rejective condition—I will bring up an example known to most of you, by which, through the repulsive efforts of the material and immaterial parts of the organization, the spirits who have once controlled a medium in the most easy and perfect manner, have been unable to approach that medium so as to influence her at all. Now we can move her arm; that is the material connection alone. We can move it as I move, but that has nothing to do with the movement and vibration of the soul. We can not approach the soul; we can not seat ourselves in the carriage and take the reins of the mind and drive thought through every part of the spheres. The coursers are there, and so is the carriage, harnessed and ready for the journey; but the driver is in the repulsive condition, which repels us.

Now be it known to you that the soul is organized in its material connection with the body. This is a new idea, which has been revealed to us lately.

The soul enters the embryo ready organized, or it could not grow; and when it leaves its material organization, and steps over the threshold of eternity, it is ready organized and prepared to encounter all that is before it.

There are therefore two distinct organizations: one the material body, and the other the organic soul. Now to convince your minds that the organic soul may be improved distinctly and independently of the body, we will offer as an example this fact, known to every one who has watched the phases of organic life and the manifestations of the soul. Take a tree, and you can shape it into what form you please by grafting on its branches another and a different kind of fruit; you can raise the most delicious fruit from another and a different kind of vegetable. Then you can, from one vegetable of a very inferior quality, generate the most acceptable kind of fruit or food known to man. You can improve the breed of your dogs in their fleetness, shape, scent, and all the properties belonging to this particular line of life for which it is designed. And so you can sheep. You can improve the breed of sheep, and make that which is lean remarkably fat, and from sparse wool produce a luxuriant growth in fineness, length, and weight. So with a horse: from that which is an insignificant animal, you may produce the proudest specimen of animal life. You may go further, and yet your tree is a tree still; your dog yelps his characteristics; your sheep bleats his cognomen and race; your horse, the noblest, is but a horse after all. But when you communicate to the organized soul the knowledge received through the material parts, you make that which was man a very God; you send his thirsty soul up to the source from whence it sprang, and it comes back stamped with all the attributes of its origin.

Thus it is that the soul, developed in its connection with the body, grasps with the arm of almost Almighty power the deepest secrets of nature, and sports with their dark mysteries as with a toy. It takes from heaven the emblem of His awful power, and tames it to the workings of its own convenience. Man spans the earth's surface with his iron bands, and binds distant parts together, and makes them citizens as of one family. In the smallest pebble that he crushes beneath his feet, he, in the omnipotence of his mind, extracts the principle of laws which he adapts to his own exigences and necessities.

What can the horse impart of his own knowledge to another? Can he impress on the mind of another the image of thoughts in his own brain? But the soul of man, starting from a given epoch, sends to the future that Almighty knowledge which thrills in the hearts of men in all time. Is that material, that thought which excites thought when ages shall have passed away, and even the name of the man have perished in the past? Has God done more than this? Has he not done just like this? and when we see nations, continents, the world itself springing into life, and grasping these thoughts, and adapting them to their own condition and age, shall we not say that this universal principle has more of life than all God's earth on which man lives, and even his own body, for that dies, but the thought of his soul is eternal. This, then, it is with which we commune. This it is now that I am impressing; we impress, by our own thoughts, the soul of the medium; every vibration of his own soul is syncronous with vibrations of our souls. You can feel the pulse beat within its vessels, and time the smallest beat of the heart; but you can not time the vibrations of the soul. Its mainspring is the God who made it; but he made that same principle to move your souls as well as mine.

The soul is organized, and its special organism is what I influence. I enter into that soul by that receptive principle existing there, and when there, that soul, through its material organization, responds my thoughts the same way it responds to its own thoughts, and I become its soul —my mind is its; but when I influence its body I use material means known to every one present. How vast their

own power and yours! yet the door is but partly open,
and you are peering over a vast country which lies beyond
—looking through a small space to an inconceivable space
beyond. This is our first step toward heaven and its mysteries. Then, friends of the sacred circle, chosen as you
are, favored with opportunities far beyond those which are
given to many of your race—ponder well what you have
heard—for it is not a sprinkling of knowledge and wisdom
you have had, but a copious shower, which will germinate
the eternal seeds of wisdom in your own souls, if you will
but unite with us in their cultivation.

What say you? Can you comprehend all that is said to
you? Are you satisfied that you have probed to the bottom every principle, and sentiment, and thought so lav-
ishly poured on you? Yet your soul manifests its divine
attributes in its thirst for more; and may I say to you, it
were well if you understood it all? I am standing on a
plane that overlooks the glorious beauties of the spheres.
I see the radiant glory of divine light that sheds its gorgeous hues on every flower, and tree, and plain, and mountain. I see millions of spirits, who once inhabited your
world, wending their way, 'mid this brightness, to that spot
where every spirit concentrates. I look back, and this
dark ball is rolling in the space to which its orbit is circumscribed. I see your mites of bodies toiling on its surface, delving for the petty things there to be gleaned; but
ever and anon the divine emanation of the soul starts from
your dark atmosphere, and, obtaining its ultimate height,
sparkles and bursts in the midst thereof, sending forth its
brilliant sparks. Thought is God, for it controls all nature, and penetrates all the laws by which God has made
that nature. I tell you, then, stand ye not still, for every
thought of mind, whether of great or little import, yields,
either on earth or in the spheres, its diamonds to enrich
some mind which shall have found and taken possession
of it.

23

Section Forty-five.

Thursday, Dec. 29, 1853.

The circle met at my house—all the circle being present.

The question was asked—What is the physical condition in which we must be placed in order that spirits may communicate with us?

Through Dr. Dexter it was answered:

CHILDREN, you talk about love, and you imagine that through the spheres this eternal attribute of God is made manifest, and yet you suppose that this divine attribute is in every heart, and that from the beginning God endowed the spirit with that which is a part of himself, as an element of his origin. This may be true. It would seem that when God gave forth the soul, with that soul there came the same attributes it possessed when incorporated with the germ. And it is true that every soul on this earth, and inhabiting the countless worlds above and below, has this eternal principle in its nature; but there is one important lesson to be understood, and the facility with which I can communicate to you by this means enables me to occupy a moment or two to tell you what that lesson is.

What is this love? Is it that which will make us work for others—suffer for others—give to others? All these things, these efforts of the mind and body, may arise from an entirely different source or principle.

What is love, and what its influence on our souls? There are as many different minds in all their phases, all their actions, all their manifestations, in all their passions, in all their affections, in all their tastes, their likes, and their dislikes, as there are differences in the stars; as one star differs from another in glory and brilliancy, so does mind vary from mind.

God, when he stamped the impress of his sentient particle which came from him, endowed it with the almighty attributes of his nature; claiming kindred with himself, it claims kindred with the minutest and meanest thing he has created.

Then in this difference lies all that we know of the influence of this principle of love. In some, starting from the hour when the body first enters this world, it burns in its physical existence like a bright and glorious light; dimly and feebly flickering in another, it lingers out a miserable existence, feeding not on that which is congenial to itself on earth, but on its own nature in itself. It seems as if there it could find nothing to assimilate with on earth. Daring and bold, flashing and sparkling in another, it seems to sweep every thing away from its path till it reaches the verge of this existence, and then finding itself free from its mortal trammels, it ushers itself into the next existence in one glorious and gorgeous manifestation of its divine nature.

But, then, what of all this? Shall we, who know and feel what this love is, shall we feel it—know it—live by it —enjoy by it—rise by it—and ascend to those glorious spheres by it, and neglect to tell you what it is? Is there a mind among you, my children, that can answer me this question, What are the duties which love requires of you? And, my children, though I have come to you, though the intercourse I have had with you has even on my own nature had its blessing and its profit, can you not feel that this is an important question? And then are you to love the world, and in that love be willing to do them good, to labor, to give, to feel, to suffer, to sympathize, to heal, to assuage, and yet not be willing to do yet more? Think you that these efforts are enough?

Why say you, God has gifted me with these various emotions of the mind, and I can not love what is distasteful to it, and yet you can love what is congenial? And is not God's creation from the zoophite to man all con-

genial to his law, and is not this love from God? Does
it not pervade his whole nature? Does it not emanate
from him in radiant streams of light to each through the
spheres, lighting up those glorious abodes with the very
holy light of himself, and make it all one on this platform?
What heart, then, sends its cold chill of uncongeniality because it feels it can not have the same tastes, and likes,
and hopes as another? Is not his gorgeous bow the very
arch of love through which all must rise from one sphere
to another? And when the million souls that are now
wending their way to the eternal spheres shall arrive there,
will they not bask in those glorious beams that make no
refracting ray?

Then shall it be said to that heart which yearns for another's love, that it shall not be given to him? If you can
love, you can love one as well as another. And yet, O!
let me ask you, Have you loved truly, holy, purely, and
well? The divine law which says, Love ye one another!
comprises what I have said; but I charge you, oh! my
children! dear to me as the summer breeze to the brow of
the sick man, or as the perfume of the morning flower as it
sends its essence up to God! O, how I love you! How
my heart opens to you, as if in itself it could shelter you
all! How much joy I have felt in coming with my friend,
and this man's friend, and all your friends, and aiding your
advance and progress in the truth! But I charge you—beware! I charge you once again, and I do the work of my
Father when I say to you, Beware! for ye canst turn love
into that which is worse than hate. Guard this attribute
which is coexistent with your birth, but do not foster it to
gratify that which arises from no heavenly source.

Children, I bless you, and O! may the sweet calm of the
spheres rest on each heart, and may your life here be one
of holy joy till I meet you in the spheres.

After a brief pause it was said :

Judge, Sweedenborg has been talking now. He has occupied some little time. Shall I go on, or not?

I answered Yes; and then through myself it was said:

Do you not all perceive that your soul—the life-princi-ple—call it what you will, has, during this primary exist-ence, as it were, two existences? One, if I may so say, living in the material body, deriving its thoughts from ma-terial objects and through material organs, and the other existing independent of the body, deriving its thoughts and its knowledge from sources unconnected with it?

How can I make you fully understand a proposition so important to be understood? Let me take this as an illus-tration. Go with me into one of your churches. You see beauty of proportion, massiveness of structure, elegance of taste, and conveniences for animal comforts. These are ideas you derive from your physical senses. You see and feel these things.

Directly by the side of that building there is another, in which you see the same massiveness and beauty. Thus with your material senses you go in those buildings, but there is something in you which enables you to go a step further, and while you stand looking at them, taking in these ideas, you do not stop there—you go beyond the senses. Your mind looks upon one as a spot in which the worship of God is had, and the other as a gambling-house. While thus looking, neither is in actual use, yet to you one is holy and the other repulsive. Why is this? What is it that makes you see this? The dual existence of the soul independent of the body.

You are the master of a ship out of sight of land—what directs you to port? Your mind.

It is with this existence that we commune. First with the material—then with the spiritual or higher nature. How it is that we thus commune, I can not now tell. In time it will be made known to you. But it is this some-thing which is of you, which, like your other faculties, im-proves by culture, which enables us to commune with you. Unless you have analyzed and studied your own minds you can not comprehend this. But those of you who have turned your thoughts within yourselves and learned to understand your own powers and attributes, can well look up beyond the material objects which surround you, and comprehend the source whence the soul may derive its inspiration and its divine knowledge.

Is there any reason why we may not, as well before death as after it, thus commune and thus approach that invisible Source of light and knowledge?

Look within yourselves, and trace the association of ideas. Follow a thought with all its strange connections, through all its devious windings, back to the concealed recesses of its origin, and see how often it is that that origin is not of this earth, and springs not from any material object, but from this communion of spirit with spirit.

This, which seems so strange to you, is very clear to us, and we know how far more close the intercourse will hereafter be, for we know how much more intimate is the connection between the two existences, the material and the spiritual, than you do or can well conceive.

Much, however, depends upon yourselves—make yourselves accessible to us, and we come—make yourselves inaccessible, and we are obliged to depart from you. And O! believe, much of your happiness hereafter must depend upon your intercourse with the brighter spirits, who, in the performance of their mission return to earth to guide, direct, and enlighten you.

Section Forty-six.

Monday, Jan. 9, 1854.

The circle met this evening at Dr. Dexter's. After sitting a short time, Sweedenborg came and spoke to us through Mrs. S. as follows:

DEAR children, the love I bear you is this night strength-ened by the childlike patience and earnest hope with which you await our coming among you. The spirit of peace and calmness shall overshadow your spirits in their communings of love and wisdom with the gentle spirits who now surround you, and love and joy shall rest upon each one present as a white-winged dove, sent with glad tidings from the celestial mansions of holiness. Many of your spirit-friends are present now. Each and every one has a word which he would like to say. They have not yet decided on the course they will pursue, but wish you to have an opinion about it yourselves and speak your wishes, and if we see they are governed by wisdom we will comply so far as we are capable of doing.

The circle now requested that the teachings might be of a general character, so that others also might be benefited by them.

Sweedenborg replied:

That is the best to begin with, and then, if the medium is willing, the friends will speak. Gently and lovingly their influence would surround her, not to annoy her in mind or body.

O my dear children, the atmosphere here to-night is so calm and gentle—An angel might soar through it with unruffled pinion, where human hearts are in such beautiful harmony with spirit-presence.

Sweedenborg now left, and the medium was influenced by another spirit. She was made to kneel and bow her head to the earth, and went through the pantomime of putting handsful of earth upon her head. Rising, she uttered the word, "Friends." Again kneeling in our midst, with the utmost humility, she again seemed to put dust upon her head. After which she arose and said :

Dear friends, I have been sent here this evening to tell you how the proud spirit and haughty will have been humbled.

When I dwelt on the earth, people called me a queen. They humbled themselves before me—they approached me with deference and respect. Oh! they honored me highly because of my high station. Yes, the mighty men of the nation honored me, and kings paid me homage! They called me wise and beautiful—they said that virtue and wisdom shone in my countenance, and that love and charity were my daily companions. O yes, they said I was possessed of every gentle virtue and every trait lovely in woman! And still they knew not my heart. . They knew not the love of applause, the feelings of ambition and selfishness which reigned in my bosom, nor the feelings of revenge which I cherished toward those who thwarted me in my imperious will. And while the nation were lauding my goodness beyond all human comparison, my heart was naught but the abode of earthly and vain passions. It is true there were times when my better instincts would assume their sway and admonish me in my wrong-doing. But the still; small voice was quickly hushed by the continued sound of flattery and empty show which surrounded me. Surely it was not much of an effort to smile and look gay when every face took its reflex from mine; for the voice of grief or suffering was never permitted to reach my ear, save when my own spirit groaned in bitterness, warring over the pent-up fires of my own raging heart. For there were times during my life when, had I been free and unattended, I would have cast myself into the peaceful waters of the river, so that the former

struggles and passions might be buried forever in oblivion.
And what was religion to me but a cloak? The holy father
who confessed me dealt leniently with my most serious
offenses. He smiled upon me and called me the anointed
of God; until there was no sanctity left to shroud religion
in when I was brought before the judgment-seat of the
church; and I always felt as one who was licensed to
commit sin with a high hand; no word of reproach or
censure was ever given me. But still my spirit felt its
own blackness and impurity. I knew how far separated
from the pure and beautiful visions of heaven were my
vain, earthly thoughts. My childhood's moments had been
innocent and pure, and with a spirit joyous and happy I
had gloried and reveled in all things beautiful in nature.
These thoughts, these halcyon hours of pleasure left no
sting behind. They were now the only rays of sunshine
that came across my brief career, as some dim and half-
forgotten dream of Paradise. The hours of my childhood
now, indeed, seemed as a fairy dream in their purity and
happiness, compared with the hollow world which surrounded me. My soul had once drank deep draughts of
joy and consolation from the perusal of the works of the
good and the pure who had lived before me. And I remembered the past pleasure with which I had communed
with the thoughts of those spirits who now dwelt, I knew
not where. I indeed conceived it to be all a dream, a
pleasant, a deceitful dream; for nowhere could I now turn
to find the sympathy, the communion of which I had once
partaken. I knew my imperfections, but, alas! they would
not let me speak of them. When I spoke to my spiritual
adviser of the sore trouble and travail of my spirit because
of her sinful bonds, he, presumptuous man! forgave me
my sins. Oh! he did not remove the load under which
my spirit groaned! He only moved the surface, he only
caused the voice to sink deeper within, so that its tones
sounded not so loudly without. And when my life had
been spent thus far in doing much that was evil (I now

feel thus), and little that was really good, my spirit passed from my temple of clay. O yes, surrounded by weeping minions—supported, and consoled, and strengthened, as others thought, by the pillars of the church, the anointed ones—surrounded on all sides by a profusion of wealth, and ostentation, and honors—forgiven my sins at the last hour of my life by one as erring as myself, I departed, soon to be forgotten by those who had professed to adore me, who had almost worshiped my very footsteps! But the spirit had fled—naught but the dust remained; and how soon that dust becomes a loathsome thing to those to whom it had once appeared as the most beautiful thing in existence!

When I entered the spirit-world, I thought I should still be a queen, not of a nation, but still a queen of subjects. It seemed that I had been formed for a queen—that royal blood coursed in my veins—that my ancestors had been kings and queens far back in the archives of time; and it seemed a birthright which I never should have to forego, not even in heaven. I had pondered much on the state after death, during my life, but my ideas had never been clear in this respect. What I learned was mostly from the study of the Scriptures. The teachings I listened to spoke not much of a hell, but described heaven; and my weary heart had oft wished for the rest of a heaven; and I had also felt that, impure as I was, I could be no fit inhabitant to enjoy so pure a place. And now, as I gazed about me in that land of shadows (as it seemed), how rapidly all these things ran through my mind! I felt as though I must be cared for—I must be caressed—I must be welcomed, because of my former station. I looked about me in vain to find some vast assembly of persons coming to honor me—coming to convey me in triumph to my destined home. But I saw none, and I wandered along in doubt and uncertainty, first gazing here, and then there. My steps were wonderfully upheld. I knew not upon what I was treading, and yet I was traveling rapidly in a new and unknown place, and frequently I became tired and weary, for my journey seemed to lengthen, and my prospects grew no better. I thought within myself, they have not. been apprised of my coming, they have not expected me, or some of my former friends would come and welcome me. And now I grew sad. I had gone a long distance, moved by the invisible power which upheld my footsteps, but I had been cheered by no ray, and I sat down by the wayside and wept bitterly, O how bitterly! I felt so lonely and deserted! I was no queen now, with willing subjects to obey my look and nod. There were no submissive attendants to minister to my weariness and despair; none ready to raise my drooping spirits with music, or their counsel, or comfort. But here I sat all alone and deserted by the wayside! yes, as lone and wretched as the veriest beggar that had ever prayed for bread at the gates of my palace! And now I was filled with anxious reflections. I seemed to look back upon my past life, and compare it with my present existence, so new to me, and to ask myself, who, indeed, am I, and what am I? Am I not more than the common herd? Am I not still a queen above my subjects? Oh! how my proud heart swelled nigh unto bursting, now when I felt how insignificant I was when stripped of all my surroundings! My tears were those of anguish, and shame, and rage, and disappointment. Long time I mused and wept. Finally a calm, a change seemed to pass over my troubled heart, but I felt, oh! how deeply, every unworthy act of my past life. My former misdeeds, the effects of my baser passions, which had left their impress upon others, now stood forth before me in bold relief. I now felt that every good deed, every gentle feeling of love, or charity, or mercy which I had been led to perform or indulge, cast a heavenly calm upon me, and took away the fierceness and the anguish of my bitter grief. The remembrance of these was clothed in a soft, silvery light, O how beautiful! Those deeds of mercy now cheered and comforted my troubled spirit; and again I wept; but they were tears of penitence, of contrition, which soothed and quieted me, and brought up a hope from the lowest chambers of my soul that I might yet be able to perform something more worthy those pleasures I had experienced. While indulging in these thoughts and wishes of what I might do, and regrets of what I had done, I looked up, and beside me stood a female. She was exceedingly fair and beautiful to behold. There was a look of heavenly dignity and beneficence in her face, and her whole being seemed pervaded with such gentleness that I was encouraged to speak. She held forth her hand and called me sister. She asked me if I was weary, in such mild and gentle accents, that my tears flowed afresh, and I yearned for her sympathy. I now poured out my sorrows, and begged her to lead me to some more genial spot. I told her I had been a queen on earth ; and when I said this she smiled sadly, and said, "There are no queens in this our country, save queens of love and purity—those who excel in love of their fellows, and whose good works make their faces shine with wisdom, and who are ever bearing good tidings to those on earth. These are the only queens we have here."

I was amazed at her words. I had not conceived that I should be as the commonest subject of my kingdom, unnoted and unnoticed. I spoke of many who had gone before me, and wished I might be led to them. I spoke of the joys and dazzling beauties of heaven, which had been described to me during my life. She told me that my former friends were all engaged in different occupations. I was surprised again, for I had not supposed an occupation was consistent with heavenly enjoyment; for the manner in which she spoke led me to suppose that the occupations consisted of labor more than enjoyment. She gazed in my eyes, and told me I was but an untutored child in the knowledge of the life which was called the hereafter. She said that my spirit's best intuitions had been repressed, that the baser part of my nature had been called forth and developed by my worldly career ; and I must now begin to live truly the life which leads to eternal happiness. She said my friends were all progressing in their eternal journey, and that I must follow them, for they could not return to me.

I questioned her about my former life, and found she knew every thing concerning me! She told me she had been my guardian spirit while I inhabited the body, and had endeavored in manifold ways to approach me and whisper gentle words of admonition and warning in my ears. At times she had led me by the spirit of gentleness and love. At times I had repelled her by my own evil conduct, and had allowed spirits who only loved darkness, and to deceive men's souls by their arts, to approach me with their counsel and advice. O how I wept when she told me these things? And she moreover said I must forget that I had been once a queen on earth, for none but the humble in spirit might hope to become even as a little child in this land of love. I now saw I must lay aside all my former dignity and love of flattery, and be led by this lovely spirit's counsel. We walked until we arrived at a pleasant mansion, wherein we entered. I was here greeted by several spirits who welcomed me candidly and pleasantly, but paid me no deference, and seemed not to know I had been a queen. And the spirit who had conducted me, said, "This is the dwelling wherein you must take your first lessons in self-denial, and in divesting yourself of those worldly notions which will be so prejudicial to your future happiness. Those persons about you will be ever willing to assist you with kind and gentle words when you need such help; but you must perform the labor of reformation for yourself and within yourself; you must become as lowly and as loving as those who surround you; you must even become as the little flower whose head is bowed toward the earth, as if in humility, lest the sun's rays might fall upon it with too great and overpowering a a splendor. My dear child, your heavenly nature was formed to be pure and gentle—to be loving and kind—to benefit others by your gentle counsels, and to sympathize in the sorrows of the human heart. But the world placed you upon a dangerous pedestal, which only made you wretched and unhappy. Your higher and better nature was ever struggling to gain the ascendency over the material grossness which surrounded you, and the mighty conflict only sickened and wearied your spirit. And this is why life seemed so hateful and hollow at times. The sin was not yours, my child, but it was the sin of circumstances and of corrupt teachings, of fawning counsels and of selfish aggrandizement. These obstructions, connected with others, are now removed; but, my child, all the earthly clouds of error which an earthly existence developed are still within thine own bosom, and it is now thy labor to erase them all, until there shall not be left the faintest trace of their former existence. These will pain thee and harass thy soul's comfort, and, until they are all effaced, will still give thee the same sad feelings which they did on earth. There will be no outward foe here to battle with. Within thyself must the victory be obtained. Then tarry not, my child, but begin thy labor immediately; and when thy heart becomes so filled with the love of God that thou shalt want to go forth and take the beggar, and the lame, and the blind by the hand, and feed the hungry, and bind up the broken-hearted, and say to the erring: 'Sister, I am thy sister and friend, and will lead thee in the path of love and goodness,' then wilt thou be fit to mingle with the loving spirits who do their Father's will; and then shall thy face and thy whole being shine with far more transcendent beauty than that which was upon thee when thou wast clad in thy regal robes. When thy good works shall have purified and refined thy being in this sphere, O then, thou hast in prospect a glorious flight to another. There shalt thou see the heavenly city whose foundation is made without hands. There shalt thou mingle with the pure in spirit, whose voices will greet thine ear in tones of music soft as an Æolian harp. Oh! what joy and glory, what rapture and delight await the transfigured soul! Thou shalt mingle with beings whose purity will shed a light about thee, and cause a heavenly glow to pervade thy whole being; and thou mayest walk by the shining rivers of love and lave thy body in their placid waters; and weariness shall not overtake thee, no sorrow shall enter that place. The love of the most high God dwells in and pervades all things here, where no grossness can enter. The elements of discord and inharmony approach not that place, but the voices of angels, singing never-ceasing praises, are borne down on every breeze, and find a glad response from every heart which dwells therein."

Oh! now I wished I had never lived, I had become so wrapped in wonder and amazement while she spoke of that glorious place; and then the long-forgotten dreams of childhood stole softly across my memory. Ah! then I felt it was true. I felt that in the purity and happiness of my childhood's home the bright angels from the far-off realms had whispered those thoughts into my heart, for I was then less material, more natural. The connection between that glorious land and my spirit had been more close in my childhood's hours than when I had mingled with the world and partaken of its character.

And now she breathes a blessing upon me; she tells me to labor, to love, to persevere; and she leaves me to return to her bright reward far beyond me. But she says I shall see her when I have worked out the mission which it is my part to perform. She bids me be careful, be watchful, for there are earnest eyes and loving hearts gazing down and beckoning me upward. Oh! who would not labor; who would not be a beggar; who would not forego all earthly honors, that they might hereafter be permitted to be only one of the least in the house of God, in the gates of Heaven?

Previous to the communication being finished, Mr. Warren asked what her name was? She now replied by saying, "My name is Humility; once it was Pride"

Section Forty-seben.

The circle met at Dr. Dexter's house.　Present, five of the members, as at the last meeting.

The following was given through Mrs. S. :

A POOR old man comes in your midst, bending beneath the weight of a heavy load, and surely he looks as though he would rather part with life itself than with that dearly-loved treasure.　He comes to you bearing the same appearance he did when he left your earth.　He was not of your coun-try nor kind, but lived in a distant part of your globe. We well let him give his own history.

The spirit said that the miser did not influence the medium himself, but gave his history, which was repeated by the spirit controlling the medium.

Fellow-mortals, I have been instructed to come here to-night and give a brief sketch of my former and present life.　I do, indeed, come with my much-loved treasure in my arms.　I come, bearing the empty emblem of that which constituted my all-engrossing happiness while on earth—the gold, the yellow gold, which alone my soul craved "as its food and its drink," as its highest felicity and joy.　With what bitterness and regret I look back upon my earthly career.　Ah, me ! I must look back, there is no help for it.

I bowed down all the energies of my soul to the accu-mulation of this one idol.　Ay ! my very soul itself bowed down daily and worshiped it as a God, whose possession would confer happiness and joy upon my whole existence. The predominance of this passion, repressed all that was

good and noble within me. It made me grasping and nig-
gardly—it made me deaf to the voice of sympathy and
love—it chilled my very heart's core with its golden, its
false glitter. And when a soft and gentle voice within me
besought a hearing, I would lock myself up within the
glittering walls of my treasure and shut out every emotion
save that of avarice and penury; for this, alas! was my
daily companion. I used not the comforts which God had
strewn so bountifully around me. My heart was too sordid
to part with one penny, unless it was to keep me from actually starving. O how I loved my wealth! O how I
gazed upon it! How I gloated over it daily and dreamed
of it nightly, and hid it away, lest any should steal it out
of my possession! And often, during the hours of my un-
quiet slumbers, I would start up frantically, thinking some
one had stolen my treasures. Wretched, miserable miser
that I was! I deserve the frowns and dislike of every honest and generous heart while I make this humiliating confession. But how I loved that dross I alone can tell—I
alone have felt the pangs which I have endured in consequence of that base passion. But finally disease took a
strong hold upon my enfeebled and emaciated frame. O, I
was no proud subject for death to triumph over. In all
my misery and rags, in all my wretchedness and filth, there
was but one warm spot within, and that was where I felt
the strong love of my gold. O how I hated to die and be
buried beneath the surface of the earth, and leave that
treasure above it! I longed to carry it with me, to rest
my head upon it, that it might be my comfort when I
waked in the world beyond. And that waking! That
dreadful, dismal waking! O how it makes me shudder
now to think of it! My first consciousness was that of
being in darkness and coldness, and having lost my treasure. My treasure! O how I groaned, and wept, and
begged for that which had been the comfort of my life!
Every thing seemed gloomy and cheerless without it; and
when I at last became fully conscious of my position, how

dreadful, how terrible were the thoughts which filled my soul! Oh! no. No bright spirits approached me, no kindly looks welcomed me; but beings as repulsive as myself stood and beckoned me to their company. And I said within myself, O wretched man! thou hast doomed thyself to eternal misery, because of thy love of earth's base metal! There was nothing inviting or pleasant in the company of those miserable-looking beings. Their countenances expressed no other emotions save those of sensual gratification; and all their propensities seemed to be groveling and earthly. The eyes of my soul were now opened. I saw myself, my former life reflected back in those beings who were near me. They wished my society, but I did not wish theirs. As dark and repulsive as I felt my own soul to be, their horrible appearance made me rather wish to fly from them than to approach. On gazing at them more closely, I saw that they held tightly within their grasp treasures of gold. I saw them hug them up to their bosoms and then they would look toward me and point toward them. Yes, it indeed seemed to be part of that I had prized so highly, and which I still coveted so ardently. I was tempted to go near them when they showed me the treasure, when a bright form, which I had not before perceived, in a warning voice bade me beware how I trifled with my eternal happiness. But the love of gold was so strong within me, that I could not resist its pleadings, even for the voice of an angel. I had known no other God, and my heart yearned only for its earthly idol. Tremblingly I approached those miserable beings, and then, O grief and sadness! their arms contained naught but an empty show, no gold in reality, nothing but that which wore the semblance; for when I touched it, it melted from my grasp, its very touch scorched my fingers, and then it fell away from my hungry view. O, then I felt how lost and wretched was my condition—then I wished that I might sink out of sight, or be carried away where I should be remembered no more. But such was not my fate. O

how they laughed at me with a fiendish joy. They mock-
ed me, they bid me behold the fruits of my long labors.
There was a look of exultation, of triumph in their countenances as they witnessed my disappointment; and yet
they, poor wretches, were ever grasping at the unreal
phantom—the empty treasure. And I stood as one lost
and forsaken of God and man. Who in this vast space
around me cared aught, or knew aught, about a poor, insignificant soul like me? None seemed to think of my existence save those poor wretches, who seemed even more
unhappy than myself, for while I knew how unreal their
treasures were, they were constantly grasping up that which
was naught but empty air. They never looked up, and
when a kindly voice was wafted to their ears on the breezes,
they heard it not. No joy, no comfort for them save in
that unsatisfying labor of accumulating and always losing.
And now I sank upon my knees and buried my face in my
hands. Yea, I bowed my head to the very earth, and prayed in bitterness and grief that God would have mercy upon
me, worthless worm of the dust. O how prostrate my
spirit now laid in its dejection and sorrow! "Lost, lost!"
I exclaimed; "no light, no mercy will beam upon me—
no bright angels will come near me, no kindly voices will
cheer the solitude of this awful place." And then a voice
said in mine ear, "O, you will have gold, heaps of gold;
cheer up, man, for you shall dine on gold and sup your fill
of it every day. You shall revel in it, for we have been
many years here. We always loved it and craved it, and
don't you perceive how much of it we possess?" I turned
shuddering away, for it was one of those dark, fiend-like
beings who had spoken in my ear. "God help me," I
said, "for I am lost eternally, lost for my love of gold."
And then a deep, calm voice spoke loud and clear. It
said, "O mortal, not lost for eternity, only thou hast lost
many years of joy and happiness in thy spirit-life. Lost
eternally? O no! not eternally, for our God is a just and
merciful God, and he forgives the sins of his erring chil-

dren when they come to him in meekness and humility of
spirit. But, mortal! thou hast lost all the joys which thou
wouldst have experienced had thy hoarded wealth been
given for the good of thy fellow-man—had thy cherished
treasure only been made useful in any way, thou wouldst not
now feel the weight of sin and degradation which prostrates
thy soul so low. And now, frail mortal, canst thou give
up thy gold, or must thou, like those poor darkened souls
on the other side of thee, still hug that senseless treasure
to thy heart? Are thy thoughts still wrapped up in the
joys of that possession? If so, thou must be like those
upon whom thou art gazing. Poor spirits, how darkened
are their souls! and yet they are not lost, no, not lost, but
they have not yet thrown off the love of earth and earthly
gratifications. Their aspirations are not for the good and
the pure. They think of naught but gross animal pleasures; and as long as they desire such, as long as they seek
no higher—as long as their souls are wrapped up and lost
in such illusions, they can not be less degraded than they
are. O pity them, mortal! To think of the many precious
hours they are losing in worshiping their earthly pleasures! And let it carry a deep and lasting lesson to thee,
ignorant, selfish, vain mortal that thou art! for thou must
now see thyself in thy true colors. Repent and be converted; thou hast many long hours, ay, years of labor
before thee. Why, thou art little better than the animal
which bore the animal's form and feature while on earth,
and walked in a lonely position. Thou hast never shown
that thou possessed one attribute of a God-like soul; thou
didst, if it were possible, disgrace thy immortal spirit by
the way thou didst insult and keep it hid beneath thy
earthly covering. It is even now all blurred and dimmed
by the impurities of thy earthly life, and it can not stand
forth in its true dignity until thou hast labored long and
ardently to wash away thy former sins. It lies with thyself; begin now, choose the way of hardship and labor,
for hardship it will be for thee. Or stay here and grovel

in the dust, until thy soul shall become so wearied and worn with its profitless existence, that thou wilt be glad to begin still farther off than thou mayest do now, to wash out thine iniquities, and cause thy light to shine. There is much for thee to do which must be done. And when thou hast overcome the follies and sins of thy past life— when thou hast gained confidence and hope even in thy ignorance and unworthiness, thou must again descend to those poor spirits who are still in so much misery. It is thou who must stretch forth thy hand and assist them, for didst thou not, in thy earthly life, encourage them by thy acts? And thus shalt thou blot out the memory of thy sins until they shall darken thy sight no longer. There will be no lack of instructors and kindly words of encouragement. Gladly will good spirits approach all who do not repel them. But the labor lies within thyself. Thine own hand must hew down the mountains which rise to bar thy progress to that world of purity and holiness which lies far beyond."

He ceased speaking. O blessed and hopeful words! That I am not eternally lost. My resolve was long since taken, friends, and so far have I profited in my toilsome but thankful journey, that I have come to you in humiliation of spirit and with thankfulness to God, who has permitted me to testify to his boundless love and forgiveness even to such a wretch as I. Good-night.

Section Forty-eight.

Thursday, March 30, 1854.

The circle met at my library. All were present, with the addition of Mr. and Mrs. Gay, and Mrs. Leeds, of Boston.

The five mediums present—viz., the Doctor, Mrs. Sweet, Mrs. Leeds, Laura, and I—were seated in an inner circle by ourselves, pursuant to directions written through the Doctor:

The manifestations began by my seeing and describing some of the spirits who were present.

Among them I saw Charlemagne, Voltaire, Woolsey, and Mary of Scotland.

CHARLEMAGNE spoke to me, and reminded me of the lesson which he had given me at Chicago, for it was as important to us as it was to them, and we ought to be thankful for the advantage of learning it during our primary existence. Each owes a duty to his fellow-man, to aid in his elevation and development, and it was the greater or the less, according as each was placed while on earth in a condition to perform it, and sooner or later, on earth, or in the spheres, it must be performed. Hence, they who, when on earth, were in situations which gave them great power over the destiny of man, had devolved upon them a greater duty than those who were born to a humble and obscure condition of life, and more was exacted from them. Upon them rested a greater responsibility, and hence it was that it was they who now so frequently appeared to us, when the opportunity to approach man was at length afforded them. And it was a sad truth that while they were thus drawn back to earth by the stern dictates of this duty, there were many, very many, who in life were obscure and humble, who now were far in advance of them in the spirit-world, because within their limited spheres they had performed their whole duty to man, to the extent of the means within their reach.

This law, he said, applied to all, and upon us, who had been favored above our fellows with the knowledge now pouring from a divine source upon the earth, it devolved a responsibility far beyond theirs, and it behooved us to understand it well, that when we cast off our mortal forms, we also might not be recalled to earth, to battle again with its passions and perversions, because of duties neglected or responsibilities slighted by us while here.

Then, through Laura, it was said:

Do you understand the objects of self-progression? Why do you desire to become good? alone that you may do good to others? alone that you may be elevated in intellect, in knowledge, and all wisdom? That you may associate with the good, the pure, the holy, the wise? That you may draw up with you others to the same level? For general good and general purposes, or because in being good you may develop in yourselves the capacities to do good to others?

If this last remark be true, it is important that we examine the conditions, and means, and results of our own individual progression.

Do we, when we have felt our own unworthiness, our own short-coming, our ignorance, and yet felt we had powers of mind capable of improvement, of progressing, do we contemplate the effort and result for man's general good alone, or does the deep yearning of the heart wake up a desire, first of all, for our own good, that when we have learned to be pure, holy, and wise, and to love, we may be able to disseminate these attributes for the good of others? When conscious that we are progressing, shall we assume prerogatives and rights that belong to God? Shall we judge as God judges, and punish as he punishes? In making a law for ourselves do we do away with the laws that God has established? When making a path for ourselves, can we avoid the highway which alone leads to Heaven? Can we arise upward and onward to God, acquiring in our progress all the attributes which make us what we should be, and yet sacrifice the least of the feelings of those around us?

Seek we for truth? Search we the hidden mysteries of our own nature, and say we shall be true in every thought and in every thought's utterance, and yet violate before God the principles on which truth is founded?

Then, through the Doctor, it was said:

How sweet is the air—how balmy the breeze which is laden with the perfume of Heaven's own flowers! Underneath the shade of a tall tree whose branches spread so wide, and afford such cool, grateful shade, there, on the bank of a gurgling brook, with flowers springing up all around me, embowering my seat with their many-colored petals, and their perfume so sweet—there, where the birds warble their songs to God, and spirit-voices catch the tone, as the spirits upward fly and take the hymn to God's own footstool—where a mellow light steals softly in and gives a saddened, sober hue to every thing—there, where spirits are pure as that beautiful breeze, and as that bright light where they sit, hand in hand, talking of God, of love, of truth, and working for themselves and others—oh! there, where every feeling is truth, is harmony, is joy, seraphic and supreme, have I lingered, loth to quit, reluctant to come to earth.

I have sat on that seat listening to the gurgling water, drank in the beautiful air, listened to the songs of bird and spirit, and felt my whole nature moved in me as it took its upward flight to Heaven.

How strong, then, the claim which could draw me back to earth—back past all that is so bright, so pure—past all the associations which make life one glorious day of joy ecstatic!

I have not been with you often of late, but I bring with me feelings fresh from a locality as pure, as kind, as charitable, as harmonious, as merciful, as loving as exists.

Oh! will you take them? Will each feel my blessing, filled with a spirit's love and faith, as it descends on each?

What come I for? There are stern duties which call us back to earth. It is long since ye all met as ye have now. How many feelings have grown up among you in that time—how many that were good and noble—how many that were evil—how many that retard—how many that advance your progress?

What seek ye the communion with spirits for? for knowledge, for wisdom, for truth, for love? And out of this, which prize ye most? All of you have some aim in searching out the mysterious truths of spiritual intercourse, which may benefit yourselves and others.

But the intercourse would be as worthless to ye all as the wildest doctrine founded on no truth to the heart that hungered and thirsted for righteousness, unless ye had some motive for self and others. Spiritualism, as it should be taught, comes to each as a direct mission from God. To each it brings its tribute of love, of grace, of kind encouragement, of strength, of chastening or reproof, or of direction.

How has it been with you since last I asked the question? Have you done only that which you are willing to lay open to the broad daylight? Has your intercourse with the world been such that it might be as open as the sunshine? Have ye had no concealments that ye dare not tell? Have you sought for truth, and gone along, boldly raising your head to Heaven, and claiming of God the light his mercy could shower on your path?

The heart may yearn for truth, but, muffled up in its own mantle of righteousness, and choosing its own path, it can never attain His high purity and love.

I am impelled by my mission to direct the heart that struggles for light to open doors and let the prisoned soul go free, to remove the shackles that fetter the mind, to breathe words of hope to the desponding, to teach that truth is to be attained only by truth. You can not make the truth false. The law of God is supreme, and whatever runs counter to it in its demonstration, perverts that which might perfect ourselves or others.

What is our duty? Can we fashion it ourselves to suit our tastes and purposes? The soul that receives truth in its inner self needs no law to govern or direct it. The law springs up in itself, and the truth lights it to its proper demonstration.

After all, God indeed knoweth our secret thoughts, and I tell you that the thoughts of you all are known to some spirits, not, perhaps, to one, or any of your usual number who surround you; but there are spirits who know them, and the act which militates in this day, with all appliances of spiritual intercourse, will surely be found and sent back to the heart whence it sprung. But there is a nobler object, a higher, holier purpose to govern you—the desire to make yourselves holy and pure, even as He is pure; and when you give evidence of all those attributes which belong to the Father, how little you feel of earth! The soul, indeed, casts off its shell and stands in its own individuality free, but bound by cords stronger than human ingenuity ever devised to the eternal Source of Truth and Love · forever.

You can not advance when your path is tortuous. Flatter yourselves as you may, you will return to the same spot whence you started in spite of all your efforts.

No, there is no need of tears to mark the spot where spring the eternal waters of life within you. Why looks the soul back on earth, drawn to the hearts there waiting and languishing by ties so tender and strong? Why looks the soul up to heaven and turns back to earth, sighing to be once more among its friends? The bond that binds affection there is the very bond which keeps all nature in its action—that keeps the Eternal One on his throne—

moves life in all its action and demonstration. Weep not, O spirit, for very soon you shall be able to make him you love so much feel you are near him, and whisper to him consolation that the world can neither give nor take away.

SWEEDENBORG.

P. S.—While I was writing out these minutes on this day (April 1), Mrs. Leeds, Laura, and Jane sitting on the sofa, Mrs. L. was thrown into a trance and said she saw a spirit, clothed in ancient armor, with a drawn sword in his hand, walking backward and forward. After a while he moved away from her, and she followed him until he arrived at a bridge, very beautiful in form and of Gothic architecture. He paused on the bridge and beckoned her to approach, and raising his sword, he exclaimed, "Onward, to conquer." She hesitated about advancing, saying, that if she crossed, she was afraid she would not be willing to return. She finally crossed, and the bridge turned into a large revolving wheel. "Thus," he said, "it is with existence."

His garb was then changed, and he now wore a mantle thrown over his shoulder.

Something was said between us, in the pauses of her trance, in the course of which I spoke of our finding in the spirit-world all the animals and material objects we saw in this life, and said that death is but a release from the trammels which bind us to this planet and a transfer of our existence to a more refined element. That it was like the grub which lives in the baser element, the earth, and dies by rising in a new body, the butterfly, destined to live in the more refined element, the air.

She was again thrown into a trance, and seizing my hand she said, "That is true, and you are the only man that understands it." I said, "No; I had instructed many in the thought, and some, doubtless, had received it." He answered, "Yes, but with you it is a firm faith, and with others merely speculative." He then went on to say that his change of garb was intended to convey this idea to her.

He then requested her again to go with him, yet she hesitated, because she could not see his face. He asked her if she did not trust in God without ever seeing his face, and would she not trust him? He then took another female on his arm and said to her, "This lady, at least, will go with me." She replied that that made no difference to her. He offered his other arm to her and she accepted it, and thus, arm-in-arm, they entered a magnificent Gothic temple.

He asked her to bow. She refused. "Why," he said, "this other lady bows!" "But," she answered, "I will not bow." "See," he said, "she kneels." But she answered, "I will not kneel to any thing but my Maker, and to him I will lift up my mind in silent prayer."

She had previously asked him if he was a Catholic? and he did not answer. She had also said to him, that that other female was going with him because she valued the honor of his company, but she did not.

He then pointed out to her a long path, and said that was her way unless she knelt there, and that she could go to Heaven only by that path. She answered, "Then we will not go to Heaven together." He then told her the other female had done penance, become pure, and passed on. She answered, "Do you think so? I do not."

Then the altar changed to a dazzling brightness, all shining with gold, and he asked, "Will you not now kneel?" She answered, "No." Then the altar changed to a single eye, and he said to her, "Let us pass on." They then entered a building, which she described as too vast for mortal eye to comprehend, and here he led her to a flight of stairs, and with great politeness and courtesy of manner bid her ascend. She expressed her dislike of that manner, saying it was a mask, and was not fit for the spirit-land. She wanted to see his real feelings. He told her she was high-minded. She said she did not intend to be, but only sincere.

They ascended the flight of steps, where he opened a door, and beneath her, in a pit, she saw various animals— wolves, leopards, boa-constrictors, etc. She asked what they did in the spirit-world, and if they were alive? He told her to descend and see. She declined, saying, she had just come away from such animals in the shape of men and women. Suddenly she turned to him and asked where that other woman was? He answered, "She has gone to look for popes and priests, while you are looking at your hobby on earth to see if there are animals in spirit-life."

He then showed her a beehive, and she asked him what that was for? She did not want to see such things in the spirit-world. He answered that she was too impatient, that the hive told us that we must ever work.

He then appeared to her again clad in armor, and told her he had three garbs upon him which yet to her he would put off, and let her see the inner man of Charlemagne. He then took off his gauntlet and laid it upon the floor, then laid his sword upon it, then kneeling gracefully on one knee, he reached out his hand to me, and said, " Friend Edmonds, they are for you, lift them up. Through you and yours I shall yet atone for the wrongs I have done my countrymen. Through you I will yet atone to your countrymen the wrongs I have done to mine. This great truth, now given to you, shall be a ball of light to my country, and spread from pole to pole."

Then turning to Laura, he said, " Lady, I too have been a Catholic. Catholics here have altars and cathedrals in plenty, but I have passed from sphere to sphere and found no pope or priest! Hold you fast to your present belief and great will be your reward."

He spoke a few words to Jennie, telling her that Laura, ere long, would require her sympathy, and entreating her to sustain and strengthen her with her gentle love.

Then kneeling before us, he uttered a short prayer, that through me he might be permitted to atone to my countrymen for the wrongs he had done to his own.

Section Forty-nine.

Friday, April 7, 1854.

This evening, through Dr. Dexter, in my library, it was said:

How difficult it is for the will to change the habits the mind has acquired by years of one kind of thought, by years of one kind of association! To me, even now, the effects of habits acquired on earth, whether for evil or for good, are the most difficult things in this life to alter or change. It is so, not only in regard to habits of thought, but equally so in reference to our affections—perhaps stronger, in reference to the affections, than almost any other of the functions of the material body. Sure it is, that when the mind acquires a habit of thinking a certain order of thought, the effect is perceptible in the acts of the individual's life. Thus we train ourselves on earth to live, to think, and to love with a greater or less degree of intenseness according to the habitudes of our minds. What, then, should be the relationship between mind and mind on earth in its various properties and attributes?

We talk of our affinities, of our sympathies, of correspondences! How often is it that our affinities are fashioned and directed by habits! How often are our sympathies with another's mind and opinions governed by our habits! the habits which the soul for years has acquired, bringing as an offering its richest tribute of affection, leaping over the bounds of time, and, still in the spheres, lavishing its treasures of love upon that object with which it was so long and so closely associated on earth! Oh, we talk of our affections, of our love! I tell you affection and love teach us in the spheres to crucify that which is selfish, and to love, even if loving produces the intensest suffering; for there are times when the soul pours out its affections like running water, and the tide, instead of being received in another's soul, is suffered to run waste, until its waters are drank up by the thirsty earth. We meet this even in the spheres.

It is exquisite pain to feel that love like this is wasted, and yet affection, true love, is tested only by its tenacity of adhesion.

Does not He who made us love? when every morning's sun shines forth new evidence of his affection, and even night's darkest pall gives evidence that love is still there twinkling in the thousand stars that stud that mantle? No; no action, no words, no suffering, no treatment can stay that feeling in its utterance. To bear and forbear, to suffer and endure, and yet to love, is the attribute of the progressed soul; and he who stops on earth, because his affections are not appreciated; because the love he proffers has been rejected; because it is not properly appreciated in himself; because his sympathies are not understood or his motives recognized; because he was not known; because for the love he had he was misrepresented; because there was no return but harshness, sternness, and the proud spirit, in its upward reaching, was crushed and sent back to earth; if he falters, if he withdraws his love back into himself, he has progressed only so far as his own condition of mind was tested by his own selfishness; for when we live here we shall learn that that which is pure and holy, that which is of God and to him, that which is righteous, that which is without spot or blemish, that which is high, noble, brave, gallant, proud, that which is learned, wise, profound, beautiful, consists in loving forever.

Section Fifty.

Sunday, April 10, 1854.

At the circle, this evening, we had a new manifestation, which was repeated on several evenings. Mrs. Sweet and my daughter Laura were both influenced at the same moment, and saw the same objects. They conversed with each other concerning what they saw, which seemed, from their conversation, to be the ruins of a buried city—the relics of a people and an age long since passed away.

A memorandum of their conversation was made at the time, from which Mr. Warren afterward wrote out the account of it. Laura also wrote her account of what she had seen; that precedes the dialogue, and even at the hazard of a little repetition, it is all inserted, as from it all we derive a very interesting view of man in one condition of his progression to his present state of refinement and civilization.

Laura's statement is in these words :

SITTING at the circle, Mrs. Sweet and myself were entranced so deeply, that we lost all consciousness for a short time. The first I recollect was Mrs. S. calling me by name, and asking me to go with her ; the spirits were sending us on a mission of love, and now we would start. · Suddenly was opened to our view a city tumbling to ruins ; spires were tottling, and here and there were the pillars of some splendid abode, standing like monuments of the past, silent in their grandeur. No sound could be heard save the winds. No life was there. ·

We descended slowly until we reached a dark entrance, and as we entered, it seemed as though a city was before us, buried 'neath the dust of ages. We clambered over the ruins, and entered a large subterranean passage or chamber, and on every side were statues sculptured exquisitely, mostly female figures—some were still perfect—some broken and crumbling to dust ; all were covered with a dark mold ;

every thing was enveloped in gloom, and we were enabled to see the surrounding objects by a light, bright and clear, that seemed to follow us and illuminated the objects of our attention, while all besides was shrouded with the darkness of the tomb. As we advanced, there was a chill that pervaded our frames, showing that the sun never penetrated there, and every thing was covered with a mold, cold and clammy to the touch. As we proceeded into the interior, the cold, damp atmosphere increased in its chill, and there was a feeling of oppression, as though the winds of heaven seldom found entrance there. Beneath our feet were stones, apparently blocks of marble of various hues, but covered with a slimy substance, which rendered it difficult for us to walk. Between the heaps of stones was a species of rank grass, growing stiff and reed-like, with sharp edges, resembling wild swamp-grass. We noticed in the first chamber that a portion of space was devoted to religious purposes. A singular, frightful-looking image was there, and its bright-red eyes glared at us as though it deemed us intruders in that city of death. Before drawing near, it appeared like some hideous animal crouching in suppressed fury; but upon examining it, our fears were dispelled, for it proved to be an idol formed of a dark, metallic stone substance; and the eyes that appeared to glare proved to be large jewels of a clear crystalline red, resembling ruby, but much purer. It had ears like those of a spaniel dog, in which were hung massive gold rings about five inches in diameter. Its face resembled a human being, with a head of the shape of a dog. There was before it an altar made of crystallized salt. It appeared to me broken, but still perfect enough to judge what it was. After having examined this creature carefully, we turned to the left and beheld the figure of a lion with wings; it was rough in its beauty, but very natural. I could not tell what kind of stone it was of, for it was covered with dust and slimy mold. Near it stood antique vases about five feet high, some composed of yellow marble, and some of a flaky, glittering crystal substance. Their bases were square and smooth, and the vases slender, gradually increasing in size, and much resembled the imitations we now have. Some were with handles on each side, and some without; they were delicately carved with fruits and flowers. While gazing upon these objects, and viewing the works of human hands, we saw advancing in the distance the figure of a man, and my companion remarked that it was strange to see a living being in so desolate a place. As he approached we discovered he was a spirit; his figure was tall and slim, and his face was dark and forbidding; sorrow seemed to have reigned supreme with him for ages. His look was that of amazement, mingled with fear. His garb consisted of a dark, ragged mantle, wound around him with a majestic air, but it had the appearance of decay like the objects surrounding us. Upon his head was a coronet of tarnished hue. It seemed frail and crumbling, and where jewels had once sparkled, were the hollow sockets glaring as though in mockery of the past. His hands were long and shriveled, and he moved with a slow tread, gazing sadly and sternly upon the ruin around him. My companion addressed him. As we passed into another chamber, we noticed the atmosphere was colder and more oppressive; the wall on the left side of the inner apartment was covered with what appeared a painting, but upon examination it proved to be mosaic work, representing a man on horseback. The face of the man was coarse, and very like an animal, and the expression was cruel and stern, and very disgusting. He wore a skirt of various colors falling to the knees, and thrown across his left shoulder was a circular mantle covered with grotesque figures. On his head was a singular-looking cap, which I could not fully describe, as some of the mosaic work had crumbled to dust. It was the life-like portrait of the unhappy spirit we had before met.

We passed on, and immediately before us were various garments, some falling to pieces at our touch. One in particular attracted our attention: it was a short, full skirt; the fabric consisted of gold and silver threads, interwoven with some kind of wiry material. Its fastening was by gold cords passing over the shoulder, and crossing in front. Then there was a waist about a quarter of a yard in depth, a strait piece hollowed under the arms, presenting a grace ful appearance, fastened behind by golden strings inter laced. I should judge that it had belonged to a female. We both noticed that after having described it, and turning to look at it, all sight of it had disappeared; nothing remained.

Our attention was then attracted to a staircase, broken and rough, presenting a dingy, brown surface, smooth to the touch; but when examining the material, we saw it was the white, transparent, flaky stone we had met with in the first chamber. Toward the right of the stairs, against the wall, stood a dark stone table, highly polished. It was filled with goblets and cups of gold and silver, exquisitely wrought; the largest goblet resembled those of the present day, differing, however, at the top; instead of the top being a plain ring, its rim curled over about an inch, with silver pendents made to represent bunches of grapes, solid and massive; it was used, I should judge, for flowers. The cups were small but very heavy, of different shapes, some plain, some goblet form. There was also a square plate with deep sides, which consisted of copper, beautifully figured, engraved as it were with some sharp instrument, but it was so covered with mold that it was difficult to decide its purpose.

We then passed into another chamber, which appeared in better order than the first; it was paved with marble of various hues, inlaid in figures, diamonds, circles, squares, etc., somewhat broken, however, and the center of the apartment was covered with pebbles of various sizes and beauty, which seemed like jewels. The windows were Gothic shaped, about three feet in height and two wide. The substance was not glass, but something soft and transparent, and colored red and green, and various other hues, blending most beautifully. Each piece seemed about two inches square.

We concluded to ascend the broad staircase, frail as it was. After much difficulty we found ourselves on a broad platform, or balcony, formed of this singular white stone. It was all one solid mass, unlike the pavement below. As we stood there, we saw a garden below us; it was an inner court, surrounded by buildings. In the center was a fountain, dried up, but the basin showed that water had flowed there for a long space of time. Around this fountain were statues of various sizes; some had fallen down; some were wanting a head, some an arm—one leaning against a tall figure of a man, the face all perforated with age.

To the left was a temple of dark shiny marble, round at the top, supported on fluted pillars, in the center of which stood a frightful image, roughly made, but too far destroyed to describe. He had been called the god of the land, and ruled the elements.

We turned from this scene to descend the stairs, and to the right we could see a long corridor, on each side of which were white marble columns, some broken, but pure and beautiful. We turned to the left, and entered a room with a low ceiling; but what was remarkable was its singular appearance. The walls and furniture were all alike, of smooth, polished stone, resembling in color and substance blue vitriol. In one corner was a couch of the same material, long and solid; a square block, highly polished, answered as a seat. One side of the room was covered with frescoed images, and heads with wings. We entered another room, and there the walls were of a light drab color, and singular, unknown writing was on all sides. At the extremity of the apartment was a fresco scene standing out in bold relief. It represented a very beautiful female resting on the left knee, her hands crossed and tied, resting on her right knee, her head bent over her hands, and her hair flowing and black. The face was exquisite in form, and the expression was far more elevated than the race that appeared to be natives of this region. I should judge she was a Georgian or Greek slave. Her form was delicately shaped, and the perfect poetry of beauty. We were told we might leave now, and as we turned to go, I saw a vase of iron filled with coins. We descended and passed through the same apartments, but noticed that large toadstools and mushrooms, larger than any thing we had ever before seen, were growing amid the ruins in corners, but, strange to say, there were no reptiles anywhere visible. We passed out, and oh! how grateful was the pure air of heaven to the two shivering mortals! It seemed morning, and we knew nothing more until we found ourselves seated in our library with wondering faces around us.

The dialogue, reported by Mr. Warren, was in these words:

MRS. SWEET.—Sister spirit, are you willing to go with me to explore a scene of ancient ruin, so that we may describe it for the benefit of our friends?

MISS EDMONDS.—Yes, I am willing to go, if it will do any good. I am willing to do any thing that will be of service to mankind.

MRS. S.—Well—come with me. I don't know what I am to go for, but I am impressed that we must go, and that it will be of use. The spirits will probably guide us; though I don't see any spirits with us.

MISS. E.—We seem to have arrived at a most dismal place.

MRS. S.—Why, what an ancient place it is! It is all in ruins. I can hardly see, every thing is so gloomy.

MISS E.—Are not those that we see yonder towers?

MRS. S.—Yes, they are towers that are broken and tottering to their foundations. It is a very gloomy place! The rank grass grows up amid the rocks, that seem to have been hurled over by some mighty force.

MISS E.—Where are the people that belong here? But people could not live in so desolate a place. It is deserted.

Mrs. S.—Yes, it is indeed deserted. Can you see any human being?

Miss E.—No; none.

Mrs. S.—The air is chilly, it strikes to my heart.

Miss E.—Yet there must be inhabitants somewhere about, though I can not see any. Here is a great building, partly in ruins.

Mrs. S.—Let us enter at this door, or rather the opening, for it seems more like going into a cave, it is so dark. Part of this building is standing entire. What massive work! Look at these marble halls—these figures sculptured in stone—that broken fountain. Observe the perfect beauty of these statues! All that the art and industry of man could do has here been done.

Miss E.—Yes, the works of art around here in ruins are truly wonderful. They must have been made in an enlightened age of the world.

Mrs. S.—Man's spirit must have been highly developed before he could from the cold stone fashion such forms of beauty!

Miss E.—But he did not look *up* from these forms.

Mrs. S.—Oh, Laura, something was wanting and wrong, or this mighty city would not have fallen. What a chill pervades all things here! Look there! yonder is a figure. It is a living being. I will inquire of him what all this means.

Miss E.—I see the figure. Let us go to him.

Mrs. S.—But be careful, we shall stumble over the rough stones. See what blocks and fragments are scattered about! It is difficult to find places for our feet. I am afraid there are wild beasts among these ruins. See! that person is coming toward us.

Miss E.—Do not fear—he will not harm us. Surely the spirits that brought us here will protect us.

Mrs. S.—But, Laura, see! that is a spirit. See what a dark robe or mantle he has around him! I am afraid of him—how do we know what he is? See! his head is bowed down, and he seems oppressed with some great sor-row. Are you willing to speak to him?

Miss E.—Yes, and I think it is our duty to speak to him. I do not fear him.

Mrs. S.—But I am afraid to go near him. What do you think it is? Is it a human being? What if it should be some dark spirit? that mantle is so black and so myste-rious!

Miss E.—We are in good hands. Do not tremble. Those who brought us here will protect us.

Mrs. S.—See! now he raises his head. What a face he has!

Miss E.—He is himself a ruin. What wretchedness!

Mrs. S.—See! the flesh seems wasted off his bones by grief. He is indeed wretched.

Miss E.—Let us speak to him. Perhaps we may com-fort him.

Mrs. S.—Spirit, speak to us.

Miss E.—Why are you here? what is the cause of all this sorrow which is so visible on your countenance? Why are you wandering in so dismal a place?

Mrs. S.—See, Laura, there is a crown on his head—some of the jewels are gone from it. He was a king here in times gone by. He does not look much like a king now.

Miss E.—He is to be pitied. Let us go to him, and talk with him. Perhaps we may learn his history.

Mrs. S.—See! he approaches us. We will talk with him. He is about to speak. I hear his voice—it is hollow and low. Tell him not to come any nearer—I shudder at his presence. He repels me with an icy coldness. His voice strikes a chill through me. I am afraid.

Miss E.—I do not fear. I will stand between you and him—and the spirits that brought us here, will they not protect us?

Mrs. S.—Look at his crown, or that which once was a crown. See how moldy it is! The jewels are gone or faded—for there is no brightness or beauty to the gems.

Miss E.—He is like the other ruins about here.

Mrs. S.—Yet perhaps we can help him. Spirit, can we render you any service? Don't injure us, for we came on a mission of good—we will be useful to you, if possible. Spirit, if we can aid you in any way, tell us how, but don't approach us.

Miss E.—Do not fear him—he will do no harm. See! he is weak as a child.

Mrs. S.—He speaks. He says, "Blest messengers of Heaven! have you indeed come to the scene of my former greatness and splendor, to behold my present sorrow and humiliation? Have you come like me to gaze upon the fragments of that splendor and power which once filled my soul with rejoicing and gladness? Have you come to behold my weary spirit retracing daily and nightly the scenes in which I used to reign a king supreme over all?"

Miss E.—Poor spirit! sorrow is in every feature, despair in every tone. We should be glad to render you happier, if in our power.

Mrs. S.—Why, that is our mission here. Look on his face, Laura; every feature is imbued with suffering. I feel now that we can approach him safely. Listen; he speaks again. He says, "I was cut off in the midst of my glory and greatness; my splendor availed me not when the summons of death came and laid me low. But my spirit chafed with anger. Oh, how I hated to leave the scene of all my power and grandeur! I have wished for no heaven, for my hopes of happiness were all upon the earth, and I have lingered about this city of my love and my earthly idols, and watched her decline. I have seen her greatness and her power fade away as gradually as the light fails at set of sun, till all that was proud and beautiful — all that was noble and magnificent in this wonderful city—has sunk down into the dark waters of oblivion till even the remembrance of her power is lost forever."

Miss E.—Let the spirit cease to mourn. Sorrow is unavailing. Let the morning succeed to the night. Let the past remain buried; come to the present and live. Suffer us to lead you to that light where a new course is opened for your spirit.

Mrs. S.—He speaks, "Oh, yes, I have too long lingered here, and wept amid these ruins of my power. My spirit has thus been chained down by my love of earth, and I have grown familiar with this desolation. This lonely place has been all the heaven there was for me, till the light has grown dim, and my spirit has almost forgotten there is a brighter place, and quite forgotten how and where I may seek it."

Miss E.—But thou hast not been forgotten.

Mrs. S.—He speaks again: "No, for they begged me to leave; but I have wasted long and precious years in mourning over my lost greatness."

Miss E.—Mourn not for what is past. Listen to our counsels. Come with us, we will guide thee to happier scenes, where thou shalt forget this sad waste of mournful ruins that only keep alive thy sorrows, and we will show thee the loving friends of other days, and thou shalt be more blest than even in the days of thy proudest power and grandeur.

Mrs. S.—He says, "What sounds are these? Why, mortals! did you come with angels to comfort and bless a poor child of earth? Did spirits of Heaven send you to me with these words of hope."

Miss E.—Bright spirits knew thy condition—spirits that wish all to be saved. They sent us to thee, to bid thee rise with new strength, and press upward and onward in the race, to tell thee to let these stones crumble and rot while thou shouldst soar on the path of progression.

Mrs. S.—He says, "Yet I see angels have come with

you. Bright beings! how beautiful they look! I am dusty and ragged. I have grown to be myself a ruin of the same color as the ruins around me, and as unclean. Will these bright beings receive me?"

Miss E.—Yes, they will, and joyfully. Cast aside this timidity—this feeling of distress. See! they approach thee. They are thy friends.

Mrs. S.—He says, "Oh, Heavenly Father! hear thy penitent child, and let those happy spirits who have come on an errand of mercy lead me away from this scene of desolation!" Laura, he is gone. Those spirits have conducted him away.

Miss E.—That was our mission here. It is happily fulfilled.

Mrs. S.—Did you see those spirits at first?

Miss E.—No, not at first. They followed us hither.

Mrs. S.—What a place we are in! There is so little light. The grass is white—the plants all look sickly.

Miss E.—It is because the sun never shines here.

Mrs. S.—If I were not afraid I should like to examine this. But it feels so cold here and so death-like. No human beings have lived here for centuries.

What singular-shaped windows! They are of many colors—made in figures. How beautiful they are! Look at those great, tall vases of white marble, so curiously wrought. See! they have fallen about in every direction. Look how they are sculptured. There are little figures and scenes carved on every side. See these vases that have handles on each side, with figures sculptured on them. They are very old-looking. Here is a massive figure cut in stone. It is a lion. It must have been made to set upon a building. It is very roughly cut, and yet it is very perfect in form. There are shining stones throughout its substance. It is so dark here I can hardly see any thing— and only one thing at a time. Those invisible beings who are behind us, shed their light so that it shines right between us, and we see only that upon which it falls. All else is wrapped in darkness. It is so difficult to walk here, too. The grass hurts my feet. Every blade seems to be a thorn.

Miss E.—Come on this side and see this.

Mrs. S.—I don't know what these things are—they are crawling reptiles—I am afraid of them.

Miss E.—I'll go first. I am not afraid. I am sure nothing will hurt me.

Mrs. S.—What is this before us with such glittering eyes? I am sure it is not alive. Let us look at it. What unnatural-looking eyes! They seem made of red stones. Don't go near it. What can it be? The face is long, and yet round—its hair is hanging down.

Miss E.—It is an ancient idol. Who could worship such a thing as that? See, it has rings in its ears. Its long hair hangs down.

Mrs. S.—It has an awful face! The stones which serve for eyes are red as rubies. How large they are! The figure is monstrous indeed.

Miss E.—See what a pedestal it is placed on! It seems to be a crystal marble. Look! here is an inclosure. It is evidently for an altar. It is broken, and the ornaments are scattered. Let the light shine upon it, so we can see.

Mrs. S.—I can hardly see it.

Miss E.—We have seen enough of it.

Mrs. S.—It is so still and death-like here, it seems as though we were in a tomb. It sends a chill over me to look round. I seem to be amid graves. It is so dark and cold, and there is no life around.

Miss E.—Look here! See this curious piece of mosaic.

Mrs. S.—I should have called it a picture.

Miss E.—It is the most interesting thing we have seen. See! it is made of small stones of different colors. Some of the pieces are gone. They must have been advanced in the arts to be able to do such things.

There is the figure of a horse. See that cloak—I never saw such a cloak. It is thrown over one shoulder. Look at this cap with the gems round it. Why! this was a palace, and this represents a king with his crown on. I do not wonder things are so strange.

Do you see that great flight of marble steps yonder? See how wide they are—many men might walk up them abreast. The railing is also of marble. But the steps are cracked, and rusty, and dirty.

Look at these windows. How different they are from ours! The panes so small and so numerous, diamond-shaped, much broken.

Look here, too, at these old garments. This was once very rich stuff. Now it is moldy and crumbling to dust.

This place is very close. It oppresses me. I would not stay here, but we have been brought here to see these things and report what we have seen, so that others may profit by the lesson.

This is a female's garment. It is a short, full skirt. It has silver and gold threads interwoven in it, so that it is stiff and heavy. It is very rich with the precious threads, but it is now discolored. The gold and the silver glitter, but the rich stuff has decayed. I can see how it was put on. Two cords went over the shoulders and crossed in front. It has a very little waist, only covers a little in front—no sleeves—something like a child's apron. It did not reach half up the waist.

Do you notice those things we have been examining are all gone? They seem to have been brought for us to look at, and then taken away again.

Look at these heavy goblets—what curious shapes! The lip curls over. They have grapes sculptured upon them. They are very unlike what we have. How heavy they are! And here is something peculiar. They look like plates of copper. They are very rusty now. This must be the place where that spirit lived.

Let us go up stairs—it is so close here. We should get fresh air there. Let us go—there by the broken columns.

Mrs. S.—I fear to go up those stairs. They look so

crumbling and so rotten, and yet they can't fall, for the spirits would not let us go up any dangerous place. Come, Laura, we will go up.

What a beautiful scene! It looks into the court. Look at that fountain in the center, surrounded by figures of statuary. The grass and shrubbery have almost overgrown it.

Here is a room different from all we have seen. Every thing is of one color—all a light-blue, like the sky. These things are made of some kind of earth by chemical process. The room is filled with things made of it. They are smoothly glazed like china dishes—but they are all blue, and of the oddest shapes.

There is but just light enough to see. There are two recesses or panels in the wall, on which are sculptured bas reliefs. They are covered with dust.

There is a little figure of blue crystal. It has a strange look—like its inhabitants, I suspect.

Here is a square block—a sort of seat. It is smooth on the top—it is all blue, and carved on the sides.

Miss E.—If we should go into that other chamber we should get another sight.

Mrs. S.—I am tired. Let us finish this exploring. This spirit who is with us, does he wish us to look at these things any more? Will it do any good to be here?

Miss E.—He smiles and says, "Look and record what you see for the use of the world."

Mrs. S.—I am afraid to remain here any longer. We may meet serpents. I am not easy. It is so dark here. I don't know why, but there is an impression of something bad in every thing about us.

Miss E.—They who dwelt here lived only for sensual gratification. See! 'twas to gratify sense they had these pictures. All shows their sensuality. Can you read those characters on these walls?

Mrs. S.—No—those inscriptions are Greek. Yonder is a vase. There on the walls you see letters cut in the same characters. It is doubtless part of their worship—a book always open.

Miss E.—Just observe that picture. The prominent figure in it is a slave. What a pitiful look! How different the dress is from the others in the picture. It is one of some subjugated nation, brought from a distance. It is a female, and very beautiful. They must have been very barbarous here.

Mrs. S.—She is not like our slaves—she is white, her hair straight, and she has more soul in her face and more cultivation than her conquerors; but she is a slave from her dress. Let me look at her features again. This was a captive taken in war.

Look at that man on horseback. How cruel, how gross and animal!—his horse looks better than he. Badness is expressed in his face. He was a miserable wretch. He is the same one we saw.

Miss E.—He was bowed down. He does look like that image.

Mrs. S.—Let us go—it gives me pain; or let us look at something more agreeable—let us seek flowers.

Miss E.—There are no flowers here.

Mrs. S.—Do you see that beautiful plant—crushed down like a lily—like a cup in shape—of a white color? The sun don't shine here. These are curious plants.

Miss E.—They are mushrooms.

Mrs. S.—I don't like this place? I fear there are snakes.

These were once beautiful walks. They were covered with small pebbles of various colors, like jewels. And here is a bouquet basket.

Miss E.—What is this place built here, with a figure inside? It is a garden idol. It is not so perfect as those inside. He was supposed to control the elements.

Mrs. S.—Let us return—we have gone far enough.

Miss E.—Must we go back? We shall have to come again, and we shall yet see beautiful sights.

Mrs. S.—But I am very tired, let us go. Oh, now that

we are outside, how pure the air feels! What a soft, warm glow! I don't want to go in there again. Next time let them send some one else. Do you suppose we have done any good?

MISS E.—Yes, of course, we have done much good. I suppose they thought that we had curiosity enough to wish to see all those things. We certainly did good to that unhappy spirit, and we have observed the things shown to us, so that they might be recorded, and we have done our duty.

Let us return.

Section Fifty-one.

Thursday, April 14th, 1854.

The circle met at Mr. Sweet's. All present except Dr. and Mrs. Dexter.

Mrs. Sweet and Laura were influenced, and carried on their dialogue nearly in these words:

MRS. SWEET.—Now we are drawn down into that dark place again..

LAURA.—It is not as cold as it was before.

MRS. S.—Turn and look at the spirits, and see who are with us.

L.—The same there were before.

MRS. S.—A whisper comes over my shoulder, saying, "We used to live here." Could bright spirits ever have lived in such a gloomy place? He says, "It was not so gloomy and ruined a place when we lived here. It was then a city of splendor and magnificence, of riches, and of mighty men."

L.—In what were they mighty? In the arts?

Mrs. S.—Yes.

L.—And in war?

Mrs. S.—Yes, and more especially the latter; but in the arts, see what beautiful ruins are still here, after a lapse of so many ages. Behold the crumbling ruins of what was once so beautiful!

L.—Are we in the city now, or only in the outskirts? Methinks we are in an outer building.

Mrs. S.—It is growing colder. The spirits are taking us in a different direction.

L.—It is a long avenue that seems to have no end.

Mrs. S.—Isn't it a long avenue? I don't like to go.

L.—But let us try and see.

Mrs. S.—It is winding, and leads into darkness. Will the spirits go with us and lead us? it looks so gloomy.

L.—Oh, fear not; they will guide us well, and show the way.

Mrs. S.—Don't you see? we will have to stoop down.

L.—Oh! how dark and cold it is here!

Mrs. S.—See! the stones of this entrance appear to be great blocks of granite or red freestone, with shining specks in it, veined in places.

L.—Yes, it is most beautiful to behold.

Mrs. S.—Would you not like to gather specimens of this stone?

L.—Yes. Shall we merely stand on the threshold of this subterranean passage, or shall we penetrate and seek the entrance? Let us try.

Mrs. S.—We shall never get through this dark place. There must be a gate.

L.—How slippery it is here! every thing is covered with slime and a cold sweat.

Mrs. S.—Oh! feel the stones; the moss on the walls is of the same slimy substance. Take care, or we shall meet with reptiles of some kind.

L.—There is nothing that can live here: have no fear.

Let us proceed and hasten through, that we may find the light, and not tarry here in trembling.

MRS. S.—I am afraid to go there, it is such a long, long passage. Oh! the spirit by you has his hand on your shoulder. I wish they would come as close to me.

L.—Let us hasten on.

MRS. S.—Oh! do you see that gate before us? We must pass through that entrance, and I see a faint glimmer of light.

L.—The gate is very massive, and appears to be locked; how are we to open it? There is a secret spring, and I should judge this was the dividing line between two sections of country.

MRS. S.—Here we are by the gate; how does it open, I wonder?

L.—By touching the spring, and pushing it up.

MRS. S.—Is that the way they open gates here? I never saw such curious locks, if that is one.

L.—But it is all rusty, and I don't see how we are to open it. Come help me push it up; it is too massive for us to move it.

MRS. S.—Wait. Spirit-guides are coming. There! one has opened it.

L.—Oh! how simple is the operation; they are familiar with every thing here. Oh, see! we will have to pass quickly, or the gate will close and catch us. I think this must have been a secret passage for the monarchs to traverse throughout their dominions.

MRS. S.—It seems to me that we have entered a different country; just look back upon the dark pasage we have left. Do you see the globe suspended from the roof of the entrance before us? and there is a face carved in stone, and heads of strange-looking animals. How curious!

L.—Yes, and how beautiful and perfect are the figures! And there is an animal resembling a goat, yet appears to be a cow. How unlike any thing we ever saw before!

Mrs. S.—There is a bird with horns; he is as large as an eagle.

L.—How beautiful is the workmanship!

Mrs. S.—It is better walking here; the road is well made and smooth, and there is grass growing here.

L.—Yes, it is delightful, and every pebble glistens as though each was a precious stone. Oh! there are flowers here, some very singular in their appearance. There is one which is formed of a tall stem, resembling the sugar-cane; it is about three feet in height, and at the top is a large bell-flower, with rounded edges, and is of coarse texture. It looks hardy and tough; the leaves grow at the base of the plant.

Mrs. S.—Let us go on. I see houses in the distance. The sun shines here. Where is the sun? I see the light, but not the sky or sun.

L.—Do you not see that the light only penetrates in spots, and illumines the place here and there only? This must be a buried city.

Mrs. S.—I wonder if the place is inhabited! What a queer shaped house that is!

L.—It is an octagon-shaped building, the roof round, and gradually formed to a sharp point, and a golden ball at the top.

Mrs. S.—Let us enter that building and examine it. Now just open the door. How massive it is! It must be very old.

L.—It is made of bamboo, or something resembling it.

Mrs. S.—Those spirits follow us here. There are figures cut out in the walls, birds and beasts, and even fishes; the walls are of a substance resembling plaster.

L.—Do you see the fish have horns? Oh! there is a body—a figure crouching in the corner. There has been death here. It is the body of one of our attendant spirits. It is not very beautiful.

Mrs. S.—I wonder if the spirit brought us here to see his bones!

L.—I hope he is better-looking now, for that is a horrid-looking figure.

Mrs. S.—The spirit says we are not able to judge of his spirit by seeing his bones. Just wait till we see him in the spirit-world.

L.—I want to examine those bones; let us go shake them.

Mrs. S.—Oh, there are seats made of stone all around the room, and there are windows here resembling those we saw in the dark building.

L.—Do you notice that it is not glass, but a soft substance resembling glue, and is very richly colored? and though the light penetrates, yet you can not discern objects through it.

Mrs. S.—It is not as transparent as glass, and is much coarser. The spirit is speaking again; he tells us to go in further to another chamber.

L.—Oh, see! the walls of the apartment are of blue stone—very beautiful, are they not?

Mrs. S.—But this is a pretty place. There is a fountain in the center of the room; and do you observe? there is a figure of marble in the middle of the basin, and all around the room are figures of females and children projecting from the wall. The females have on curious garments.

L.—Yes, and the skirts are like those we saw when we were in that dark palace; even the texture is the same, and it is wonderful how the colors have been preserved, so gorgeous and rich as they are.

Mrs. S.—Why don't they have representations of angels, instead of those females? I don't like the looks of those.

L.—Because they knew not of life hereafter, and their tastes being sensual, they gratified them in this manner. Did you observe, sister-spirit, the design of the fountain? The water is led up the center of the body, flows from the heads, and falls on the outstretched hands.

Mrs. S.—Oh, those figures are disagreeable, don't you think so?

L.—Yes, their faces are coarse, with protruding lips, broad noses, and round-shaped faces; they were very animal in their natures — very little spiritual about them.

Mrs. S.—Do you see? there has been a stream of water running through a marble channel, and fishes of every kind were here. Why, Laura, they worshiped the fishes, the birds, and these figures. Oh! what a religion was theirs! Hark! the spirit is speaking; he says, "They had very crude ideas of divinity, they worshiped him in all sorts of distorted forms, and through all sorts of fancies, their imagination running riot, leading them into monstrosities." I would like to leave here. The spirit says it makes him gloomy to remain here, because memory is refreshed, and he thinks of the days he spent here; he would be glad to go too.

L.—I should think he would be, but it is our duty to examine all. I should think all would appear strange to him.

Mrs. S.—"Hark!" he says. "This place seems no more natural to me than it does to you. I have lived beyond it, forgotten it, save as a spot where my spirit first received its earthly tenement, and was divested of its horrible and sensual grossness."

L.—Oh, let us pass from this apartment now.

Mrs. S.—There is something else to look at, he says, before we go; it is the figure of a female with a babe in her arms; her hair flows to her waist; she is tall, noble-looking, but gross, and far from delicate. Notice her dress— her breast exposed, arms bare, and only covered with ornaments. Oh! see, there are strange-looking musical instruments in the corner; let us examine them.

L.—There is a triangle formed of a very beautiful, light-colored wood of great fragrance, and there are strings attached to it, and there is also a long pipe, three feet long, with a trumpet end, all perfect, but somewhat discordant in sound.

Mrs. S.—See! Laura, there is written music; I can not decipher it.

L.—It is written on parchment with a mineral which resembles coal, and therefore the letters or figures are large and black.

Mrs. S.—I guess they did not have printed music then.

L.—Observe the floor of this room; it is wood inlaid, and very beautifully polished.

Mrs. S.—I thought it was marble, but I see now that the wood is inlaid so as to represent flowers, animals, etc., and is of various colors.

L.—Judging from the splendor here, the spirit must have been one of the grandees, if this was his abode. There is a secret door at your left; they must have been an intriguing people, for there are so many secret passages and doors, they must have loved deceiving.

Mrs. S.—The spirit says they were an intriguing people, and needed all the mysteries of art and evil-mindedness to conceal their evil deeds. They were very sensual, loving the worship of idols better than what was professed at the altar where their prayers could be answered by the most high God. The spirit seems very solemn, folds his hands, and says, "Ay! you would be solemn, too, could you stand and gaze on ruined houses where you once enjoyed life in its fullest sense, andcould you feel having lived only to enjoy the present, never thinking of the future, you had been called suddenly away, and beheld in an instant the great ignorance and evils of earthly life. You would mourn as I do, on gazing on the graves of so many unrisen souls who yet remain far down in ignorance and darkness."

L.—Tell him not to feel so sadly; there is a chance for such spirits to rise. Tell him to look on the scenes of bygone days with more cheerfulness; there is hope for all.

Mrs. S.—I wish he wouldn't feel so gloomy. But he says it is for his people he mourns. He knows there is hope, for by looking and striving he has redeemed himself from his crushed and darkened state; and in order to advance, he has been sent to guide us, and show us how he lived when he had thought of nothing beyond a luxurious and licentious life.

L.—Will he allow us to leave here now, and examine the interior of the building?

Mrs. S.—He says Yes, he is going to conduct us to the place of worship. We are only on the first floor—we have not ascended the stairs yet.

L.—Had not this spirit once a title? for here all is splendor.

Mrs. S.—Yes, he was one of the king's counselors. Here is an altar made of stone, upon which is placed their chief idol.

L.—And it is covered with jewels; it has only one eye, which is in the center of the face, and resembles a bull's eye.

Mrs. S.—Oh! it is a horrid-looking image, and what a terrible atmosphere pervades the place! The spirit says it is difficult even for him to remain here.

L.—Do you see? there are many idols surrounding the chief one. They are the minor gods, and were supposed to be ruled by the chief god.

Mrs. S.—At the other end of this apartment is a dark stone altar on which ashes are scattered.

L.—By the appearance of the whole altar, they must have sacrificed human beings.

Mrs. S.—Oh! do let us leave this place; don't go there.

L.—Oh, yes, I must, for there is so much to learn that is interesting. Come; if you do not wish to go, stay there, and I will go alone.

Mrs. S.—The altar is about ten feet long, and at one end there is a huge caldron. At the other are the bones of the victims. Laura, have you seen any iron here? I have not, every thing is stone.

L.—The caldron is of copper, and is a receptacle for the animals sacrificed.

Mrs. S.—They put in the animals when they worshiped; they put in spices and bodies of beasts anointed with
sweet-smelling odors. They took out the entrails mixed
with spices, and the odoriferous incense scented the air and
affected the senses of the worshipers, and they were filled
with delirious joy and praised their idol.

L.—Once a year the people were allowed to enter and
prostrate themselves in gratitude for the great privilege.

Mrs. S.—Why, they used to sacrifice slaves here!

L.—Yes, they captured the most beautiful females and
children, and sacrificed them to their gods as the greatest
offering.

Mrs. S.—Oh! let us leave here, 'tis too dreadful to
think of.

L.—Do you see that bright spirit, that beautiful female?
It is one that was sacrificed here.

Mrs. S.—Oh, I must leave here, for methinks I hear the
groans of the dying mingled with the adoration of the
people. When the victims were burned, they strewed the
ashes upon the worshipers. I want to leave very much.
It makes me feel bad. It seems as if I can see crowds of
spirits sad and gloomy. I see now that bright, beautiful
spirit! Ask her to speak, you saw her first. Her hands
are folded on her breast. What a heavenly expression!
she will speak to you.

L.—She is very beautiful. She says, "I was indeed one
of the fair daughters of a race of beings celebrated in war.
I was captured by these people—a rude and cruel race—
was torn from the dearest ties that bound me to earth, was
sacrificed on this altar, and when the breath left the body,
I felt I was leaving for a better land; for often, when gazing
upon Nature's works, I knew there was bliss yet unfolded,
that there was a better, brighter land. And when my
body was tortured, my spirit was rejoicing with the bright
ones unseen. There are many spirits here, and those beyond you, oh mortals! to whom I come. They had one
talent, and many used it to their best knowledge, and some

neglected it. My mission now is to them. I come to tell them I forgive them. I come to point the way. See you not that upon their brows is stamped the mark of my ashes long since placed there, and now I will guide them onward and upward."

Mrs. S.—See what a gentle spirit she is! She truly loves her Creator, smiling on these poor creatures. See their saddened faces! she is leaving flowers for them. Were we brought here to see this and tell of it?

L.—Yes; does not this lesson reward us?

Mrs. S.—See! she has gone. Why are our feet so cold?

L.—It seems as though the winds of heaven never penetrated here.

Mrs. S.—It does not seem as though there could be spirits down in this dark, dismal place, here, where she was sacrificed. And she has come to aid them! Oh, how dead the air is around us.

L.—Let us leave here. We have seen enough of this.

Mrs. S.—The spirit says, "Ascend the stairs and gaze around the country." The stairs are broad—broad as our house is wide. Steep, unlike ours.

L.—The stone of which they are formed is the same pure crystal that we saw before.

Mrs. S.—There are holes cut in the steps; why are they so?

L.—That the air may have vent from below, it preserves the stone.

Mrs. S.—The spirit says, "Observe the lines drawn on each side of the steps; the slaves were obliged to pass on the outside, and were not permitted to step on the center, so great were the distinctions between the classes."

L.—Let us ascend and view the surrounding country.

Mrs. S.—Oh! what a scene of desolation and ruin; some buildings fallen, and half covered with sand.

L.—Do you not see some houses standing partly covered with stones and lava, a black-and-red matter crushed in masses; some are white, and there are trees growing amid the ruins.

Mrs. S.—There are flowers and plants here very beautiful. It looks as though an earthquake had visited this place, and many buildings are untouched. How can any thing else live here in this desolation? Look! there is a singular garden. What is it?

L.—It is an ancient hanging garden, and on every side are drooping vines looking as though they sprang from the air. See that temple beyond; it is formed of different colored stones. Let us look at it; in its center is an image with eyes in the side of the head, with ears hanging to the shoulders, the nose flat. What is in his teeth? fruits of the earth. They offered to this idol the first fruits in every year, in order to propitiate him.

Mrs. S.—What an old temple it is! that image has wings. On each side of this god is a little image.

L.—Do you see what they hold in their hands? hearts. In the spring of the year the youths and maidens were betrothed here before these idols, and they offered them their love.

Mrs. S.—Oh! what looking things they are. They must have appreciated the offerings. What little imps they are! The spirit says, No scandal of his gods. They used to consider them beautiful, and young maidens used to do homage here.

L.—How winding is this path! let us seek it.

Mrs. S.—Take care, you will fall. There is something buried in the sand. Stop until I see what it is. I have got it out; it is a stone foot, very ugly. It must be that of an idol; oh! it is so ugly. Come away! I don't like these things. The spirit says I am a coward.

L.—I am going back to get that foot. See, it is of stone, broad and flat; it was their god of the minerals. On the sole of the foot are jewels.

Mrs. S.—Let us go from here, now. The spirit says that the foot was supposed to preside over all things. Their divinities were always tangible as well as worshipers; every thing was external and gross.

L.—Are there ever moon and stars visible here?

Mrs. S.—The spirit says, "Go on, and you will see some of our ancient paintings."

L.—Oh! that will be interesting. What makes it so rough here?

Mrs. S.—It is the ruined temples and stones crumbling to dust. There is a house with the door open—a very low, square house of a yellow color.

L.—Let's go in. There is a queer picture gallery of parchments hung up all over. There is moss hanging from the roof—very beautiful. There are figures on the wall—a horse standing on two legs. There is another, it is that of a man, and his head is shaped in a peak, like the roof of a house.

Mrs. S.—The spirit says this was the rendezvous for the higher classes; there were not many such places in the city, for the class of minds who were attracted by these things were few. The paintings were performed by natural genius, prompted only by love of them—not having in our city such regulations as you have. Slaves performed most of the work, often excelling in the labor and purity of conception. They were of a different race, and were prisoners of war put to menial occupations.

Mrs. S.—Do you see how the paintings are fastened?

L.—Yes, they are parchments stretched across at the sides upon wooden frames.

Mrs. S.—There is a scene of the people sacrificing slaves, a representation of the manner of which we have been told. I do not admire the conceptions, but the colors are very rich.

L.—The flowers painted are very coarse, and merely sketched. Shall we leave here for home now?

Mrs. S.—Yes; if you wish we can go home and come again; he will tell us more next time. He can not in our language call things by their proper names, but he will speak as plainly as possible. He says he could show us many things that would frighten us: then I don't want to see them. He says I must do many things I don't like, and I'll be glad of it afterward. He is taking us out by the gate.

Section Fifty-two.

Thursday, April 20, 1854.

The circle met this evening in my library, all present except Mrs. D. It was first written through the Doctor:

I WISH, dear friends, that you could see the faces of the many spirits that are with you, lighted up by a feeling that imparts such a radiance, that they sparkle like stars. 'Tis for joy that you are once more together* and at work; 'tis for the future; 'tis for the great good that will be done; 'tis for time; 'tis for eternity.

I can come nearer through you, Doctor, with your present feelings, than I ever could before, and I know that we have all progressed, or this could not be.   BACON.

Through Laura it was then said:

We come from our far-distant homes to bring truth in every form, and now will we come, like harbingers of morn, and tell of the triumph of truth. The birds, at early dawn, carol their sweet songs to awaken nature from her repose, and in one voice send up to God their glad tribute of praise. As dawn passes on, each warbles its notes to Heaven; and

---

* The long absence of the Doctor and myself, on our Western mission and other causes, had interrupted our full meetings for a period of over three months.

as night approaches, and all nature retires to rest, the warbler continues his song till the last hour of day, when relieved by the bird of night, whose hooting sounds from hill to hill, and echo sends it back again.

Thus it is with truth. Morning dawns again, and the song reverberates. It has risen with the morn, and is sounded abroad in the earth; everywhere its notes are heard joyful, solemn, deep in tone—different, yet blending and making one harmonious song. Man has arisen, awakened by the sound of truth stealing on the ear with its gentlest musical tones. Whence comes the sound? From the far-distant spheres it comes, and he enjoys it. The weary, way-worn traveler, seeking the path to a safe haven, hears its loud whistle. It is music to his ears, and reminds him of his childhood, and truth, dawning upon his soul, reigns triumphant. The busy man of the world, heeding only himself, looking only to gain, hears the deep-toned hooting of the midnight owl, and he starts anew and asks what is it? It is truth, with all its solemnity, visiting his heart. He stands and listens, yet heeds it not; but ever and anon it reaches his would-be-deaf ear, and he can turn nowhere that he does not hear the sound.

As noon arises he is surrounded by the sounds from every tree, and shrub, and flower, and heart that is throbbing around him, that truth is triumphant. Prepare the way for its coming in all the glory of heaven. Yet still hardening his heart, he pushes his way on, stumbling, falling, weary and worn, and sits him down by the way-side. Travelers pass him by, each with a palm of peace in his hand. He wonders where they received the boon? and the answer is, It was given by Truth.

Young childhood hears the whisper of the winds and the gentle notes of the birds, and listens with joy, for he knows it is the voice of Truth, and he travels on, rejoicing evermore.

The sorrowing female, bowed by grief and cares, sees no noon for her; all around her are clouds and darkness. All nature seems wrapped in mourning, and as she sorrowing treads on her weary way, the sweet, joyous song greets her ear, bids her hope, and tells her it is Truth passing and surrounding her, and she must embrace it if she would behold nature clothed as of old. She starts, and cries, "Whence that voice ?" Cherubs answer, "Beloved mother, we come to bring you of that blessing. We come to tell of a land where thy lost ones are. Embrace the new gift, and to thee too will be given the palm of peace, and thou mayst go on rejoicing."

Thus shall it be. Truth shall go from clime to clime. You shall never see its setting sun, but it will be a beacon-light to all—to each a staff to aid up the hill of progression. Treasure the precious boon of Heaven. I thought I had the gift, but I had only the outside bark ; now I have the staff itself. The covering has crumbled, and now I lean on the pure crystal staff. Oh ! let me ever grasp it tighter, and it shall be my guide to my God.

Then, through me, it was said :

I am borne far off into the regions of space, amid the countless worlds that roll through the vast expanse. I stand alone, surrounded by the blue ethereal—illuminated only by the sparkling worlds rolling round me—some near— some far off—with inconceivable velocity, and yet in direct obedience to the will which has fashioned and speeded them on their eternal way. I see them of various sizes, of many hues, of every conceivable variety of intensity of light. Amid this vast and living universe I stand alone. But a voice speaks to my ear, "Seest thou falsehood here? What speak these mighty creations of His hand but His truth ? As they move on in their eternal paths, they carry the truth as His messengers throughout His boundless creation. They proclaim truth as they roll. Emanations as they are from Himself, from His inconceivable wisdom, from His boundless power, they are the embodiment of His truth, and ever speak it to the universe through which they are wending on their never-ending journey. Pause! oh, mortal! and behold, if thou canst, how vast, how omnipotent, how enduring, how unwavering is the truth which they proclaim, and canst thou conceive that amid these rolling orbs, falsehood can find a resting-place? That it can speak to the intelligence that emanates from God himself aught but truth? Pause yet awhile, and grasp within thy mind, if thou canst, the mighty lesson of truth which these countless worlds, spread out before you like a spangled carpet, are teaching to you and to the myriads of sentient beings, who, like you, are of Him and to Him. And standing thus amid a boundless universe of truth, breathing thus into thy nostrils an atmosphere which is truth alone, imbibing from its life-giving qualities the very spirit of truth, canst thou conceive of the mind that would seek for falsehood here, rather than truth? Enter one of these glorious orbs which roll around you, and view its habitations and its inhabitants, see how lovely is the scene which opens to your view! See how gorgeous, and yet how grateful is the light which rests on that scene! See how pure, how bright, how full of love toward each other are they who inhabit there! See every heart beating for its fellow! See how every thought is laid bare to the world around the instant it is born, and canst thou find here, amid this beauty, this purity, aught but truth? Look upon the broad plain spread out before you, redolent with perfume, and resplendent with nature's brightest hues, and see if thou canst find there the dark footsteps of falsehood? Go with those bright spirits from their resting-places abroad to the tasks that are before them, see them marshal worlds in their orbits, evolving new worlds from the disjointed matter scattered through space, and developing from it new souls, candidates for immortality, and see if in aught which they perform here or enjoin there, thou canst find even the germ of falsehood! Roaming thus through His vast creations, looking upon man in his brightness and power, thou canst find naught but truth.

"Dost thou ask where, then, is falsehood to be found? Hither, mortal! and I will show thee. Descend with me from these bright abodes. Let us find a world yet imperfect and undeveloped, recently only ushered into being from the universe of matter! and perchance we shall find there a being who does not emit from himself the light which surrounds him, who perchance is dependent for his light on some material object near him—who is bound to the matter in which he grovels by chains so gross that you almost marvel that he is not fastened, like the rock or the tree, to the planet of which he is a part. Alas! you see that his progress in the path of his ultimate destiny has been so limited that he is incapable of comprehending even the material light by which he sees ; and that not only has he not advanced far enough himself to generate his own light, like the bright spirits whom you have just seen, but it is difficult for him to comprehend that it can be generated by any ; and when that material light in its daily revolutions disappears from the world which he inhabits, it leaves behind it a darkness even more congenial to his nature than the splendor of its noonday. Canst thou not, O mortal! here find the germ of falsehood? Canst thou not, amid the material and moral darkness that broods over their undeveloped minds, perceive that falsehood may indeed flourish and be most potent?

"Go with me still further down. Behold those, who have passed through that material existence, after having yielded to the mere animal propensities of their nature— after having denied that there was light, and even that there was a power that could speak it into existence. Go among them, bearing as they have, into their present existence, the darkness which they hugged to their bosoms. See how gloomy is the air which surrounds them! how murky and how black is the atmosphere in which they grovel still on! See how the darkness of their existence has even discolored their material garments! Seest thou not amid them the birthplace of falsehood? Seest thou not

that their whole life is a living falsification of their nature
—almost every breath of air they inhale—every thought to
which they give birth—every act of their existence is
stamped with the falsehood of their dark abode? Thus,
oh, mortal! have I shown you man in his extremes, and
hast thou capacity to comprehend the lesson?

Thy nature gives the choice, and it is in thy power to select
between the brightness of truth and the darkness of falsehood. What is there to prevent thee from choosing wisely
and well? Thy God has endowed thee with the capacity
to choose. Wilt thou choose in obedience to the immortal
instincts of thy nature? or wilt thou acknowledge the vas-
salage of thy material propensities? Answer for thyself,
for thou canst; and remember, that while Truth has her
abode amid her votaries in those brighter realms, Falsehood
ever dwells in the darker regions, to which she is full
mighty to draw down her worshipers."

Through the Doctor it was then said :

The history of national and individual sacrifices given to
us in the Old Testament is a beautiful illustration of what
is required of the human heart in its intercourse with God.
A sacrifice in ancient days of a lamb, a goat, or an ox was
in itself considered an atonement for many sins which had
been committed ; and when the Father saw fit to indicate
his recognition of the sacrifice, then the individual knew
he was forgiven. The illustration is most beautiful, for it
shows us that in these days, instead of a sheep, a goat, or
an ox, the searcher after truth should lay his own heart on
the altar and offer it as a living sacrifice.

Why wanders the heart so far away from that which is
true? Are there falsehoods that come direct from God?
Can he who made us deceive us? Would there be any
untruth if the heart did not fashion it out of its own grossness and sensuality? What! to profess to love God—to say
that we feel the desire to be pure—to pray to God that he
would make us pure, and then to use the reason with which

we are gifted, the high attributes of our nature, our instincts, tastes, education refined as they may be—all the means and appliances which surround us to deceive ourselves and others? Professing that God is very beautiful, and his creation teeming with all that is grand and glorious, then, O! then, in the face of all we profess, basely to betray ourselves, our God, and our principles?

Yet this is the truth that half the world live upon and dare to die upon. O! I pity that man's heart that professes love to God and man, and yet builds up between himself and heaven a wall of adamant by the perversion of his own nature. I tell you that the spirits who visit that man—what shall I say? they'll make a hell in his heart that will pour out a bitter lava worse than Ætna. O! then, the wrongs done not only to his nature, but to the eternal principles which God has established! Holding up between the light his own base nature, the false diamonds he sells for truth, that some straggling ray may catch the eye of a deluded follower, they pilfer all that is good, all that is sacred, all that can be relied upon, and very complacently say, I do indeed love God and my neighbor!

There is more of evil in the world that grows out of hypocrisy than almost any other one cause, and one of the greatest punishments which an evil spirit encounters when he enters the spheres is the knowledge that he can not trust a single soul he meets. No wonder the wail of an agonized heart wends its way to Heaven. No wonder that the soul, conscious it has done wrong, pours out bitter tears of unfeigned repentance. No wonder that it draws from the brighter spheres those souls which catch the falling tear and bear it where it is prized above rubies. No wonder that when the soul wakes up to a sense of the wrong it has done—its own falsehood and deceit—the storm of desolation prostrates every thing there. The heavens might be black—they might fall, yet not atone for that sin.

Yet why, to-night, do the spirits speak of truth? Why has the lesson been inculcated with such force? It is that you may be true and perfect; for I tell you that unless you become living evidences that the love of God is shed abroad in your hearts, prompting them to truth, it will be more terrible for you than to call on the rocks and mountains to fall on you. For if you lie, it is not our fault, but your direct punishment. If you are hypocritical, it is not the spirits who have taught you to be so.

If you live not up to the faith you profess, do you not lie to them and to God?

Spiritualism is a religion, and it enjoins on its followers a greater regard for action, for in that is the whole incentive to progression. The pains and penalties denounced against the world the world fashions for itself.

Your light should indeed come from yourselves. You should not, like the moon, borrow it, but it should be of itself and for itself, because of God. It should beam forth and illumine your path. It should be a light to your feet, lighting you up to Heaven.

Section Fifty-three.

Monday, April 24, 1854

The circle met this evening at Mr. Sweet's. All were present except Mrs. Dexter, and there were present the two Mr. M'Donalds from Glen's Falls, N. Y.

After some general instructions for the proceedings of the evening through Dr. Dexter, Laura and Mrs. S. were influenced to continue their description of the buried city, as follows:

LAURA.—They wish us to go to that buried city again. Come, let us go. It is so dark there and cold, darker than ever before. They lead us to the right.

MRS. S.—Laura, you will have to lead me. I can't see. Just look and see if these spirits are with us.

L.—Oh, yes, there they are; they say it is rendered darker by the influence surrounding the place being of that nature. How cold it is! Let us hasten on.

MRS. S.—Spirits, won't you go before, and show us the way? Laura, are you not afraid?

L.—No, not afraid—they will lead us on ; but this cold, damp air chills me. Let's hasten on. I will lead you— the spirit says he will not let us injure ourselves.

MRS. S.—He puts his hand on my shoulder. I feel stronger now.

L.—This scene strikes terror to my heart, it is so dismal. This must be one of their secret dungeons. Do you see that faint light far ahead?

MRS. S.—Yes, but it is very distant. Take care. You will fall. What is that in our way? This is some horrible thing!

L.—Let us seek it. What is that in our way? It is so cold here.

Mrs. S.—Let us go around, and not near it.

L.—Let us see what it is. Shed a light upon it. What is it? It is square. Oh, I see.

Mrs. S.—I can't see, it is so dark!

L.—It is a square trap-door of stone, very hard. Do you see? The spirits told me to touch the spring. Oh! horrible!

Mrs. S.—Oh, it is terrible here!

L.—There are bones piled up here. This is some place of punishment.

Mrs. S.—There are bones of animals here of all sorts.

L.—See! bones of children, men, and women! Why are they here? Ask that spirit, perhaps he will tell us. It must have been a living tomb!

Mrs. S.—The spirit says it was to put people in alive, and let them perish, as a punishment, when they had committed any great crime against the gods. They put a number in together, and also wild animals to devour the victims. Oh! let him shut the door, I don't want to see more.

L.—He will allow us to pass on now. See! what is that?

Mrs. S.—It looks like green grass beneath our feet—it is moss.

L.—It is much pleasanter here, and the moss is so soft, so velvet-like. And now we can go on, for we have had enough of those dismal sights; but it was necessary that we should see them all. What is that at the left?

Mrs. S.—I was going to ask you if it was not a spirit about to guide us?

L.—It is the figure of a woman standing with her arms folded.

Mrs. S.—The spirit says she is a spirit come to guide us on further, to show us what to do. She wants us to speak to her.

L.—Now I understand why we are brought to these darkset haunts, to reassure the unhappy spirits loitering here.

Mrs. S.—I did not think there were people here.

L.—I see that black building we are leaving.

Mrs. S.—Oh, don't look back, we have reached the entrance! See! it is bright, and observe those massive images—they must be idols—they can not be human beings.

L.—Do you see one figure, very black in appearance; it resembles a centaur, but is coarser, more disagreeable.

Mrs. S.—It has no clothes on. I do not like it.

L.—It sends a chill over me to look at those figures. What degraded tastes! What could this place have been?

Mrs. S.—The spirit says it was near the palace; they did not term the building palace, but a name we can not understand. He beckons us on. Shall go in? We must go up those steps.

L.—Oh, what figures are here! faces fierce, firm, gross, and sensual, and the expression of countenance denotes every passion in which man is capable of indulging.

Mrs. S.—Don't look at them; they are very vulgar, I think. Look! that female spirit has passed on before us. This place looks like home. See those images around the room—casts of human beings placed in niches!

E.—The walls of this room are sparkling with jewels laid in figures; and observe that image with two faces, one each side, male and female in one. What could have been their ideas of nature?

Mrs. S.—There is one worse than that; it has the form of a female, with a horse's head.

L.—See the next one to it! a man with two horns; the one on the right side is two feet high, and on the left one foot.

Mrs. S.—Can you read that strange writing on the wall? It is the queerest writing I ever saw.

L.—I have seen those characters before. The spirit says he will tell us what this room was called.

Mrs. S.—Each dignitary had a peculiar divinity of their

own to worship, and the name of each is written above the image.

L.—That accounts for there being so many dotted round the walls. I see paintings. What beautiful works of art! The walls are of fresco; the ceiling shaped like a dome.

Mrs. S.—The paintings are beautiful, but coarse-looking. And Laura, see those birds! they look as though taken on the wing, they are so natural.

L.—They are the best we have seen yet—such rich colors. And do you observe the windows in the dome? They are formed of different colored stones and crystals, and the light shines through most beautifully, all the colors blending. I like this room. That female will take us to a still stranger place. The door shuts with a spring, and has a sharp blade of stone attached to it. Every door has that blade to prevent intruders. Those who understood its management were not injured, but those who didn't, woe betide them! 'Twas lucky we had aid to open them.

Mrs. S.—The spirit says these things have not been penetrated into to the present generation. She lived in this city herself. Laura, we must follow that spirit; she's dressed in white. I like her looks. We are now in the room above the one we left. Look in the middle of the room! What is it? A throne? It's a singular thing.

L.—See! it is a square piece of stone, carved with ungainly figures. What could it have been?

Mrs. S.—Do you see that railing around the throne? It is composed of the whitest, purest stone I ever saw. I wonder what it can be?

L.—It looks more like crystal. What is the name of it? Can't the spirit tell us?

Mrs. S.—He says it's a stone peculiar to the country. It was found buried in the depths of the earth, and taken from thence, and for ornamenting and beautifying our cities' noblest buildings. They also used to form their idols of it. This is the room where the females worshiped

—where they had all sorts of revolting ceremonies, and even sacrificed their slaves, while performing their horrid rites.

L.—Do you see that repulsive scene enacting? I never could imagine half that is presented here. There they are cutting a female slave into quarters, and figures are dancing round and bathing their heads in the blood of the victims. Innocent little children were bound to sticks of wood the same size as themselves, and thrown into the fire.

MRS. S.—See! they had something that they drank during these ceremonies which made them almost frantic.

L.—The drink was composed of the juice of a coarse plant, the same that we have before described; the stem yielded a rich sap, which was boiled with spices, and they drank it thus.

MRS. S.—And that was given them to drink by the priests. Slaves were not permitted to enter here unless to be sacrificed. See their horrible actions; they had forgotten their delicacy.

L.—They acted as though possessed; they had slain a child, and were playing foot-ball with its body.

MRS. S.—I can't see it; don't ask me to. I want to leave this place.

L.—No; we must remain and see all. These were their greatest ceremonies and sacrifices to the gods. They were excited to it by this drink. There is one cutting off the head of an old man, and children are playing with it.

MRS. S.—They allowed the young maidens to come in and join in all these things! No wonder they had lost all traces of female delicacy and refinement. Oh, horrid is the sight! Let us leave this place. ·

L.—Yes, but go first to the other end of the temple. See! in that corner is an image of a human being with four legs, head pointed, eyes staring without lids!

MRS. S.—I can't see it, it is so dark here. I don't see how you can laugh at it; it makes me shudder. Did you notice the fireplace?

L.—Built for sacrificing human beings! There is nothing left of human feeling here. They delighted in taking life in every form, even the females.

Mrs. S.—There is something else to be seen before we go.

L.—See that spirit! so beautiful and bright!

Mrs. S.—'Tis the same that brought us here; she is very beautiful.

L.—She says, visiting these scenes she once frequented, and which she dreaded to recall, has enabled her to progress, and her translation to a bright sphere takes place on this very spot.

Mrs. S.—Oh, she is a pure-looking spirit; I wish she would not leave us.

L.—See, she goes upward, and as she goes throws flowers in our path. She says, "I go to my happy home, for my mission is done, and Heaven is won." If we are thus rewarded at the end of our mission, does it not encourage us?

Mrs. S.—Something to work for, something to look forward to. This is worth working for. They say we must return to this place again, for there are some things to be shown us which will not be known for generations to the world, if not disclosed now, and we have aided them much.

L.—We will help them; assure them we are willing. The one behind you has placed a star on your forehead, and says it shall remain there, and he will know you by it in another land. He will be first to greet you when you come home.

Mrs. S.—Your guiding spirit says he will conduct you to many places. He says he loves to conduct you, you are so willing. I hope he will bring us to the air again.

L.—If I can, I will be of service. I am ready. Here we are in the air again.

Then through myself was presented the following

VISION.

They have taken me to the darker spheres. There I see countless numbers of spirits, of various hues of blackness,

amid that dark and murky atmosphere, so dark and thick
that it would seem almost palpable to my senses.

There, amid that cold and watery and cheerless air, amid
that repulsive gloom, I see those countless myriads, boiling
up, as it were, under the influence of the darkest passions
and vilest propensities of the human heart, like a seething
caldron filled with human misery and set into never-ending
motion by the lurid and enduring flame of human passions.

Spread out before me is a vast country, its surface level,
its soil bleak and desolate, with naught to relieve its dreary
monotony, naught to indicate life in itself, but a few sickly
and disgusting plants, that seem to have sprung up and
grown in darkness.

There is a restlessness about those inhabitants that is
terrible to behold, for it speaks of the worm that never
dies, it tells in language not to be mistaken, that its gnawings are incessant, that its torments never cease. That
worm is memory, and with all who people that immense
desert, it is ever busy in discharging its duty as a minister
of the Most High God, ever active in the performance of
its terrible task of retribution. Like a hissing serpent, it
is ever following the heels of those whose past was evil.
Like a consuming fire, it is ever at work at its task of burning and purifying the heart. Like the dread of impending
evil, it is ever throwing upon the corrupted heart the numb-
ing chill of its fear. Like the air they breathe, it is ever
infusing into them its deadly venom. Like the life-giving
principle which surrounds them, it is ever imparting new
life and activity to its office of punishment for sin.

It needs the aid of no material flame to infuse suffering
into the heart. It needs no chains of earthly iron to bind
the fallen soul to the dark soil in which it grovels. It
needs no galling fetters to have its iron enter that soul;
but, alone, unconquerable, unceasing, ever active, from its
blasting embrace there is no escape, from its devastating
breath there is no refuge. It thrills the ear with an acute
pang that pauses but to increase its might with renewed

effort.   It flows in upon the eye but to light it up with a lurid flame, glowing like a burning coal, and relieved only by its center-spot of intense blackness, which proclaims the hue of the soul that looks out through it upon the world around. It invades the taste, and while its sweetness tempts to indulgence, the bitter and burning feeling that follows but speaks of the inner condition still.   To the nostrils it is pleasant and captivating, but it ever leaves behind a putrid and offensive scent that speaks of the corruption that is festering within.   Felt throughout the surface as a cool and inviting breeze, it instills into every vein, infuses into every bone, pours upon the extremity of every nerve torments that rival the agony that is buried deep beneath that surface.

Thus the faculties which have been perverted to purposes of selfish indulgence become ministering spirits to the demon of memory that ever haunts them, and bear to the suffering heart, to the deepest recesses of the polluted and fallen soul enduring streams of agony so intense, so overpowering, so omnipotent, that it tells the soul upon which it is exerted, the awful lesson, that nothing short of Almighty power could inflict it.

Oh! could mortals see in the flesh, and ere it be too late, how sad is the ruin the soul can bring on itself, how terrible is the agony which the memory can inflict, how incessant and how insatiate are the senses, in bearing within the soul the punishment that must ever flow from their perversion, they would recoil affrighted from the contemplation of a condition so infinitely more horrible than aught the wildest flight of the imagination ever pictured!

It is now shown to me in this vast concourse before me —in the mass and in each individual.   It is seen in a restlessness, a discontent with the present and its employments, a desire to escape to something else, an uneasy and impatient seeking for some relief, which mark the conduct of all who are before me.   They are ever seeking for something, which, alas! they found too often on earth—

something that will enable them to forget. But oh! how vain now the search! The material surroundings which, in their earthly life, through the intoxicating cup of pleasure in its various forms, aided them to drown the voice of the monitor within, have now all left them, and it is in vain they fly for refuge—for they find none. The intoxicating draught can no longer stupefy the senses, the maddening love of pleasure can no longer by its indulgence conquer the reason, and even death, to which so many of them looked for relief, afforded them none when it came, and answers not now to their call. No night with its slumbers comes now to aid them. No insanity, even, can be invoked as a refuge from thought. No excess of passion, though here it rage with tenfold fury, can bring them the coveted blessing of gratification. And thus they exist, day by day, age upon age, century after century, living monuments, speaking lessons, of the curse of perverted faculties.

And what adds infinite horror to an existence so terrible, is the conviction, instilled into their minds, by their earthly teachings, that it is for eternity.

Toward man, in or out of the form, their hearts burn with a bitter and concentrated hatred, which finds no relief but in inflicting suffering upon each other. Toward the fair face of nature, whose beauties they slighted, whose lessons they disregarded, their feelings are those of abhorrence; for every feature of it, from the rolling orb that speeds its way through space, to the blade of grass that protrudes its tiny head from the crevices of the rock, is ever proclaiming in their ears the lesson that nature ever speaks to nature's God. Toward the Great Creator they look with mingled feelings of defiance and of fear—defiance which has followed them from their mortal existence, and which here, as there, is displayed in disobedience of his laws, and fear, lest the power which is full mighty to inflict upon them what they suffer, may yet visit them with even greater misery.

Such is the scene spread out before me. If I ask those who are thus suffering, if there is no refuge? no hope? every heart answers None. I raise my eyes and ask from above, Is there no hope? Far distant I see a faint light. Reposing in its beams I see many pure and bright spirits, who seem hovering o'er this dark abyss, from which they are repelled by its gloomy atmosphere. From them comes my answer, "Yes, even for these there is hope—even for these the Infinite Father has provided a redemption—even for these he has vouchsafed a Saviour; for even in the darkest and vilest heart there, perverted, misshapen, and degraded as it may be, His spirit still slumbers, and it will yet answer to His voice as it speaks from above. In each soul is the power of its own redemption, and the hour of its redemption will be when it shall have learned the lesson so important to man in every stage of existence—so much easier to be learned and to be acted upon in his primary existence—that he must work out his own salvation."

And now there appears to me from that distant light a bright and pure spirit, whose countenance bears the impress of deep grief, and yet of unbounded love, and he says to me :

"Mortal! proclaim this truth to thy fellow-man. To many of us the learning of it has been a long and bitter trial. See that it be not so to you by neglecting the instruction when it can be most available to you ; and fear not to proclaim it by any dread of the manner in which man may receive it, for when thou shalt have passed to this sphere of existence, thou wilt meet with many a human soul whose gratitude or whose reproach will attend thy footsteps in thy passage through eternity, as thou dost faithfully perform or basely betray the duty imposed upon thee."

Section Fifty-four.

Monday, May 8, 1854.

The circle met, and through Miss Laura Edmonds as medium, the following was given:

I AM going over a long bridge. The abutments are tottering and decayed, and I fear to cross it. As I ascend it, it trembles; yet I must go over it. A spirit near me whispers that I shall fall. I can not see his face, and can not tell if I should trust him. I must however try, for I have been sent for that purpose, and I must go alone.

That spirit discourages me. But there is another at some distance before me that I can see, who beckons to me to come. I will go over the bridge, though it looks very dangerous. The scenery beyond is beautiful and grand. I should have been satisfied to have viewed it from this distance, and would have returned, but the spirit before me says " Come."

As I descend from the bridge it is steep and difficult, but it is passed. I look back, and that which at the time of crossing it appeared to be a steep and slippery bridge, made of frail materials, of rotten and broken timbers, tottering, ready to fall, and with an abyss on each side of it, is no longer the miserable structure I supposed. It is a work worthy of the greatest architect. The foundations are broad and strong, its proportions are graceful and true, and it is built of the purest white material that ever met my eyes. What is strange! it is divided in the center by a thin transparent partition. On the right I see bright forms crossing it; on the left I see mortals crowding forward.

The bridge is new, and its beauty and strength have attracted crowds from the adjoining land, and its singular structure has excited the wonder of many spirits, and they are flocking to see how well it is used.

The old and decayed appearance of the bridge was an illusion. It seems to all who cross it that it is tottering, and that they shall fall, and they have so little faith in the guides who lead, that it seems to them to be very dangerous, while it is really perfectly safe.

There is an old man stands on the entrance of the bridge who offers to every mortal who wishes to cross, a staff. I notice that those who accept it, and hold it firm, cross in safety, and without fear.

I asked him the meaning of this? and he says, smiling, " Child of earth! the staff I give is perfect faith. Those who use the staff go safely, and without fear ; those who use it not, slip and stumble in walking, or stand gazing at the evidences of decay, and tremble for their safety.

"Take in your hand the staff of faith, and it supports you in the passage across the bridge."

Section Fifty-five.

Monday, May 15, 1854.

The circle met at my library. Through the Doctor the spirit of a female, who died many years ago, began her autobiography as follows:

To the old, the recollections of childhood are the happiest remains of life. Mine was a happy childhood, with loving parents, kind and affectionate brothers and sisters. I passed the early days of my life in almost uninterrupted happiness. Ours was a noble house, and I was the eldest daughter. I lived in the closest intercourse with my mother, and I revered my father, for I loved him as he deserved to be loved.

You all know how stern were the laws that gave control of the child to the parent in those days; but my mind, indulged in close and affectionate intercourse with my parents, was permitted free range, untrammeled by any fetters of domestic tyranny. Oh! how I loved my father's gentle voice! How I loved my mother's gentle tones! and the years I passed on earth were an assurance how affectionately I regarded my brothers and sisters. God! that the agony of earth should still cling to this heart, shriveled as it has been by so many years of separation from earth! I lost my father and mother just as my mind had begun to assume its own individuality. With him our house tottered; but when my mother died, it fell prostrate. Canst thou not, oh my Father! canst thou not yet permit the agony to pass from me?

I left my father's house; my brothers and sisters were separated, some with one relative, some with another. I went to my father's brother. Kindly he received me, gently and lovingly he treated me, brought me up as his daughter, and gave me all the education the circumstances and times permitted. His was an enlarged mind that was in advance of his time. He saw far into the future, and calculated the advantages I should derive from possessing a mind educated, cultivated, and refined. I went into the world, flattered, petted, sought after. I found no heart to whose care I was willing to trust my own. But at length, being on a visit to a friend, I there met him who was afterward my husband, and on him I lavished all the deep, gushing affection of a heart that I thought knew how to love. His indeed was a nature on which God had stamped the image of some of his own attributes. Proud, yet not haughty—noble and generous, yet impetuous and impassioned—with a mind clear, distinct, and comprehensive, quick, frank, confiding, tender as the summer morning's breeze, yet so excitable, that his nature would become clouded as the summer sky with the thunder storm, and yet pass away like that summer cloud—every attribute was beautified by the contrast.

He loved me. Even now the wail of that spirit which I sacrificed comes up before me, and I, silent, self-convicted, hear it, and find no escape from the agony it inflicts.

I married this man. I knew his nature, but he did not know mine. I thought I loved, and was willing to sacrifice my own happiness for the happiness of others, to sacrifice my feelings and desires for his gratification.

I thought my will should be exerted in contributing to his advancement and welfare; but oh! when his nature was galled and excited and irritated by collision with the world, instead of throwing oil on the waters, I added to the tumult of passion. Oh! how I could have guided him; and that love which I sacrificed might have been a guiding star to my progress through eternity! Oh! the storms I might have quieted! the passions I might have soothed! His mind, stretched to its utmost tension 'mid all his disappointments and trials, turned to my love as the needle to the north. My smile in his affliction I knew was like a ray of sunshine to his heart for days.

Even when our child was grown up, and I in the middle of life, I suffered my heart to be turned from child, from husband, from God. I did not sin, but I suffered the opinions and prejudices of another to worm themselves into my mind, to change my affection, and take it away from him whose life was in my smile.

Father! thou hast vouchsafed to me, this night, tears! This spirit whose heart is marble, has found percolating through its texture drops of water from its flinty heart—a heart of stone dropping water! And how, think you, that noble man received the words with which I pierced the gentlest, softest, noblest heart God ever gave to woman? Conscious of his own imperfections—conscious of his variableness and excitability, he said to me, "You have crushed me; but the love I bear you bids me hope, for if wrong has been done, God himself who bids us live, that we may repent, will justify my efforts and give me comfort in your love at last. Wait, and this nature shall be changed. I'll fashion my heart to suit your affection."

Pale and trembling, bowed down as he was, the hopes of half a life blasted in one instant, I turned away and told him, "Never!"

And this man who had instilled his insidious poison into my heart was scarce half mine own age!

I can't go on; some other time I will tell the rest.

Through Laura the following communication from the comedian Liston was given:

Sir, my life was an eventful one. It was a mixture of all the scenes that pass before the human eye. I was born in humble circumstances. My mother was a mother to me indeed. My father was a stern, cold man, caring little for his children, striking awe to their tender hearts when they approached him, and yet there was affection in his heart

for them, but they knew it not. I did not love him much.
I could not.

My childhood was spent like other children's. I was allowed my own free will most of the time. And they
called me "Funny Tom"—that was my nickname.

My father would often say, "Prayers, now," and that
was like a death-knell to us: we would fall down on our
tender knees, and our cries would be elevated with his,
but our wishes would be leveled at his unfortunate head.

Thus was spent our childhood—not always on our knee-
joints though. I grew up, not caring for the future, hating
the sound of prayers—and well I might—for I always saw
fun in every thing; when my father would flog me, I derived infinite fun out of that even, for I pictured to myself
what a beautiful sight it must be to see a fat man sweating
over a dancing young one!

I grew up hating what ought to have been loved, yet
with a heart throbbing with tender affection, longing for
some fond heart to rest upon, and as I passed on through
the world, I still felt that longing desire for something,
deeply and tenderly to love.

I saw in nature many beauties that satisfied for a time
that longing. I went forth into society. I was courted,
fondled, laughed at for my keen wit and satire. I found
friends everywhere, and I rushed on through life excited,
and enjoying the applause of man ; but when I returned
to my home in the still hours of the night, then I felt that
wit was not my happiness. I would go forth again the
next day with my heart bleeding—like a wanderer in
the desert, seeking for some cooling spring whereby to
quench my thirst ; and I would quell those feelings, cover
them up with a light, laughing manner, and the smile
would wreathe my lip, and joy pervade everywhere,
while my heart was weeping the keenest tears of sorrow
silently within.

I would hear my friends say, "What a happy fellow;
the world goes well with him !" The mockery of these

words was agony to my soul. I would rush forth into dissipation, try to drown my cares, and appear to my nearest friends the same as ever. I would go forth on to the stage, and I enjoyed it. I entered into the very keenest of the satire. I was happy while I was giving vent to my mother wit. It afforded me excitement and pleasure—more at times than at others, for I could not always be seeming; it was not my nature. I had troubles in my own home that well-nigh weighed me down, and I would leave my domicil with an aching heart and go on to the stage; the curtain would rise, the house soon resound with laughter, and my buoyant spirit for a moment reign supreme. For the time I would be happy, but when the curtain dropped I fell too, and was the sad, gloomy man again.

I hated myself and the world, but I never expressed it. I felt alone. I was happiest when in the society of the truly refined and delicate, but then my life was such that I felt out of place when in the society I most enjoyed. I would rush forth into witticisms, and cover up the deepest feelings of the heart. I cursed the hour I was born. I cursed myself, for I was not happy, and I knew not where to find happiness.

Oh! friends, you may see a smile on the stranger's face, but it does not always speak the heart.

The call-boy is coming, and I must hasten away.

Sir, this is a long story, and I must give it in piecemeals. I hope it will be of service. I will finish another time—now it makes me too gloomy for the medium.

Here he closed, and through Mrs. Leeds it was said:

I see a bright angel descending, laden with a precious treasure. He is robed in ethereal blue. On his brow is a coronet of sparkling gems. He has a silver breastplate, on which are letters of glittering, burning fire, and around each letter is twined a vine.

He comes in majesty and glory, surrounded by a gorgeous light. In his hand is a staff, glittering, sparkling, and bright. As he advances, majestically, beautifully, yet humble in mien, his appearance is sublime. The letters on his breastplate are HOPE.

He speaks to me : "Child of earth ! I was in my happy home, far away among the spirits of brightness and love, and the words came to me, ' Arise ! leave thy happy abode, and to earth. Thy companion, Truth, has gone forth and is triumphing there. The angel of Love is gently descending, following Truth. Mortals have greeted their treasured gems and gathered them close to their hearts, but they are mortals still. With truth they have evil ; with love, hate ; and as Truth dawns on the soul, Evil whispers his fiendish words, and makes them doubt. As Love has gone forth, Hate has stepped in, severed the links the bright spirits have woven, and made them doubt each other's truth. Now thou must go forth. Mortals are weary. They need more aid. Thou, beautiful one ! must go forth and tell them the door is open for evil and for good. Both have entered freely, and they are discouraged. They have seen the evil and missed the good, and felt as if there was no hope.

"But thou wilt whisper gentle words to them. Thou wilt shower treasures on their hearts. Tell them to hope through all ills—to hope on and ever. Thou hast been sent by a Father's hand to bid them look forward to the future. Though the ills of life may disturb them, there is something beyond that will triumph over all.'

"I went forth the Angel of Hope. I come now to bid mortals look forward to the future, and though evils may creep in, to have charity, to watch with brotherly care that the evil may be eradicated.

"May my influence cheer the wanderer. We three will go hand in hand, and mortals will feel it. Love, Hope, and Truth unite in singing, ' The hand that made us is divine.'"

There is another angel hovering near. He is clothed in white, with a crown of lilies. His mantle is spangled with stars. He is Charity. He says to man, "Take my mantle, and though thy brother try thee, clasp it tighter to thy heart!"

O! could you see the spirits about you! As I speak, they are forming a happy band, singing praises, whispering blessed teachings, and praying you may receive their lessons; for remember, mortals! God has willed it and pronounced it good.

Section Fifty-six.

Monday, May 22, 1854.

The circle met at Mr. Sweet's. The Belgian lady spoke through Dr. Dexter as follows (it being a continuation of her story):

IT is not because the spirit feels and endures his own suffering that he is punished. Suffer he must, from the knowledge that he has sinned; suffer he must, to feel that he is cut off from the enjoyment of those scenes of happiness that others partake of, but which he can not approach. But more keen is the suffering, because he knows that the whole spirit-world can see his sin written on his face, and feel that his punishment is just. How I have suffered, no one can tell! Where is the sun that used to shine so brightly on my face, that every thing had the hue of Heaven upon which its rays lighted? Where is the carol of the birds? Where that beautiful music, which caught on its dying strains the echoes of my own heart, and floated in harmony up to God? Where the trees—where the flowers, I loved so well? Great God! where are those whom thou gavest to me—precious, precious jewels! my children? It seems as if I hear their wail coming even now from above, reaching me here with a voice that never can die, "Mother! mother! where are you? O, come to us, leave us not, mother!"

I have a view of that which is before me. I see the right—I see the path! Just so I saw it when I was on earth. Even now my soul asks of itself, Is this punishment for wrong, or is it the working of that never-ending principle that pervades nature everywhere—the principle of reparation? I am not punished, for there is no hand that controls me—no hand that guides me; and yet I can not do otherwise than I do. O! Thou whose resting-place is in heaven—whose eye seeth all thy created works—whose being is so pure and holy—whose law is so supreme—whose power so infinite—whose love so great, and whose mercy is never-ceasing! if the agony of a suffering heart can reach Thy throne, Father, forgive, forgive the erring soul!—erring—willful—bitterly willful!—that will that crushed every thing between it and heaven, and made its step to hell out of the deepest feelings of its nature. Erring! So Satan might have erred, if he knew that if he raised his hand, the unerring hand of God would smite him. I was told that in spite of his knowledge he raised his hand against his Creator! What did I do less? Why, the long years I have groped in darkness so profound, that not a ray of light penetrated it, was exquisite happiness compared with the light that unsealed all the secrets of my soul to the spirits around me! You may talk of patience—you may whisper words of gentlest consolation to the drooping heart—but he that does a wrong, knowing it to be wrong, and persisting in it, not only feels the fearful consequences of that sin, but, in addition, there is the whole weight of that heart's agony which he has wronged.

Section Fifty-seven.

Thursday, May 25, 1854.

The circle met, and through Laura it was said:

I STAND on a plain. It is a green field, with short grass, and on my left it extends like a prairie, far into the distance. Immediately in front of me is an immense mountain, covered with short, green grass, which gradually ascends from where I stand.

The whole mountain has the appearance of a triangle, round in front, but without a tree or shrub on it. There is a pathway, which leads up the mountain straight to the top, and on its summit stands the figure of a man.

There is a pale pink light all over the mountain that comes from behind it, and casts its hue on the sky, and fades off into a golden tint, and so on to a deep yellow.

I look back, and see a mass of faces as far as the eye can reach, and I hear a rustling sound as of many persons. I look to the mountain again, and now I see the sun rising slowly, high, bright, and clear, behind the man, and throwing a splendid, bright, clear, pink light over the whole scene. It is ascending higher and higher, and becomes brighter and brighter.

I am directed to look beyond the mountain, and there I see myriads of spirits approaching, bearing each something in his hand, and rapidly advancing. They come in bands, and there is a bright white light around them. The rustling sound grows louder.

I am now told to look to the left, and there I see a spirit approaching, holding in his hand a scroll, on which is written, "Liberty of Thought." To the right I see a banner, far distant, but approaching. On it are words in gold within a myrtle wreath, "God is Truth. Onward! still onward! for Truth shall prevail. Hope on! Hope ever!"

And now I hear the softest music, gentle, rich, melodious, indescribable—not instrumental, but rich enough to be so. I ask what it is? and the spirit answers, "Child of Earth! 'tis the voice of prayer, blending and resounding through space, which in this gentle, harmonious manner wafts its way to the Godhead."

And now all is hushed, and I see two figures on the hill. He who came last has a scroll, on which is written, "Rise! thy faith has made thee whole. Thou art a leper no longer." The other, with his hand uplifted, speaks thus: "Mortals! brothers! you see the rising orb before you— you see the light penetrates space. Arise from your darkness. Behold the light of heaven which is for one and all! See the armies of God's messengers hastening to the rescue. Arise! Gird on the armor of courage! Behold that banner! Ponder on its words, and forward! for this mount must be ascended, in order to see the fair scene far beyond it. Let your voices be blended harmoniously in one universal prayer for light and truth, and the restless murmur which now pervades you be turned into a song of rejoicing to Him who said, Let there be light."

Now I am borne away from this scene, and I feel a grateful perfume. I ask what it is? and it is answered, "See you not flowers springing up everywhere? Read what they say, 'Charity to all and for all. Hope! courage! faith! Love for all. Throw the mantle of charity over every one, for it covereth a multitude of sins. Act each for thyself.' Heed well these simple lessons, for in their simplicity there is much weight, and the perfume of thy daily acts shall ascend a grateful incense to Him who has given thee these flowers. Away to earth again. Give what thou hast seen, and heed the lesson well."

Afterward through me this was given:

From Heaven's high throne the word has gone forth.

From the inconceivable brightness around the great I AM, flashing in its dazzling radiance, the mandate has issued, "The work of man's redemption has begun, and it shall be finished."

Peters may deny, Judases may betray, the affrighted herd, terrified at the cruel cry of "Crucify him! crucify him!" may flee at the approach of danger, but one will again be found to plant the cross on the summit of Mount Calvary, as a beacon light to future ages, though he bear it alone, and there water it in his own life-blood.

You, who are chosen ministers of this great Truth, are free to labor or to flee.

If you flee, calculate first the consequences to yourselves and to those who have intrusted you with their confidence and love.

If you labor, let it be with stout hearts and unfearing minds. Let not the toils, the trials, or the temptations of life impede you, and to you be all the glory.

And know ye all that it is not for yourselves ye toil, but for Him whose ministering servants ye are, and for the countless hosts of immortal beings who in future ages will approach His throne, redeemed by His love through your ministration.

Section Fifty-eight.

The circle met, and through Mrs. Leeds, as medium, " The History of a Philosopher," as he called himself, was given as follows:

I WAS so bitter to the human race that I led a secluded life—a hermit in every sense of the word. I grew up savage to meet an eternal God. I was bred in affluence, and my parents left me a heritage. I was courted. They called me manly-looking, and added the appendage, intellectual. I met, at twenty-three years of age, a lady, not fair to look upon, but she was intellectual, graceful, and all I wished her to be. I lavished all my affections upon her. She took them, and I thought her the beau-ideal of perfection. I was sure she would sympathize with me, and take my last breath when leaving the world. One day, walking in the garden (I remember it well.!), I saw her and a friend on a balcony approaching the spot where I was. I stood behind a tree, unobserved by them. They came and sat down by the tree. I intended in a moment to step out, and amid the chat appear before them; but I heard her say to her friend, "I could love him better, but he is too lavish with his affections; it is almost insipid." I turned. The serpent was in me. I had no more love for her. My brain reeled. I know not what else she said. I had heard enough. There was only one human being that I still loved—that was a companion of my youth. My brain reeled with madness. I passed on, and the lady was never troubled with my affections. When the rose withered, she withered. I know not what became of her, and care less. I plunged into dissipation, from sin to sin, with my friend. I played deeply. He was always my friend. Reckless, I stumbled and fell. One word from him would have saved me from destruction; but no! he turned from me also— left me poor, degraded, and disgraced. There was no one human hand to stretch out and say, "Be of good cheer." I traveled bare-footed until I reached the summit of a hill which overlooked a city; I looked around and bid farewell to all mankind. I led a hermit's life, and treated the human race as scorpions or adders, and if they passed my hut and were thirsty, I did not aid them. No! a drop of water was too cool to give. I would have sooner given a coal of fire to make their misery more! So I lived—so I passed into eternity, not expecting to have my eyes opened to any thing of a future life. No! annihilation, I thought, was man's destiny. I acknowledged a First Cause, but naught else. At fifty years of age I was launched into eternity, and the first that met my gaze were friends I had left on earth whom I had hoped never to meet again. I was taken with despair and remorse of conscience. I was amazed. I looked upon myself—enough! for the serpent was stinging me. I was clothed in the human form. What! was I not dead? Had not I gone? Was I in a phrensy? Was it imagination? I know not how long I thus mused, when I was conducted to the earth. I looked and saw a form clothed with rags and vermin. I looked and saw I was living, and seemed to have a body still, and in anguish I cried, "Oh, is there no death or grave? I am, then, with my kind again; but I see no plain to retire to from all around me," for I was surrounded by adders in human form, and oh, what a hell! Your imaginations could not picture such a hell. Twenty years have I been here, and the first ray of hope that dawned on me was but a short time ago. My mother! my mother has given me three flowers; I have not seen her, but I know it must be her. When I drank deep of anguish, I saw a flower in my path, and on the leaves were written the word "Hope." After many of your days I found another flower. On it was written, "Your mother." I cried in my soul, "Come to me, my mother!" After waiting long, another came to me, on which was written, " Catch at the ray of light, and you shall see your mother." In my loneliness I saw a distant ray of light and a form pointing ; I followed by instinct, as the hound follows the hunt. I knew not for what I came. It was to earth, among mortals again, I was to mingle, and tell them of my fate, in order to reach my mother. I was told I must come gently. I was attracted to you, my young friend. I liked not the instrument, because she awakened in me an interest. I did not want to find another of her sex to feel interested in. Then came another flower, which said, "Tell your griefs to mortals, for by it you shall progress, and we will travel on together."

I came to you, first telling you of my being by the seaside. Watching the ocean, and taking up a pebble, I would throw it into the water, and as I threw it, it would make a circle, and thus I philosophized : " Thus it is with the human race, soon to be no more ; they will soon be gathered to their fathers." But I find it different ; for what you leave undone on the land which your God giveth you, you must do when in eternity. He gives you talents and every faculty, and if not well used, and your duties fulfilled, he sends you to earth to perform them yet. I hear a voice, and it says, " And in thus coming, you will engender better feelings, and you will learn to feel affection for the human kind. 'Tis even so," she says, "and you will wish to do them good, and when you shall save one soul you shall be raised from despondency to the summit of a hill." I shall come again to finish. Had I but stretched forth my hand to save a child, even in the streets, from harm, or allayed one pang, this would not have been my fate. My mother has sent another flower, on which is written, " Have patience and hope, my son." My name was Bernard Carlisle, of Freyburg, Germany. My mother was Scotch, and my father a German.

Through Laura, the spirit of Queen Elizabeth of England came and said :

I have rode in state, and cut down the noblest of souls,

men and women ; and now the beggar, that looked on me with awe, is far above me.

If all monarchs knew their fate here, they would be as humble as the meanest peasant.

I was reared unfortunately for myself and my nation. In my youth I had all the feelings, all the tenderness of girlhood. Few thought it. But my father's proud, stern nature was in me, and as years advanced, his pride grew in me ; the affections were quenched, and I became an iceberg.

I ascended a throne with many good impulses and intentions, but some around me took advantage of my weakness and betrayed me, and then I became hardened. They called me Good Queen Bess, their much-loved sovereign, but I saw beneath it the dark current of hatred, and my heart hated in return.

There was a fair daughter, reared in luxury, who was my bane. I slept not at night for thinking of her who could easily supplant me, not on the throne, but in hearts I would fain have had love me. She came to claim her crown. I little thought in depriving her of an earthly crown I was giving her a resplendent, heavenly one that I could never take away.

What atoms are men! They think they are moving nations—performing mighty deeds. When laid in the dust, they will see to what small things they were turning their attention.

I lived a reckless life, yet within me was a still, small voice, saying, "Beware." Years rolled on—laws were made—deeds done—would they had never. been done ! And I saw my rival laid in the dust at my command, and I gloried. But peace was never mine from that hour. 'Twas hell on earth. History too truly tells my character —too truly records my deeds. I can not bear to look on the past, but I must tell my story, in order to progress.

The day came when my sun was to set, and truly it set, as I thought, never to rise again. I withered away like the merest shrub.　I, the Queen of England, died like other mortals; I had to sink into the grave.　I found myself dying, and with what horror I thought of leaving life! for in my youth I had been taught the Catholic faith, yet found many things more acceptable in the Protestant faith, and scarcely knew where I stood when on the threshold of life.

My subjects flocked around me.　I felt there were many who sorrowed; but I had sinned against God, and what was my crown to me?　I heard them say, "She's going—send the tidings."　I could have got up and throttled them.

Breath left me, and, horrors on horrors! I found myself in a dark, dreary region.　I heard voices in every direction, but not the soothing ones my soul craved.

I saw spirits garbed in dark colors approaching me, and who, do you think, was their leader?　Tall and commanding, but sorrowful, and coming with all the passions of man—'twas my father!　I could have groveled in the earth, and hid my face, for I beheld I was darker than he, and he was dark enough.

They spoke to me, hissed in my ears, and some said, "Where is good Queen Bess now?"　I saw at a distance a beautiful spirit coming toward me.　I could have sunk into a chasm.　You can guess who it was—it was the sainted Mary of Scots.　She was the first to offer me a heavenly crown.　She stood ready with it in her hand.　That was more punishment to me than being in such a dark, dreary home.　Yet I felt her gentle influence and her silvery voice, and I did not resist her or go with those who were hissing in my ears and coaxing me on.　She saw in my thoughts the wavering state of my soul, and she said,

"Sister, arise! I await thee.　My love! despair not; there is hope for all."　And again came all the beautiful, pure impulses of my childhood, and with them humility and remorse, and I crouched at her feet and wept.　She still stood there, and other bright spirits flocked around her. Some I knew. They would not leave me. My father stood anxiously looking as if his fate depended on mine. A crowd of bright spirits flocked around him, took him by the hand, and we ascended together; and slowly have I ascended since, but that bright spirit has never left me. I could not progress fast, I had so many earthly feelings. I felt I was a queen. How it retards progress! As I go on, I leave the queen behind. All grows brighter, but what a distance I have yet to climb! And spirits have told me that, to climb faster, I must return and review my life, and do what I had never done—some good.

Now I must leave you. This night will be eventful for me, for I shall have taken a step onward. And when you think of spirits, think of unfortunate Queen Bess, and pray for her—you'll all have brighter crowns. I hope to meet you one day. Farewell.

Section Fifty-nine.

WEST ROXBURY, MASS.,
Saturday Evening, August 19, 1854.

This evening a circle was held, consisting of the Doctor, Mrs. Hall, of this place, Mrs. Leeds, of Boston, my daughter, my niece, and myself. And it was written through Dr. Dexter, that Washington wished to speak to me. And then through me it was spoken:

OF what moment would be a revelation from the high court of Heaven itself to man if it were not to affect and control his daily walk in life? Of what value would be a religion that is assumed as a holyday garment only, and laid aside 'mid the daily duties of your earthly existence, or that would consist in mere profession without action? How imperfect and unavailing the regeneration of the human heart, unless it were shadowed forth in your every act! If the great object of the mighty movement which is now upturning the foundations of the moral world, is to prepare mankind during their primary existence for an eternal one, then it must, in the very nature of things, in order to be effectual, stamp its impress upon every thought of the mind, on every feeling of the heart, on every act of the outer and inner man. In all his relations, domestic or public, civil or religious, affecting himself alone or in connection with his fellow-man, its influence must be felt, and must be all-powerful. Man's regeneration can not be confined within the limits of profession, can not be circumscribed by a portion only of his earthly duties, but it must reach every act, must extend over every relation, must embrace every duty. How otherwise can this life be a preparation for an eternal one? How can man fitly prepare himself for the countless ages of eternity, if his primary lesson be devoted more to his material gratification than his spiritual elevation? How if he at the same time attempts to serve the world with its perversions and sinful propensities, and with only an equal devotion dedicates himself to his higher moral duties to his great Creator? Nay, it can not be, and one of the fallacies which have flowed from the evils and misdirections of the past, one of the false teachings which have sprung from the same womb that has given birth to the infidelity that is so wide-spread among men, that it has traveled with its twin-sister down the stream of time, is the dogma that Religion and Government have no connection with each other.

The government that repudiates the dictates of religion, that repels from its action the moral lessons which descend from heaven to earth, can not look to realms above for its origin or its inspiration, nor can it claim the aid of the bright and holy spirits who in obedience to His will are now shedding his light abroad on the human heart. The government that refuses to acknowledge the higher moral influences that are ever at work among men, builds its foundation on the sand, and invokes to its destruction the frightful current of selfishness, violence, and corruption, which have so long marked the dominant powers of the old world, and have already made a frightful inroad upon those institutions built by your fathers of the last century amid prayer and thanksgiving to God. No wonder that the happy land, where freedom hath her abiding-place echoes now so loudly with the iron tread of the slave-holder. No wonder that the power and position of your rulers are held up to your people as the spoils of a sacked city to gratify cupidity, and to corrupt the hearts of the people. No wonder that the sacred fane of your freedom to which the eyes of the world have so long been directed, and around which cluster the hopes of your spirit-fathers gone before, is polluted by the presence of the money-changers. No wonder that again is demanded some fearless one to overthrow their tables and purify the holy temple of God. No wonder that alienation in the hearts of your people has taken the place of that brotherly love which once marked you as a united people! No wonder that discord has stalked abroad in your land, and seated itself in the high places by the side of power, and held it trembling in its seat. No wonder that now, broadcast in the hearts of the nation is a feeling of despondency in reference to the future. No wonder that men are calculating the value of your union as they would the value of cattle in your markets. No wonder that the enemies of freedom throughout the world, and in the spirit-land too, are gloating over the scene of corruption, of slavery, of discord, which my unhappy country now presents in the presence of man and God.

Oh! could you feel; oh! could you see the anguish that wrings the hearts of those who toiled to make you free and happy—could you witness the gloom which the prospect of the future casts over their minds—could you behold the sad anxiety which now pervades the spirits of countless hosts who are engaged in this mighty work—could you feel as we feel the dark cloud that ascends from your midst to Heaven, bearing toward his throne the impress of man's most evil passions, and repelling from your midst the holier and purer aspirations that are ready to descend upon you, you would start back appalled at the prospect, and lifting up your hands and hearts as we do to the throne of the most high God, you would unite with us in beseeching him to have mercy yet on our common country, and on mankind; beseeching him to drive far from you the destroying angel that is reveling in your midst, sapping to their foundations the institutions which were consecrated by our blood and our toil. Deeply interested in the welfare of my country, bound up as my heart even yet is in the continuance of its freedom; looking on its institutions as the great fountain of freedom that was yet to flow over the whole earth, I ask myself, "Where now is the spirit that made us free?" and from dark and dismal depths alone a voice answers, "Here, buried beneath the load of oppression and selfishness which has grown up and overwhelmed us." The voice that once proclaimed freedom, and sent its glad shout through illimitable space to the footstool of God, and brought thence its echo proclaiming emancipation and happiness to man, is now but faintly heard beneath the overwhelming load that is heaped upon it, and drowned as it is by the clanking chains of the slave and the lash of his master, fail to keep pace even with the dark cloud your corruption has sent up.

Standing high amid the light which falls from Heaven's throne, and casting my view back to the spot I love so well, I look in vain for the bright and beautiful light that ascended when I did, and bore me companionship in my passage to the realms of the blest. Oh, think not, my friends, that this is fancy's sketch. Deem not that it is a picture of a diseased imagination. It is a sad reality in

your very midst, witnessed by God, by spirits, and by
men; mourned over by the good, exulted over by the
evil; and casting over the prospects of the future its dark
and gloomy cloud. Ask yourselves if it is not so? Ask
your hearts to speak their fears as to the future? Ask
the enemies of freedom upon earth? Ask the down-trodden millions who have ever looked to you as their beacon light, and see if there will not come up from all
these sources one general response. "Alas! alas! it is
true." And if it is, upon what foundation do you rest an
expectation that your nation and its cause can merit the
favor of God? Upon what basis can you build your hopes
of its perpetuity, and what is there to keep burning before
the world the light of your freedom which we kindled for
man?

The high destiny prepared for my country, its onward
progress toward eminence and happiness, the influence of
its example on the world, the spread of its important lesson
of self-government, where now are they? Spread abroad
on the face of this vast continent, flourishing in full vigor
of young manhood? Answer me, for ye yourselves know.
For our part, instead of hearing the voice of your happiness, your virtue, and freedom ascending from a thousand
altars and meeting us on our approach to earth, we have
to dive down through the dark clouds you send up, and
exhume it from the prison-house in which your perversions
have pent it up, and unless your downward progress can
be arrested, unless you can be returned to the purity with
which you started, unless the heart of the nation can be
awakened to the fearful prospect that is before it, better
far would it be that the land should again become the habitation of the wild man of the forest, and the beasts on
which he preyed. Better far that it should be so, than
that now, when the corrupt and crumbling institutions of
absolutism throughout the world are tottering to their
very foundations, the appeal of the oppressed of other
lands can meet no response from this. Better far that the

pestilence which walks at noonday should sweep through your habitations, than that you should be incapable of cheering on their upward way the oppressed of other lands on whom freedom is fast dawning.

Oh! I once thought that when this time should come (and well did my prophetic soul know it would come), that then my beloved country would stand out in the face of mankind a bright and shining light, not only proclaiming throughout the world the reality of freedom, but pointing the way to its sacred temple; that it should stand at its very portals prepared to assist their feeble steps up its toilsome ascent, and welcoming them to the fellowship of freedom and the emancipation of man.

Then through the Doctor it was written:

This first part of our treatise on government, as the preamble to fact, is most finished. Washington says he then wishes to give you a vision of what exists here, to draw the comparison with earth, and then shadow forth the true government that ought to rule in your land.

BACON.

Section Sixty.

WEST ROXBURY, *Aug.* 21, 1854.

The circle being assembled, through Dr. Dexter it was said:

THE progressive demonstration of the works of God is better evidence of his power than though he had finished them at once. Had the world been entirely finished, there would have been no new developments. Nature, instead of putting forth new forms and shapes, and every new form and shape manifesting an attribute in advance, would have gradually decayed, gradually retrograded, and thus, at this period of the world's history, the whole of its surface, and even its depths, might have been in a stage of decay.

One of the higher purposes which the Creator has manifested in his design is the ability, the power, inherent in every created thing, to exist, as it were, by the very principles of its creation. Thus, instead of the world's decaying, instead of its mighty mountains crumbling to dust and disappearing from the surface of the earth, whatever change takes place in matter, it always enters into some new form of combination, or the constituent of old combinations, and thus lives, grows, develops, generates, by the inherent properties or principles of its creation.

This is evidence, too, of the great power of Him who fashioned every thing. And it is no more singular in reference to inanimate matter than to animate matter, that this principle of inherent progression is visible in every animal which has existed or does exist on the face of this globe.

Singular as it may appear, and the remark may be trite,

for the fact exists on your earth, there are men, learned
men, too, who deny the possibility of any progressive development either in animals or matter. And yet were it
possible for man to penetrate into all parts of the earth,
to examine every locality, every situation which offers any
inductions of interest, were it possible for him to separate
from the strata in which they are imbedded the fossil remains of the earliest animals which lived on this globe,
and trace their comparative advance and progress in the
scale of existence from that period up to this time, it would
satisfy the most skeptical, that where one animal has been
developed as the germ, that animal has, in the progress of
advancement of time and circumstance, put forth new attributes and assumed new combinations within itself, and
thus has gone on increasing, progressing, step by step,
until this day.

But the question arises in our minds, What is all this for?
Can you show us, in comparison with man or animals, any
other part of nature which progresses in the same way?
Yes, the answer is very simple. There is not a department
of nature, animal or vegetable or mineral, that is not in-
delibly stamped with proof of its progressive advance, and
what is also the fact, that the different climates, modes of
culture, and soil, in which they may be planted, so modify,
so change the original nature of the vegetable, that when
a vegetable indigenous to India is transplanted to Canada—
if you can make it live in another climate—in the course
of a few years it assumes distinguishing characteristics
that entirely divest it of any semblances to its former appearance and attributes. So with the animal, whether you
take the fox, or go from the fox to man. The farther you
go north, the more do these animals, corresponding to the
same genera or species in warm climates, change their external features so as scarcely to be recognized.

Again, the question is suggested to your minds, Why is
this so? I answer, that to the inquiring mind, to the
searcher after truth, it was this display, these evidences of

external progress in material things, that was the hand-book in which might be read the same condition of things existing beyond this world.

The question, too, is asked, How far back into the years which have passed since the earth was fit for man's abode shall we go for the first evidences of man's existence? at what period of time did man first stand on this earth, so much in advance of all created things, and so much more omnipotent than any other animal by the possession of a living soul? If we plunge into earth's center and raise the deepest strata there buried to the surface, we find the time is not indicated there. Descend ocean's depths, and its dark bosom gives back no answer to the inquiry we make. Ascend the highest mountain, the evidences there are still barren of answer. Go where we will, seek where we will, we can not tell at what period of time man made his first appearance on earth.

To the really shrewd and analytical mind—one that searches, investigates, and compares, man, boasting and boasted man, he who claims to rule the earth by the power of his mind and his affinity with God by the connection of his spirit, would seem, by the variety of properties which he manifests, the similarity of attributes and passions which he indicates, to have been the joint product of the aggregate development of every animal that lives and breathes on earth; for in the vast and multiplied demonstrations of his mind, in his anger, his revenge, his lusts, and desires; his cunning, his ingenuity, his boldness, and courage; his craftiness and hypocrisy; in his affections and his jealousies; in his envy and his pride, he assuredly gives evident token that he has something of almost every animal in his combination that lives and dies on earth.

Section Sixty-one.

WEST ROXBURY, *Aug.* 22, 1854.

At a meeting of the circle this day, through the Doctor it was said, as from Lord Bacon:

WHETHER it can be proved to a positive demonstration that man was the product of this progressive principle, existing everywhere in nature, I know not. What spirit ranging now either through bright and beautiful fields of the holy spheres or the dark and gloomy habitations of the evil, can point to that time in the history of the world's progress when man, as the result of these inherent innate powers, sprang forth like a flower opening his attributes— his mind—to the reception of truth, and appropriating those powers to the government of animals and matter around him?

Certain it is, that as in the logic of the schools of my day and of the present day, the argument by analogy was considered the most perfect and conclusive, so, as we can not by positive proof show the time or the progress of man's development, we have the right to rest our argument on the analogies which bear so forcibly and which connect so powerfully every event in the chain of circumstances, from creation's first manifestations to the present hour.

I reverted yesterday to the idea, that if all the intentions and designs of God had been accomplished, perfected, finnished, man, instead of evidencing his connection with God and the powers and attributes which characterize him through his works, would have made no more advance in the scale of existence than has or does any animal around him. Suppose the work was accomplished, was done—

that nature had yielded her fruit and the ripened seed was dropping to the ground—what then? Was there a new existence to spring up? Were there new properties and powers to be developed? Were there new organizations to be created? No, the work was ended, and every time the principle had accomplished its object the end had come!

Now let your minds contemplate the effect this would have produced on man's physical, material, mental, moral, civil, and political advance. Nature having finished her labors, came trembling and faltering, shriveled and decrepit as an old man to the grave. No young life bearing up within itself, and creating new existences as the old ones passed away. No spring-time, with its budding leaves and blossoming flowers, but existence had passed over the earth, and wherever its footsteps trod, death marked its progress. No! man then would have lived in caves and clefts of the rock. The work was done. What chance was there for progress? What chance that the Godlike attributes of his mind should have stamped their image even on creation's progress itself? Dwelt in caves and clefts of the rocks? Ay! he would have been the companion, the associate, by the properties he would have developed, of the very beasts who had their habitations in the same places with him. No proud temple would have reared its towers to heaven. No broad and beautiful fields would have blossomed with his handiwork. No ships would have crossed the ocean. No railroads would have spanned your earth. No paintings, the evidences of the Godlike capacities of man's mind, would have imaged forth the inventive and conceptive beauties of his mind. No machines would have been invented to lessen the labor of his hands. No government would have been instituted. No sciences would have originated. Earth and men would have grown old the moment they were born.

Think you that the germs which are reflected from the great principle, the Father of us all, when sent to earth to mingle there with the bodies of men, would not have returned to him who sent them, and said to him, "Father! thy work is ended there, what need of us ?"

Stand ye here on this high mount and look back on the picture I have drawn. Each morning sun would have arisen later; the evening shades would have grown darker; the decaying forest; the crumbling mountains; the rivers shortened in their course, and lessened in depth; the ocean contracting its vast waters; the sun shorn of its brightness, and the moon casting no reflection; the stars refusing to twinkle their light; where once the rose-tree blossomed, yielding no more flowers forever; where earth had once yielded her treasures of grain and corn, no seed germinating in its barren womb again. Man, earth, beasts, creation—all would have given but one dim flash of its Creator's power, and then shrank back into the constituents of which they had been fashioned.

Look you again at the picture. Springing into life as the race-horse, who springs forward to reach the goal before him, every advance toward that end but increases his power and his speed.

So with creation. No spear of grass waved by the wayside but felt the necessity of companionship. No tree that sprung up but bore within itself the power to germinate its kind. No flower opened its petals to the breeze but dropped its seeds, and there sprung up its brother and its sister. The birds which kissed its blushing leaves bore to other localities the seeds which they stole in that embrace, and dropped them, there to germinate, to grow, and to blossom into beauty and grace. No ray from the bright god of day fell on the earth but what it nourished into life a thousand forms, a thousand new germinations. Each day the sun rose brighter and brighter, for each day developed new creations, new existences. Not a drop of rain that fell on earth's surface but infused this principle throughout its very depths.

Through me, and from the spirit of Washington, it was then said:

There is no perversion more firmly seated in the minds

of my countrymen—none more injurious—none that is calculated to be more lasting in its effects, than that which
attaches to the purposes of government the idea of aug-
menting wealth alone, or, in other words, that the chief end
of government is to increase the wealth of the community.

Appealing, as that idea does, to the selfish propensities
of the human heart, binding man in subjection by the
cords of corruption, it has been cherished, fostered, and
propagated by those who, clothed with power, have ever
cared to exercise it rather for themselves than others; and
it has been the chief instrument of maintaining the fatal
fabric of absolutism in all ages of the world. It has been
most effective in enthralling man, and binding him in submission to the domination of his fellows. .

Throw your mind back on the history of the past, and behold how frequent and successful has been the appeal of
power, on the part of the governors, to the cupidity of the
governed. It has laid at the foundation of all tyranny;
has characterized the structures which absolutism has
raised, and has ever stood in the way of the progress of
true freedom. And even when freedom has leaped the foul
barrier and moved abroad among men with cheering hope,
it has often been arrested in its progress and turned aside
from its high and holy purposes by this same appeal. It
has been with anxious solicitation that in all countries and
in all times the apologists for arbitrary power have inculcated this principle as most vital, and as the end and aim
of government.

It is not alone amid the shadows of absolutism that it has
found its home; it has stolen into the temple of Freedom
and taken up its abiding-place even in the presence of
its holy altar, mingling its selfish aspirations with the
prayer for liberty that would otherwise have ascended un-
tainted—mixing its polluted breath with the incense that
would otherwise have arisen in grateful perfume, and unit-
ing its discordant cry with the cheering song of liberty
among men.

Its deformity hidden by the disguise which man's perverted vision has rendered practicable, it has too often
been welcomed as a fitting guest in the mansion of Freedom, and been warmed into life by its fires, until it has
been able to strike in its fangs and diffuse its poison on all
around.

Unable, openly, to withstand the onward march of freedom which has sprung from man's progressive advancement, it has "stolen the livery of Heaven" to serve the
purposes of evil, and covertly worked its way and infused
its poison until the bloated and corrupted mass of humanity has yielded to its silent inroads, even while boasting of
its victory over its open attacks.   Stealthily, silently, yet
with the tenacity of death, it has wound its way into the
very body of Freedom, substituting the convulsions of disease for natural action, the hectic of consumption for the
glow of health, the appearance of prosperity for its reality.

Such have been its inroads in my country; and as time
has rolled on, casting around her institutions the protecting
embrace of power and permanency, the invasion of this
principle has been silent, though sure, until many, very
many, unmindful of the great lesson inculcated by our
Revolution; with thoughts directed only to the accumu-
lation of wealth; with energies bent only to the increase
of temporal prosperity, have taught themselves to look
upon all government as having one legitimate object alone,
that of increasing individual, material wealth.   Hence it
is that there has been so great a departure from the principles which swayed the minds of the fathers of our nation,
and a substitution in its place of the corrupting and de-
basing principles of action which distinguish absolutism
everywhere, and which cast their taint even upon our institutions professing to be free.

Do you ask, why I dwell with so mournful a tone upon
this sad picture?   Why my mind broods over the future,
which it shadows forth?   It is that we may try, ere it be
too late, to restore the virtue of the past in the place of the

corruptions of the present; bring back our government to its original purpose, and once again impress on the minds of the people the legitimate and proper object of government, that in the exercise of their rights as freemen they may be swayed by purity of principle, rather than the cravings of cupidity.

Oh! could my countrymen descend with me into the hearts that are petrified by the exercise of unlimited power either on earth or in the spheres—could they with me penetrate the deepest recesses of the minds which sway such power, they would start affrighted at the advances, however disguised or covered they might be, of the feeling which is engendered. Oh! could they penetrate into those darker spheres where, in unprogressed man, vice is ever festering, and where the dark clouds of selfishness, of cruelty, and of intolerance are brooding over the unhappy scene; where the love of self swallows up all regard for the future, all remorse for the past, all reverence for God and all aspirations for purity, they would find the birth-place and the home of the principle whose inroads they have permitted among themselves.

Could they ascend with me into the brighter spheres, where love, and purity, and happiness shed their mellow light over each heart, and send their gentle tones of sweetest harmony upon each ear; where man's progressive advance toward high heaven is the daily object of desire and of view, they would behold that that principle has no abiding-place there, but is banished those happy realms. O! could they thus range through the spheres and o'er earth, and thus behold beneath the deceptive surface the reality that is working among men, they would become conscious, as we are, that it is time to sound the alarm, that it is time to marshal the forces for the conflict; for on its event must depend the great question whether freedom shall continue to inhabit with us or take her flight to regions more congenial; they would feel how imperative is the duty upon every one to arrest the progress of a princi-

ple which is sapping our national freedom to its foundation, and assimilating our institutions and our fate to those
which we have been taught to abhor, and which we so
loudly profess to avoid.

Remember ever the great lesson which you are taught
by your intercourse with the spirits of the departed—
so different from that which human teaching has so long
infused into your minds—namely, that life in the spirit-
world is but a continuation of life upon earth, and that the
legitimate object of the one is but to prepare for the other;
that time—your time on earth—is but a stepping-stone to
an eternity in the spheres; that the bias and direction of
the mind, and the affections which obtain on earth, make
their impress upon your existence after you have left it;
that the perversions and misdirections which you imbibe
during your primary existence affect and direct your life
after it; that the truths which are planted in the soul
while it inhabits its tenement of clay accompany and cheer
it on its way through the long ages of eternity; that there
is now dawning upon the earth a light which can not only
dispel the darkness which surrounds you, but can open to
your view the life after death, its impulses, its duties, and
its destiny; that you are receiving instruction and knowledge from those who have penetrated the future beyond
the grave, and who are now permitted, in the providence
of God, to return and teach to you the great lessons which
are opened to them through the portals of eternity; that
standing amid the brightness of His wisdom and the softening influences of His love, receiving, as they become
more perfect, the brighter and better lessons which flow
from the storehouse of his Almighty mind, they are permitted to open to your view the pages on which they read
these high and holy lessons, and are rendered capable of
advancing you in virtue, in wisdom, and in happiness, and
that, by unfolding to you the knowledge which experience
in spirit-life bestows upon them, they can advance you
too, upward and onward in your high destiny—can aid

you to cast óff the perversions and errors of life, and even upon your earth assimilate your condition to that of the spheres.

And know, that as in the form of your government you have.imitated the work of His hand, as displayed among the worlds that sparkle in the heavens above you; as you have thus learned in form to imitate the creations of His wisdom, so you may be taught to progress still further, and learn to infuse into that government—thus in form assimilating to your planetary system the order, the regularity, the wisdom, and the love which bind these systems together as one harmonious whole, and maintain them, ever moving in dumb yet joyful obedience to His commands, so that you too may move on in your enduring orbits, progressing ever onward, developing ever the great properties which slumber within you, unknown even to yourselves, and diffusing abroad in the universe through which you move the blessings of your obedience to His laws, and of your advance in His love and wisdom.

Section Sixty-two.

WEST ROXBURY, *Aug.* 23, 1854.

The circle met, and through the Doctor it was said:

AND if this was the influence upon inanimate nature, how much greater must be its influence upon man himself; for it is a law that when man has devised and originated any particular thought or invention, and has successfully achieved the result he had in view in its construction, it increases his desire and his power to invent and contrive other and more advanced thoughts and inventions. Thus, as in creation's development and progress, the manifestation of this principle reveals the spirit which controls it, so in the advance and progression of man every step exhibited the pure power, the energy, the capacity of his spirit that was born of God. And here is the separate and distinct manifestation of one cause operating upon and controlling man and matter; and it shows, too, the independent, individual powers of that spirit which impelled man to act separately and independently. Now when we recur to the past, we are struck with many of the great incidents of time, that seem to show us that this law, this principle, was interrupted in its proper and direct application and effect, for here sprung up a nation whose people, whose laws, whose government, whose arts and sciences, whose commerce and mechanics showed the force of this mighty inherent impulse, and yet standing as the very landmarks of what this principle could do—they sparkled and flashed for a time, and then went out and left a darkness more profound than before. The traveler, as he passes over that country once blossoming in every part like a garden, once exhibiting the care and the providence which ruled it in its roads, its aqueducts, its canals, its walls, and its various cities, looks in vain now for any evidences of the power, the wealth, and the wisdom that once distinguished it. Where the fig-tree blossomed and gave forth its fruit; where the clustering grape showed the evidences of knowledge and of taste; where the beautiful grove sheltered in its shade the tasteful residence of some rich man; where the stately barge was lashed at the mole or pier; where the waving fields of grain showed the industry and care of man; where the proud temple lifted up its towers to heaven in capacity and splendid grandeur, surpassing that of any modern creation; where the teeming thousands mingled together in the daily avocations which belonged to their life, is now desolation and solitude. Where now are their roads and canals? Where the waving fields of grain? Where the home of the peasant, or the palace of his employer? Where the cities, the vessels, and the millions of men, women, and children who peopled and directed them?

The desolate temple is made the den of the lion or the tiger, and the courts of their places of worship are tracked with the slimy trail of the hissing serpent. Solitude and desolation are stamped on the face of every thing which meets the view. The dark and silent waters of some sea or lake cover, like a shining mantle, the spot where erst there flourished a nation, and its bitter waters bring back to the mind the recollection of those causes which we have presumed swept them from the face of the earth. But is this an evidence that the world has retrograded? No! no! for what has been lost in one locality has been a thousand times more developed in another. What are a few spots on the surface of the other continent, from which have been swept away nations and cities? Is there less of man, of cities, of nations, of wealth, of power, of commerce, of arts and sciences, of inventions and contrivances, of that which adds to the benefit and happiness of man, of that which controls nature in her manifestations, of that which enables man to act even here as the instrument in the development and the legitimate application of those laws which God has established, and in the development of his own nature and power, in his capacity to act as God's vicegerent upon earth; in the certain, unalterable, undeviating progress which he makes to accomplish his destiny here? But what if nations have been lost in time, and their works annihilated? The winter's ocean, with its storms and waves, has not obstructed man in his passage to a world lying in eternal silence, and solitude, too, and from the depths of its vast forests to develop power, might, magnificence, and real glory that have astonished the world.

Then through me it was said :

I am beholding the internal organization of a commu-

30

nity in the spirit-world. I am beholding the locality which
they occupy, and it is a place as much as any we occupy on
earth, having all the material surroundings which we have
here, with its mountains, fields, and vegetation, with its
animals and its residences. It seems in many respects like
an earthly scene, yet with additions, new appliances, and
attributes necessary to and flowing from a superior refinement and development of matter. Thus, I observe, that
some of this matter is transparent ; so, too, I see that locomotion is sometimes by the use of the limbs as with us,
sometimes by floating slowly through the air, and at others
by darting with lightning speed from place to place. So I
see what seem to be clouds, having the form and shape of
those we behold in our atmosphere, but which are in fact
aggregations or banks of light. So, too, I perceive that
the light resting upon the scene, varying in hue and intensity in different places, is not an emanation from a material
ball like our sun, but is produced, self-generated by every
inhabitant of that locality—the hue of the light which
is emitted from each one varying according to the predominant feeling or propensity of each individual, and
commingling with that of others, produces an endless variety and ever-changing colors. So, too, I perceive novel-
ties to me hitherto unseen, and unimagined existences in
man, in animals, and in inanimate matter. Thus I see cor-
uscations of light unlike any thing we witness here, too
brilliant and intense, and too delicate and refined to be
perceptible to the mortal senses ; and I behold in inanimate matter many things which I can not stop to describe,
which are unlike any thing ever beheld on earth, and
which I am told are created for the purpose of contributing
to the happiness and enjoyment of the sentient beings
around. The air, the water, the earth, the living, moving
beings have all of them attributes and properties unknown
to us on earth, but which seem to be necessary to and
commensurate with a more refined and elevated state of
existence.

I give a sketch thus general of what is before me, because I am so situated that I have a bird's-eye view of this whole community and its surroundings, and I am told by the guiding spirit* who stands by my side, thus to behold, as a whole, and not to permit my attention to be drawn to individual or isolated things.

He says to me, "Can you convey to mortal minds a just conception of that which you behold here, and especially that which you on earth call space and distance? You measure that on earth by a standard peculiar to your condition there, and you can readily perceive by what a different standard you must measure it here. Thus, for instance, you perceive those buildings stand apart from each other, you would say, by your earthly standard, a few rods apart. Can you conceive or describe how far apart measured by our standard? To make yourself understood, speak, then, the language and use terms and phrases with which you are familiar. It will be enough to convey your ideas, and leave the reality to be appreciated by you when you arrive here and find yourself sufficiently elevated to comprehend the new state of things to which you will be introduced."

This spirit further says: "I see you are asking in your mind, why have buildings here, houses and residences, where there seem to be none of those atmospheric changes which render them necessary on earth? Let me ask you in reply, do your mansions contribute to your happiness and enjoyment only by protecting you from the changes of your earthly atmosphere? Why is it, when the air is balmy and pleasant, and you require no roof to cover you from its influence—why, in the pleasant twilight of your day, or in the soft moonlight of your night—why, when the temperature is just at that standard when it is most grateful to you, do you still cluster together in your mansions, and form a happy group around your hearth-stone,

---

* I afterward learned this was Howard, the philanthropist.

rather than wander away alone, enjoying the nature that surrounds you? It is because in the idea of home and its associations there is something pleasant to the human heart. That pleasure lives with us in the spheres, and is not dropped with that outer garment which required protection from the weather. During the intensity of sultry heat, during the peltings of the storm, amid the icy chills of the northern blasts, your material bodies might demand the protection of a house; and if that was all there was about a house, or its uses or advantages, you might well ask, why have houses in the spheres? But as those moments when the house is a protection for the material body are but few in comparison with the period of time during which you are otherwise enjoying your homes, so it can not be difficult for you to conceive that a mansion can contribute something more to man's happiness than merely shielding him from the weather. Turn your mind back some forty years in your material life, and see how much happiness you derived from the recollection of the happy hours you spent in your father's house, see what memories cluster around you, and how effectively they can protect you at this moment even, from the corrodings of present cares and anxieties. Step across the grave, and think you that these memories die and are lost to you? And do you not perceive that in those memories is involved a source of happiness connected with your earthly home that is something more than its mere protection from the weather? Turn your mind back, he says, to some of the scenes which you have yourself witnessed in the spirit-land: why did the hunter and his Indian companion erect their log-cabin under that grateful shade, nestling near that over-hanging rock, by the side of that bubbling spring, and in view of that dense forest? It was because it recalled the recollection of their happy home on earth. And be it ever remembered that in the memory is your heaven or your hell. In the spheres, as on earth, the rustling of the leaves, the dropping of the water over the little fall, the footstep of the approaching Indian, were in themselves comparatively nothing; but, as they carried the memory back over the vista of many happy years that had passed, they filled the heart with happiness, and brought up from its deepest depths, feelings of gratitude and love toward Him who had permitted and toward them who had shared that happiness. Think for one moment how entirely the nature, the habits, the propensities, the deep-seated feelings of those two beings, which by time became engrafted on their very existence, must have been changed, to have enabled them to have found happiness in any other form—that happiness which is the object and end of spirit-life.

"As on earth, so in the spheres, God bestows upon man the freedom to choose his own path to happiness. And as no two beings are constituted precisely alike, so no two find their happiness in precisely the same objects or occupations. Variety—infinite, unbounded, illimitable as space and enduring as eternity—is marked upon all God's works, and is overpowering evidence of the extent of his might and the depth of his wisdom. And that variety is found, not only in the form of creation, but in its never-ceasing action and motion.

" Proceed yet another step in the retrospection of your visits here. Why the beautiful gardens, the fragrant flowers, the grateful lights, the pleasing variety of scenes that were spread out before you and unfolded to your view? That they might contribute to man's happiness, and by their infinite variety afford aliment to every heart. And pray tell me, if you will not consent to this form of existence in the spirit-world, in what shape you will present it? What other form can it assume that can in any way connect it with your life on earth ?

"Why was the mansion, occupied by your spirit-companion here, so like that in which she had taken her departure from your earth ? Her life here was but a continuance of that which had began with you, and he who will read the human heart can easily appreciate the feelings which prompted her to cluster around her home in the spirit-world the memories which had formed so great a part of her previous existence. The change in her must have been marvelous, and, unlike any thing we know of in nature, that would have taken away from her the pleasure of those memories, and even the statue of penitence that was placed amid that shrubbery pointed to the past and to the future more than it did to the present, for the reason that man from his very nature—that nature which is divine in its origin and in its destiny, and which elevates him above the animal creation—lives and enjoys more in the past and in the future than in the present.

" So, too, in your travels through the spirit-land, in one place you found a castle tenanted by those who took pleasure in magnificence; near it, you saw the humble cot, occupied by those of a different temperament, who found happiness in quiet and in obscurity. In one place you found a mansion surrounded by stately trees, because its inhabitants found pleasure in their grateful shades. In another, instead of trees, you saw an unshaded garden, filled with flowers and shrubs, and the thousand things that go to make up a beautiful parterre, and that was because its proprietors thus enjoyed themselves; you found one man toiling in a peculiar task for the purpose of elevating his fellow-man to his own condition of happiness; you beheld all the members of a family laboring together for the good of a whole community. These things were so because they thus found their happiness. You saw evidences of advance in the arts and sciences; you heard music, vocal and instrumental; you saw teachers engaged in giving instruction; you saw communities engaged in consultation, because in all these things they found their happiness, and that variety which is thus stamped on all God's creations. Why! you saw wild animals coursing through the wood, and birds floating in the air; you heard the murmur of the running brook; you beheld the spray of the sparkling fountain. Nay! you saw, and as in your earthly life you

used, the gallant horse, because in those things happiness
and enjoyment were found. And while in these, as it were,
earthly objects, you discovered there was enjoyment in
the spirit-land, so, too, you beheld that these objects were
ever lifting the heart in gratitude to the bounteous Giver
of all, and were but the means by which the soul was elevated to the contemplation of scenes and existences still
higher, still more elevated, still more bright and beautiful,
which were within their daily view; and amid it all, from
the sea-shell which rattled beneath your tread, through all
nature, animate and inanimate, which surrounded you, up
to the bright and shining worlds flashing in the far distance, you beheld that the beatified spirits who inhabited
them were ever learning the important lesson that God is
over all. Boundless in his love, illimitable in his wisdom,
he has bestowed upon man the capacity to live with him
forever, and has endowed him with the ability to understand and obey the law by which that existence can be
made happy; and throughout all this you have beheld the
demonstration of the momentous truth, that existence in
the spheres is but a continuance of that on earth, and life
on earth is but a preparation for that in the spheres.

"In giving to man a revelation so important as that which
embraces a knowledge of the reality of the life into which
he is to be ushered, the spirits, as the ministering servants
of Infinite Wisdom, have entered upon their task with a full
knowledge of the difficulties which attend not only its being
given, but its reception by man. Conflicting, as that reality does with the crude, vague, and fanciful ideas which
have so long obtained in men's minds, they are conscious
how much error is to be unlearned before the truth can
be welcomed; and they are aware that much time must
elapse before the mortal mind will fully receive the momentous truth. Intangible, imperceptible to the senses on
which man has been taught to rely for his knowledge, the
difficulty of working out a conviction of the truth has not
been overlooked by them. They do not ask that this

revelation shall be received as authority, but they appeal to man's reason; they ask the exercise of his judgment; they direct your minds to all of nature that is around you, and they bid you behold how consistent this revelation is with every manifestation of nature in all her works; and they rejoice that it is not through the lips of one alone, but of many, that it can be given. They have approached their task with a realizing sense of its vast importance to man. Ages have rolled away while he was preparing to receive it. Sparsely, and at long intervals, has divine truth been given to him—here a little and there a little— while his mental capacity has been growing up to the ability to receive it. At length the hour has come, so long anxiously waited for by spirits in the spheres; and now that it is given, many a heart, while it is lifted up in thankfulness to God, trembles lest man in his darkness may yet once again reject it.

"The event is in His hands, but as His ministering angels do we toil. We may plant and we may water, but it is He alone who can give the increase. To Him we commend you, and the divine cause in which you are engaged. And to Him we pray that in His fitting time he may bestow on weak, faltering man the capacity to receive a truth which can elevate him so high in his onward progress to the Godhead, and so prepare him for the mighty destiny that is before him."

Section Sixty-three.

WEST ROXBURY, *Aug.* 24, 1854.

At the circle it was said, through Dr. Dexter:

AND what are the effects of this great law of progress that have been apparent in every epoch, in every race of man in the world's history? The question is answered on the consideration of fact; for this is true—that which is crude, is polished; that which is the germ is made to develop the thing; that which is imperfect approaches perfection. And it matters not how small the evidence of progress may be which we detect, as year after year and age after age passes by, if there has been but one step forward either in man, animals, or matter—one evidence, one proof that this is so, that which we have taught you as truth must be admitted, must be recognized to be so. Look abroad, compare the past with the present—has the world deteriorated? Has man, as its recognized head, lost any of the high capacities and powers which God bestowed on him when he was developed into being here? Say, has he lost any even of his physical powers?

Perhaps that may seem so when we view the past in one aspect alone. But as it is the effect and tendency of this law to refine, to sublimate, to perfect, it follows that although the grosser properties of matter may be removed from it, it does not take away its legitimate and innate virtues. Hence, when you remove from one locality its aborigines to another country, they may die, or may contract disease which debilitates their physical powers, but the amalgamation with the inhabitants they find there, develops a race of beings whose mental attributes and properties are infinitely superior to those which characterized either. For they can invent, and contrive, and execute; they can bring around them the means, the properties, and the powers of material things, and so combine them, so arrange them, that they become the very appliances which enable them to begin and finish plans and purposes which would, from their vastness and their legitimate goodness, overwhelm their progenitors on either side with astonishment and wonder.

Now, say I, when you realize this fact, you can understand that though it might be true that the physical development as to size and muscular strength of man may be less at the present day than that of men living five hundred years ago, yet to-day he possesses the ability to contrive and execute works and objects that it would have been impossible for man to have conceived at that time, much less·to have executed.

To-day, man, by the force and power of his genius and his inventions, has rendered it unnecessary that he should display the vast amount of physical strength which was required to execute the commonest necessities of life in ages that are past. The fruits of his mind stand as evidences of this truth; for what was the labor of thousands of hands, and could scarcely be accomplished then, that which required years to perform, is now the mere playwork of a simple machine, with a boy or a girl to manage it. Talk of the Pyramids of Egypt! Could we have but witnessed the length of time it required to build them, the immense and almost incalculable number of men who were coerced to labor there, the sacrifice of life, the vast amount of treasure expended, and compare those vast, those truly great and enduring monuments of the olden time with one invention of man's mind at the present day, we are overwhelmed with the ideas that the comparison suggests. Compare the Pyramids with the locomotive engine of the present day, and then ask the candid mind if that engine is an evidence of man's retrogression? Standing solitary and alone, the Pyramids—these vast mementoes of man's power and greatness—to-day keep the same watch and guard they did when they were finished. Designed for two purposes, one of which was a depository of the dead, the Pyramids lift their cold, gray points to Heaven and fulfill the second object of their erection, inpreventing the sands of the desert from sweeping in and making desolate that which was once called the most fruitful, the most productive part of that country. And this is all.

The dead have been buried there for ages. That purpose has been fulfilled and ended. How much of good they accomplish to-day, you can judge as well as I. But what end is to be fixed to the varied, the infinite, the incalculable benefits and advantages which this engine has already produced, and which the world has the right to expect it will continue to produce as long as it is in the power of steam to turn its wheel. With a single pair of hands to guide it, and two simple bars of iron upon which it runs, it "girdles the earth in forty minutes," and like a true and good spirit it brings the benefits and products of one section to interchange with them the benefits and products of another.

It opens to the enterprise of men sections of country which would have remained deserted and desolate; it causes cities to be built and flourishing towns to spring up where erst nothing but a dark and silent forest existed; it brings together man and man; it engenders comparison; it begets association; it stimulates enterprise; it fosters industry, and gives to man and nature a power and advantage they never before possessed. The Pyramids, as evidences of man's might ages ago, have accomplished, perhaps, the design for which they were created; but they can develop no new properties, neither have they the power of accomplishing any other design. But in the vast and almost inconceivable change which has taken place in almost every part of the world since this engine was invented, in the powers conferred upon man by its means, in the new evidences which are flowing in upon the world every day of the new powers, benefits and advantages which man and nature are deriving from it, what is the world to expect, and what and where will be the end? Is it necessary to pursue this comparison further?

Thus the necessity which laid the physical powers of man under tribute, although just as imperative to-day, are met and mastered by those attributes which his mind has generated in his progressive advance from that period up to the present.

As the spirit of man progresses, so does the mind, its instrument, also become strengthened and developed, and there is opened to the mind's comprehension the true purposes and objects of creation—matter as it exists in its general arrangement and in its individual combination, the specific capacities of each constituent, and the various forms under or by which new combinations may take place, which shall strengthen man's dominion over every created thing, and which shall, by-and-by, from man's consummate knowledge, from the refinement and sublimation of his various attributes, enable him to say, " I will," and it shall be done.

The spirit here asked me if I remembered, last winter, during our travels, calling the Doctor's attention to a deep cut in a railroad track over which we were traveling, and telling him to see how we were constantly, in all our operations, assisting nature in the great work that is ever going on around us, that of leveling the rough face of the earth and fitting it for a residence for a more refined and progressed race of human beings. Every road we built, as well as every rain storm that came upon us, was performing a part of this work.

And then he resumed :

It is not only in laying railroad tracks or in clearing off vast forests, in leveling mountains and filling up valleys, in constructing ships, in contriving the most intricate mechanism, that man exhibits the intimate connection that man and his spirit and its instrumentalities have with his God. But it is, when he, standing in the place of his God, takes hold of the very laws which that God has established, and wields them by his will in developing out of the harmonious relations and combinations which he himself devises, and producing from this new and harmonious arrangement a result in advance of the properties which distinguish either constituent originally in that combination; I say, when he does this, he of a truth becomes a god, for he makes the very laws of that God obedient to his will. Well has one of your wise men remarked, that he who makes two blades of grass grow where but one grew before, is one of the greatest benefactors of his kind.

But I say to you, he who does this manifests the ability to do more, and can make the laws under which he lives obey his will in devising new and more perfect creations.

The advance which has taken place in the vegetable department of the world is almost inconceivable to you. It is but a few years since that many of your commonest vegetables were unknown to man, and but a very little time has passed away since many of the fruits and the flowers which adorn your gardens had no existence on earth. They have been developed, originated, from the skillful combinations which man's genius has made: thus making the Law a servant of his will. He who could stand on an elevation overlooking the past, and which gives him a view of the present, would strangely wonder that each epoch of time has left such Almighty monuments of its progress. Time was when the vegetation which covers this earth was so coarse, and rank, and so abundant that it covered its face in every part where a seed could take root; but how coarse, how crude, how unfit for the support of life!

Through me it was then said, as by the spirit of Washington:

Having thus paused a moment to review the realities which have been laid open before you, and to contemplate how much life in the spirit-world is but a continuance of that on earth, let us recur to our original purpose, and see

how man, in his political relations in the spheres, as you
would term it, is still the same being, possessed of the same
attributes, and affected by the same tendencies.

As with you, so with us, in proportion as man advances
from the mere savage condition of living only as an animal, so does he develop the necessity of government. And
the nigher he approaches toward the Godhead, the more
does he recognize the duty, the necessity, and the obligation of order, regularity, and obedience to law and its ministers. It is only when you descend to the level of the
mere brute creation that you behold a condition of no
government. When there is infused into man the intellect
of the immortal soul, there is impressed upon his instincts
the necessity of government, and that necessity, I repeat,
is more and more recognized as he advances upward toward his high destiny. And again, it is as man thus advances upward that his government becomes one of law,
and not of absolute and uncontrolled power. It is man's
degradation, his retrogression, the growth and preponderance of his evil propensities which pervert that government from its legitimate form of law to its degrading form
of despotism; for it will soon be found that absolutism
comes as the legitimate offspring of anarchy and disregard
of law, and sinks and dies in the presence of law and its
domination.

Hence, in the history of your earth, you will observe
that all those arts and improvements which have tended
most to elevate man intellectually and morally, have flourished most where power was regulated by law, and that
those works which have most manifested the might of
man's physical nature, have found a fitting existence
amid the stern sway which has made the minds of the
many bow to the will of the few. And it will be seen that
man has most advanced in his career upon earth, when the
government under which he has lived has aimed more at
his intellectual and moral nature than his physical.

You will observe this in two ancient and cotemporane·

ous nations. The whole purpose of the government of Sparta was the development of the animal nature, and all that history tells of Sparta is, that she produced good soldiers and plenty of slaves. In Athens, on the other hand, attention was more directed to man's spiritual nature; and when history speaks of Athens, she points to her painting, her poetry, her eloquence, and her philosophy, and traces their current down the stream of time, leaving on future ages, centuries after, the impress of the thoughts then developed.

So it is in the spirit-world. When you have been in those darker regions where despair and desolation reigned together, you have witnessed the rule of force, the government of absolute power, the domination of individual will, and you have beheld at once the degradation of submission with the debasement of the man, or, to use a passage in your mind which now rises to your memory, you have seen how "Submission to the tyranny of man is commensurate with rebellion to the sovereignty of God."

Now behold government in the brighter spheres—not the most elevated, but in those conditions which are manifestly above your condition on earth, and see if, in the contemplation, you may not learn some truths that may benefit your fellow-man there. Hereafter, perchance you may behold government in still higher conditions of spirit-life, and beholding how it, too, is impressed with the all-pervading law of progress, you may, step by step, witness its improvement, and perhaps in time be able to demonstrate to man on earth that obedience to the law of his moral and intellectual existence may be as instinctive as that which is witnessed in the hunger and thirst of his physical nature. But of that hereafter.

Now look upon the scene spread out before you, and of which now, as yesterday, you have a bird's-eye view. Behold! this community is not so large but that every member of it may be personally known to its rulers. Thus the characteristics, propensities, attributes of all—the governor and the governed—are known to each other. There is no reaching forth here of the arm of power beyond the scope of knowledge, so that it may be exercised for the benefit of the ruler, with but little regard for the welfare of the subject. But the great end and object of its exercise is the advancement and happiness of all; and power here extends its authority no further than it can be beneficially exercised for the benefit of all who may be subject to it, and who may come within its scope.

And observe—for you will see this principle everywhere —that the great object ever in view in the exercise of power here, is to enhance the happiness of man, by promoting his progress, intellectually and morally; by advancing him in purity, in love, and in wisdom, and thus surrounding him with the product of their combination, which is Heaven, wherever it may chance to be.

Now go with me and enter that hall. What see you there? There is a convention of a limited number of persons, both male and female. They seem to be both aged and young, possessing, apparently, the wisdom and sobriety of age with the enthusiasm and energy of youth.

There is one man presiding over the assemblage. His occupation seems to be to preserve order, and infuse regularity and system into their deliberations. Hear you not the subject of their deliberations? You will perceive that they combine within themselves the advisory power of an executive council, the enacting power of a legislature, and the dernier resort of a judicatory.

I remarked to him, That is a combination of power which requires great wisdom and virtue, for the danger of temptation must be very great? He answered:

Yes! but is the combination incompatible? May not man advance to such a state as to become a safe depository for such powers? And if he may, do you not see that the combination in the same hands will enable them to temper justice with mercy, to enforce the stern mandate of authority through an appeal to the affections?

But, I inquired, Do they execute as well as enact, perform as well as adjudge?

No, was the answer. Here the progress is not so great as to warrant that union, and consequently here the executive is in a great measure, though not entirely, separated from the judicial and legislative power. We will, by-and by, observe the executive, but let us pause a moment longer here.

These men are selected for the task you see them performing, by the free, open, unbiased voices of the whole community, male and female—for here woman stands by the side of man, the equal child with him of one common Father. When I say open choice, I mean as in contrast with the secret ballot which taints your earthly institutions, and which is as frequently the instrument of deception as it is the protection against oppression.

They are not selected for any definite period. So long as they discharge their duties well, the duty rests upon them. But each is ever subject to a public scrutiny of his conduct, and at any time the voice of that community may be taken, whether the individual shall continue longer in the position to which he has been elevated. The power of removal exists with the power of appointment, and may be exercised whenever it is demanded. I see you ask in your mind, What is the qualification which elevates one to position here? and I answer, All other things being equal, he who is most ready to sacrifice self to the good of others is the choice of the community; for these men are at once servants as well as rulers, and feel ever that the great obligation is to exercise power for the good of others, and not for selfish purposes.

Mark the character of their debates. You have been listening to their discussions. Do you behold anywhere the display of that intense selfishness which at once tramples under foot all regard for others, all obligations of time, all convictions of duty, that so often convert your earthly-forums into the semblance of dens of wild beasts?

Do you behold here the love of sarcasm and retort that rejoices in inflicting suffering, and that revels in the laugh which more frequently springs from gratified malevolence than from innocent enjoyment? Do you behold here the turmoil, the confusion, the uproar, the disorder that seem to flow from the madness of intoxication, mental or physical? Do you behold here the eternal strife of man with man, that reminds one rather of the gladiatorial exhibitions of old than the deliberations of the Sanhedrim or the consultations of the Areopagus? If you do not, if the clouds which thus obscure the atmosphere of mortal power do not here find an abiding-place, to what will you ascribe the calm, the repose, the benign antatmosphere which rests upon this spiritual scene?

Look! in every heart you will find written, more or less distinctly, yet ever there, controlling, quieting, directing every thought and feeling, the injunction, "*Love one another.*" This command, which with them is a reality and not a profession, has become to their hearts a disinfecting agent that has driven away the malaria which in your earthly halls make the mortal heart boil and bubble with the malignant passions that you have seen playing their part even in the spheres, and performing there their terrible task of inflicting misery upon man.

You will observe, too, that there is nothing secret in the deliberations of this council; every thought is open to the inspection of others and to the observation of all who choose to look on. Disguise, concealment of thought and purpose! they are unknown here, and no duty is more imperative than that of driving them away from their deliberations. They think openly before the world in which they live, and with them language and countenance are instruments of conveying truth, not concealing it.

Mark, too, another characteristic of their deliberations —the extreme deference they pay each other. No matter whether the speaker be young or old, a novice among them or one long seated there, mark! how deferen-

tial they are to all he says. And can you not see the effect
which this produces upon him, prompting him every moment to imitate the example thus ever before him of disregarding self in his regard for others?

I inquired, Have not these people some peculiar privileges, some ex-
clusive right, as a reward for their toil for the common welfare? He
answered:

There speaks the taint of earth, which can not appreciate
that virtue is its own reward, and that the virtue of self-
denial is one, of all others, most prolific of happiness to
the regenerated man! No! they have no privilege but
that of washing the feet of those whom they serve, and in
return may find their own bathed with the tears of penitence, whose flow they have encouraged. They have the
privilege of enhancing their own happiness by toiling for
that of others—the privilege of advancing themselves by
aiding the progression of all around them—the privilege
of learning in the common cause to be meek, gentle, humble, in the exercise of power, for thus was He who came
to save man by unfolding to his view his true destiny.

Through Mrs. Hall, by impression, it was written:

In view of these great inherent principles of the soul,
where shall we look for their legitimate and successful results but in that state of existence where they can be fully
developed and exercised? The experience of the long
lapse of centuries testifies, that here on earth they are but
feebly and imperfectly shadowed forth. If matured in any
one degree, it is at the sacrifice of many others. Can the
reasoning, philosophical mind rest satisfied with this imperfect manifestation of what is pronounced the noblest
work of God? It opens the half-blown flower or the stint-
ed and shriveled vegetable, yet these are more perfect in
their kind than the majority of the living, sentient beings
who call God their Father. Is not the earthly parent ambitious and earnest for the welfare of his offspring? does
he not, overlooking the comforts of his present state, lav-

ish all, if need be, on its advancement and improvement?
Love is given and emulation excited, that it may meet and
answer these expectations. Whence springs all this devotion, this self-sacrificing affection, if not from the breathing,
loving heart of the great Parent Cause? Every principle,
every law originating in him, bears upon it the impress of
his nature, and shall it return unto him void? Shall the
great circle of his holiness and perfection be broken?
Can the passions and sins incorporated into man's earthly
nature overcome its fountain Source? As well might the
trembling rill check or divert the ocean in its surging roar,
or sooth the cataract in its awful play. Rather let its bubbling rill be submerged and lose itself in the bosom of
omnipotence.

The mighty reservoir of redemption and purification is
opened for the healing of the nations. Its ebbing current
leaves the shores of eternity, and it shall flow on till the
calmness of an eternal peace rests upon its waters, for the
lost sin shall have been thrown upon its surface and washed
with the tear of repentance.

But bound not this vision of purity and blessedness by
the small advance made upon earth, for we tell you it is
the work of an eternity, even the process of purification
before that of embellishment and adornment begins. The
soul must be re-created into the living principles of divine
holiness and love, and the evils incident to its mortal existence be purified even as by fire. Having then the original, unadulterated properties of the true metal developed
and strengthened by its sojourn, it shall assume forms of
beauty and loveliness before unknown, and participate in
enjoyments whose exquisite satisfaction the loftiest imagination never conceived.

It has struggled thus far, through life, a mystery to itself, an enigma to its fellows. It has gleaned some lessons
from nature that have soothed and comforted it. It has
worshiped God in the sun and in the stars, and the flowers
have been as angel-breathings, softening it with the dew

of Heaven. The God of the soul has spoken in the thunder, and the song-bird has warbled his praise; their echoes have thrilled it with living life, that it has grown. Now, putting away childish things, it demands the food, the pleasures of manhood. Like the oak of the forest, it would rise to Heaven and point the way. It will remain no longer at the base of the mountain of truth. It would mount its rugged sides. Though early prejudices and dearly-cherished opinions fall bleeding by the way-side, leaving deep scars upon the heart, it will still press onward and stand proudly at its summit, for it knows and feels within itself that there is a glorious view that will gratify its longings and expatiate its desires. It feels a God above, around, and within, and it would cleave the heavens, that it may know of Him, of itself, and trace out that lineage which binds it a link in this unbounded chord of harmony and love.

It is this great want of the human heart whose suppressed cry has penetrated the celestial heavens, and fallen even upon the throne of God, mingled with the ashes of penitence, that has roused the Spirit in his home of purity and love, to come forth and answer this demand of suffering humanity. God has said, Let there be light in the moral and spiritual, as well as in the material world, and light has come. It already illumines many hearts. It is yet in the mists of the morning. The heavy clouds of the long night of error and superstition are slow to disperse, but the rainbow of promise spans the sky. It encircles earth and pervades heaven. Its colors shall radiate with deepening power and brightness, ray meeting ray, till it becomes a perfect halo of light, an arch of beauty and majesty, reflecting the glory of God and the purity of man.

Stand firm, then, ye faithful laborers in the vanguard of God's holy truth! Though the mists of the morning envelop you, the sun of regeneration, which sets only behind the throne of Omnipotence, has arisen in your land; and through you its beams shall be transmitted to all generations.

God works by laws through those means best adapted for the fulfillment of his designs. The time has come when the perfection of his laws demands new and extended channels of operation. The earth has been upturned from its center—its different strata analyzed and resolved to their common elements. Man comprehends how one formation produces others, and he stands proudly lord of its secret workings. Throughout its opening pages he reads the progressive spirit of creation. He turns to the world within himself, and he would understand its deep mystery. The shell of his existence is cloven. The divinity entoombed there cries aloud for its right, also, in the great scale of progression.

The soul has a right to demand for itself its birthright. It is not denied to the animals and inanimate formations of the universe of God, and shall his breathing spirit be quenched when it is capable of assimilating itself with Him, working with and for Him in the reproduction of beauty and order ?

It is for this that the silent stream of thought, originating in the great heart of love, escaped the boundary of Heaven and wandered to earth. It is meandering through the glades of evil; it fertilizes the plains of benevolence and affection ; subdues the mountains of passion and will, till at last it shall bear back the rich tribute of a' subdued and submissive world, ready to yield to its Author the rich fruits of its harvest-gatherings of gratitude and love.

It is this advanced state of the soul, its ability for still further progression, that has brought its kindred soul from its spirit-home, to lead it on, to guide its researches, and prepare it for its future destiny.

Thought has penetrated eternity, but, like the impatient child, blindfold amid living beauty and life, it stretches forth its groping hand, and that hand is now grasped by a spirit-brother. It no longer is alone and sightless, but is rejoicing with confidence and hope.

Grasp ye, then, our hand firmly. We will bear you

safely over the yawning gulf of death, and induct you into life everlasting—the spirit-life, that life that is gushing up within your soul, and has been forced back upon itself till its living fires must either find rest or consume the very element of its own being. The Ætna of the soul has burst forth, not with the lightning fires of destruction, but the soft and mellow light of spiritual truth and regeneration, which rises like the beacon star of hope, and shall again guide the wanderer as did the star in the East.

Emanating from the throne of God, it rekindles the wandering spark of earth, that they burn on together, and their united flame consummate the glory of God and the resurrection of man. Ministering spirits of his angel-children have descended, bearing the torch of love and wisdom. As they ignite the combustible materialities in their path, what wonder that affrighted man exclaim, Behold! the destroyer cometh! He has come—to destroy—to save! When the smoke of the great conflagration now raging upon your earth is dissolved, instead of mourning over the ruins of the past, the glorious future shall fill you with enraptured hope. The lifting clouds shall reveal such beauty, life, and harmony, that the eager hand shall stretch itself forth to pluck, even now, the flowers of Paradise that overhang the scene, revealed by the clear atmosphere of truth and love; and they will yield their fragrance to refresh and strengthen the soul for new and still higher attainment.

The dark shadow of death, which has rested like a pall upon the breaking heart of the world, shall fade away, and the clear river of life flow in, bearing away only the materialities of earth to conduct it onward in the progressive scale of being, wherein to bask in the new-born, unfledged hopes of its new existence. The dream-land of youth shall have become the reality of age, the mother of its love, sitting side by side, talking of God, and truth, and duty; while the father, strong in principle and fervent in action, shall say, My son, thus can your life glorify God and benefit man.

The trembling penitent shall come and be again enfolded in the embrace of hope and affection—the tear of sorrow, falling only to purify—and the wayward be brought back to duty.

The sad, unfinished picture, abruptly terminated in its rudimental state, shall again be placed upon the living canvas of the heart, with its pencil dipped in the fountain of eternal truth and justice, portraying the lineaments of spirit-life and spirit-land beyond the grave. The eye of love shall detect its own, but so beautiful, so chaste, so pure, it shall bow down with reverence and gratitude, and say, My Lord and my God!

Children of earth! the home of the spirit is now being made known to you, that you, as in the olden time, may bind on your sandals and prepare for your journey. There is so much of adornment and beauty you can now place there, so many dark clouds you may dissipate, that God in his mercy has permitted the vail to be lifted. And beware how you, in your short-sightedness and worldly wisdom, ruthlessly destroy the vision. You act for your own soul and its eternal destiny. You can enter now the mansions of eternal blessedness, or you can stand shivering among the cold vanities of earth till life shivers into eternity. But even then you must take up its tangled thread and weave from its disjointed fibers the texture of immortality. You stand alone accountable before God for the use you make of the great privileges bestowed upon you, and in this individual responsibility it is given you.

We, the spirits, love, advise, and counsel you. Before God, we are true to you, true to ourselves, and faithful to duty in this matter. Judge ye.

Our instruments that we have chosen are like yourselves, of the earth, earthy; with much labor, and sacrifice, and toil have they been prepared to transmit to the world the truth of the living God, through the testimony of his ministering spirits. They are freely offered as burnt-offerings upon its altar. They work for us and with us, and well they know that with us they stand or fall. They, with us, feel the sustaining power of God, and His truth, and whether comes weal or woe, we say with him of Nazareth, "Thy will, not ours, be done."

Section Sixty-four.

WEST ROXBURY, *August* 24, 1854.

At a meeting of the new circle, through Mrs. Leeds it was written :

THE spirit to remain inactive after the body has fallen asleep and gone to the grave? O! man of earth! ask reason, and consult the throne of judgment, then commune with thy God, for he is always near to inspire holy thoughts into the soul of his creatures who have emanated from the Godhead. Why put from you His divine hand? It would elevate and lead you back to purity, love, and truth. God, in his infinite wisdom, would give man of the Tree of Life in this existence, so as not to go into eternity with so much darkness around and about him, but rather like the prophets of old.

It is their teachings you take for a guide at this day. Has God the Father lost all power? given his creatures the ascendency? for they say in their pride, "There can be no communication with his ministering spirits, and even if there can, it must be evil;" forgetting that the good and evil are always put in the reach of mortals for them to choose, and by the fruits shall ye know them. Beware how the light is neglected, for we compel not; we only invite you to view the path of wisdom and truth before you, to lead you from darkness into marvelous light. Yes, we would give to you the bread of Life. Ask and you shall receive of the truth that surrounds earth. You have the evidence of our being with those who will inquire how to attain the realization of our communion. Come, learn of that joy—the joy of knowing that departed friends are ever anxious to speak of the life beyond the grave—to give of the evergreen of Hope, and bring the myrtle of Love, the olive-branch of Peace. Will you refuse the Dove who would tell you of the dry land that we have reached, and would come on angel-wings to bring glad tidings to every heart? Oh! come! drink at the Fount, and thirst no more. It is the well-spring of everlasting joy.

Now we will explain what these joys and pleasures are, and of what they consist in the spirit-spheres—that which is congenial and profitable, and will aid in progression.

If one of the partners of your joys and sorrows is called first, he can wait by some clear stream and tarry the coming of the other. The same occupations and delights can be enjoyed there. The halls of memory can be consulted, and oh! how they should be decorated on earth, that when visiting their apartments, there shall be no shadow of remorse to mar the temple of immortality. There, in the garden of Contentment, await the loved ones, to reveal to you the treasures not hidden, but ready for the coming of spirits to the homes of the children of God. Heaven and earth rejoice in the light given them.

Then followed this dialogue through Mrs. Leeds and Laura, spoken by them on two or three different days, and written down by others.

HELEN.—This path leads to a beautiful scene; it is that of a village.

LAURA.—A cord draws me back as I get on that path.

H.—I know what it is. Think not of that cord; it is not broken.

L.—What is it? It seems I get so far, eager to go on, and then I fall back.

H.—Think not of it, for we are delaying these spirits in

the form and out. We will describe that village, and all you see, and explain it through you.

L.—I am going up a hill, wending my way among bushes, in a narrow path, and I should judge——.

H.—Have you to judge? There is but one Judge. He judges all. You must go in that path, and make the best of your way onward. Now go, and with me describe the village and the scenes therein.

L.—I have reached the summit of the hill——.

H.—There are myriads of forms here! Are they spirit-forms? See how busily they are engaged in their different occupations!

L.—Each one seems to be deeply interested in his work, and I notice on every face the same expression of peace.

H.—And as you gaze on this scene, ever and anon these spirits welcome to their homes a new face. Some of those new comers look weary and worn, as if they had had much pain. There are little children here of every size and age. It makes no matter whether they are strangers or not, for this village is called BENEVOLENCE.

L.—I see at one end of the village a large temple.

H.—But you have not seen with how much tenderness and care they treat these strangers who come to their village; and when they look up and ask where they are? they tell them in the kindest accents to wait till rested, and they shall travel farther onward. Then the spirits take it upon themselves, each in their turn, to administer to the wants and comfort of those intrusted to their care. Love beams on every face, and the weary are soon restored to strength.

L.—I notice that this village is situated on a side hill, and the mansions are varied in architecture, but very beautiful, each dwelling-place suiting the taste of the occupant, and I see a beautiful stream running gently at the foot of the hill.

H.—See how busily the spirit-forms are filling goblets and carrying them to their homes to refresh those they have under their care.

L.—See! there is a dwelling open in front, and it is large and beautiful. A spirit tells me it is of Grecian architecture, and I see, as those strangers approach, some are ushered in there, and the beautiful spirits of the place draw near to them and are endeavoring to rouse them to vigor; and now I see those cup-bearers bringing of the cooling stream.

H.—Yes, and if you will look above you will see spirit-forms floating in the air, all ready to take the spirits, as fast as they recover, and carry them in their arms to another village more beautiful. As they enter this village, what see you at the entrance? It is an eye. What is the meaning of it? They will tell you.

L.—It signifies that even in this resting-place He dwells as he does in all space and in all eternity.

H.—But here you will see them looking over books, as if they wished either to recall or see the record of those who have gone before them. Then, as they look, there is a spirit that comes forward and tells them there is the eye to behold every footstep they shall take in progression, in order to be prepared to see the loved ones who have passed before them; and as I look I perceive, as they run their finger down the list of names, there are names of friends they have known on earth, and the names they bear in the spheres. Then they look in another book, and it is very large, and there are laid out plans of what they shall do, in order to go from this village to one even more beautiful. That village is called CHARITY.

L.—O! I see a spirit that has just arrived; she is decrepit and old with grief, and she looks submissive, but as though sorrow had weighed her spirit nigh unto the dust.

H.—Well, she will not look so long, for every thing beams with benevolence and charity; and even as she looks on that arch in front of that beautiful home (for it has " Home" in beautiful letters over it), it attracts her attention and inspires her with confidence.

L.—Hark! she speaks.

H.—She forgets she is old and decrepit.

L.—She stands erect, and says, "My God! my God! thou hast not forsaken me. My soul has indeed found its resting-place."

H.—As she enters that dwelling, familiar voices say to her, "This is a home for you, but you have not to cease working yet."

L.—Why does she start? She replies, "Work! I will ever work, to repay a Father's tenderness and mercy to me."

H.—She inquires what is the work? Her guide then tells her to first come in and sit down and feel at home.

L.—And is that the way mortals are received when leaving the form?

H.—If you will notice, you will see she has much work to do.

L.—Why is that?

H.—Because she must not only have freedom of mind to feel she is at home, but must act accordingly. You see she has benevolence and charity. This is her work, for her to extend mercy to all who come within her home. She is the sole occupant there now, for those familiar faces are gone. They were only there to welcome her.

L.—O! what a happy entrance into the spheres! and she feels that while working there, and greeting others, she is fitting herself to meet those loved ones; and there we will leave her.

H.—Do you see how beautiful, how quiet the village is? Every thing is so in order, but full of spirit-forms. The air about them is—what?

L.—And is it only that light cloud, that mist, that separates them from another sphere?

H.—And riding on that cloud are happy, smiling faces, and they are ever inspiring those in this happy village with exalted thoughts.

L.—But see, there is a child about leaving that place. Let

us watch it. They all know it is going away, and there is not an expression of regret or selfishness there. The beautiful little one laughingly bids them adieu, and they all with one voice raise a chant.

Hark to the words! " We praise thee, O God, we lift our souls to thee." Borne on a silvery cloud, the little one passes from their sight, and they return to their peaceful labors.

H.—Now we will go a little farther—for distance is nothing here—and look into that city. It must be a city, it is so much larger.

L.—And what is it called?

H.—The architecture of the buildings is beautiful, and as you enter beneath the portals of the gate you look with awe.

L.—Sister spirit, they tell me I am to describe that place? May I do it justice.

H.—You have first to tell the name of the city.

I will give it to you in a few moments, and then you can go on. A spirit, robed in silvery garments, holds a wreath in its hand. It is formed of jewels, very beautiful and dazzling to the sight, and as you gaze, you will gather strength.

The name of the city is LOVE. You can now enter and describe the interior.

L.—The country before me is very beautiful. There are many paths leading to the gateway. The gate I have seen before. It consists of gold, a glittering gold, light, and not so gross and material as our gold. It is a very large gate, and has an arch over it formed of the same material —transparent gold; the device is a grape-vine, the leaves and fruit closely intertwined, and the two ends held together by a jeweled bird. The gate is opened, and I see, a bright spirit standing at the entrance, who ushers us in.

H.—Now we will advance, so as to inform others what the buildings are and of what use they are, for here great numbers congregate.

L.—Sister spirit, what is that shining light before us?

H.—That is the beacon light to the city of Love.

The buildings are most beautiful, but the order that reigns within is more so. Tell thou what thou seest to those who are waiting to hear the news of this city.

L.—And joyous news it will be, for there is perfect love reigning here!

H.—And other combinations, no doubt. Love of excellence and wisdom.

L.—And truth.

H.—And do you perceive how many spirits recognize familiar faces? How content they seem? and how intent in the pursuit of knowledge?

L.—They beckon us.

H.—Yes, for I see their thoughts. It is not so much for what they shall cull for their own use, but to enable them to progress others in all the branches of learning in which they are engaged.

L.—Now they are drawing us from the portals of that city up an avenue leading to a large building far distant.

H.—The motto over that building is, "Liberty to all who enter this city."

L.—Great quiet reigns here, no discordant sounds, no inharmonious greetings.

H.—For every thing is done decently and in order.

L.—As we advance toward that building, see the numerous spirits thronging there of every age and size. Pray describe it.

H.—It is a circular building with twenty-four galleries. It has no roof.

L.—Why, it resembles an amphitheater!

H.—In front of the speaker's desk there are guides, each one having in his hand the motto of his class, and as each speaker advances to the desk, he addresses his class in a specific manner, and in such terms, that it impresses them more forcibly than others in the building, so that each guide instructs his own sphere of spirits, although they meet in this temple of learning in such a mass.

L.—I notice that they are very attentive and intent on what he says. A look of perfect content pervades the whole assembly, and as each finishes his discourse, he stands aside, and another teacher takes his place.

H.—They are not arranged as mortals are in their places or classes, but seemingly float on the atmosphere, and combine together so closely that a very large number of spirit-forms can be admitted within the building.

L.—I notice one feature here in this hall, and that is, on the surface of the ground, which seems so transparent, a great many flowers are growing.

H.—The city is built upon ethereal clouds, surpassing in beauty every thing that can be brought to the view of the material eye. Mortals can have no conception of it! for one sphere is built on another in an ethereal atmosphere, and is alive with spirit-forms, keeping together in perfect order.

L.—The city spreads out to a great distance, and its whole appearance is ethereal — nothing like our earthly material about it. There is a delicacy, a transparency in the objects that is past description.

H.—And the exterior of their dresses, countenances, buildings, every thing, has this most beautiful, refulgent light, that passes all understanding, except of those who can be permitted to enter the interior state, or, in other words, pass from the normal state with spirit-guides by spirit-laws beyond the valley.

L.—Why does the light here change so much? Do you notice it?

H.—No, I am trying to see what they are showing me about this valley, I have not advanced as far as you yet.

L.—I will wait and help you.

H.—No, I do not wish you to do so. The valley of *Courage*—for it requires much courage to penetrate beyond the material life, to behold the mysteries, the beauties, the glories of the eternal life. And it is not denied to any of God's children—they can all partake of this spirit-life, and it will strengthen and invigorate the mortal body, and fit it and prepare the spiritual body for all the dangers it must undergo to meet the forms of those so loved on earth. Now, if you will come with me, and look particularly at the other buildings in this city, we can learn what the spirits have to occupy themselves about after coming out of this temple of wisdom and learning.

L.—We will go. Now I see a large building of purest white material. It is circular, and the roof is supported by columns elaborately wrought. I can not count them, there are so many. The roof resembles layer upon layer of smooth, frosted snow, and at the top is a beautiful bird, with wings outspread, and in his beak he bears a small tablet, on which is written, "Truth."

H.—I also notice that all the birds are of a golden hue; their plumage is very beautiful. They are not entirely useless, for each bears in its bill a bit of tissue or transparent paper, on which words are written, and they go to other spheres and let fall these scraps. The spirits there take them up, and read thereon words of encouragement and hope, and thus the spirit-friends in the spheres are cheered and progressed, and so these little songsters are employed, and they carry music that doeth the spirit good, their notes are so melodious and are in such perfect tune and keeping.

L.—I observe that in this are the same class of spirits the first speaker was addressing. Some are conversing, some inscribing words on bits of paper; and as the words are written and the papers filled, some spirit near takes the scroll and gives it to a bird, by whom it is wafted away.

H.—Let us follow that bright messenger-bird and see where he will carry us, for he looks round to see if we are coming.

We draw near a sphere. On the outside are stationed

bright spirits, with golden robes tinged with blue; around their foreheads are halos of light. Going round to the entrance of this city, I see over the gates the words engraven, "THE CITY OF HAPPY CHILDHOOD." No mortal eye can conceive of the beauty of the spirit-forms which come to greet the little cherubs who are entering the city the same time we are.

L.—'Tis Heaven, indeed!

H.—A mother's heart must thrill with joy when she hears of this city.

L.—I hear music. Oh! it swells on the ear gradually louder and louder, and dies away with joyous notes as melodious as the woodbird.

H.—There are flowers here of the same hue and brightness as the spirits themselves. And oh, see! the little cherubs twining flowers. They look up, and their happy faces are lit with holy light. When they get a garland or wreath woven, these little birds take it from their snowy hands and bear it to another sphere to encourage a mother who is struggling to see her dear one, or bear it to earth to whisper in the mother's ear that it is not dead, but twining brightest flowers in the spirit-spheres to greet her coming, and they are ever active in twining these flowers. They laugh so childlike and so happy, for they are perfection here, it would seem to us. As I gaze, I see spirits with the same dress coming to this city, and look around, but it is in order with all. Then I see, as I saw before, a class, but not so many, arise from their position and float with their guide, for they can leave this city, and so he leads them along in a train. They touch at every sphere, to the planets, and meet other spirits who take them in charge: thus they can go everywhere and anywhere, for they have more liberty than those spirits who have arrived at a more mature age.

L.—I notice that when the spirit-guide conducted them from the city they looked upon him with great joy and confidence, and seemed to anticipate pleasure. As they separated from him, and laughingly bade him adieu, they floated out of his care, but not out of his sight.

H.—I believe that the little cherubs have but one prevailing thought, that is, to go to and from this bright city with flowers.

L.—Whither are we going now?

H.—I am watching these little angel-forms; they are so happy, I could never tire looking at them, and seeing them with their little messenger-birds floating in the air, for they go with them.

L.—We must away, for they beckon us. We must leave this heavenly scene.

H.—As I look at other parts of this city, I see spirit-forms larger than the first, and they are, as it were, going to school. They have guides the same, and as I look I see a train coming from school; and another train separating, each going in a different direction, as if there was an attraction that drew them to all parts of the universe. As I examine their features closely, I see there much intelligence, far beyond mortals' idea of children.

L.—I notice one feature—it is this: the mind of the spirit-child is so cultivated that all its latent powers are developed gradually; those that were most developed on earth are not forced beyond the other powers, but their minds are so trained that all the attributes God has given them are perfected; therefore that aspect of intelligence—that deep look that belongs to eternity.

H.—And each of these spirit-forms—for there are not one or two, but millions—can leave their spirit-spheres, and with their guides hover near mortals for a stated time. I have watched them closely as they come near our planet Earth, and observe they go to those about their own age.

L.—Why is that?

H.—When they see the young tempted by other spirits around them that always hover near earth, they take from their guides the same scraps of paper that I have noticed in the little beaks of the birds, and read them aloud. If the mortal hears them not the first time, they read them seven times, for they do not become weary or discouraged; and when they perceive that they can not reach the germ within the casket to impress it aright, they offer up a prayer—not a prayer to leave, but to come again, that they may have strength to resist the temptation around them in their own natures and the affinities that impel them. They do not look sad, for even after they have endeavored with all their spirit-power, there is a smile of resignation and trust that they shall be able yet to make mortals realize the goodness of God in so letting his ministering spirits come to them and lead them from error to truth.

L.—We are on the wing again. Where'er we turn our eye we see perfect system, perfect order, perfect beauty.

H.—And there is no trying to outdo one another. All is in such perfect harmony that one and all are anxious to know what they can do for the spirits at their side; it is almost too much for mortal senses to believe.

L.—Why is that clear fountain there, at the entrance of the City of Childhood?

H.—It is the fountain of Jewels.

L.—For what purpose is it?

H.—Do you not see the little cherubs run and pick up the jewels as they fall from the fount, bubbling and sparkling, toss them in the air, and catch them as they fall? Then they look at them, and the jewels speak to them in these words, "Such are ye: be pure, and mar not our beauty. We will let you play with us until you shall be as bright and pure as we are, that you can enter with us, for we will be your passports to the gate of Heaven." And the little cherubs look around, and their thoughts say, "Can there be a brighter place than this!" The words uttered by the jewels are engraven on them. I never want to go away from this place; there is no guile or sorrow here; all is pure, bright, and holy.

L.—Following that bright light, a bright form appears

floating before us, and I see a band of bright little spirits coming toward us. Shall we not go toward them?

H.—They wish us to follow the spirit of a little child to the childhood spheres. I am borne to a room where there are many mortals standing around a little couch. As I look above the sorrowing minds, I see a perfect semblance of a little child, in airy form, in the arms of one of those bright ones I saw a little time ago. He smiles and wishes me to go and see how this little child employs its time. She is joyous, though just taken from the arms of a fond mother. She is attended on every side by those little birds. She thinks not of earth, or that she ever existed there; but as the spirit floats on this bright cloud, it ever and anon whispers in the child's ear, "Thy father and mother of earth you shall see again. Do not forget them. You shall come with all these little birds around you, and whisper love into their thoughts. You will float near them with all these little birds, and they will give them those little scraps of paper, so that they can read and understand them; and as you grow—as you would have done on earth—the papers and the birds will grow larger. Forget not thy father and mother of earth."

The child looks up without wondering, but seems to understand by instinct what the spirit says.

The little child is attended by tiny birds opening their beaks, and that enchains its attention· so that it keeps a constant, fixed gaze. I see in the beak of those birds a small scroll. The birds have the same golden plumage, and send forth such notes of love that the child asks for the scroll, and the spirit gives it to her.

They have now almost arrived. I know the road—I have been here before. They meet a train of cherubs about the same age, three or four years, who seem to rejoice that another is added to their number. They know the child is just from earth by the scroll and the little birds, and as they approach the gate where is so much splendor and beauty, it does not dazzle the eye of the child, for all the way they have been preparing its spirit, and it feels composed, and with all its childlike glee begins to pick up the jewels. There is not one thing in this home but what bears the impress of intelligence—every thing seems almost to speak.

The child plays with the jewels as with its toys on earth, and when tired rests on this cloud of light. It requires not much time to recruit, for, like a child on earth, its mind is ever active and restless after some new toy.

From jewels to flowers, it passes the first day of its existence in this form.

Then, when it looks around, it finds itself clothed with a new form. It looks at its hands, and now first beholds the children surrounding it. It claps its hands with a merry peal of laughter, and says, "I'll have a good play now with all these little boys and girls." It has not yet changed any of those childish words which it was accustomed to use on earth. And as I gaze, I see there are spirits ever whispering in the ear of its parents on earth, and the same spirit which bore the child to its home, goes back to the mother, and that links the chain of affection that is never to be broken. That spirit tarries with the sorrowing mother, and prepares the atmosphere around her for the little cherub to bring the mother flowers, and for the little birds to sing their notes of love with these words, "Mother! look up, my spirit is here. I love my happy home, and my spirit can come so near, and bring all the bright flowers that grow in that garden and give them to father and mother, who so loved me on earth."

The spirits are constantly showing the children various and beautiful forms of flowers and jewels to give them instruction, which they are ever receiving in the sphere of childhood's home. So that the child loses not one lesson, although it hovers near its mother. And then it wings its way back, so that it is constantly and ever growing, as if on earth, in form and beauty, in wisdom and love; and thus every little spirit-form is conducted by the divine laws to the light everlasting, preparing not only its own progression but even that of those on earth.

They are improving and arranging the flower-beds, which are laid out with such care that it is no labor, but a pleasure.

It is not what we would consider a city of buildings, streets, courts, and alleys, but it is made up of spirit-forms, who stay their allotted season, and are relieved by others taking their place, and go forward in their sphere of usefulness.

The children never tire, for in every object that the spirit-child gazes upon, it beholds beauty and intelligence. It does not look around for something to amuse the mind as when on earth, for every care is taken by the Father of all that the little cherubs shall be ever learning that it is a delightful pleasure and no toilsome study. There is no morning there, no night, but one continued day, and so the time passes in eternity, as we have tried to describe to you, without too much dazzling the mortal eye. But as this glorious truth opens to the view of mortals, they shall know more of spirit-laws and spirit-life. It shall be given in such a manner that all minds can understand and appreciate the operations of the spirit on the natural laws, so that it shall not mar the mortal temple to understand the secrets of the immortal tabernacle that is raised in every sphere after passing from this terrestrial existence.

Section Sixty-five.

WEST ROXBURY, *Aug.* 25, 1854.

The circle again met, and through me it was said:

· I WAS again in the legislative hall of that sphere, and my spirit-guide, who, it seemed to me, was Washington, standing by my side, said to me:

You observe this community is large and numerous. The higher powers of its government are exercised by representatives, chosen from and by the mass, but it is divided into many smaller communities, and each one of them into others smaller still, till they are reduced to circles or bands of from twenty to fifty each.

The whole community meets only by its representatives. The smaller communities often assemble together to receive instruction and to deliberate upon matters connected with the general welfare.

Each one of these communities has its presiding and ministering spirit, its secretaries to record its proceedings, and its own place of meeting. Each member of the communities is not only instructed but practiced in the art of self-government, not only of the community, but of each individual member: it laying at the foundation of their system of self-government, that each first learn to govern himself, and he who permits himself to lose self-control is at once deprived, and that by his own consciousness, of the power of interfering in the government of others, until a proper frame of mind is restored to him.

This process of purifying the governing body is one of the most interesting and important institutions that obtain among them, and it is exercised chiefly by the individual who is affected by it. I say chiefly, because there are times when he is obliged to invoke and receive the aid of others in restoring his mind to its proper bias; and that aid is given as from brother to brother, and not as from ruler to subject.

It is attended with no harshness, has no form of punishment, but is kind, gentle, forbearing, and comes as aid to the distressed. In communities as near the mortal sphere as is this which you are now beholding, this purifying process is frequently resorted to, and with some one or other it is almost always in exercise. But as you advance higher it will be less frequently seen, and gradually disappear until you arrive at spheres where it is unknown, because unnecessary. It is frequent where you are now looking, because there lingers around the individuals yet so much of mortal taint and earthly passions. With some it is long before that taint wears out, and they who are afflicted with it are to their fellows objects of compassion, not of condemnation, and instead of the hisses and the yells of disapprobation which you hear at times in your mortal assemblages, you will here see the starting tear and the trembling lip pervade a meeting at the exhibition of the propensity which sets this process in motion. And in him who offends, it is not a feeling of anger that is aroused, but emotions of shame and sorrow that he should thus have touched the hearts of the brotherhood around him. The agony that in his breast follows the consciousness of error is known to and recognized by every one, and awakens in them emotions of sorrow alone, shown by the sympathy, the active comfort and consolation which are on all hands proffered to him in his distress.

On earth you would call this punishment, but we better understand here that it is the inevitable result of law, which is never violated by the conscious mind without bringing suffering in its train. You have in your material existence the same law, both morally and physically. You recognize it in its physical aspect. You know that you can not pervert any of your material organs from their legitimate office without inflicting pain. If you thrust your hand into the flame, it smarts. If you take poison into the stomach, it destroys. If you imbibe that which impairs and disturbs the action of the brain, you suffer, not mentally only, but in your whole nervous system. Thus, in your material being, you recognize, through the instrumentality of your senses, that evil and suffering flow from the violation of the law of your nature. Some of you are so far advanced as to recognize this truth as equally applicable to your moral nature. With us it becomes a self-evident law, ever at work within us, morally and physically; and one most prominent result flowing from your death is the capacity to understand this law and the causes of its operation. Hence, with us, we require no judges to condemn, no chains to bind, no prisons to incarcerate the offender. The judge of the offense and the executioner of the law reside together in the heart of the convict, and instinctively perform their function. Every man is a law unto himself. Man in the spheres, in all the relations of spirit-life, bears about him ever the avenger of broken laws; whether he is groveling darkly amid the depraved and unprogressed, or is working his toilsome way upward, he has within himself the consciousness of violating the laws of his Creator, and that consciousness works out its own task of retribution, and finally of purification. It will sometimes start from its course, and seem to wander from its proper path—sometimes inflicting suffering too severe and enduring, and at other times relaxing its rule, so as to fail in producing a lasting impression; then comes the duty of the governing spirits to return it to its pathway and keep its action within due bounds. This is manifested, not merely in their political relations with each other, out of which now this lesson has flowed to you, but in all the relations of spirit-life, and you must readily perceive that the happiness of our spirit-life must increase as we advance beyond the reach of these mental aberrations, and must diminish in proportion as we yield to them. It is so in your life—invariably so, however much external or apparent prosperity may hide from your material vision the gnawings of the worm within; and with us the same law operates only the more forcibly, because of the removal from its operations of the obstacles which your material nature so often present.

Now you have seen and have' had told to you the great principles which mark political government in the spheres. There is, however, one more consideration which is not a matter of positive enactment, but the result of circumstances with us as with you on earth, and that is, goodness is rewarded as well as vice punished. That reward each earns for himself. He asks it not from those around him; he reaches out no hand for it beseechingly to his rulers, but claims it as his due, lays hold upon it as his right— the more certainly and the more effectively that he is at length free from the material appliances which on earth so often stand between virtue and its reward. Hence it is that with us we need no judicatory to inflict punishment for error, or administer reward for rectitude. Each man bears the court in his own bosom, aided and supported at times from without, but always open and at work within.

Now look at the executive department of this government, and you will see spirits presiding over the whole community, over each division and subdivision, revolving each like the stars of heaven in their orbits, marked out for them by the same Wisdom which has fashioned each and started them on their eternal path. You will observe that the great duty of those presiding spirits is not so much to rule over as it is to serve their fellows—that the passport to those positions is not so much a capacity to govern as it is a willingness to serve; and that the positions are assumed, not so much from the love of power as from the desire to do good to others. Hence you will see throughout this whole community spread out before your

view—partially progressed only as it is, and bearing about
it still much of earthly taint—that the predominant feeling,
cultivated and existing, is the desire to benefit others, and
on that predominance is erected the happiness they enjoy.
And you have already seen, in your progress through space,
how the prevalence and domination of that feeling have
made the realms you have beheld, one above another, more
bright, more beauteous, more happy, more joyous, so that
long before you could even in imagination approach the
gates of Heaven, you have beheld man enjoying a beati-
tude far surpassing what poets have fancied, or the imagination has ever painted, as the happiness of Heaven itself.
So, on the other hand, you have beheld, as you have descended amid darkness, misery, and despair, that the absence of this feeling, this disregard of law, has been commensurate with the enduring suffering you have witnessed.

Now, child of earth! pause thus on the threshold of eternity, and ask yourself if man on earth is not capable of
making his mortal existence an epitome of that darkness
on the one side or of that brightness on the other? If he
can not drag up, on the one hand, the seething caldron of
boiling passion and suffering, or draw down, on the other,
the realization of the peace and happiness to which man
can attain? See! if, when imitating the wisdom of God,
in the form of your government, you can not infuse into it
his principle of attraction, binding each member to its place,
and thus making a harmonious whole. Tell me if wisdom
shall thus speak from on high to mortal ears in vain. Tell
me if the lesson of virtue and happiness which is spread
out before you shall fall powerless upon the human heart?
Tell me, will you still seek, amid the shades below, for the
example of your lives? Shall virtue and its rewards, joy,
and wisdom, and happiness, descend from the bright spheres
above, in vain on your earth? Shall they float over a drowned
world, and return to the ark bearing no olive-branch, indicating a subsidence of the flood? Shall Heaven's gates be
open toward earth in vain? Shall its holy light be yet

again repelled by the darkness you yourselves create around you? Or are you, at length, ready to plant in your midst the standard of his Almighty love, and rejoice as it unfolds itself to the breeze of Heaven? Will you receive it as the brazen serpent, erected in the wilderness of your mortal propensities, to heal the sting of the thousand mortal reptiles that have followed your footsteps so long?

Choose ye! for the freedom of choice is yours. Choose ye! the road in which you travel; but in making that choice, oh! my countrymen! remember that the day once was when God shed abroad on your happy land the benignant light of his own freedom—that he gave it to you in charge for the benefit of mankind—that the responsibility of keeping, of sustaining, and of fostering it rests upon you—and upon you and your children, to more than the third or fourth generation, the consequences for good or evil must flow. Choose ye then wisely and well, and may He in His love and mercy aid you to attain the destiny that is within your reach—that of being the beacon-light of freedom to an enslaved and benighted world!

APPENDIX.

Appendix—A.

Thursday, July 28, 1853.

AT the circle this evening only three were present—the Doctor, Mr. Warren, and myself.

When we first got together I told them how singularly uncomfortable I had felt for two or three days. I had been unable to feel the presence of good spirits, except occasionally, and the rest of the time my mind had been filled with doubts and fears, and once the attempt had been made to impress me with the notion that the withdrawal of my wife's intercourse had been produced by her anger at having heard of something I had done, and to awaken in me, in consequence, a feeling of resentment, which in former times I had been too apt to indulge in. I had resisted that feeling as to her, because I knew better what her feelings really were, and I had looked upon it as an attempt of attendant spirits to cure me of a proneness to indulge such emotions. But I had, notwithstanding, felt very unhappy and desponding, without any visible cause for being so.

The Doctor soon began to feel the spirit-influence. He said it was a novel and unpleasant one. I remarked, I supposed it was an undeveloped spirit, and if so, I added, let him come, he can do us no harm, and we may do him some good.

After a good deal of struggling, he wrote in large, coarse letters :

You are smart men. Don't you think you will do great things? Who are you, Judge E., and who are you, Dr. D., and what fool is that asleep on the lounge? Go to the Devil."

These few words occupied a whole page, and were written with violent contortions, and several times the pencil, paper, and books were thrown at my head with great violence.

At length, however, the writing was completed, and I read it aloud.

I then said : You have chosen of your own accord to come here, and now you must tell us who you are and what you have come for? This I demand in the name of God, and you must obey.

The contortions and violence of gesture were renewed and augmented. The books, paper, and pencil were repeatedly thrown at me with great violence : his fist was doubled and thrust out toward me, as if he wanted to strike me, and once or twice he looked at me with a concentrated feeling of hate and defiance. I sat by the table opposite to the Doctor, leaning my arms upon it, looking him steadily in the face, and saying to him several times : It is no use struggling. You must obey. After some time, and with many interruptions, he wrote :

I have been around and somewhat near you for a day or two. My name is ——— ———.

As soon as the name was given I recognized him as one of the last ones whom I had tried for murder, and who had been executed the past winter. He had been a short, burly English sailor, who without any provocation had cruelly killed a policeman with a cart-rung, beating him with it even after he was dead.

I asked him why he came? He answered :

I was sent here.

For what purpose?

To annoy and worry you.

But wasn't you sent here that I might aid you and do you some good?

No.

But can't I aid you? If I can I will with all my heart.

I don't know what to say.

Tell me who sent you, and then I can tell what to do.

Spirits opposed sent me to you.

But do you like the society in which you find yourself?

Yes.

Your condition must be an unhappy one. Do you not want to change it for a better one?

Yes, if I can.

Well, now let me try to help you. I know I can, and I can invoke the aid of others to assist, and if you will allow it, we will do you some good.

Let me go to-night. I will come to-morrow night, and tell you all about it.

Very well, we will be glad to see you and talk with you as long as you please, if we can only do you any good. But when you come to-morrow, will you not come more gentle? You see how violently you have used the Doctor, and you can talk just as well without tormenting him. Won't you do so to-morrow?

Yes.

Then good-bye now, and I reached out my hand, took his, and shook it, saying, It is the hand of a friend and a brother. Come gently to-morrow, and you will find us so.

Then he immediately left.

It was altogether a very extraordinary manifestation. It was conducted throughout with unusual and indeed unknown violence. He took entire pos-session of the Doctor, not merely of his arm, as others did, and the Doctor said he felt an almost uncontrollable inclination to strike me, and to commit acts of violence, and he felt the controlling power of my will over and over again, so that after catching my eye once or twice, he could not again lift his eyes to mine.

After the spirit left we had the following communication from Sweedenborg

Hark! my friends, and listen to the strains of glorious harmony descending from above, filling the lower spheres with music so divine, that even the earthly spirits, dark and undeveloped, yield to its gentle soul-subduing strains, and wish they too could sing such notes of joy. Why is this? It is because in the conflict with self a victory has been achieved, and the mind prone to err has been brought to the stern obedience of wisdom. If you had not permitted this fellow's interference he could not have possessed the Doctor; but it is well it is so, for in this manifestation you learn, that even in the spheres there are those opposed to the de-velopment of truth and the intercourse of spirits. This is the true history I mentioned in my teachings, that spirits gross and mis-chievous occasionally arose from the dark spheres, and visited the earth. Here they congregate with those undeveloped spirits who cluster around the earth, and finding that the open and facile inter-course of the higher spirits with those in the form on earth, in removing the errors and mischievous purposes of many spirits belonging to this association, giving a new direction to their thoughts and aspirations (and it is the first step toward progres-sion), they have contrived in various ways to interrupt our com-munion, and to vitiate the object of our teachings. In fine, they have tried all sorts of plans to dispossess us of the affections of our friends, and to instill into their minds vague as well as positive suspicions. Under this state of things, they have really organized a direct opposition to our efforts, and have selected some of the shrewdest of their number to visit circles and individuals, and by covertly and insidiously instilling into their minds unpleasant thoughts about propriety of action, the faith of spirits, the purity of purpose, and the many secret motives known only to their own hearts, they thus strive to destroy what we have built up.

This man is one of the number, and though I knew he was here, I did not suspect him of the intention of influencing the Doctor until he had hold of him, and the Judge expressed a wish to have him go on. With this liberty, he tried to deceive you, but being commanded in the name of God to tell his name and object, he was compelled to tell the truth and thus expose his designs.

However, he will come to-morrow night more gently; as he has left us with an admonition from me, he can not refuse to obey.

I can only say, God is always with us.   SWEEDENBORG.

I here inquired whether our mode of dealing with him had mollified his feelings any?
It was answered :

I only wish you could have seen the countenance of that spirit, when firmly yet gently you brought him to yield to a higher will than his own, and too, when instead of violence you so kindly desired to do him good, and expressed that desire in such a way that he knew it was true. The spirit fairly and positively turned pale with the powerful emotion those words of love and hope produced. Yes, you have probably shortened his probatory state many years by your treatment of him to-night.

I inquired if during the two or three days that he had been around me my wife had not been with me, seeking to counteract his influence, for it seemed to me that I had several times felt her presence ?
It was answered :

Yes, Judge, your wife, Bacon, myself, and other friends have been with you. Mr. Hopper has been with you. Now this plan was concerted, and they did not know that, seeing their thoughts we understood all that these undeveloped spirits designed to do. Thus when this man, who hated you, was sent to disturb, etc., we assembled around you, your wife approaching sometimes quite near to comfort you; but presuming we could draw out of this evil purpose an effect for good, by changing and diverting its influence, we permitted him to go on, but you now see that though you have been made quite uncomfortable, yet in the good you have done and will do, you will have accomplished an object for which years of suffering are no recompense.

You will have raised from bondage a spirit free, and opened to his vision and choice the eternal action of hope and the immortal liberty of progression. Is this not worth being annoyed for a day or two?

I asked: Shall we then give him the interview to-morrow night, as proposed?

It was answered:

Yes, if agreeable.

I should like to have you meet here again to-morrow night, to greet Mrs. Dexter, and have Mrs. Sweet here also, Judge. I would suggest, that if you have time you would see her, and tell her about this visitation, and have her present to-morrow night. I think a very great lesson can be gleaned from our meeting, and joys unspeakable to all. Good-night,

SWEEDENBORG.

— — —

Friday, July 29th, 1853.

This evening we met by appointment at Dr. Dexter's. Present, the Dr. and Mrs. Dexter, Mr. Warren, Mr. and Mrs. Sweet, and myself.

The communication began as follows, through the Doctor:

He is here, and in quite a different mood from last night. He is actuated by two opposing feelings toward you, Judge. He is vindictive, and yet struggling with a newly-awakened desire, of which feeling he has had no knowledge before. Now, friends, after he shall have written through the Doctor an answer to questions, I propose that, under our direction, he manifest himself through Mrs. S. This was my object last night, and in so doing, I think the very nature of the spirit may be probed.

I bless you all, and I earnestly call your attention to the great feature of this teaching, which is, that love, pure love, in its effects on the heart, of both spirit and man, is the only true incentive to progression. SWEEDENBORG.

It was then written in large, coarse characters:

Now, what do you want to-night?

I told him that last night he had said that he had been sent here by those opposed, to worry and annoy me, and had promised that to-night he would tell us all about it. He answered:

Well, I can talk better.

I told him he might talk to us through Mrs. S. if he would be gentle with her.

He said he would, but then acted through the Doctor with great violence. He grasped my hand, and squeezed it with a violence that caused me pain for several hours.* I asked him why he did so? He answered:

I don't know. I feel you have injured me.

I told him I was unconscious of having done so, and he knew better than I did whether he had been unjustly convicted.

The effect this remark made upon him was very great. He immediately ceased his violence, and seemed to withdraw his influence from the Doctor. The Doctor said the influence upon him was, that, whereas he had felt very hot before, now a cold chill ran all over him.

Sweedenborg then wrote:

The Spirit is silent and astonished.

Now we will permit him to influence Mrs. S.; but we will guard him, so that he can not do other than gently to move her. He may say many things undoubtedly through her, but he can not disturb her, other than the impress of an unprogressed spirit; but in your efforts for truth and good, you should not object to come in contact with such a one.

Then, after a good deal of a struggle he got possession of Mrs. S., and for more than an hour talked to us through her. I endeavor to give a general view only of the manifestation; all its particulars would occupy too much room. He began by saying:

That is damned hard work.

And after a while, he said:

Well, what have you got to say?

I replied: You said just now that I had injured you?

So you did.

I am not conscious of it. Wherein did I do so?

That is a pretty question to ask, too. You had no right to do as you done in regard to me.

---

* I did not recover from the effects for several months.

But you were dealt with according to the laws you had violated.

Yes, I know; but I'd been here yet but for you and the laws. Damn the laws! I liked the world, and do yet.

But do you not see something better than this world, which you can obtain?

Nothing I can get at very handy. I tell you what it is : I led a jolly good life, and wasn't willing to leave it ; and I am bound now to stay and torment a good many, you among the rest. I was happy enough when they took me away.

But said I, Can you not see something before you more attractive than that?

Before me? My God, before me! Thunder! Do you think I look before me? No; damned if I do. I belong away down where it is so dark.

Mr. Sweet asked him about his childhood. He replied:

What do you know about me when I was a child?

Nothing, said Mr. Sweet; but I suppose that you were then innocent and happy.

So I was.

Well, then, said Mr. S., don't you want to bring back those happy days?

I aint a fool. No; I am not. As a child I was innocent, but I don't want to be a child again. I have become a man, and am a man yet.

As he said this, he arose and stood erect before me, looking at me with an air of fierce defiance.

I said, That may be; but do you not want to make your manhood as happy as your childhood was?

Don't I want what I can't get?

But you can get it, that I know.

Yes; you say you do. You wouldn't talk that way with me before—but now I'm a spirit. Then I was a poor guilty wretch. That's what you done.

Then walking backward and forward before me, with an impatient stride, he exclaimed:

Now I am as good as you, if you are a judge.

Are you sure of that? At least, you are not as happy.

That won't go down. I was happy enough when I lived here,

and would have been happy if it had not been for you. 'Twasn't my fault I was so bad. Myself had nothing to do with it. Did I make my character? 'Twas as much as I could do to get enough to eat. 'Twasn't always I got that, and then folks said I stole; and I did. I say I did, and would do it again.

But surely such feelings can not give you happiness?

Talk about happiness! It is very little I ever saw of it yet.

Seek it now, then, and you can obtain it; and I will help you, if I can do you any good.

If you can do me good, just do. Now, I tell you, I am in a very bad state. Oh, my blackness within! I could do any thing to be revenged on man who made me what I am. Change the blackness of my heart, my bad passions to purity and goodness? Oh, no!

Mr. Sweet asked him if he could not forgive?

Oh, if you only knew all the injuries I have to forgive, you would not think it so easy.

I said, Forgive us our trespasses as we forgive others.

I knew that when I was a little boy. If I only had the pure heart I had then, I would not be here breathing revenge and despair. If you could look around and see my blackness compared with the brightness of those spirits, you wouldn't say I could ever be like them. I am a foul blot compared with them. I forgot all the charity and goodness I ever knew. I feel it, and see it, and hate myself, my black, degraded myself. Why didn't God cut me off years ago? Why leave me to become so black a plague spot, and in hell, too? for I am in hell. The torments I endure are so agonizing that I know I am in hell. Would you like to see the place I dwell in?

I told him, No; his description satisfied me.

Thank your God for that. I wouldn't wish my worst enemy to know it; to hear their cursing and wrangling in the fury of their black passions, made blacker still by indulgence. Reptile, as I am, I feel that I must fly from that bad place, but where to fly to?

Fly to the aid and protection of the brighter spirits around you. See you not many here?

Yes; hundreds, hundreds. Judge Edmonds, do you think those

bright beings would touch me, covered as I am with darkness and iniquity? When I touched them I would leave a black spot on their bright robes.

Fear not; you can not taint them, but they can brighten you. You have but earnestly to wish it.

Yes, I see them smiling; but they smile at my filth and misery. I may be an object of curiosity to them. I am out of place, like the man in the play, and when the curtain falls, I return to my old state again.

We told him he need not return, if he but earnestly prayed to be delivered.

It is a long time since I prayed. Many miles from here is the place where I learned to say a prayer.

Who taught me? My mother, my mother!

Do you not wish to see her again?

Of course I do; but I am so far separated from her.

You can diminish the distance if you please.

I would I could only believe it.

But look around you, think of what you have seen, and judge for yourself, if it is not so.

Yes, yes; I've seen many strange things since I've been here and I have seen them led off far away from us, and, as we were told, to a better place.

Well, you ask and strive, and so it may be with you.

Well, I will, if I can. I tell you what, I have a friend who is a good deal better off than I am. And I believe he interceded for me that I might be permitted to come here to learn a lesson. But after all, it is only preaching, and bad as I am, I have heard good preaching in my day.

But I have, and can have, no object in misleading you.

Well, I don't know as you have; I was told you meant kindly by me.

By whom?

I was told so by a stranger, who sent for me and brought me here.

Is he here now ?

I haven't seen him, but should like to. Oh! if any body could certify to me that I should not return to that dismal, hellish place that I left! You say, I must pray to get out of my misery? Is not that the way? I don't want to go back among those vicious, miserable black devils. I'm bad enough, but I don't want to go back there.

He then fell upon his knees, and earnestly prayed to God and the bright spirits not to let him go back. When he arose from his knees, he said :

You can tell me more than I know, and can assist others who are with me. You can come nearer than the bright spirits.

He then paused a few minutes, and gazing intently, he said :

One of them comes near me, and says all you have told me is true, and that if I am willing to like goodness and purity better than my wretched companions and evil passions, he will lend me a helping hand. But he can't get as near as that yet.

Be patient, and persevere. He will come yet ; it is your own will alone that keeps them off.

Judge, if I only thought they could come near me—if I only could get over this—yes, yes—this stubborn wickedness—could only get on—they would come near me. I am stubborn, I always was. I'll tell you what it is, I never undertook any thing but I went through it.

Yes, that we know. Enter, then, on this work with all your energy, and see how fast you will go.

Years ago I had better feelings, and now see what a man I became, and what an end I made of it. Well, Judge, you have been very patient with me, more than I expected. I came here with all the ugly feelings I left the earth with. But I don't know as it amounts to much after all. But I should like to have people overlook my faults and pity me. I did not have so bad a heart. But they made me mad, and I drank rum, and it made me crazy, and I went on from bad to worse. No matter, that's over now. I want a friend, I want friends in the spirit-world.

Look around you, then. They are at hand if you will but merit their aid.

They brought me here to hear a good lesson, and now I could profit by it, if any body would help me to do what's right. I suppose I must tell the truth here. I hate the place I was in enough, if that is all. I am tired of it, if I could only get rid of it. I'll struggle to do so. He says I need not go back so far. How that eases me. You are very kind to me. They told me you would be so, but I did not believe them. After all, I am a poor, helpless wretch. I hope, Doctor, you will forgive me for my violence. I came here with revengeful feelings. I wanted to let you know I had some power as well as the bright spirits. If you only knew how much better I feel because I have not to go back there, it is such a dark, dark place. See, here's one coming close to me, his cool breath comes so pleasantly across my burning heart. And I need not go back! And how many I have left behind me! Judge, they tell me that if I do right I can go back and bring them up. Well, I will do all I can. I will be a man yet. They say they'll help me. Every body will help me. I feel it in my heart that I am not as bad as I was. Well, that is glorious, and I am not dreaming. I have never had a pleasant dream since I have been in that dismal, gloomy place. Oh! how pleasant it seems to me to be out of that dreadful place! Oh, these wise, majestic-looking people begin to smile upon me. They beckon me, and speak kindly to me. How lovely it looks over yonder! I am getting ready to go there, it is so beautiful. Is it a dream of heaven? I could never dream of any thing so beautiful! When I was a child I used to dream of such things. But this! Oh! this is something real, and I feel it. Why, what a calm light seems to come from that place! O! bright spirits, do not let me turn back, but assist me to look that way, that I may go even whence that light comes. Can it be possible that such a wretch as I was, ever existed? I am not the same person I was when I came here. Why, I look different. The roughness that covered me as a garment is gone. I am more refined. I feel so humble. Can it be that I am changed from so loathsome a being to being fit to mingle with pure spirits? am I so suddenly transformed?

Oh! forget me, Judge, as the miserable being whom you condemned to death for raising my hand against the life of a fellow-being. Think of me only as the humble, the penitent, the grateful spirit, who, through your kind assistance, has come out of the blackness of despair and death, and who is now beginning to walk in a smooth and pleasant path, with his face toward the sun. Oh! my heart is very thankful. I humbly beg your pardon for any thing I have said amiss.

I have recorded his language as if spoken without interruption. But it was not given thus. We conversed with him all along as in the beginning of the interview. But I have thought it enough merely to record what he said, as thus the progress of his mind can be as well understood as if I had written also what we said to him.

There are one or two things which I may mention here as well as in their order.

When he was talking in the earlier part of the evening, with a revengeful air of defiance, Sweedenborg wrote through the Doctor :

Judge, command him to observe the regard due to God and to the laws respecting man.

I did so, and from that instant his manner changed.

He swore several times at the beginning. By-and-by, in one of his fits of impatience, he said :

I want to swear, but they won't let me.

Later in the evening, he said :

I had like to have sworn, but I'll never swear again.

Once, in describing the horrors of his home, with an intense look of agony, he said : that the horrible scene of his death on the gallows was ever before his eyes, was painted there, and was constantly acted out before him by his companions to amuse themselves, and they laughed at the agony it caused him to suffer.

At length it was written, through the Doctor :

Let him now retire. You can call him again some other time, that he may literally report progress.

I said so to him ; and he replied :

Oh! yes, I have no desire to stay, I am so anxious to go, for I see the way. I was going to ask permission to come again. Good-night. The way before me looks so bright ; I have left the darkness all behind. I now can see. I once was blind.

Then, through the Doctor, it was written :

My friends, you have the lesson ; improve the teachings in your own cases and others. Good-night.

Appendix—B.

It seems to me that it would be well to add here the result of my inquiries on this same subject, at an early stage of my investigations. I was then receiving my communications from the rappings and the tipping of a table.

From my notes of Sept. 8, 1851, I first extract:

In order the more clearly to understand your instructions on that subject (death), I had proposed to myself to ask you questions in reference to your own death. May I do so?

Yes.

What was the last event which you can recollect as having occurred before your death?

I can scarcely tell—death is much like sleep in that respect.

Is there a space of time between the moment of death and the entrance of the soul into the spiritual world?

There is.

Is it perceptible to and recognizable by the one who dies?

A faint and doubtful affirmative was given. The alphabet was called for, and it was said:

All bodily pain ceases in proportion to the nearness of the disunion of the body and soul.

Does all consciousness cease at the moment of that disunion?

Yes

Were you conscious of Dr. Gray's entering the room?

Yes.

What was the first event of which you were conscious after the disunion?

The first event of which I was conscious was that of seeing you and Dr. Gray conversing about me.

Was that after your entrance into the spiritual world, and seen by you with your spiritual sight?

I can hardly tell, but think it was with spiritual.

I remarked here in a low tone to Dr. Gray, who sat next me, " that I was sorry I had entered upon the subject, that I was afraid it gave her pain, as it did me, and I believed I would cease my inquiries. She immediately said:

No; go on.

resumed. What event first made you conscious of being in the spiritual world?   •

No particular event. I became conscious gradually.

Was there any suspension of your consciousness?

Yes.

How long did it continue?

I have no means of telling how long.

What was the event occurring here of which you were first conscious, after you became conscious of being in the spiritual world?

It was you and Dr. Gray's entering the room and conversing about me. But I do not know whether you had before that entered the room or not, but I think not.

Is the suspension of consciousness of the same duration with all persons?

It is various with different persons, depending on circumstances —longer where the death is sudden; each one has his own time.

How were you received or attended when you first became conscious of your being in the spiritual world?

Five and five only meet next Monday, and you, as well as we, will be better prepared to continue this subject

----

September 15th, 1851.

Five met as directed. The alphabet was called for, and these sentences spelled out letter by letter.

Friends! the bright and freedom day is breaking. Horrid death is being revealed and demonstrated to be but a glorious birth; the gloom which now attends the chambers of death, the stifled sobs and the darkened windows, shall ere long be exchanged for serene, pure, heavenly delights; weeping shall give place to cheer, and the pure zephyrs of Heaven shall waft through open windows to bathe the brow of the toppling and almost deserted tower. The music of the spheres above will greet the senses of the enraptured inhabitants of earth. Then mournful lamentations shall be no more known. Now in the gray twilight of morn, the dewdrops are descending almost insensibly upon all things. But the influence of the rays of the rising sun are required to give life thereunto. The dewdrops are Truth—the sun is the Understanding.

We paused for a time for the teaching to continue, when it was said:

Ask questions.

What ones?

Yours, that you have prepared.

On what topic?

That of death.

I then recurred to the written questions on that subject which I had prepared in the recess. My first one was this:

I again ask (in the hope that in the interval your memory may have been refreshed), what was the last event occurring before the disunion of the soul and body which you can now remember?

No answer.

Do you remember my lying on the bed beside you?

Yes.

(I did so lie till she breathed her last.)

Do you remember Laura's fainting away and our carrying her from the room?

No.

(When I perceived she had ceased to breathe—and I could perceive it only by putting my lips to hers—I said, "She is gone." My daughters were kneeling by her bedside; and as I said this, Laura fainted and was borne from the room.)

Do you remember Mr. Houghton's administering the communion to you?

No answer.

Do you remember your sight failing you and your saying, "It is growing dark, but it is death, I suppose?"

Yes.

I then remarked to the circle, in order that they might comprehend the conversation, that these were the last words she had spoken, except a faintly whispered " amen" to one of Mr. Houghton's prayers.

The alphabet was called for and it was spelled out:

It was not to his prayer that I said Amen, but expressing my resignation to the will of God in taking me from you.

I then asked:

I do not exactly understand whether your seeing Gray and me was before or after the disunion of the soul and body. I infer that it was after. Am I right?

William Penn, who was present at the time you allude to, says you are right.

I then remarked to the circle that these answers enabled me to ascertain the precise time, or very nearly so, that she had remained unconscious; that she remembered and had mentioned the last event which did occur before she breathed her last, and the first event of which she became afterward conscious, and that about one hour had intervened between those two events.

I then put several questions in order to ascertain, if I could, how long it was that she was thus becoming gradually conscious of her being in the spiritual world, but I got no answer except that I understood her to say, that while undergoing that process she was not conscious of what was going on here, and of course could name no events known to me by which I could measure the period. She added, however:

I was fully conscious of being in the spiritual world at the time of the deposit of my body in the grave.

Thus two events were given me by which I could approximate to a result, for I knew that about forty hours had elapsed between the time when Dr. Gray and I entered the room and the time of her funeral.

I proceeded with my inquiries, and remarked how difficult it was for me to ask questions as to what occurred in her sphere, upon her being ushered into it, from my having but imperfect ideas of the change wrought by death; but I recurred to the question I had propounded at the last meeting, viz.: How were you received or attended when you first became conscious of being in the spirit-world? The answer was:

Ask questions.

I asked, Which of your friends there did you first see and recognize? Your father?

No.

Our children, and which of them?

Our children first came to me; I recognized them at once when they came.

How did you recognize them? and in what form did they appear?

By knowledge, and not by looks. I felt their presence.

Were others also present?

Yes.

Who?

A great many. Our children and their circle.

I remarked that I wished I knew how to inquire what was said or done then? It was answered:

When·there is more time we will give you a·detailed account of it.

Let me now, however, make this inquiry: Did you undergo any formal trial and judgment for the deeds done here?

No—very distinctly and decidedly given.

The alphabet was called for, and it was said:

Friends, we must now go to the Harmonial Foli. ˙Good-night.

September 22, 1851.

The same circle again met.

I referred to the word "Foli," used the other night, and inquired what language it was?

It was derived from a sound used by the Marsanians.

Marsanians? Pray, who and what are they?

Inhabitants of the planet Mars.

What does the word denote?

It implies something which can not be expressed in your language. It is a meeting of worlds.

For what purpose—worship or improvement?

Improvement.

What do you mean by "worlds?"

Inhabitants of other planets.

Of planets, besides those in our solar system?

Yes.

Some remarks were made among us as to who met—those who were in harmony with each other, or all? Mr. Partridge inquired if all were not harmonious?

No.

Edward Fowler said he supposed that some had not progressed enough yet to be harmonious with others?

Yes.

Dr. G. remarked that it would take 200 or 300 years yet before the Malays or Fejee islanders would be as much progressed as we were.

Not so long as that, Doctor.

I then recurred to the topics at our former meeting, and asked if I should proceed with them?

Yes.

Which topic? Death?

Yes.

I then remarked: At our last meeting you said that at another time you would give us a detailed account of the manner of your reception in the spirit-world. Will you do so?

Yes. Ask questions.

Who was it besides your children who met you?

All my friends from earth met me, and, accompanied by some friends from Mars, as guides (they are great travelers), I was conducted to the different worlds, and had explained to me the manners and customs of the inhabitants of each, and the uses of many of their implements.

To what end was that done?

To make me become acquainted with the different inhabitants of space, and enable me to travel alone.

Did you after that travel alone?

Yes. I now go where I please, alone, without difficulty.

For what purpose do you thus travel.

One purpose was to show me the contrast that exists between this earth and its inhabitants and others.

What "others" do you mean?

Saturn, for example; thereby disengaging my mind from the short-sighted policy of earth. Another purpose was to enable me to choose where to go, and whom to associate with, and to receive superior instruction.

To be continued. Good-night.

September 29, 1851.

The same circle again met.

I proceeded to business by calling attention to where we left off, and asked this question:

Can you give me an idea now long you were thus occupied in surveying the universe? That is, how long was it before you got through your journey through the universe?

No, my dear husband. I hope I may never get through.

During your survey did you still notice the affairs of this earth?

Yes.

Dr. Gray remarked, he supposed that during it, she was still doing good to others?

Yes.

I then asked several questions together, thus: After that journey was over, what next occurred? Did you settle down into your destined position? How was that pointed out to you? Were you permitted to select for yourself? If so, upon what principles did you select it?

I have a natural affinity toward the inhabitants of Mars, but being there much of the time does not prevent me from recognizing and caring for what transpires on earth.

Is most of your time spent in the vicinity of Mars?

Much of it is.

Dr. Gray remarked: With the spirits of that planet, you mean?

Yes.

More so, I asked, than with the spirits of this earth?

Yes.

Why is that so?

Because I am nearer their plane of development than that of this earth.

Is that higher than ours?

Yes; but a great many of the earth's inhabitants have an affinity for the plane of Mars.

Were you permitted yourself to choose that?

Yes—with marked emphasis.

Has your position changed since your entrance into the spirit-world?

Yes, to one higher circle, and partly to one higher still.

In what circle are you now?

You will understand that there are innumerable circles above and below your plane. When we speak of Circles No. 1, No. 2, etc., we speak comparatively, taking earth's plane as the starting-point—as No. 1. There are no absolute numbers, nor any absolute lines of demarkation between the different circles. The spirits of a comparatively low plane can not enter into the pleasures or uses of those of a higher plane here any better than they can there. You could perform the duties of a street-sweeper, but he could not perform yours as a judge. It is a moral division, and voluntary.

What has caused your change?

I have been developed, and am making progress.

Did any ceremony attend your elevation from one circle to another?

No. It was gradual.

Do you remain still with those who were your companions at first?

I partly change them as I progress. Some do not progress so fast, and remain behind. Some of my old acquaintances are my companions still, and our children are in a measure so.

What are your occupations?

I am a compiler of planetary history, and a teacher thereof.

Was this selection of the topic of your studies your own choice?

Yes.

What induced the choice?

It was a favorite study of yours.

It was then from your regard to me, and to fit yourself to be my companion in the spirit-world, that you adopted it?

Yes.

In what does your happiness consist?

Only in doing good to fellow-immortals.

What do you mean by immortals?

All on earth and all above it.

Dr. Gray added: And below it?

Yes.

When any one dies, is it a duty of some one or more in the spirit-world to attend him and lead him to what is right?

Not made a duty, but a pleasure.

What I mean is, is it always done?

Yes.

Appendix— C.

THE SELF-SATISFIED.

October 16, 1853.

AT a meeting of the Circle of Progress, through Mrs. Sweet the following manifestation was made:

Friends, I would like to give you the first experience of a man in the spirit-world who left the form satisfied with himself, satisfied with his prospects of heaven, satisfied that his life and actions had entitled him to the fairest seat in the land of gladness. He lived a smooth and pleasant life, in conformity with all the forms and ceremonies required of him by the church where he paid his weekly worship. He gave alms to the poor, assisted the needy, upheld with his means all societies which seemed to be of a goodly character. Thus he lived a pleasant and easy life, in anticipation of a pleasant and easy entrance into the heaven which his mind had dwelt upon as the incarnation of every thing beautiful and holy.

Having passed the shadowy gates of death, he supposed he should be at once taken on high, and he stood waiting for some one to accompany him there. He was approached by one whose countenance showed deep thought, high resolves, and mighty attainments. By him he was welcomed and led upward, till they came to a strange-looking country, and he asked his companion why it was that it should look so uncultivated? It seemed to be a beautiful land, abounding in hills and dales, and with diversity of scenery; but there was a rough look, a want of cultivation apparent. Its inhabitants seemed honest and industrious, but they bore the same rough, unfinished appearance; and he asked why every thing was so crude? His companion said he would soon explain it, but that was to be his home—he would become an inhabitant there. "But," he added, "let us hasten on, I have

much to show and tell you; but when thou shalt return from our
journey, thou wilt see the propriety of what I have said."

So they continued their journey to countries smoother and more
highly cultivated.

After a great length of time apparently to the stranger—for he
was made to see the distance with mortal senses—they arrived at
a beautiful city.. Now, indeed, thought the stranger, I have found
heaven What a glorious place it is! He was led around and
through the city. What grandeur and sublimity everywhere met
his eye! How perfect and uniform every thing was! Spirit-
hands alone could form it. Behold how beautiful the trees! how
inviting their shade! how grateful their color! He begged to
stop and lie down in that shade, that he might enjoy the happiness
that everywhere invited the weary traveler to repose of mind and
body. But his companion led him on. And he gazed up into
the sky, where clear and beautiful seemed the pure vault, studded
with stars shining like gems of rare brilliancy. There was such
an air of repose, of heavenly calm resting on all things, he fain
would have tarried to enjoy its beauty.

They arrived at a land where the broad and beautiful streams
were dancing in the moonlight, and where there seemed to be
sounds of music and of joy constantly wafted from their ripple.
How gloriously bright was every thing there! A soft, silvery
atmosphere seemed to pervade it, clothing it in a mellow and heavenly beauty, yet bright and clear as though bathed in the light
of the noonday sun. Presently his ear caught the sound of soft
and gentle music. How softly it fell on his senses, and lulled his
passions to rest, by its purity elevating his soul to a communion
with worlds yet unknown beyond the stars, to a communion with
something still higher, the great Fountain of purity and light, the
Center of love, that great Divinity which fills the universe!

Then he indeed began to feel as though he was an unfit inhabitant for that lovely place. He was approached by several spirits.
They gazed kindly upon him, yet as if he was a stranger. They
did not seem to recognize him as one of themselves, and he
moved along with a lonely feeling. He noticed that all seemed
intent on some purpose, or were busy in some errand of usefulness
for their fellow-beings. He seemed the only idle one. He saw,
also, that they were clothed in bright and flowing garments, which

seemed to float around them as with a flood of light, but which did not encumber their progress, seeming to be a part of themselves, and making up the form of the spirit. How expressive were their looks, and with how many different emotions !

As the stranger passed along with his companion, he said to himself, " This is truly a more elevated heaven than ever my weak imagination could paint; it is ten thousand times more beautiful than my soul ever conceived. Yet it is no place for me. I look so coarse, so unlike every one here, that my soul shrinks within itself, nor wishes to mingle where all seems to bear the impress of wisdom and elevation far beyond me. Can it be that I am not prepared for heaven ? How sad it makes me feel ! I thought there was prepared for me a mansion in the heavens. But the more I gaze about me, the more I feel my unfitness to mingle with' the bright throng—to inhabit this bright land. My soul seems very small. Its coarseness appalls me, and seems to shut me out from all these vast and glorious scenes. It can not surely be that those who inhabit here ever possessed souls so narrow as mine. They must be from other planets, from other worlds, where wisdom has developed them. Their countenances are so beautiful, so highly exalted in expression—their tones are so mild, and yet soft as music, they seem to penetrate my soul like angels' voices. Their proportions are so perfect, their motions so graceful and easy ! Oh! take me back ! Take me away from this glorious world, with my dark, gross body, back to that rough country. I feel I belong no part or parcel with these glorious beings, whose beauty sheds light on all around. They can not mingle their beauty with my deformity. Their purity overshadows me, and mingles not with my grossness. Lead me away ; I am unfit for this place. I entered it with a proud and pleased and happy heart, for I had an idea that the beauties of heaven were to be enjoyed by me. How humbled I feel ! How unfit I know myself to be to tarry around these pure spirits !"

The spirit who had acted as his guide heard him in silence, and led him slowly back toward the country which was so rough and uncultivated, where, having arrived, the elder and more experienced spirit thus spake to his companion :

" My son—thou hast been permitted to see thyself as thou art. Thou canst judge, without being told, how suitable to thy spiritual development would be the country and companions thou hast been introduced to.   Thou canst see to what a point of development thy spirit has reached in its upward aspirations after the pure and holy truth which comes from on high.   Thy life and education, if they have not led thee into many great errors, have deprived thee of many great advantages.   Thy soul has been merely taught to look up, as the heathen does to the Sun, to the Great Spirit, and ask protection, mercy, and forbearance.   Thy prayer has been selfish in many respects.   Thou hast prayed only for good to thyself, and to those who, as thou thought, were like thyself.   Thou hast gone through with forms and ceremonies in obedience to the law of man.   Such puny laws never emanated from a higher Source.   His laws rule the universe, are illimitable, never-ending, unceasing and glorious in all their searching and working.   Beginning with time, they end but with eternity.   But thy soul was taught to respect man's puerile laws, to give heed to their teachings, and thou shut out from it the bright and glorious revelation which is open to the inquiring and earnest heart of every seeker, who reaches up to seek it at its fount.   Man's spirit in all ages and nations hath ever mounted up, broken away from the conventionalities of customs and laws, and has been gladdened by showers and streams of glowing light and beauty from the great Fountain itself.   Canst thou not see where thou wert a sluggard, sleeping on a bed of roses—and while others were pointing thy way to heaven, thou foundst it an easy way ?   The good thou hast done shall be rewarded.   No· good thing is overlooked by the great Father, for goodness brings its own reward.   Dost thou not feel how much of heaven thou hast lost by leading a sensuous, material life—the life of a happy, contented Christian as you called it.   The mind of man should never be contented to remain stationary, but be ever grasping for higher and nobler things, ever untiring, for thus it will be ever advancing to attain some new idea.   And now, my son, I see that thou art fully awake to thy true position, and have learned a profitable lesson, and I see high and holy resolves budding forth within thee.   Had thy mind been opened before, had some impulse been given thy soul, how it might have grown in wisdom !

"This country is like thyself and thy companions.   It possesses every attribute of beauty and usefulness, yet how rough it seems !   Thou perceivest it has not been made useful.   Every thing is in its first crude, unpolished state. Even so is thy heart. Thy spiritual body is in just such a position. All around you have been taught the same lesson, and whether they have profited by 'it thou canst tell from their progress.

"And now thou mayest begin to develop the spiritual part of thy nature, which is so gross as to disgust even thyself. The beautiful country shown thee is indeed a heaven to those who dwell there, because their lives, the growth and development of their spirits have raised them to that sphere, and thou likewise must labor and progress as they have done, until thou shalt attain to gifts which have become their heritage.

"Think not the glories and joys of heaven are but formed to please the sensuous eye of man, to feed his appetite for ease and comfort. Think not that the life of the pure and good is spent only in praying and praising God. Oh, no! The beatified and purified spirit is one continual prayer, a never-ending adoration of the Majesty of the Most High; but there are other duties and objects. The immortal soul has other work than singing and praying forever. It has a grand labor to perform, which begins with its entrance to the spirit-world, carries it from one stage of progress and perfection to another, until it becomes pure and beautiful, and divested of all earthly grossness and passion, and approaches nearer the great Center of light and universal love.

"Oh! it is a mysterious and glorious life which the immortal spirit enters on when freed from its earthly body!"

And now what grand and beautiful thoughts arose in the mind of that spirit! He exclaimed, "Oh! my life was indeed a short dream, even a dream without one pleasant vision, save a heaven of ease. But now I begin to realize I am indeed an immortal soul, one who by his own efforts must rise, learn, walk, labor, and work out his own salvation. I now feel that I have indeed an inheritance in the skies, incorruptible, which will be mine, but I must labor to attain it.

"How pleasant will seem that labor, and how thankful my spirit feels even now, that I am not obliged to mingle with the dark and unprogressed minds that annoyed me on earth! I have great duties to perform, great lessons to learn. Oh! what a field there is before me—what a land of promise, glowing with immortal light, immortal reward, and a glorious certainty of attaining what I labor for. Could I return, I would speak in tones of thunder to earth. I would bid them throw off the shackles which have so long bound them to earth as beasts of burden. I would bid them soar with me into realms of space and light, to be free and glad in their boundless liberty, and laugh with joy as little children, because of their new-found happiness.

"Oh! heaven is near, and yet far away. It is in the human heart, where light from heaven flows, but the actual heaven is far distant from this gross and darkened body of sense and matter, as far off in its majesty and purity and glory from sight, as the fartherest star the eye can see—the fartherest flight of imagination. Purify yourselves then, prepare to enjoy that beautiful country, and your lives shall be an unending hymn of thankfulness and joy to your Father in heaven."

Appendix—D.

THE ARCHITECTURE OF THE SPIRITUAL SPHERES.

GIVEN THROUGH OWEN G. WARREN.

[MR. WARREN, who is by profession an architect, and who has been a member of our circle from the beginning, was, during the summer of 1854, partially developed as a seeing medium. He is alone when he sees, and the objects which he beholds agree so well with what is seen by other members of the circle, that the corroboration was deemed valuable enough to warrant him in writing out a portion of his experience, which he has done in the following paper.]

In answer to a request which I made to certain spirit-friends, that they would show me scenes and buildings actually existing in the spirit-worlds, I was on many different occasions put under spirit-influence, in order to show me that which I had desired to see.

The visions presented were numerous and varied, the prominent object being generally some building, the arcnitecture of which I was called to notice. In every instance the scenes were unlike any thing I have ever seen, or could have imagined; for though they corresponded in general to things upon earth, yet in all cases they were distinctively different, embodying to me new and strange ideas.

The series of visions here described was preceded by the information, spelled out, that my friends would be assisted by KÖTZE-BUE in their efforts to represent the architectural examples; and as an introduction to him, I was shown his face and figure as he now is, and then, to indicate portions of his history on earth, he was shown to me in his youth or middle age, mounted upon a horse, and wearing the military costume of a Prussian officer. Then followed a scene in which there was a large number mounted, constituting the staff of a commanding officer.

A public building was shown to me, apparently constructed of gray stone. It was square, each side being about eighty feet. At the four corners were buttresses, surmounted by crocheted pinnacles. It was four stories high, with wide windows of a Gothic pattern, the jambs splayed, and the opening crowned with a four-centered arch. There was a hip roof, quite high, giving the whole a pyramidal effect.

I saw a dwelling-house which appeared to be constructed of iron. The supports were slight and simple. The sides were made of a sort of lattice-work of iron, as it were of hoop iron, crossed, leaving the meshes about six inches square. Vines and flowers were trained upon the building. The inner part of the walls was made secure by some filling in.

A square dwelling-house was shown to me, apparently made of wood. The four sides inclined in, so that the windows of the three stories, being flush with the sides of the building at the sills, stood out at the top like dormer windows.

A row of laborers' cottages was shown me. They were white, one story and a half high—gables to the street—two windows reaching to the ground, one of which served for a door, and an upper window in the gable. The whole plan seemed to be ten by fifteen feet.

I saw a cottage ornée, built of polished marble, of the collegiate Gothic style. It was an indistinct vision, but the general impression I had was that of an extensive dwelling, very beautiful and, very picturesque. I saw near it a plant somewhat resembling the variegated century plant (Agave Americana); but the stem was larger, and imbricated in a peculiar manner.

I saw a Roman Catholic cathedral of large dimensions. It was of Gothic design, of the general character of the Strasburg. The material of the external was very rich. I noticed particularly one of the spires. It was faced with blue enamel. The four angles of it had, in place of crochets, foliated ornaments of gold, very elaborate—a sort of wreath of leaves pointing upward. The upper portion of the spire was of a similar character, wearing the general appearance of the stem of the palm, except that it was more openly imbricated. Upon this sat a golden cross, of Gothic pattern, very elaborately cut.

The interior of the cathedral seemed more extensive and grand than that of St. Peter's at Rome. It was rich in sculpture and decoration beyond the power of language to express. It had a nave and aisles, and a clerestory, with choir and chancel. The chancel window, of stained glass, was of extraordinary dimensions, and richer in color than words can describe. The stairs leading to the pulpit and the drum or sounding-board above it were miracles of high art in carving. They were of a rich wood, not so dark as ebony, but darker than rose wood, I have never seen any work so elaborate, nor ever imagined any thing equal to it. Upon the rail of the balustrade was a spiral (like another rail wound in corkscrew form) that ran from the newel to the top. The richness of this work excited my wonder. I have omitted to say that upon the four sides of the spire that I examined, there were mosaics in oval and lozenge-shaped frames—the frames of gold leaf-work, like the angles.

I saw a temple to science and art, of Corinthian order, cruciform in plan, with a large dome in the center. The dome was hemispherical. There seemed to be a central square building, crowned by the dome, and having a species of low towers at the corners; and then, extending from the four sides of this, were peristyle temples. The whole had a pyramidal effect from the size of the dome and the mass of the central building. The temple seemed to be the center and crowning glory of a vast space where the arts of landscape gardening and architecture had combined to create a scene of sublime beauty, of which my language could convey no idea.

I saw a series of pretty cottages, of many beautiful styles. I noted most those which were new to me in character. I noticed that one was built of rubble in pretty large stones. The stones were as irregular in their outward projection as possible, having no appearance of art. Some stuck out of the wall like a bushel basket; others were sunken in; all were jagged and different. The jambs of the openings were clean cut and regular. ·

In a beautiful grove, where all the ground was close-shaven grass, a road wound along, apparently much traveled by horses and equipages. In an opening, upon a sunny slope, I saw a cottage of peculiar character. It was a story and a half high, of English style—a semi-Gothic. It was covered upon the sides and roof with green moss. Every part was a vivid emerald green. I saw the four sides, which were all different, and liked the design much.

I saw the pleasure grounds of a gentleman's estate—a landscape garden of the most magnificent proportions. Every possible variety of form and color seemed represented in the different departments. Vast clumps of trees of well-contrasted foliage, alternated with lawns and isolated trees of beautiful figures. Beds of flowers in geometrical forms were interspersed, and canals or water-courses meandered among them. A lake seemed covered with aquatic plants and flowers, and a fountain rose to a grand height, scattering far and wide its shower of spray. Fruits of rare form tempted my sight, and flowers were everywhere in profusion. I have never imagined a scene of such heavenly beauty.

A fence that surrounded a garden of flowers took my attention in another view. It appeared to be, not a fence, but a row of beautiful plants growing as a border, crowned at the top with flowers.

I saw a building whose general character was that of an extensive warehouse. I was shown the interior, and it was full of goods, lying upon shelves and counters. There were rolls of cloths, flannels, silks, velvets, muslins, etc., in endless profusion and variety. My attention was specially called to a quantity of ladies' shoes, and I was made to inspect them narrowly. They differed in no respect from the morocco slippers I have often seen. I was made to observe that the soles were of leather, and a little thicker than usual.

I saw a vast extent of country like a prairie, and near me was the track of a railroad. While I looked, a train of cars approached with terrific speed, and passed. The locomotive was in the form of two gigantic white horses, whose forms concealed all the works of the engine.

I found myself looking down upon the deck of a ship. I noticed the windlass, which was of the common form. I then saw the vessel at a distance upon the water. It was a barque of elegant proportions. She approached near to me, and I saw that the bow was remarkably sharp.

When all these things had been seen and examined minutely, the spirit-relative who had caused them to be shown to me (that is, had brought the spirit who had done so), affixed, as it were, her signature to the series of views. I saw placed before me a tablet, on which was written her name.

On other occasions there have been presented to me other kinds of structures. On one occasion I was shown a small private garden, along a wall of which were trained grape vines, very thickly covered with light-purple grapes of the form of the Malaga variety. Many other kinds of fruits were there, but I did not know any names for them, nor could I describe them. One kind looked something like a pear, but was evidently something very different. The stem was about six inches long, and there were four leaves at the foot, forming a cup. In this garden, which was also richly embellished with rare flowers and laid out with regularity, there was a summer-house of peculiar character. It was circular on the plan, about twelve feet in width. It had four circular pillars, which supported a dome-like roof, the eaves of which projected some two feet and curved upward. On the under side of this cornice or turned-up roof was ornamental painting, not unlike in character the painting seen on the antique Etruscan vases. The colors, too, were similar. The pillars were decorated with ornamental figures of the same general character. At the time I saw this summer-house there was shown to me a school-house. It was a Gothic building, two stories high, made of a yellowish brown sandstone. I saw only the exterior. It was not remarkable for size or beauty.

I was shown the interior of a conservatory, seemingly all made of glass; on sides and upper part were trained a variety of vines. The trees which I saw surrounding the various buildings—of which I examined minutely at least a hundred—were all different from any I have seen upon earth, both in foliage and flowers, and still more in the general character. All were, as a rule, more beautiful than I could have imagined. One tree had leaves which seemed convoluted like those of a species of Malvus, only it was more compact. I have seen also as large a variety of flowers as of trees, and have made drawings of some of them. Amid all the trees and flowers, I have not seen one specimen which could be classified with the Flora of Earth.

Of the fruits, I saw none resembling any I have seen on earth, except the grapes, which were shown to me in great numbers, not differing essentially from many kinds here.

Having often requested my sister to show me her residence, I at length obtained several views of it. It was in extent a suburban villa, with the character of a cottage *ornée*. It was of an oriental style of architecture, something between Saracenic and the florid Gothic. It had high verandas on two sides. There were also balconies of various styles. There was a light and airy appearance to the construction of the verandas, they being made of ornamental wire-work, over which climbing plants were trained.

I was shown the interior of the house, but saw it indistinctly. I noticed a clock hanging upon the wall. I saw in the drawing-room the hearth of the fireplace, which was of a variegated marble, black and white, and very beautiful. The hearth-rug was a rich piece of work, very similar in character to the velvet tapestry or Axminster rugs. The floor had no carpet. I was told that it was removed because it was the summer season with them. I saw an embroidered screen, and an ottoman covered with elaborate embroidery.

The general effect of what I saw was not unlike that of houses on earth. The arrangement of the furniture was similar to that found in first-class houses here. I was promised a more complete exhibition of all these things.

After I had seen and examined the various parts of the house shown to me, my sister opened a wardrobe and showed me her dresses. There was quite a variety of them. They seemed chiefly of silk. I noticed one dress that was evidently a special costume. It seemed Persian or Turkish.

I was then shown her husband's wardrobe. I found that it did not differ in any essential particular from the clothing worn by gentlemen here. I noticed one vest that pleased me. It was of the form now worn here—double-breasted. It was of velvet, beautifully figured, black and purple.

Other articles of clothing were shown me which I can not particularize. I asked if she would show me the plant of which they made linen, or that which corresponded to our linen. She showed me a plant about two feet high. (Leaves lanceolate, acute, branching at top into six or seven flower stalks, upon which were yellow flowers. Calyx deep and ribbed, petals collapsed and convoluted. Its common name is Socelcia.)

Partridge & Brittan's Spiritual Library.

Our list of Books embraces all the principal works devoted to Spiritualism, whether published by ourselves or others, and will comprehend all
works of value that may be issued hereafter. The reader's attention is
particularly invited to those named below, all of which may be found at the
Office of The Shekinah and Spiritual Telegraph. The reader will perceive that the price of each book in the list, and the amount of postage, if
forwarded by mail, are annexed.

The Shekinah, Vol. I.

By S. B. Brittan, Editor, and other writers, is devoted chiefly to an Inquiry into the
Spiritual Nature and Relations of Man. It treats especially of the Philosophy
of Vital, Mental, and Spiritual Phenomena, and contains interesting Facts and
profound Expositions of the Psychical Conditions and Manifestations now attracting attention in Europe and America. This volume contains, in part, the Editor's
Philosophy of the Soul; the Interesting Visons of Hon. J. W. Edmonds; Lives
and Portraits of Seers and Eminent Spiritualists; *Fac-similes* of Mystical Writings, in Foreign and Dead Languages, through E. P. Fowler, etc. Published by
Partridge and Brittan. Bound in muslin, price $2 50; elegantly bound in moroc-
co, lettered and gilt in a style suitable for a gift book, price $3 00; postage 34
cents.

Nature's Divine Revelations, etc.

By A. J. Davis, the Clairvoyant. Price, $2 00; postage, 43 cents.

The Great Harmonia, Vol. I.

The Physician. By A. J. Davis. Price, $1 25; postage, 20 cents.

The Great Harmonia, Vol. II.,

The Teacher. By A. J. Davis. Price, $1 00; postage, 19 cents.

The Great Harmonia, Vol. III.,

The Seer. By A. J. Davis. Price, $1 00; postage, 19 cents.

The Philosophy of Spiritual Intercourse.

By A. J. Davis. Price, 50 cents; postage, 9 cents.

The Philosophy of Special Providences.

A Vision. By A. J. Davis. Price, 15 cents ; postage, 3 cents.

The Celestial Telegraph.

Or, secrets of the Life to Come, revealed through Magnetism; wherein the Existence, the Form, and the Occupation of the Soul after its Separation from the Body are proved by many year's Experiments, by the means of eight ecstatic Somnambulists, who had Eighty perceptions of Thirty-six Deceased Persons of various Conditions ; a Description of them, their Conversation, etc., with proofs of their Existence in the Spiritual World. By L. A. Cahanet. Published by Partridge & Brittan. Price, $1 00 ; postage, 19 cents.

Familiar Spirits.

And Spiritual Manifestations ; being a Series of Articles by Dr. Enoch Pond, Professor in the Bangor Theological Seminary. With a Reply, by A. Bingham, Esq., of Boston. Price 25 cents ; postage 3 cents.

Night Side of Nature.

Ghosts and Ghost Seers. By Catharine Crowe. Price, $1.25 ; postage 20 cents

Gregory's Lectures on Animal Magnetism.

Price, $1 00 ; postage, 17 cents.

The Macrocosm and Microcosm;

Or, the Universe Without and the Universe Within. By William Fishbough. This volume comprehends only the first part, or the Universe Without. Paper, bound, price, 50 cents ; muslin, 75 cents ; postage, 12 cents.

Arrest, Trial, and Acquittal of Abby Warner,

For Spirit-Rapping By Dr. A. Underhill. Price, 12 cents ; postage, 2 cents.

Physico-Physiological Researches

In the Dynamics of Magnetism, Electricity, Heat, Light, Crystallization, and Chemism, in their relations to Vital Force. By Baron Charles Von Reichenbach. Complete from the German second edition ; with the addition of a Preface and Critical Notes, by John Ashburner, M.D. ; third American Edition. Published by Partridge & Brittan at the reduced price of $1 00 ; postage, 20 cents.

Spiritual Experience of Mrs. Lorin L. Platt,

Medium Price, 20 cents ; postage, 3 cents.

Spirit-Manifestations:

Being an Exposition of Facts, Principles, etc By Rev. Adin Ballou. Price, 75 cents; postage, 11 cents,

piritual Instructor;

Containing Facts and the Philosophy of Spiritual Intercourse. Price, 38 cents postage, 6 cents.

The Spiritual Teacher.

By Spirits of the Sixth Circle R. P. Ambler, Medium. Price, 50 cents ; postage, 7 cents.

NEW AND VALUABLE BOOKS

Religion of Manhood; or, the Age of Thought.
By Dr. J. H. Robinson. Price, 75 cents; postage, 12 cents.

Philosophy of Creation.
Unfolding the Laws of the Progressive Development of Nature. By Thomas Paine, through Horace G. Wood, Medium. Price, 38 cents; postage, 6 cents.

Epic of the Starry Heaven.
Spoken by Thomas L. Harris in 26 hours and 16 minutes, while in the trance state; 210 pages, 12mo., 4,000 lines. Price, plain bound, 75 cents; gilt muslin, $1; morocco, $1 25. Postage, 12 cents.

Astounding Facts from the Spirit-World,
Witnessed at the house of J. A. Gridley, Southampton, Mass. Illustrated with a colored diagram. Price, 63 cents; postage, 9 cents.

A Letter to the Chestnut Congregational Church, Chelsea, Mass.,
In reply to its charges of having become a reproach to the cause of truth, in consequence of a change of religious belief. By John S. Adams. Price, 15 cents; postage, 4 cents.

Rivulet from the Ocean of Truth.
An interesting narrative of advancement of a Spirit from darkness to light, proving the influence of man on earth over the departed. By John S. Adams. Price, 25 cents; postage, 5 cents.

Voices from Spirit-Land.
Through Nathan Francis White, Medium. Partridge & Brittan. Price, 75 cents; postage, 13 cents.

Arnold, and other Poems.
By J. R. Orton. Partridge & Brittan. Price, 60 cents; postage, 9 cents.

Spiritual Telegraph Papers.
Vols. III. and IV. Edited by S. B. Brittan. Embracing the selections from Nov., 1853, to May, 1854. Price, 75 cents; postage, 20 cents each.

A Review of Dr. Dods' Book on Spiritualism.
By W. S. Courtney. Paper bound. Price, 25 cents; postage, 3 cents.

The Tables Turned.
A brief Review of Rev. C. M. Butler, D.D. By S. B. Brittan. Price, 25 cents; postage, 3 cents.

The Sacred Circle.
A monthly periodical. Edited by Edmonds, Dexter, and Warren. Price, single numbers, 25 cents. Two Dollars per annum.

Lyric of the Morning Land.
A beautiful poem of 5,000 lines (253 pages, 12mo), dictated in *thirty hours*, printed on the finest paper, and elegantly bound. Price, plain muslin, 75 cents; muslin, gilt, $1; morocco gilt, $1 25.

Lily Wreath.
A beautiful gift book, made up of Spiritual Communications read chiefly through the mediumship of Mrs. J. S. Adams, by A. B. Child. Price, gilt, $1 00; full gilt, $1 50; postage, 15 cents.

Humanity in the City.
A series of eight lectures, by E. H. Chapin, delivered in New York for the purpose of applying the highest standard of *morality and religion* to the phases of every-day life. Price, $1 00; postage, 14 cents.

Light From The Spirit World.
Being written by the control of Spirits. Rev. Charles Hammond, Medium. Price, 75 cents; postage, 10 cents.

The Pilgrimage of Thomas Paine.
Written by the Spirit of Thomas Paine, through C. Hammond, Medium. Paper price, 50 cents; muslin, 75 cents; postage, 12 cents.

Elements of Spiritual Philosophy.
R. P. Ambler, Medium. Price, 25 cents; postage, 4 cents.

Stilling's Pneumatology,
Being a Reply to the Question, What Ought and Ought Not to be Believed or Disbelieved concerning Presentiments, Visions, and Apparitions according to Nature, Reason, and Scripture. Translated from the German; edited by Prof. George Bush. Published by Partridge & Brittan. Price, 75 cents; postage, 16 cents.

Voices from the Spirit-World.
Isaac Post, Medium. Price, 50 cents; postage, 10 cents,

Dr. Esdaile's Natural and Mesmeric Clairvoyance.
With the Practical Application of Mesmerism in Surgery and Medicine. (English edition.) Price, $1 25; postage, 10 cents.

Also, Mesmerism in India.
By the same Author. Price, 75 cents; postage, 13 cents.

Fascination:
Or, the Philosophy of Charming. By John B. Newman, M.D. Price 40 cents; postage, 10 cents.

Shadow-Land:
Or, the Seer By Mrs. E. Oakes Smith. Price, 25 cents; postage 5 cents.

Supernal Theology.
Alleged Spiritual Manifestations. Price, 25 cents; postage 5 cents.

Messages from the Superior State.
Communicated by John Murray, through J. M. Spear. Price, 50 cents; postage, 8 cents.

Love and Wisdom from the Spirit-World.
By Jacob Harshman, writing Medium. Price, 60 cents; postage, 11 cents.

Seeress of Prevorst.
A Book of Facts and Revelations concerning the Inner Life of Man and a World of Spirits. By Justinus Kerner. New Edition; published by Partridge & Brittan. Price, 38 cents; postage, 6 cents.

Philosophy of Mysterious Agents.
Human and Mundane; or, The Dynamic Laws and Relations of Man. By E. C Rogers. Bound; price, $1 00; postage, 24 cents.

The Science of the Soul.
By Haddock. Price, 25 cents; postage, 5 cents.

Sorcery and Magic.
By Wright. Price, $1 00; postage, 19 cents.

The Clairvoyant Family Physician.
By Mrs. Tuttle. Paper, price 75 cents; muslin, $1 00; postage, 10 cents.

Answers to Seventeen Objections
Against Spiritual Intercourse. By John S. Adams. Published by Partridge & Brittan. Paper, price 25 cents; muslin, 28 cents; postage, 7 cents.

The Approaching Crisis:
Being a Review of Dr. Bushnell's recent Lectures on Supernaturalism. By A. J. Davis. Published by Partridge & Brittan. Price, 50 cents; postage, 13 cents.

Practical Instruction in Animal Magnetism.
By J. P. F. Deleuse. Price, $1 00; postage, 16 cents.

Spirit-Minstrel.
A collection of Ninety familiar Tunes and Hymns, appropriate to Meetings for Spiritual Intercourse. Paper, 25 cents; muslin, 38 cents; postage, 6 cents.

Spirit-Voices.
Dictated by Spirits, for the use of Circles. By E. C. Henck, Medium. Price, paper, 38 cents; muslin, 50 cents. postage, 6 cents.

Buchanan's Journal of Man.
A Monthly Magazine, devoted to Anthropological Science, by which the Constitution of Man is determined through Phrenological and Psychological Developments. Price, per annum, $2 00; single copies, 25 cents; postage, 3 cents.

Beecher's Report on the Spiritual Manifestations,
To the Congregational Association of New York and Brooklyn. Price, paper, 25 cents; muslin, 38 cents; postage, 3 and 6 cents.

The Ministry of Angels Realized.
By A. E. Newton, Boston. Price 12 cents postage 1 cent.

Amaranth Blooms.
A Collection of embodied Poetical Thoughts, by Mrs. S. S. Smith. Price 62 cents, postage 8 cents.

Reply to a Discourse
Of Rev. S. W. Lind, D.D., President Western Baptist Theological Institute, Covington, Kentucky, by P. E. Bland, A.M., St. Louis. Price 15 cents, postage 2 cents.

The Harmonial Man:
Or, Thoughts for the Age. By Andrew Jackson Davis. Price 80 cents, postage 6 cents.

Biography of Mrs. Semantha Mettler,
And an account of the Wonderful Cures performed by her. By Francis H. Green. Harmonial Association, publishers. Price, paper 25 cents; muslin, 38 cents; postage, 6 cents.

PARTRIDGE & BRITTAN, Publishers,
No. 300 Broadway, New York.